Sporting Dystopias

SUNY series
on
Sport, Culture, and Social Relations

CL Cole and Michael A. Messner, editors

Sporting Dystopias

The Making and Meaning of Urban Sport Cultures

Edited by

Ralph C. Wilcox

David L. Andrews

Robert Pitter

Richard L. Irwin

State University of New York Press

Published by
State University of New York Press, Albany

© 2003 State University of New York

For information, address State University of New York Press,
90 State Street, Suite 700, Albany, NY 12207

Production by Michael Haggett
Marketing by Jennifer Giovani

Library of Congress Catalogining-in-Publication Data

Sporting dystopias : the making and meaning of urban sport cultures /
edited by Ralph C. Wilcox . . . [et al.].
    p. cm.—(SUNY series on sport, culture, and social relations)
  Includes bibliographical references and index.
    ISBN 0-7914-5669-2 (alk. paper)—ISBN 0-7914-5670-6 (pbk. : alk.
paper)
    1. Sports—Social aspects.   2. City and town life.   I. Wilcox, Ralph C.
II. Series.

GV706.5 .S73898   2003
306.4'83—dc21
                                                                2002030976

10 9 8 7 6 5 4 3 2 1

Contents

Sport in the City

Cultural, Economic, and Political Portraits

Ralph C. Wilcox and David L. Andrews

Fueled by the accelerating tumult of modernity, the universal emergence of sport has paralleled that of the city. From the earliest city-states of Western civilization, to the great urban gateways of Renaissance Europe, the smoke-stacked city of the industrial world, and the postmodern cosmopolis of today, sport has wrought its indelible stamp on both the physical structure of the city and civic consciousness. This is perhaps not surprising, since modern sport and the modern metropolis share certain characteristics. Both may be typified as expressions of particular cultural, economic, and political arrangements, each structuring relationships between people and space, representing collective attitudes, values, and identities, and embodying the perpetual dynamism so characteristic of modern existence. Moreover, both sport and the city are frequently, if not unanimously, reified as expressions of the progress, vibrancy, and eternal optimism that characterizes all things modern. This book seeks to provide a better understanding of these complex issues and phenomena and, in so doing, it hopes to further the understanding of the complementary relationship between sport and the city within the North American context.

As recently as three centuries ago, less than 2% of the world's population lived in scattered urban areas. Spurred on by the genesis of industrial capitalism in late-eighteenth-century Britain, and first sprouting from the fields of Northwestern Europe and then towering along the shores of the Northeastern United States, cities soon became a symbol of the changing structure and experience of modern life. By the beginning of the twentieth century, 15% of this planet's people were urban dwellers. This transition, from a rural to an urban existence, has accelerated as we enter the third millennium for, as David Clark suggests, "The last decade of the twentieth century marks a major watershed in the evolution of human settlement, . . . it encompasses the period during which the location of the world's people has become more urban than rural."[1] Today, while this shift continues worldwide, across all continents and even in countries

with a deep and resistant tradition of agrarian dependency, the impact of urbanization on humanity varies dramatically. While some people readily absorb
such change as a matter of course, others struggle with the pains of cultural
dislocation, economic upheaval, and associated ills, for it cannot be said that the
shift to a universal urban existence has been heralded or, indeed, experienced as
a sign of progress in all quarters.

If urbanization is the process, then the city is the product and one which,
by definition, conjures up images of large numbers of people huddled together
in a socially constructed and cramped urban space. The city was earlier characterized by Max Weber in 1899 as "A locality and dense settlement of dwellings
forming a colony so extensive that personal reciprocal acquaintance of inhabitants is lacking."[2] Molded by the hands of industrial capitalists, David Harvey[3]
argues that the modern city grew out of a convergence of the unmatched
human migration from rural to urban living, industrialization, and mechaniza-
tion. Furnishing improved access to communities of production and consumption and creating previously unimaginable economies of scale, the city
nonetheless spawned such seemingly inevitable ills as overcrowding, unemployment, homelessness, crime, poor health, and pollution at levels theretofore
unwitnessed in rural life. Quite remarkably, while volumes have examined the
birth and development of the modern city, along with the associated process
of urbanization, relatively little has been written about the place and role of
sport in the emerging city.[4] Accordingly, this book seeks to fill such a void
through a collection of multidisciplinary analyses presented by international
scholars grounded in anthropology, business, cultural studies, history, media
studies, public and urban planning, and sociology.

Once the seat of pharaohs, emperors, and monarchs, the ancient and medieval city hosted a myriad of sporting rituals and celebrations over time. Frequently sponsored by the urban elite, yet increasingly practiced and consumed
by the populace, the ancient city skyline became dominated by sporting venues
and monuments, perhaps no better exemplified than in the towering structures
of the Coliseum and Circus Maximus in Rome. Yet it was with the emergence
of the modern city in eighteenth- and nineteenth-century Europe that sport
and urbanization became so inextricably entwined. In the United States also,
adds Steven Riess, sport "has been shaped, reshaped, and further molded by the
interplay of the elements comprising the process of urbanization. . . . In addition, America's sports institutions have . . . deeply influenced urban change
. . . in distinctive and visible ways."[5] Various explanations have been advanced
to further explain this interconnectedness. To Dale Somers, the rise of sport in
late-nineteenth-century New Orleans could be best attributed to the need for
an antidote to the problems, pressures, tensions, frustrations, and pent-up energies associated with the newly experienced patterns of urban living. He explained: "Sports rose to prominence . . . in large part because they provided a
social safety valve that allowed great masses of people to blow off steam in a

relatively harmless way."[6] Helen Meller, in her broader study of leisure in Victorian and Edwardian Bristol, England, offered a different argument, claiming that "the modernization of the city contributed to a new self-consciousness about urban civilization."[7] Suggesting that sport was part of a larger urban revolution in the provision of leisure (which included public libraries, art galleries and museums, swimming baths, parks, playgrounds, and missions), she argues that municipal governments, middle-class reformers, industrial philanthropists, and socio-religious and labor groups joined forces in an unprecedented and a collective demonstration of civic consciousness to address such urban ills as disease, pollution, mortality, and the prevailing sense of helplessness. Stephen Hardy's study of sport and community in Boston (1865–1915) appears to support Meller's thesis as

> Concerned residents examined the city and found it physically debilitating. Clusters of wretched housing, poor sewage systems, and polluted air made the city ripe for illness and disease. . . . Worse than the destruction of individual lives was the shredding of the city's very social fabric. . . . It was against the background of real concern over the city's physical environment, its social life, and its image that public and private sport and recreation promoters fashioned their arguments.[8]

In conceiving of the city as a purely physical space, sport can be said to have had a significant impact upon molding the structural and spatial constitution of the urban environment. At the same time, the phases of urban metamorphosis have quite clearly been manifested in the changing form and practice of sport for, as Riess contends,

> The process of city building influenced sporting developments in nearly every conceivable way—most notably, changing spatial patterns, expanding municipal operations, the formation of class and ethnically defined neighborhoods, innovations in public transportation, the rise of political machines, the development of voluntary status-oriented sports associations, changing value and belief systems, . . . and evolving forms of individual and group behavior on playing fields and in the grandstands.[9]

Perhaps just as important was the fact that as people left behind the vast, open spaces of their rural existence for the cramped confines of the city, so they demanded new arenas for the pursuit of those healthful physical pastimes that had become so central in their lives. The narrow city streets and congested urban spaces were indeed dangerous and unhealthy playgrounds for this new and relocated generation of urban dwellers. Before long, urban parks, playgrounds, gymnasia, stadia, and arenas emerged as necessary "breathing spaces" for the production and consumption of sport and as theaters of cathartic outlet from the stresses of urban life, so molding cityscapes forever.

Earlier scholars have clearly established the essential ingredient that city building provided for the modernization of sport. In essence, a previously unmatched base of urban participants and consumers flooded into industrializing cities demanding a suitable replacement for the utilitarian physical pursuits practiced in simple, agrarian society. Challenged by the relative monotony and boredom associated with life in the industrial city, seeking a panacea for declining health among the workforce, and building upon the emerging traditions of mass production and improved communication, social reformers, capitalist entrepreneurs, and municipal and industrial leaders sought to exploit the increasing levels of discretionary capital and more widely available free time to develop, refine, promote, and deliver services and products which, in totality, came to represent the foundation of the sports industry as we know it today.

While the chronology may vary from city to city and country to country, the sequential growth of urban space presented by Van den Berg, Drewett, Klassen, Rossi, and Vijverberg,[10] represents a most useful framework. Growing out of the quiet thoroughfares and the green remnants of the medieval feudal common and frequently bounded by the unpolluted rivers of modest marketplace settlements, the industrial "walking city" became home to a rapid influx of rural settlers as workers sought refuge in close proximity to the means of industrial production. Labeled by Van den Berg et al. (1982) as the process of "urbanization," this first stage was perhaps the most dramatic as a large segment of humanity was first introduced to a lifestyle to which it was unaccustomed and for which it was quite ill prepared. For instance, during the Colonial and Early Republic years in the United States, 95% of the population lived an agrarian, rural existence. However, with the rapid acceleration of American city building after 1820, both the number and size of urban settlements grew. At the outset of the Civil War, there were more than 100 cities with more than 10,000 residents. Though small by contemporary standards, a new and unique urban industrial experience began to emerge, a life characterized by overcrowding, poverty, crime, disease, poor health, squalor, and a deep sense of anomie, all within a stone's throw of the central business district, ironically the focus of urban renewal today. This early urban condition was perhaps no better described than by Clarence Cook who, in 1869, writing of New York, found

> . . . no place within the city limits in which it was pleasant to walk, or ride, or drive, or stroll; no place for skating, no water in which it was safe to row, no field for base-ball or cricket; no pleasant garden where one could sit and chat with a friend, or watch his children play.[11]

Such a scene was, quite clearly, a world apart from that which this first generation of urban dwellers had earlier been accustomed. While public and philanthropic efforts to appropriate and preserve parklike "breathing spaces" in the overcrowded and high-priced "walking city" frequently failed, private ventures in the form of saloons, billiard halls, gymnasia, and sporting arenas sought to capitalize on the urban settlers' demand for recreation and a temporary escape from the many and unfamiliar challenges of city life within late-nineteenth-century North America. Severely limited by the availability of space for the practice and promotion of physical culture, cities soon became the crucible in which the middle-class-led social reform movement was forged. In addition to bringing public education, public health, public libraries, and public housing to the general populace, cities witnessed the emergence of public parks, playgrounds, and baths. At the same time, private, commercial enterprise responded to the demand for mass entertainment through establishing amusement parks, bathing spas, horse-racing tracks, and sports grounds and stadia along the transportation arteries. For those possessing the uncommon means to reach the far-flung periphery, exclusive, private country clubs, golf clubs, and hunt clubs willingly catered to the "conspicuous consumption" of their newfound patrons of privilege.[12]

During the inter-World War period, the process of "exurbanization" (Van den Berg et al., 1982) was initiated, as settlements extended outward from the urban hub along the transportation arteries formed by a maturing railway and road system. Eventually this transportation-led socio-spatial revolution resulted in the appearance of a postindustrial, "radial city," with outlying commuter communities becoming the forerunner of the modern suburb. Thus the "walking city"[13] was eroded both in terms of population deconcentration to the suburban margins and loss of urban space due to the demands of the mass transit networks necessary for moving the newly divided metropolitan population. Following World War II, driven by the dreams of home ownership and ancilliary mass consumption and the promise of less expensive real estate made more accessible by ever-improving spatial mobility, flight from the urban core continued through what Van den Berg et al. (1982) called a process of "counterurbanization." This represented an evolutionary stage characterized by the appearance of the modern "suburban city," peripheral settlements which, though frequently economically dependent on the capital and services offered by the city, commonly demanded a sense of exclusive removal from the parent municipality. Precipitating debates on the meaning of urban citizenship, civic responsibility, and annexation, city parks and recreation departments joined other segments of municipal government in the battle over the provision of services to metropolitan, suburban communities on the periphery. Often resulting in the incorporation of suburban communities and "new towns," and thus ensuring politico-economic and cultural insulation from the urban hub, the resulting "push and pull" of urban-suburban interdependence represents an extremely complex yet essential consideration in understanding the evolution of the modern city. Equally important, although admittedly not addressed fully in the context of this book, is the need to recognize the values, symbols, and practices associated with the [sub]urbanization of sport, which included the gradual relocation of consumer sport from the central business district to the outer reaches of the metropolitan area, easing proximity to sporting spectacles for the affluent, suburban customer.

Today's postmodern, cosmopolitan sprawl is a product of what Van den Berg et al. (1982) call "reurbanization." Characterized by a complexity of paradoxical relationships, Soja[14] offers, perhaps, the clearest understanding of this continuing metamorphosis of the city. He (1989) argues that the changing urban complexion is, in large part, a product of a shift in the economic base, from Fordist mass production and consumption to a more flexible system of production located in new industrial spaces such as the green field "technopoles" associated with high technology. Further, he identifies the rapid growth of financial services in the renovated central business district and the inner-city areas associated with low skill, low pay, and labor-intensive industry, as the other two contrasting urban, economic spatial nuclei consistent with postmodern urban cartography. Soja further argues that an ongoing process of decentralization and recentralization has turned cities "inside out" with an increased urbanization of suburbia and the city fringe, a decline in the population density of the central business district, and the "gentrification" of former working-class neighborhoods. So, while the economic, social, and cultural centers of urban settlement are increasingly flowing to the city's former periphery, the urban core nevertheless retains an important, if reconfigured, role within the life of the city. As the central business district adopts an increasingly (financially based) specialized function and somewhat surreal identity, the previously decaying remnants of the industrial city are renovated into branded spaces of festive consumption for suburban tourists and those from farther afield.

Postmodern theory has provided a new lens through which the relationship between city and sport might be examined. Characterized by the practice of urban psychology, sociology, technology, and organization, and solidly grounded in political economics, sport can be viewed as emblematic of the widespread social cleavages in gender, race, and class.[15] Moreover, the sometimes chaotic and always eclectic form of the postmodern city, devoid of urban planning, sprawls across a seemingly endless hinterland that is appropriated as ex-urban territory by its settlers. This complex, unimpeded process of urban invasion, succession, and segregation has created fragmented, polynucleic cities, in turn, resulting in a contest for space based upon social power relations. This has been manifested in sport and is most clearly exemplified through the polarization of public (parks and playgrounds) and private (country clubs) urban space, wherein citizens may interact and compete anonymously or, rather, choose to be segregated (on the basis of gender, race, class, and religion). Adopted by the Council of Europe in 1992, the *European Urban Charter*[16] recognizes that a complexity of urban problems, including inner-city decay, deprivation, a deterioration of historic centers, excessive traffic densities, a shortage of good quality, affordable housing, and high unemployment, along with noise, air, and soil pollution, has contributed to a postmodern condition of spatial and social inequality in the contemporary city. Accordingly, it has affirmed the right of all urban dwellers to take part in sporting and recreational activities, to develop their expertise in sport up to their individual potential, and to be provided safe, affordable, and local sport facilities.

Faced by a broadening gulf of social, cultural, and economic inequality brought about, in part, by the changing structure of urban labor markets, a small, though growing, technical-managerial elite, a large base of deskilled, low paid workers, the unemployed, and the homeless personify the social fragmentation, segregation, and polarization marking the contemporary city. These growing inequalities between resident classes of the city precipitate tension, leading to spatial withdrawal, insulation, and incarceration reflected by the increasing appearance of walled estates protected by armed guards, shopping malls with state-of-the art surveillance, and new sports stadia frequently located beyond the economic reach of most citizens. Of great significance here is the manner in which different groups and individuals have appropriated sport as a symbol of group affiliation and affirmation. From the affluent "soccer moms" of white, suburban America to the playground basketball tradition of America's black urban ghettos, the complex weave of socioeconomic status, gender, race, and space serves as a prime justification for the importance of better understanding the relationship between sport and the city.

Struggling to retain a sense of civic identity in an ever-changing world and desperate to escape the tensions of contemporary urban life by returning to a time of greater social harmony and civility, today's city is moving to the construction of an urban imaginary through architectural design and urban planning. Clearly, the futuristic, monolithic sports stadia (such as the Astrodome in Houston) constructed worldwide in recent decades, only to be followed by the more recent trend toward the erection of nostalgic architectural remembrances to the "golden years" of professional sports spectacles (such as Camden Yards in Baltimore), support this recent intrusion of emotive "built" signifiers into urban life.

In the United States, the urban playground tradition associated with mostly African-American, scoioeconomically depressed, inner-city neighborhoods has intrigued many cultural onlookers over time.[17] Commonly reinforcing the image of a world characterized by crime, drugs, gambling, poverty, hardships, and hopes and dreams while loudly advocating a pathway out of the ghetto, these often exploitive accounts have contributed toward perpetuating and even romanticizing a mostly young, black, urban, male construct. This is in stark contrast to the lavish, sterile, and conspicuous, ultramodern constructs to sporting extravagance, embracing a status-conscious, fastidious service culture, that greet the privileged customer of the "club" and visitor to the professional "ballpark."

In his excellent and comprehensive book, *Playing the Field*, Charles Eucher suggests "one notable symbol of a city is its sports team, which often is thought to personify the civic spirit."[18] In the same way that "The Big Apple," "The Motor City," and "The Windy City" represent symbolic images of a particular urban setting, such sports teams as Ajax, Arsenal, Celtic, the Cowboys, Yankees, and Red Sox are clearly synonymous with their municipal home. Professional sport franchises emerged in North America and Europe in the late-nineteenth-century city supported by an aggregating industrial populace that experienced an increase in both discretionary time and income. Professional sports teams were the product of an ongoing search for a proximal, socially approved form of entertainment that might serve as recompense for the monotony and toil of city life, and one that offered a sense of shared urban identity.

The power of civic association in sport becomes all the more interesting when one considers the history of widespread, sustainable relocation of teams from one city to another. The once authentic community attachments associated with sports teams have seemingly withered over time as team owners today frequently hold cities to ransom through the threat of relocation and toy with the affections of fans while seeking out more lucrative financial arrangement and markets. This has led to a tradition of infidelity on the part of North American professional sports teams, a pattern that has been devastating to the civic esteem of many urban communities. While the Brooklyn Dodgers' departure from Ebbets Field for Los Angeles in 1957 remains deeply ingrained in the mind of many New Yorkers, today one is hard pressed to identify the contemporary "home" of the National Football League's Giants, Cardinals, Colts, or Rams, given the owners' willingness to relocate their franchises as they search for the proverbial pot of gold. Of course, such is to be expected given today's free-flowing migration of people and the unfettered growth of capitalism. While in years past sports teams frequently were comprised of "home-grown" talent, the continuing search for an economic and a competitive edge has driven recruiters far afield, resulting in team membership possessing little local ties. Moreover, increasingly challenged to consider the potential "return on investment," municipal leaders are projecting the economic benefit of spending millions of taxpayer dollars to attract and retain sports teams and events to their cities, with direct sport investment, tourists, and peripheral investors (hoteliers, restaurateurs, and retail shopping) promising the largest financial returns for the host urban market. To some, the more important economic question remains, what income will be lost, or "leaked" if the city fails to retain or attract a sports team?[19]

Civic leaders are, of course, well versed in making the case that the public's financial investment in sports teams or events, as one part of the broader municipal revitalization portfolio, will strengthen the economy of the community, therefore contributing to an eventual widespread "trickle-down" effect on all facets of the city. Sadly, and in too many cases, public housing deteriorates, public parks become overgrown, and, years after "the greatest sports show" is seduced to town, often through sizable gifts of taxpayers' capital or exemptions, little social or economic amelioration is realized. In short, the likelihood of true and sustained economic gain from civic investment in sport appears to be limited and very much case specific. Indeed, the diversion of public monies from essential social services for the purpose of seducing and subsidizing corporate sport (which, in turn, profits from consumption of its product) just does not appear to make conventional economic sense. Nevertheless, strange though it may seem, Michael Danielson maintains that "cities with decrepit schools and crumbling infrastructure compete to build glittering new arenas and stadiums; [while] governors who slash taxes and cut welfare rolls commit millions of public dollars to sports ventures."[20] Indeed, the bilateral, predatory tactics adopted in the urban relocation of sports teams appears strangely reminiscent of a Darwinist struggle, as Eucher suggests, "Teams manipulate cities by setting themselves against each other in a scramble for the limited number of major league teams. While the cities fight each other, the teams sit back and wait for the best conditions and terms."[21] Moreover, the prevalence of "mobile" or "itinerant firms" in the North American sport marketplace is not expected to change in the foreseeable future, as Eucher believes "the cannibalistic struggles for sports franchises [will undermine] the prospects for local and nationwide prosperity and security," and Danielson predicts that cities "will remain very limited partners of professional sports, building most of the arenas and stadiums, paying more and more of the capital costs, and being frozen out of the decisions, profits, and equity shares."[22]

In response to a growing resistance to public spending on commercial sport ventures, civic and industry leaders are exploring alternative sources of funding ranging from corporate naming rights of events, venues, and teams to the sale of personal seat licenses (PSLs) and luxury suites. For example, Jack Kent Cooke Stadium (now FedEx Field), home of the National Football League's Washington Redskins, opened in September 1997. With a capacity of 80,116, the arena, which includes 208 luxury suites and 15,000 club seats, carried a final price tag of $180 million. Three months later, the MCI Center was opened. Home to the National Basketball Association's Washington Wizards and the National Hockey League's Washington Capitals, the $200 million building accommodates 20,000 spectators and includes 110 luxury suites and 3,000 club seats.

To this point, the contemporary relationship between sport and city has been limited to economic considerations. Less easy to gauge is the emotional and symbolic capital attached to a team or an event. Indeed, the notion of "Big League" and "Minor League" cities appears to have less to do with population and more to do with the strategic direction aspirations of the civic leadership, both public and private. While it is true that a major sport event (such as the Olympic Games) can represent a municipal "rallying point," and a catalyst to urban cohesion, such unity is frequently short lived. Regardless, it cannot be denied that both sports events and teams can provide a powerful collective identity for urban dwellers.

Finally, both Clark and Soja have recognized that the contemporary city is, above all, becoming a heterogeneic center of multicultural and international life and commerce. Frequently resulting in the appearance of ethnic enclaves, and the attendant xenophobic reaction to intergroup tensions and the threat of shifting power relations, the reality of a widening global interdependence in today's urban environment cannot be ignored. Despite a growing sense of skepticism, most "progressive" cities worldwide continue their investment in sport, perhaps in the hope of enhancing their municipal prestige or in search of elevating their sense of civic esteem by becoming a "Big League" city. After all, it is fair to say that few around the world knew of Lillehammer or Nagano prior to their hosting the Winter Olympic Games. Today, each has a clear identity, a location on the world stage, as they have emerged as a popular destination for visitors and investment. Indeed, so important is the "sport prize" to cities today, that the National Association of Sports Commissions (founded in the United States in 1992 as the overarching body for individual urban sport commissions in America) is being replicated worldwide as cities from Beijing to Toronto and Kuala Lumpur to Paris wager a significant portion of their nation's GDP in pandering to the whims of the International Olympic Committee, hoping for that ultimate five-ringed prize. Today, for a city to legitimately claim a position on the world stage, it must claim, in addition to a significant role in transnational business, international finance, and global communication, a significant place in the global sport marketplace.[23]

Based upon the recent pattern of municipal tax investment in sport, one might reasonably challenge the cities' myopic assessment of the potential benefit of sport to the cause of civic betterment. Equally important are the manifest and latent effects that even the most subtle changes in the city-sport relationship may have upon the other, creating a set of important interdependencies that underpin the very framework of this book, leading us to posit the central questions, to what extent has the city emerged as a material or symbolic product of sport, and in what ways is the changing city a producer of the evolving sport economy? While it is clear that sport has represented the glue that bound the seams across some cities and communities through their citizens' affiliation with teams, it has, at the same time, contributed to conflict, both real and symbolic, between municipalities and among neighborhoods within a city. For instance, while one's fanatical following of a local sports team may furnish a sense of social cohesion and civic or community pride so frequently identified as lacking in the sometimes anonymous life of the city, the tension or unbridled violence that frequently erupts inside and outside of the sports arena when rival teams meet in competition fuels claims regarding the criminalization and demonization of urban space. Likewise, the gambling, scalping, and public drunkenness so often associated with the consumption of urban sport further support the detractors. While sport, in its broadest sense of public provision, has sought to address the unhealthy and sedentary tendencies of life in the city, the sometimes corrupt, unjustifiable and often frivolous municipal tax spending on the construction of magnificent "sports palaces" to satisfy the passive consumer appetite of the privileged minority and perhaps even to reward self-interest and personal gain is tantamount to treason.

The real and imagined problems associated with urban life have been well documented and criticized over time and continue to be broadcast and constructed today. To many, urban living conjures up images of overcrowding, unemployment, poverty, homelessness, and high crime. All too often cities are tarnished with the attributes of racial intolerance, social dislocation, a growing sense of anomie, and political and economic impropriety, resulting in a general condition bordering on civic anarchy. The manner in which sport has helped create such an image or, indeed, has served to cure such urban ills is addressed in the following chapters. The radical transition of the industrial "walking city" to postindustrial "radial city," modern "suburbia," and postmodern "cosmopolitan sprawl" continues at varying rates and stages of development around the world. The most recent resurgence of interest in urban revitalization, the blight associated with the continuing human and structural deterioration of inner-city ghettos, and the strengthening resolve by peripheral yet urban-dependent suburban communities to preserve their dreams of an exclusive utopia present a continuing challenge to all. It is the manner in which sport has addressed these and past urban challenges that represents the particular focus of this book.

Acknowledging the integrated complexity of cultural, economic, and political phenomena that comprise the city, the following chapters, grounded in a variety of academic disciplines, examine the ever-changing relationship between sport and the city: place and process and physical structure and human experience. In particular, this book seeks to critically gauge the civic benefits derived from the mutual dependency of sport and the city and to examine sport's distinct role in the creation of utopian urban visions that all too often, and sadly, deteriorate into dystopian realities. In chapter 2, Alan Ingham and Mary McDonald examine sport's role as a form of collective representation and affiliation and theorize the relationship between what they refer to as *representational sports* and their affiliated consumer communities. The authors indicate how professional sport franchises within urban settings effectively inhibit—due to the overdetermining forces of valorization, commodification, and professionalization—the process of community formation by disenfranchising the ordinary consumer. Thus they intimate how sport has come to occupy an abstract space within the late modern city, a space of highly regulated consumption, partaken by strangers with no real sense of affiliation to each other or to the city in which they are temporarily located. While not referring to it specifically, in chapter 3 Gene Burd furthers the discussion initiated in the opening chapter pertaining to the relationship between sport and the construction of *communitas* (the instantiation of temporary group affiliations around special events such as sporting triumphs, allowing for the transcendence of everyday realities and differences). In chapter 3 Burd provides a comprehensive, critical explication of the practices whereby sport architecture, rituals, teams, and both players and coaches have been appropriated by the sports media to substantiate metropolitan images and identities. In doing so, he problematizes the place-based mythologizing centered around sport, which often manifests itself in the feel-good discourses of civic achievement, hope, and survival: something habitually espoused by city mayors looking to circumvent the socioeconomic and race-based divisions that plague most North American cities. Focusing on the urban sport statue, in chapter 4, Synthia Sydnor Slowikowski nonetheless provides a further exemplar of the signifying capacities of sporting artifacts. In her own inimitable style, Sydnor Slowikowski provides an insightful reading of urban sport statuary in which she identifies statues of athletes as emotion-laden signifiers that preserves, in embodied freeze-frame, particular socially constructed categories and ideals. However, she also offers an alternative view, keying on the notion of the urban sport statue as a fluid, cultural space providing its viewers access to liminal narratives of becoming. Herein, sport culture is less of an agent of collective affiliation as it is an expression of individual realization.

Moving from the mainstream to the margins of urban sport culture, in chapter 5 Robin Mathy exposes the plight of the homeless within major metropolitan areas during major athletic events. Focusing on Tempe, Arizona, during January 1996, the author's ethnographic investigation analyzes the effects on the homeless of staging the Fiesta Bowl and Super Bowl within a matter of a few weeks. While acknowledging the futility of direct attempts by authorities to rid the local of the homeless "problem," Mathy identifies the unintended consequences of executing major sporting events—specifically, the dearth of affordable, short-term housing, mass transport, and assistance programs—in impeding the ability of individuals to extricate themselves from their homeless predicament. From one outsider group to another, in chapter 6 Michael Atkinson furnishes an intriguing entrée into the world of the urban ticket scalper. His precise observations of the ticket-scalping culture exhume a world divided into professional and temporary exponents of this illegal practice. Refusing to be drawn conclusively on the morality, or otherwise, of scalping, Atkinson does reveal the layers of corruption and collusion between scalpers and promoters, ticket agents, and the general public that would seem to ensure the endurance of this most ingrained urban sport subculture. Both implicated in the seamier side of the sport economy, the late-nineteenth-century criminal organizations discussed by Steven Riess in chapter 7 provide an interesting contrast to the late-twentieth-century free market entrepreneurs identified by Atkinson. In his meticulous historical examination, Riess demonstrates how in Chicago horse racing became a mutually beneficial point of engagement between organized crime syndicates and urban political machines, the former seeking to nurture their gambling enterprises through the preferential treatment resulting from their political connections, and the latter offering such indulgence in exchange for much needed donations to party coffers and the timely swelling of the ranks of party workers. Interestingly, Riess's and Atkinson's work converges again on the notion of victimless crimes since, despite their respective illegality, both scalping and gambling provide services in considerable demand by their temporally and spatially respective metropolitan populaces.

Staying with a historical focus, this time shifting into the realm of ethnic sport cultures within the urban setting, in chapter 8 Danny Rosenberg recounts the sporting experiences of the Jewish population in Toronto during the first four decades of the twentieth century. Rosenberg identifies how the Jewish community formed sporting teams, leagues, clubs, and associations and revered local Jewish sport heroes. In recounting a particularly vibrant and complex sport culture, Rosenberg's historical findings demonstrate how sport became an agent for both consolidating Jewish identities and establishing commonalities with other ethnic groups within the polyethnic milieu of Toronto neighborhood life. In chapter 9, Brian Wilson and Phil White bring the discussion of urban Toronto up-to-date with their symbolic, interactionist study of the lived experiences of youth frequenting an inner-city recreation drop-in center. The authors discovered that the formally espoused regimes of freedom and responsibility created a climate within which many youth developed a more positive, proactive, and confident sense of self, as expressed in the intricacies of the unofficial peer culture that developed within the center. Subsequently, Wilson and White outline important directions for future research focused on the urban youth experience, and that concerned with identifying the benefits—or otherwise—derived from such youth recreation drop-in programming for those living in relatively violent and impoverished inner-city settings. In chapter 10, Michael Clark turns to more programmatic concerns related to the delivery of urban sport and recreation programs. The author summarizes a two-year study of sport activities available to youth in the Detroit metropolitan area, from which he makes summary recommendations based on the need to address the dearth of comprehensive activity programs in the area. Perhaps most pertinently, Clark distinguishes the need to identify, engage, educate, and reward community volunteers in order to implement a sustainable and an effective recreation program. Moving from the urban to the suburban, in chapter 11 David Andrews, Robert Pitter, Detlev Zwick, and Darren Ambrose identify soccer's socio-spatial distribution within Memphis's greater metropolitan area. The authors discovery of youth soccer's appropriation by the predominantly white, suburban middle class illustrates sport's position at the intersection of class- and race-based divisions. In this regard, they illustrate the extent to which soccer has contributed to the symbolic construction of the idealized American suburb.

Shifting the focus to the racial politics of contemporary urban spaces, in chapter 12 CL Cole and Samantha King critically engage the renowned documentary, *Hoop Dreams*, and Spike Lee's movie, *Clockers*. Focusing primarily on *Hoop Dreams*, the authors argue that this mediated, ethnographic chronicle masquerades as a naturalistic and an authentic depiction of the contemporary, inner-city experience in a manner that seemingly challenges the routine representation of America's urban spaces and populations in the popular media. Far from offering such a progressive viewpoint, Cole and King assert that the discursive exclusions that structure the *Hoop Dreams* narrative actually corroborate the middle-class American audience's preconceived prejudices regarding the African-American populace, and their own sense of moral superiority. Building upon this notion of the discursive constitution of raced urban spaces, in chapter 13 Gamal Abdel-Shehid explores the "*Hoop Dreams* anthropology" underpinning a report commissioned by Basketball Canada, looking into allegations of racism in a Canadian men's national basketball team. Abdel-Shehid exposes the racist logic—once again masquerading under the guise of liberal sentiments—framing this official statement. In particular, he critiques the manner in which the report mobilizes the seemingly benign yet highly charged notion of urban space: a de facto euphemism or, indeed, shorthand for racial Otherness. By spatializing racial and cultural difference in this manner, the report effectively erases the possibility of racism, thereby exonerating the accused. However, as the author notes, this is done in a way that both essentializes and blames Canada's nonwhite urban spaces and populations for any racial disharmony experienced by its purportedly model multiculturalism. Lastly, in chapter 14, Andrew Thornton examines the production and experience of a particular racialized urban space centered on the staging of a 3-on-3 basketball event in downtown Toronto. From his ethnographic observations, he depicts the struggle that ensued around this event over the ability to control public space, representation, and identity. Thornton identifies the competing logics that enveloped the tournament, which viewed it as anything from a form of cultural policing and conformity to a spatially contained demonstration of black expressiveness and identity. Thus like Cole and King and Abdel-Shehid before him, Thornton exposes sport's position in the urban setting as a perpetually fluid terrain of racial contestation and identification.

Notes

1. Clark, D. (1996). *Urban world/global city* (p. 1). London: Routledge.

2. Weber, A. F. (1899). *The growth of cities in the nineteenth century*. New York: Macmillan; 1962 reprint, Ithaca, NY: Cornell University Press.

3. Harvey, D. (1973). *Social justice and the city*. London: Edward Arnold.

4. Notable exceptions, characterized by the following case studies of selected cities, are: Adelman, M. (1986). *A sporting time: New York City and the rise of modern athletics, 1820–70*. Urbana: University of Illinois Press; Gems, G. R. (1997). *Windy city wars: Labor, leisure, and sport in the making of Chicago*. London: The Scarecrow Press; Hardy, S. (1982). *How Boston played: Sport, recreation, and community, 1865–1915*. Boston: Northeastern University Press; Meller, H. E. (1976). *Leisure and the changing city, 1870–1914*. London: Routledge and Kegan Paul; Riess, S. A. (1989). *City games*. Urbana: University of Illinois Press; Ross, S. J. (1985). *Workers on the edge: Work, leisure, and politics in industrializing Cincinnati, 1788-1890*. New York: Columbia University Press; Somers, D. (1972). *The rise of sports in New Orleans, 1850–1900*. Baton Rouge: Louisiana State University Press.

5. Riess, 259.

6. Somers, 275.

7. Meller, 237.

8. Hardy, 197.

9. Riess, 254.

10. Van den Berg, L. R., Drewett, R., Klassen, L. H., Rossi, A., & Vijverberg, C. H. T. (1982). *A study of growth and decline*. London: Pergamon.

11. Cook is quoted in Riess, 71.

12. "Conspicuous consumption" is a phenomenon broadly expounded upon in Veblen, T. (1899). *The theory of the leisure class*. New York: Macmillan. See also Mayo, J. M. (1998). *The American country club: Its origins and development*. New Brunswick, NJ: Rutgers University Press.

13. Jackson, K. T. (1985). *Crabgrass frontier*. New York: Oxford University Press.

14. Soja, E. (1989). *Postmodern geographies*. London: Routledge.

15. Harvey, 25, 66.

16. Council of Europe. (1992). *European urban charter*. Strasbourg: Council of Europe. Theme 4.8. "Sport and leisure in urban areas."

17. Among them, Anderson, L., & Millman, C. (1999). *Pickup artists: Street basketball in America*. London: Verso Books; Axthelm, P. (1970). *The city game: From the garden to the playgrounds*. New York: Penguin; Frey, D. (1994). *The last shot. City streets, basketball dreams*. New York: Simon & Schuster; Telander, R. (1988). *Heaven is a playground*. New York: Simon & Schuster.

18. Eucher, C. C. (1993). *Playing the field* (p. 168). Baltimore: Johns Hopkins University Press.

19. "Leaked income" refers to economic investment (both corporate and individual) that will move out of a city to a competing and proximal host market.

20. Danielson, M. N. (1997). *Home team: Professional sports and the American metropolis* (p. 305). Princeton: Princeton University Press.

21. Eucher, 179.

22. Eucher, 184; Danielson, 306.

23. These key attributes are identified and discussed in Knox, P. L., & Taylor, P. J. (Eds.). (1995). *World cities in a world-system*. Cambridge: Cambridge University Press. The argument here is that "World City" status may, in part, be bestowed on those that have hosted recent major sports events (such as the Summer Olympic Games and FIFA's World Cup), including Sydney, Los Angeles, and Paris.

2

Sport and Community/*Communitas*

Alan G. Ingham and Mary G. McDonald

INTRODUCTION

Sport, for the most part, finds its location in ordinary culture—it is either recreational or, for want of a better term, representational. Given the variable nature of recreational, that is, primarily participatory sports, we shall say little about them in this chapter.[1] By representational, we refer to organized competitive sports (amateur or professional) that in various ways act as what Emile Durkheim (1965) called *representations collectives*, signifiers of we-ness, ways in which the group conceives of itself in its relations with objects that affect it, and sources of social solidarity. As an object with which we identify, an athlete or a sports team defines as a "community" all those who relate to the object cathectically or in a possessive manner—our athlete, our team—and who introject the "representation" into their self-definitions (I am a *** fan; I wanna be like Mike [Jordan]).

In today's media-saturated, virtual society, members of representational sport "communities" do not necessarily inhabit a shared geophysical space. Fans can form symbolic "communities" in distantiated relational space. One way that this is accomplished is through communications technologies. For example, enthusiasts of the Atlanta baseball franchise can identify with their team even if they do not live in the city of Atlanta, Georgia. This identification is most notably enabled by the "sport/media complex" (see Jhally, 1989) and, in the case of the Atlanta team, by the Turner broadcasting conglomerate. The identification with a team in distantiated relational space might seem a rather privatized emotional activity. Lest we forget, Internet technologies now allow some privileged members of the collectivity to share their passions via cyberspace and to discuss all aspects of the Atlanta team. In Europe, the fanzine also assists in this endeavor. In turn, media and Internet technologies may influence the composition of the audience at the event. For example, Manchester United, the English soccer champions, have been represented in virtual reality (by SkyTel,

---

Some portions of this chapter are modified extractions from the work of Ingham, Howell, and Schilperoort (1987).

which not only televises their games but also has infused money into the premier league) across Europe and Scandinavia. Moreover, the "club" has foreign
stars on its roster. As a result of these tendencies, as well as the relatively recent requirement for all-seater stadia, the traditional spectators of the 1950s,
working-class "caps" who stood in the terraces and petit bourgeois "trilbies"
who sat in the stands, have been replaced by a more multicultural, affluent formation. If one does not possess a season ticket, it is almost impossible to obtain
entrance to the events at Old Trafford (paying the "scalper" being the obvious
exception). In short, new media technologies and changes in league rules concerning the acquisition of foreign players have their political-economic consequences. Regardless of whether we are talking about the European premier
leagues or the North American major leagues, many fans are being priced out
of the primary consumer role, yet the opportunities for secondary and tertiary
consumption (see Loy, 1968) are expanding.

Thus while representational sport allows for the creation of particular
forms of "community" anchored in the popular, cross-class alliances are formed
around the collective representation in terms of support and fandoms, but not
necessarily in terms of how this support is organized, celebrated, and understood (see Hornby, 1992; Lewis, 1992). The process of identification is not
only mediated by biography, social differentiation, and stratification but also
has significant consequences for the geophysical and affectual space of the city.
For this reason, we place in double quotation marks the concept of "community." It is a matter of debate as to how solidaristic the coalition or community
really is vis-à-vis its sporting icons.

In this chapter we attempt to theorize the relationship between representational sports and their proximal and distantiated consumer "communities"
rather than to provide numerous empirical examples. Our analysis begins with
a brief discussion of the various political and social histories which, in their critiques of capitalist relations, have anticipated the tendency for nostalgia within
rationalized capitalist societies.

ON COMMUNITY

The concept of community has a long history, but we begin our definitions in
the work of Ferdinand Tonnies (1957). His concepts of *Gemeinschaft* and
Gesellschaft (community and society) stand at the heart of sociological com-
mentaries concerning the social costs of modernization. As ideal types, they
contrast the relationships that are characterized by a high degree of emotional
intimacy and social cohesion with those that are more contractual and find
their basis in the functionally differentiated division of labor characteristic of
contemporary societies.[2] In Tonnies (1957), we can see a value-laden concern
about the deformation of community, which results from the spread of the

industrial order throughout the modern world. This concern about community deformation, now as then, is not merely intellectual: at the heart of this concern, there is a politics of nostalgia in which visions of the past stand as a critique of present forms of social association. By "visions," we imply that we recapture a past that we have not experienced in the form of a desire for what should be. This recapturing is selective. We bracket off knowledge about the political-economic organization of societies in which these solidaristic communities were located, and we forget the affectual violence that oftentimes accompanied rather intense and continuous face-to-face social interactions and the popular cultural productions that resided in such. Nevertheless, when we now use the concept of community, we do so as a symbol of the "good society" that the various processes linked to modernization have extirpated. This normative critique of present-day social arrangements also shows up in the work of Max Weber and Charles Horton Cooley.

Weber (1978) viewed modernity as the thoroughgoing rationalization of social life. Pessimistically, he envisioned abstract, functional/formal rationality to be superseding tradition, affect, and custom as the basis for social organization. Capitalism and technobureaucratic organizations would individuate in ways that threatened the substantive rationality of the individual, leading to estrangement. Rationalization, emotional detachment, and impersonality would transform communality—imperatively organized groups would replace kinships and fraternal bondings. Cooley (1967) primarily focused his critique of modernity in terms of the impact it was having on the primary group, or what George Herbert Mead might have called a "circle of significant others" (Mead, 1934). For Cooley, modernity would extenuate rather than extend moral standards derived from love, freedom, and justice. Along with Tonnies and Weber, Cooley viewed modernity as an impoverishment of human relationships: the pecuniary/instrumental nexus turned the subtle and grateful "being-for-one-another" into a highly schematized, specialized, precise, and exact mode of existence.

We must take note of the life spans of the theorists acknowledged above. They were born circa 1860 and died circa 1925. Writing some 50 years later, Louis Wirth, one of the founding members of the Chicago School of urban sociology, cast a different light on the consequences of modernity. Wirth (1938) viewed modernity not as a collapse of communal and segmental bonding but as a determinant in the reformation of the segmental community under a changed set of social relations. Wirth's argument was anchored in the concept of xenophobia, or the general aversion to the strange/different. This general aversion to heterogeneity, anchored in categorical status, was seen by Wirth as replacing the enforced homogeneity anchored in kith and kin. Echoes of Wirth can be found in the more recent work of Richard Sennett (1974). The latter also argues that the overall tendencies of mature capitalism may have deformed the organic communities of the premodern period, but that, paradoxically, they have reformed communality in highly segmented and purified forms—forms that represent all classes, not just those of the urban industrial classes, such as Wirth analyzed. While work has become increasing differentiated, our home bases are firmly rooted in our material, social,[3] and cultural capital, and our heterophobias.

These insights about community raise a continuity/discontinuity problem. On the one hand, there are those who see continuity between the structured, segmental, communal forms of solidarity of the past and the structured, co-erced, or preferred segmental bonding of the present. Presumably, since there is continuity in the forms of social bonding, there will be continuity in the cultures that segmental bonding creates (see Dunning, 1983). On the other hand, there are those who view capitalism, particularly industrial capitalism, as a force for discontinuity and disintegration. Socialized commodity production, ratio-nalized relations of production, the increasing distantiation between spheres of production and spheres of consumption, the schematization of social admin-istration and planning, and the functional division of labor all combine to form a distinctively new social order and new relations of social relations. This pe-riod of history is referred to as "modernity" or "Fordism" and is now, some would argue, being replaced by postmodernity, which is linked to a new form of capitalism, namely, nomad capitalism (see Williams, 1989, p. 124) and flexible capital accumulation (see Harvey, 1989, and note 1) which, in contemporary capitalist societies, extenuate the ties between capital and community and, through outsourcing, destroy the basis of traditional working-class communi-ties and even national working-class cultures and solidarities.

The extent of these transformations (and, importantly, their capacity to form a distinctive era of postmodernity) is still open to debate. Suffice it to say that the changes wrought by industrial capitalism do not extinguish the quest for community (symbolic or real), nor does the postmodern focus on images, heterogeneity of meaning, and the multiplicity of identity eliminate the quest (symbolic or real) for homogeneity. What they do—to reverse Durkheim's (1933) evolutionary concepts of mechanical and organic solidarity—is elimi-nate the organic, "can live your whole life in it" forms of community and pro-duce new forms of social solidarities of coerced (for the politically and materially powerless) or preferential homogeneities.

Additionally, according to Young:

> Within the context of capitalism, . . . racism, ethnic chauvinism, and class devaluation . . . grow partly from a desire for community, that is, from the desire to understand themselves and from the desire to be understood as I understand myself. Practically speaking, such mutual understanding can be approximated only within a homoge-neous group that defines itself by common attributes. Such common identification, however, entails references also to those excluded. (1990, p. 311)

From this perspective, "community" suggests both an appeal to the included and an often unspoken understanding of just who is *not* a part of our "community."

The inclusion/exclusion aspects of community have considerable value for this discussion of representational sport. Historically, sport has existed among a vast array of cultural and political practices designed to construct boundaries around particular groups of people—to differentiate between and separate certain "communities" from others. Today's highly competitive Western sport, for example, can trace its roots to an English athletic system developed over a century ago. Exclusive clubs and romantic notions of the amateur gentleman were the class-based and ideological means by which wealthy men prohibited the working class from competing on the same athletic fields (see Ingham, 1978, chap. 2; Morford & McIntosh, 1993). This elitist creed was adopted by Pierre de Coubertin and codified in practice upon the reintroduction of the Olympic Games in 1896.

The United States witnessed a similar history of class-based exclusionary practices in its adoption of the sporting forms developed in the English Athletic Revival (see Ingham, 1978, chap. 2; Ingham & Beamish, 1993). In addition, sporting practices in the United States have reproduced and reinforced status differentiations and subcommunity categorical boundaries existing within the wider culture. One has only to think of the long and sordid history of racial segregation and ethnic discrimination in American sports (see Brooks & Althouse, 1993; Edwards, 1969; Olsen, 1968; Ribalow, 1948, for general overviews). Professional baseball provides the notable example here. African Americans were once members of the major league baseball teams in the 1890s, yet prevailing white supremicist ideology forged an unspoken agreement to ban them from the so-called "national" pastime. From this exclusion, the Negro leagues took on particular significance within the segregated black "community" until Jackie Robinson "broke the color barrier" in 1947. From the perspective of the African-American "communities," it might be argued that the "breaking of the color barrier" was a mixed blessing. On the one hand, it allowed outstanding African-American athletes the social mobility that they richly deserved. On the other hand, the reintegration of African Americans into professional sport allowed whites to claim that sport was a beacon of meritocracy. Despite the presence of African Americans in elite competitive sports and the increasingly large Latino presence in major league baseball today, structural racism continues to segregate communities of people of color from whites both in and out of sport. Recent changes in the microeconomics of professional team sports, for example, have led to the situation where fewer members of minority groups are able to attend major league sporting events—reintegration on the field recently has been accompanied by segregation in the "bleachers."

Just as noteworthy is the recognition that even within status-homogeneous sub-"communities" (and in the special experiences of *communitas*, which we discuss later in this chapter), there is and has been one major source of differentiated inequality within patriarchal societies: gender. Typically when we talk about the representational sport and the community problematic, we do so through a privileged male perspective. Indeed, much of what we have to say in this chapter focuses on commercialized elite male sport, which still exists as the dominant model of representational sport. Feminist scholarship over the last 20 years, however, has not only pointed to the idea that men's pleasure is women's work but also to the idea that sport is only one social institution among others that requires radical gender restructuring both in the production and consumption sides of social relations and in the meaning of participation in the civic ritual.

Shifting gender relations and the logics of twentieth-century capitalism have combined to create new and niche markets for professional team sports for women. The fall of 1996, for example, saw the launching of the American Basketball League, and in the summer of 1997, the Women's National Basketball Association (WNBA) games premiered. Yet despite these and other challenges, representational sport is largely overdetermined by its masculinist history. That representational sport is largely a male preserve is suggested by overwhelming cultural, political, media, and economic support. Indeed, Canadian sport sociologist and political activist Bruce Kidd (1990, p. 32) refers to the Toronto Skydome as the "men's cultural center." Because of the efforts of male politicians (although some women mayors have been complicitous, e.g., Roxanne Qualls of Cincinnati) infamous for their hostility to feminist causes, public funds and tax abatements have been used to create a stage for male team games. Thus male power is legitimated and maintained as public and private investments in stadia construction (especially single-purpose facilities that give sport team owners more political and economic leverage over city officials than do their domed counterparts) prevent alternative uses of these resources that might redress the culturally created disadvantages that women endure. Recognition of this masculinist agenda exposes even seemingly homogeneous, representational sporting "communities" as being internally stratified.

These examples reveal that the forces of later twentieth-century capitalism enable and intertwine with historically forged and increasingly complex social relations. What also has happened is that internally stratified, traditional caste, and class-based communities exist alongside of and in most cases have been substantially marginalized by prestige-based communities in which consumption relations rather than production relations form the basis of social approbation. Nowhere is this more evident than in U.S. urban/metropolitan spaces, given the dramatic shifts in the economy since the 1970s.

Declining markets, unemployment, the growth of part-time positions with few benefits, deindustrialization, and globalization have all exerted enormous burdens on the financial viability of cities and their inhabitants. Since 1972, the feminization of poverty, plant closings, and neoconservative political agendas have contributed to the growing number of urban poor and to a shifting composition of the urban poor population. Indeed, female heads of households, racial minorities, and children now form a substantial proportion of those living in urban poverty.

Especially in the 1980s and 1990s, attempts to economically revitalize urban "communities" have produced new forms of construction and strategies of legitimation. In the (post) Fordist American city, those with capital have assisted in creating fresh consumer "communities" by encouraging the consumption of events, spectacles, history, and festivals (Harvey, 1989).

As a component of what can be identified as relationally abstract consumption "communities," representational sport exists as one of a series of lifestyle practices and amusement choices designed to distinguish between groups of people. As media technologies expand and as the forces of globalization escalate, status and a sense of belongingness are increasingly gained by partaking in the good life as proffered and encouraged by producers of the preferred products and entertainment. Here, consumption-based prestige is not the prerogative of just the elites, but rather it is sought in all strata and social groupings (Goode, 1978). Those with wealth can literally embody the fashionable and engage in fancy milling: they are "Where the action is" (see Goffman, 1967, p. 197). Those with less money are only able to participate in these consumer "communities" in varying degrees. Many are left to participate vicariously—in their wish-fulfilling dreams or as actors in the sideshows occurring in the bleachers or stands and accompanying the main events. Regardless, prestige communities require punctilious conformity (see Goode, 1978) in lifestyle and thus reinforce the xenophobic impulse.

Surveillance of and sensitivity to boundary lead to the defense of boundary in a way that encourages internal purification, as is evidenced in status-differentiated enclaves of lifestyle. Also, this differentiated and status-based cultural power is reinforced by state and substate policies in the allocation of the amenity infrastructures of collective consumption. This transformation in the relations of social relations facilitates the demarcation between the irreplaceable and the expendable—the wanted and the unwanted, respectively. This demarcation is especially visible in the built environments of amenity infrastructures—both in where and what is built, in the internal, social ecology of the structures themselves, and in the pricing of access to such amenities. As noted previously, many stadia have been built under the guise of urban renewal, yet those living in closest proximity to them cannot afford the price of admission. Ironically, in the case of the imposition of regressive taxes (e.g., the use of sales taxes) to fund such stadium construction, it is also the poor who bear a disproportionate burden of paying for such facilities. Moreover, tax abatements and the creation of what are tantamount to tax-free zones to entice corporate investments create shortfalls in funding for services that the poor desperately need—education, urban renewal, sewer and water provision, and public safety.

Xenophobia causes the concept of the popular to have mixed meanings—popular as in everyone likes it; popular as in, because everyone likes it, it must be inferior. Status xenophobia also has contradictions in cultural politics. Often, from an elitist perspective, "we" and "them" can articulate in the popular in various ways: we should educate them; we need them or their taxes to get what we want (a new center for the fine arts or a new stadium in which to locate our luxury boxes and our hopes for more capitalist investment in a big league city), and we need them to buy into our "community" creations and our imagined "community" to preserve harmony in status relations which, in reality, are both culturally patronizing and economically exploitative. This is the unexplored or dark side of the concept of "community"—its cultural and political abuse. In contemporary society, the economically and politically powerful with access to important signifying systems such as the media are able to mobilize the politics of nostalgia, drawing upon romanticized versions of community, just as they recreate enticing images of community in order to attract private and public investments. Yet it is doubtful that the poorest in a given urban space will benefit significantly, if at all, from these expenditures. Indeed, this shift in economic content and form has, in many cases, exacerbated poverty and status differentials.

There is more to this dark side of a concept that is unusual among the terms of political vocabulary in being the one term that has never been used in a negative sense: it is the linkage of a habit of mutual obligation to the possibility of exploitation. As Raymond Williams expressed the case:

> If you have the sense that you have this kind of native duty to others, it can expose you very cruelly within a system of the conscious exploitation of labor. And it is for a long time a very powerful appeal, one that it is still repeatedly used in politics, that you have this kind of almost absolute obligation to the "community," that the assertion of interest against it is merely selfish. (1989, p. 114)

Thus the use of the concept of "community" becomes perverse when the interests of domination are concealed in the concept, and when opposition to these interests is designated as selfish, that is, when city managers, in their role of entrepreneurs of the public interest and speaking on behalf of the community as a whole, repress and exploit communities of locality in the interests of the dominant corporate groups.

The capacity for concerted action among the rich and powerful is nowhere better exemplified than in their attempts to persuade ordinary citizens to give up some of their hard-earned dollars (in the form of taxes) to subsidize their projects. These projects are wide ranging, including the building of such temples of consumption such as aquariums, museums of history, convention sites, banks, and shopping areas. Notably, with regard to sport, the *Christian Science Monitor* reports:

More than a third of the 113 teams in the four [U.S.] major-league sports (baseball, football, basketball, and hockey) are seeking to change their facilities, according to a report from Fitch Investors Service. In almost all other cases, the team owners are trying to force local and state governments to come up with all or much of the funding for a new facility. (February 2, 1996, p. 3:3)

From the perspective of the exploited soccer fan, Hornby (1992, p. 150) sums up the case nicely: "In the end I learned, from this period more than any other in my footballing history, that it simply doesn't matter to me how bad things get, that results have nothing to do with anything. . . . For us, the consumption is all; the quality of the product is immaterial." The chains of loyalty are precisely what predatory capitalism has in mind when its representatives appeal to the bonds of "community" to make their decisive interventions into the culture of the "community as a whole." Yet is there a mighty contradiction here? Under conditions of monopoly provision (conditions that prevail for most league sports and other professional tournaments), providers raise ticket prices and demand public subsidies (in the United States, cities may even subsidize franchises for low attendance at the gate), even after losing seasons. Thus they are beginning to price out the very fandoms or subcommunities that provide them with continuous support and leave themselves prey to the new consumerist, identity-fickle audience. They may be, in this regard, just "riding a wave." After all, in a culture committed to differentiation and distinction, tastes and lifestyle choices are not static: today's private seat license or box seats or luxury box at the stadium may give way to tomorrow's hot new consumer option.

While we have noted the period during which the critiques of industrial society arose and have offered brief discussions of the problematic of community in contemporary urban spaces, we have not considered the concept of time per se. After all, "communities" are not only spatial, they are temporal. In a sense, "community" represents a temporal commitment—without the commitment to making and reproducing "community," it is doubtful that community, in the modern sense, could exist. This caveat once again moves us away from the idealized and normative definitions of community that have served to totalize and detemporalize social relations by positing a dichotomy between the seemingly authentic communities of yesteryear and the inauthentic communities of late-twentieth-century capitalism. With Young (1990), we challenge this ahistoricity and suggest that such a conceptualization obscures the contradictions and negates the possibilities of challenging existing social relations within existing consumer "communities." There is too much traditional populism at the heart of this argument and insufficient consideration for new and "media-ated" forms of populism (e.g., communication webs on the Internet).

ON *COMMUNITAS*

In his *The Ritual Process: Structure and Anti-Structure*, Victor Turner (1969, chap. 4) introduced the concept of *communitas*—a special experience during which individuals are able to rise above those structures that materially and normatively regulate their daily lives and that unite people across the boundaries of structure, rank, and socioeconomic status (see also Turner, 1974; Harding, 1983). Turner (1969, p. 132) distinguishes three forms of communitas: (a) the spontaneous and short lived; (b) the ideological affirmation of spontaneous communitas; and (c) the normative, subcultural attempt to maintain the relationships of spontaneous communitas on a more permanent basis. For Turner (1974, pp. 84–86), the forces of modernity have eroded communitas except at the subcommunity or the fragmented, segmental, categoric levels of sociality. This assertion requires some distinction between the permanent and the ideological. While we might agree with Turner that the conditions giving rise to permanent communitas have long since passed, we note that contemporary social relations present opportunities for the concept of "community," in the form of communitas, to be the object of much ideological work. Attention must focus on the concept of *civic ritual*.

The symbolism (*representations*) associated with rituals (in the form of festivals, public spectacles, and other cultural performances) has been of interest to anthropologists, sociologists, folklorists, and historians. Building on the work of Emile Durkheim, Franz Boas and Durkheim's student, Marcel Mauss, developed common themes such as the relation between ritual and identity, between ritual and the establishment of links between individuals and their subcommunities, and between ritual and the submersion of the subcommunities into a community as a whole. That the symbolism of ritual can induce communal bonding has been promoted by Turner (1974); that symbols per se can promote the imagination of community has been argued by Anthony Cohen (1985). Previously we distinguished between permanent and ideological communitas. A second distinction that can be inferred is that of structural versus symbolic communitas. We make no distinction between these distinctions, for much of representation concerning communitas takes symbolically ideological forms that are made in reference to position in social structures. We note that ideological work is being used increasingly (in television and advertising) to symbolically camouflage the lack of genuine structural reform.

Camouflage (opacity in inequality) is inherent in civic ritual, and the persistent use of civic rituals casts doubt on Turner's assertion that communitas is present only at the subcommunity level of social relations. If communitas were to be present only at subcommunity levels, then the commitments by civic leaders to use civic rituals as vehicles for its regeneration would have no meaning or function—a civic ritual would be a waste of time, money, and energy. Thus we assert that while structural communitas has eroded in its meaningful value, there is plenty of evidence to suggest that there is a tremendous amount of ideological effort to promote and regenerate communitas under a changed (structural and cultural) set of circumstances. Here it is important to understand the civic in the civic ritual. Ingham, Howell, and Schilperoort (1987) needed a term that reflected changes in the relationship between the state and civil society as reproduced in the contemporary use of ritual, especially those serial civic rituals associated with league sporting events. The tremendous articulation between the state and civil society achieved under Fordist political economy meant that classical distinction between the public and private sectors had become hard to sustain. Given the interpenetration of the state and civil society, especially in the production of rituals, the concept of *civic* ritual had to be invented. Civic ritual thus was seen by Ingham et al. as requiring the combined resources (social and economic capitals) of both the state (or substate) and private capital, and as a combination of the hegemonic interests of public officials and the capitalist business class with the view to making these hegemonic interests and the situated interests of subordinate groups and communities into a conjoint articulation or an unequal complementarity (see Hall, Critcher, Jefferson, Clarke, & Roberts, 1978, p. 156; Sumner, 1979, p. 295).

Sport and the Construction of *Communitas*

One of the key arguments made in the Ingham et al. (1987) publication was that representational sport has moved historically from social to abstract economic space, thus making it difficult for sport to be instrumental in the creation of an empowering local "community." The abstract spatiality of representational sport was attributed to changes in the value-creating capacities of representational sport—from early forms of commercialism to current forms of monopoly in the consumer marketplace and monopsony in the labor market place. Several concepts have been used to describe this change, including valorization, commodification, and professionalization. One of the consequences combining these processes is that of the changing relations between producer and consumer groups, especially the disenfranchising of ordinary people in the determination of what would be popular.

Now we do not wish to fall prey to the very politics of nostalgia that we have been critiquing all along: of course, there has never been full participation in the cultural formation called "community," nor has there been equal access to representational sport "communities." Still, following Clarke and Critcher (1985, pp. 95–97), a case can be made that the audience of professional sports has been transformed from one that had an active, membership-style commitment to the club into one that, even if it could not enjoy the status of membership, did at least expect a customer's stake in the club in the form of a producer-consumer contract. Currently denied the active commitment of membership and the informal contract between producer and consumer, the sport's audience is reduced to a dependency upon monopolistic sources of supply to which there are no viable alternatives and to a dependency that limits the audience to only one sanction against displeasure—the choice of not to buy.

The crucial question is whether representational sport remains an effective vehicle for the manufacturing of "community," or whether it can merely serve momentarily in the generation of spontaneous communitas. We argue for the latter. The die-hard fan may be there no matter what, but spontaneous communitas requires something above the mundane—a league championship or equivalent. Only the diehard can be satisfied with miserable serial civic rituals—indeed, it may be that audience subcommunities are generated from misery loves company conditions. Only the exceptional can provoke spontaneous communitas. But spontaneous communitas is fleeting and cannot form the basis for community per se. Community involves time and social commitment, and the investment of social capital. Community, in the utopian sense, involves trust and obligation, and representational sport, especially in North America, provides no basis for such. Here franchise relocations are frequent, and the threat of relocation plays a large role in the blackmailing of urban centers with regard to stadium improvements (see Euchner, 1993; Ingham, et al., 1987; Johnson, 1978, 1983, 1985, 1986; Richmond, 1993; Schimmel, Ingham, & Howell, 1993).

Thus another consequence of the transformation of sport from social to abstract economic space is in the elevation of surplus and exchange values over use-values. This confrontation between abstract surplus and exchange value definitions and social use-value definitions of sport and sporting space may lie at the heart of the private/public, capital/community contradiction that civic ideologies of urban boosterism ("We are a major league city, so invest here!"), trickle-down effects (sport franchises create jobs—albeit, we note, low-paying, part-time jobs with no health insurance or pensions), and the magical creation of community as a whole seek to mystify. Just as a class formation must be seen in terms of a founding moment, a possible deforming moment, as well as possible reforming moments or periods (see Therborn, 1980, p. 93), so too should we view "community." And in this viewing we should remember one fundamental relation between capital and "community." It is that economic capital is mobile; geophysical communities as a whole[4] (as social and cultural capitals) are not (Hill, 1983, pp. 80–125). In the United States, we also can state that sport franchises are mobile, while urban populations are not. Thus the chicken and the egg question for cities is: do "communities" deform and franchises leave, or do franchises leave and assist in the "community" deformation process? Is this question as relevant now as it was when Ingham et al. (1987) asked it in 1984? Is it now the case in the United States that, given the competition between cities for sport franchises, there will always be an incentive for relocation as long as the sport has an effective demand (see Schimmel et al., 1993)? If this is the scenario, then "communities" will be forever blackmailed into meeting the sport capitalists' and public entrepreneurs' demands. It matters little whether this involves major league teams or the public subsidization of world-scale events (e.g., the Olympic Games). The major issue for the dominant classes in contemporary society is that hegemony is incredibly fragile. Ideology work is more important than ever. The magical recovery of "community" or the manu-facturing of "communitas" is a significant component of this work. With capi-talist tennis star Andre Agassi (the Canon commercials), we might be tempted to conclude that "image is everything." Yet because we can deconstruct images and the politics involved in them, any magical "community" will soon appear fictitious. A final thought is needed concerning the articulation between com-munity and communitas. It is one involving history.

In traditional preindustrial communities, a case might be made that with-out a geophysical community there could be no communitas. In such relational configurations, community was both the *being at one with* others and where "community" *happened* (see Turner, 1969, pp. 126–127). In contemporary soci-ety, there may be instances of spontaneous communitas in conditions of excep-tional "happenings" (e.g., earthquakes and floods), but for the most part communitas has become rather orchestrated in the sense that the limbic and the ideological are combined, with the former being subsumed under the latter. Parades and celebrations are now organized. Communitas now is absorbed by civic rituals. But are the limbic and the liminal completely contained?

In our attempt to answer this question, we combine the themes of this chapter with help from Richard Sennett's (1990) *The Conscience of the Eye: The Design and Social Life of Cities.* Here Sennett (p. xii) observes that "the spaces full of people in the modern city are either spaces limited to and carefully or-chestrating consumption, like the shopping mall, or spaces limited to and care-fully orchestrating the experience of tourism." Presumed dangerous spaces, first walled off by train tracks, now are walled off by highways. Spaces once social are now neutralized. The environment is built rather than peopled. Thus the inner city and its central business district are, with the notable exceptions of areas containing the mobility frozen poor, "socially dead" once the business day ends, or when there are no tourist events to attract those who have fled city life. The construction of downtown amenity infrastructures do re-people a city, but only for the times when they are open. Thus on a typical weekend, only the tourists and the mobility frozen—strangers to each other in most respects—populate the downtown public spaces.

Civic rituals, such as the celebration of a major league championship, in-volve both the mobility frozen and the tourist. The former are there; the lat-ter visit. Sometimes such orchestrated celebrations of "communitas" turn ugly. A major league championship celebration turns violent and vandalistic. To re-turn to previous thoughts, we offer the following as a repudiation of ideolog-ical attempts to create the "community as a whole" through orchestrated "communitas." A celebratory crowd is not homogeneous. Those who unwillingly subsidize the building of amenity infrastructures and those who benefit from these subsidies may join with the tourist and the mobility frozen. Also in the crowd will be those who willingly subsidize professional sport both through taxation and paid attendance at the live event. In the celebratory crowd, therefore, there are those who maintain an, albeit, fictional belief that they somehow are investors in the city and all that the city stands for. There are those for whom the idea that they "own" the city makes no real sense and for whom a degraded urban existence shouts out "if the city stands for something, it does not stand for or by me." For those who subsidize without a return on their investment or who stand at the margins of business and tourist life, the orchestrated celebration of communitas may be ironic indeed. Under such socially stratified and differentiated circumstances, why would we be surprised that the attempts at communitas go awry, especially when the orchestrated civic ritual takes place in routinely neutral or "socially dead" space—tunnels of glass and concrete? In the articulation between representational sports and their "communities," we should be aware of the distinction, made by Turner, between communitas anchored in the liminalities of the marginalized and disenfranchised and structured communitas, in the form of civic rituals, orchestrated for the dominant by the dominant. Civic rituals, as representations of the extraordinary, are a far cry from everyday life and reveal all of the latter's contradictions. Presumed to be popular, in all of its meanings, they serve to further distinguish between the popular and the dominant—those who confront normal human misery on a daily basis, and those who, in the guise of working for the "community as a whole," add to it.

NOTES

1. In recreational sports (and we include the consumption of representational sport as recreational), one must assume that social differentiation and social stratification determine who does what, with whom, at what time, and in what spaces. After all, in recreational sports, we are forced to pay for our participation. However, when one looks at recreational sports as ordinary or popular participatory cultures, the long-term trend toward managerialism (the corporate plan, the right to manage) has the fundamental impact of decontextualizing our participation in terms of place as a crucial element in the bonding process and in the reproduction of community (see Williams, 1989, p. 242). Moreover, managerialism in the form of nationalized, cultural paternalism bulldozes the whole intricate structures of local communities in the name of a postulated universality of cultural values (see Bauman, 1987, p. 60). Managerialism, coupled with the commodification of recreational spaces, represents the redeployment of social power in the sense of the right to initiative and control over time and space (see Bauman, 1987, p. 67; Ingham & Hardy, 1984). In this regard, both public and private "community" recreational centers become estranged from their

roots in locality—they may serve the "community," but they do not promote its intrinsic value.

2. There are many descriptors being used to label contemporary occidental societies. Some talk about postmodern, others late capitalist, or postcapitalist, postindustrial, or high modern. We reject the notions of postcapitalist and postindustrial, because capitalism is alive and kicking, although in new formations, and because there remains an industrial base to capitalist production, even if much of this production is beginning to be centered in so-called underdeveloped nations. The distinction between high modern and postmodern lies in the continuity/discontinuity debate. For those who accept the argument that there is continuity between the Fordist (industrial capitalist) and post–Fordist (flexible capitalist accumulation) conjunctures, then high modern is an apt term to describe reformed political economies. For those who see discontinuity, especially in cultural production, between the two, then postmodern is more appropriate. We argue that there is continuity in both political economy and in its hegemonic institutions. However, we do note that there is discontinuity in popular cultural productions, but that this has not yet overdetermined the political-economic process: it forms the basis of a reactionary bourgeois *angst*, as evidenced in the moral rhetoric of conservative politicians. Lacking a good descriptor, we shall use the concept of contemporary.

3. Social capital has been defined as "features of social organization," such as networks, values, and social trust, which facilitate coordination and cooperation for mutual benefit. It involves responsibility for and obligation to others. It is the social effort and human care that have been invested in the making of community (see Putnam, 1995, p. 67; Williams, 1989, pp. 123–124).

4. Here we have used commmunity as a whole, because we recognize that people do migrate from one residential location to another as a result of increased or decreased affluence. To use a phrase of Goode's (albeit, out of context), there is a principle of homogamy that often contours "community" preference.

REFERENCES

Bauman, Z. (1987). *Legislators and interpreters*. Ithaca, NY: Cornell University Press.

Brooks, D., & Althouse, R. (Eds.). (1993). *Racism in college athletics: The African-American athlete's experience*. Morgantown: Fitness Technologies.

Clarke, J., & Critcher, C. (1985). *The devil makes work: Leisure in capitalist Britain*. Houndsmills: Macmillan.

Cohen, A. (1985). *The symbolic construction of community*. Chichester: Ellis Horwood and Tavistock.

Cooley, C. (1967). *Social organization*. New York: Schocken.

Dunning, E. (1983). Social bonding and violence in sport: A theoretical-empirical analysis. In J. Goldstein (Ed.), *Sports violence* (pp. 129-146). New York: Springer-Verlag.

Durkheim, E. (1933). *The division of labor in society*. New York: Free Press.

Durkheim, E. (1965). *Elementary forms of religious life*. New York: Free Press.

Edwards, H. (1969). *The revolt of the black athlete*. New York: The Free Press.

Euchner, C. (1993). *Playing the field: Why sports teams move and cities fight to keep them*. Baltimore: Johns Hopkins University Press.

Goffman, E. (1967). *Interaction ritual: Essays on face-to-face behavior*. Garden City, NY: Anchor Books.

Goode, W. (1978). *The celebration of heroes*. Berkeley: University of California Press.

Hall, S., Critcher, C., Jefferson, T., Clarke, J., & Roberts, B. (1978). *Policing the crisis: Mugging, the state and law and order*. London: Macmillan.

Harding, R. (1983). Ritual in recent criticism: The elusive sense of community. *Modern Language Association, 98*, 846–862.

Harvey, D. (1989). *The condition of postmodernity*. Cambridge, MA: Blackwell.

Hill, R. (1983). Crisis in the Motor City: The politics of economic development in Detroit. In S. Fainstain et al. (Eds.), *Restructuring the city* (pp. 80–125). New York: Longman.

Hornby, N. (1992). *Fever pitch*. New York: Penguin Books.

Ingham, A. (1978). *American sport in transition: The maturation of industrial capitalism and its impact upon sport*. Unpublished doctoral dissertation, University of Massachusetts, Amherst.

Ingham, A., & Beamish, R. (1993). The industrialization of the United States and the bourgeoisification of American sport. In E. Dunning, J. Maguire, & R. Pearton (Eds.), *The sports process: A comparative and developmental approach* (pp. 169–206). Champaign: Human Kinetics.

Ingham, A., & Hardy, S. (1984). Sport: Structuration, subjugation, and hegemony. *Theory, Culture & Society, 2*, 85–103.

Ingham, A., Howell, J., & Schilperoort, T. (1987). Professional sport and community: A review and exegesis. *Exercise and Sport Sciences Reviews, 15*, 427–465.

Jhally, S. (1989). Cultural studies and the sports/media complex. In L. Wenner (Ed.), *Sport, media and society* (pp. 70–93). Newbury Park, CA: Sage.

Johnson, A. (1978). Public sports policy: An introduction. *American Behavioral Scientist, 21(3)*, 319–344.

Johnson, A. (1983). Municipal administration and the sport franchise relocation issue. *Public Administration Review, 43*, 519–528.

Johnson, A. (1985). The professional sport franchise relocation issue. In J. Frey and A. Johnson (Eds.), *Government and sports: Public policy issues* (pp. 64–83). Totowa, NJ: Rowman and Allanheld.

Johnson, A. (1986). Economic and policy implications of hosting sports franchises: Lessons from Baltimore. *Urban Affairs Quarterly, 2*, 411–433.

Kidd, B. (1990). The men's cultural center: Sport and the dynamic of women's oppression/men's repression. In M. Messner & D. Sabo (Eds.), *Sport, men and the gender order* (pp. 31–44). Champaign: Human Kinetics.

Lewis, L. (1992). *Adoring audience: Fan culture and popular media.* London: Routledge.

Loy, J. (1968). The nature of sport: A definitional effort. *Quest, 10,* 1–15.

Mead, G. (1934). *Mind, self, and society.* Chicago: University of Chicago Press.

Morford, R., & McIntosh, M. (1993). Sport and the Victorian gentleman. In A. Ingham & J. Loy (Eds.), *Sport in social development: Traditions, transitions, and transformations* (pp. 51–76). Champaign: Human Kinetics.

Olsen, J. (1968). *The black athlete: A shameful story.* New York: Time-Life.

Putnam, R. (1995). Bowling alone: America's declining social capital. *Journal of Democracy, 1,* 65–78.

Ribalow, H. (1948). *The Jew in American sports.* New York: Bloch.

Richmond, P. (1993). *Ballpark: Camden Yards and the building of an American dream.* New York: Simon and Schuster.

Schimmel, K., Ingham, A., and Howell, J. (1993). Professional team sport and the American city: Urban politics and franchise relocations. In A. Ingham and J. Loy (Eds.), *Sport in social development: Traditions, transitions, and transformations* (pp. 211–244). Champaign: Human Kinetics.

Sennett, R. (1974). *The fall of public man.* New York: Vintage Books.

Sennett, R. (1990). *The conscience of the eye: The design and social life of cities.* New York: W. W. Norton.

Sumner, C. (1979). *Reading ideologies: An investigation into the Marxist theory of ideology and law.* London: Academic Press.

Therborn, G. (1980). *The ideology of power and the power of ideology.* London: New Left Books.

Tonnies, F. (1957). *Gemeinschaft und Gesellschaft.* East Lansing: Michigan State University Press.

Turner, V. (1969). *The ritual process: Structure and anti-structure.* Chicago: Aldine.

Turner, V. (1974). *Dramas, fields, and metaphors: Symbolic action in human society.* Ithaca: Cornell University Press.

Weber, M. (1978). *Economy and society* (G. Roth & C. Wittich, Eds.). Berkeley: University of California Press.

Williams, R. (1989). *Resources of hope.* London: Verso.

Wirth, L. (1938). Urbanism as a way of life. *American Journal of Sociology, 44,* 1–24.

Young, I. (1990). The ideal of community and the politics of difference. In L. Nicholson (Ed.), *Feminism/Postmodernism.* New York: Routledge.

3

Mediated Sports, Mayors, and the Marketed Metropolis

Gene Burd

The sprawling metropolitan areas of big cities often lack a dominant, symbolic focus and a shared, collective, common, affective experience at one place at the same time. This is difficult because of multiple centers, cultures, and governments fractured by the placelessness of expressways, strip shopping centers, abandoned downtowns, and fractured subcommunities based on race, ethnicity, age, income, and gender. There is some shared public place and life in shopping malls and town squares, but it is perhaps in marketed, mass-mediated sports spectator stadia where the disparate parts of the whole metropolis are most often bound together into one site that central city mayors rely upon for symbolic consensus in a fragmented metropolis.

Much has been said about the relationship between cities and sports (Riess, 1989; Karp & Yoels, 1990) and about the symbiosis of sports and media (Wilson, 1994; Cashdan & Jordin, 1987; Altheide & Snow, 1979; Michener, 1976). Far less has been examined on how cities, sports, urban areas, and media intersect and interact. Evidence does reveal a long history of sports and media as partners in civic boosterism and urban growth machines (Gendzel, 1995; Whitson & Macintosh, 1993; Schimmel, Ingham, & Howell, 1993; Burd, 1977b; Northam, 1977). There have been studies on sports and media as participants in civic culture (Burd, 1969b; 1969c); on media as sports promoters (Lapchick, 1986); on the dilemmas and potential for professional sports journalists (Garrison & Salwen, 1989; Burd, 1986); and on media and cities sharing a civic ideology (Burd, 1980).

One area rich with somewhat untapped possibilities for studying cities, sports, and media is that of how spectator sports are used to market civic identities and images (Burd, 1977a), especially in the ritual and ceremony at sports stadia (Burd, 1981). Another is how the projection of a civic profile relates to both those inside and outside the city (Burd, 1970a). These areas interface with the studies that connect government and religion to both sport and cities (Prebish, 1993; Sage, 1981) and the more recent appreciation of communication as ritual (Carey, 1989) rather than mere transmission of information.

MEDIA PROJECTION AND
PACKAGING OF CITY IMAGES

As a metropolitan area expands and decentralizes geographically, and as it fragments culturally, mass media in central cities retain their image-making power. They shape the focus on a central, collective place in which sports stadia, skyscrapers, and other structural symbols contribute to a dominant, reduced, single icon of the city. This kind of "civic shorthand," as described by social psychologist Anselm Strauss, provides a means for city residents inside to feel a sense of place in which they belong and can act with consensus. For outsiders, the rivals, and civic competitors, the civic profile is packaged and protected and often preconditions what visitors and tourists will "see." It can affect mayoral self-esteem, site selections for vacations, conventions, branch offices for new industry and factories, insurance rates, bond and investment confidence, and faith in a city's economic potential (Burd, 1970a).

In this process, media civic superlatives envelop a city town and team and weld them into one symbol, which is constantly replicated by boasting mayors and broadcast anchors and placed on page 1 and in film and photos. The city, team, and events are advertised as products through overhead sky scenes from blimps (selling their own wares) as well as the merits of cities. The city on camera is the site for Big League (not bush league), with bowls, tournaments, matches, marathons, and series often named for teams, towns, products, and even media. (When 10 cities competed for the new headquarters of the National Collegiate Athletic Association in 1996, journalists noted that "Prestige is not all the NCAA is selling . . . the NCAA is, from any chamber of commerce point of view, a jewel in the expanding, high-profile sports industry. The city that houses the NCAA will be a frequent dateline in newspapers around the country, as well as the scene of CBS' live and super-hyped announcement every March of the basketball tournament field" (Tucker, 1996, p. 8C). The exaggerated civic superlative proclaims the press, team, and city number 1 (Burd, 1972), and therefore Big, Super, Grand, Final, and World Class! The Olympics are the ultimate focus on one city and victor. Persons and cities seek to be on the route of the torch to the stadium dome. Whether it is Sky, Astro, Silver, King, Metro, Hoosier, or Super, it "glistens like a giant dewdrop diamond on the throat" of the city as an "awesome, sky-line crowding structure that is beyond tomorrow" (Redding, 1975). Beneath it, media capture and convey color for Big Red, Purple Pride, Orange Crush, and the Green Wave. Teams advertise legends and logos, music and mascots, heroes and hand signals, and awards and trophies for adjacent city halls and museums. Cities for teams often are an image of teams themselves: Steelers, Broncos, Suns, Rockets, Raiders, Rangers, Cowboys, Dolphins, Forty Niners, Mariners, Marlins, Brewers, Rockies, and Yankees. (Original Olympians wore olive branch crowns that ended up in the temples of the civic deity they represented. See Shaikin, 1988, p. 19).

In today's multicentered metropolis, such sports spectacles help us know when and where we are and how we want to show ourselves to others. "Traditionally, myth and ritual have played central roles in defining human time and place," while "In secular culture, 'special times' and places are increasingly marked off by media" (Real, 1990). Mediated sports "provide spatial orientation" as the sources of geographical pride for a school, a city, or even a country. "The stadium, field house, and whatever dome are the sacred destiny of pilgrims and the center of public attention for quasi-holy rituals." These "media-distributed sports have become psychosocial centers of gravity, the fulcrums around which social and personal life are organized" (Real, 1990, pp. 352–353). They advertise the city. Such structures and buildings also "speak" with the *Signature of Power*, as political scientist Harold Lasswell, in 1978, described the relationship of buildings, policy, and communication. He noted how materials and symbolism relate to city values and forces. These include wealth, resources, and markets; health and well-being; skills, occupations, and professions; knowledge and enlightenment; affection and loyalty to group symbols; respect and rectitude and class differentiation; and standards and evaluation. These are often reflected on the diamond, gridiron, track, mat, and court and create a collective civic icon more dominant than a city's main governmental structure.

"The modern baseball parks, the prestigious and elegant racetracks, and the large sports arenas constructed in major cities in the 1920s and 1930s became civic monuments and symbols of their city's cosmopolitan character" (Riess, 1989, p. 227). It has been argued that "A city needs a big public stadium because that's one of the things that distinguishes a city . . . each era of civilization generates its peculiar architectural symbols [and] . . . acquires a spiritual significance far beyond its mere utilitarian purpose." Thus "societies which built well" are well remembered for pyramids, temples, cathedrals, railroad stations, and stadia (Michener, 1976, pp. 38–39). "The process by which a place comes to represent a society's values and holds a culture's legends reveals much about that society" (Kammer, 1980, pp. 38–39). The architecture of sports stadia reflects the culture and has "assumed an almost shrine-like position in the popular mind" (Kammer, 1980, pp. 38–39). Popular CBS talk show host David Letterman (December 20, 1996) compared Yankee Stadium to St. Peter's Basilica in Rome. Stadia, TV towers, and other cathedral-like spires, especially those in the central downtown areas, are remnants of the historic spots for religious communion (Kato, 1974).

Media coverage from sports sites fits a focus on cities generally and creates civic advertisements of which both editors and mayors are proud. Architecture is perhaps the most visual and comprehensive of these many complex facets that compose a city's image, and the photographic view of the central city's central business district is probably the most common civic image projected. Both the architect and photojournalist affect and reflect the cement and camera that create the civic stereotype of the skyline as the "city of the mind" (Burd, 1977a). The overwhelming, conclusive skyline becomes the essence of the projected city. "The massed buildings, the solidity and density of the agglomeration, the gleaming roofs, the specious neatness and order that a far view lends the scene, seem to reflect all the energy, the crowdedness, the opulence and magnificence of the city" (Wohl & Strauss, 1958). This "bird's eye view" and "civic shorthand" reduce and simplify the total city beyond an individual's everyday experience, as "personal action in the urban milieu becomes organized and relatively routinized" (Wohl & Strauss, 1958, pp. 523–532). Fragments of the metropolis beyond personal experience are brought together by mass media.

The physical architecture of the stadium and its surroundings transmits far more than game statistics. The mediated photo image creates and extends the virtual reality of the game experience for both those there and those not there and dependent on others to watch for them. The "press box" and the TV "studio" become the stadium. The old, primitive, prehistorical, premodern tribal assemblage is instantly conveyed to millions not there and for thousands there who have never met and likely will never meet personally in such a single, common spot in open, symbolic interaction or warfare. This sense of place and spectacle among downtown skyscrapers or amidst suburban highway interchanges is conveyed by TV sports anchors selling and advertising cities and teams as commodities. The projected image suggests a nostalgic center of urban "Paradise Lost" in an era of decline in public space and public life often missing in multicentered cities and multiple cultures. Sports becomes the "coalition glue" in "redefining the skyline of downtown," which "holds a community together" with TV shots of the "skylines, civic fountains and monuments, and downtown parks." Such media "attention and imagery" identifies and markets the city with constant free media mention of the cities' and teams' names that a city public relations department or chamber of commerce would otherwise have to "pay to get" (Rosentraub, 1996, pp. 29–30).

Historically, communications media have long been inseparable from the experience of cities, which are networks and sites of communication. Sports are one of the ideal vehicles for connecting and conveying this function, and the domination of sports news in the media is probably indicative of "the saliency of sport in the community mind" (Stone, 1981). The growth of emotional attachment to teams and their symbols has paralleled increased press coverage of rules, records, and other organized urban social controls (Guttman, 1986). Vicarious sports viewer-participants have relied on new communication technologies to replace face-to-face relations, and "The symbolic forms of myth provide personal identification, heroic archetypes, communal focus, spatial and temporal frames of reference" (Real, 1977, p. 215). Some illustrations illuminate the marriage of city symbols and sports media.

THE MEDIA'S "ARCHITECTURAL FRAME"
FOR SPORTS AND CITIES

One way the media blend athletic heroes, teams, and cities is through focus on architectural structures as a civic advertisement for sports. The examples are numerous and frequent: downtown is the focus for most stadia, for Grand Prix races, for the Downtown Manhattan Athletic Club awarding the Heisman Trophy (on live TV), and for sports rallies and parades. City streets, postmarks, and sometimes towns themselves are named for players and coaches. Joe Namath was known as "Broadway Joe." The Associated Press (September 1988) called track star Ben Johnson the "Big Ben of Canada." Cincinnati once considered declaring Pete Rose a city "landmark." A Kansas City Chief player in 1980 shaved his hair in the shape of an arrowhead, the name for the city's stadium. Houston Rockets' players Akeem Olajuwon and Ralph Sampson were called "Twin Towers," and when another tall player joined them, "Rockets sign 'third tower'" (*Daily Texan*, October 23, 1986, p. 12.) The tall, local university footballers also were compared to city buildings, since "Houston is, after all, the city of the corporate skyscraper. But even the oil company beanstalks are dwarfed by the Cougar defensive tackles. . . ." as "Skyscrapers (are) harder than ever to top" (*Dallas Morning News*, August 26, 1980, p. 3B).

When *Sport* magazine profiled ex-Los Angeles Laker and African-American Kareem Abdul-Jabbar in 1974, its cover showed him reaching out of the downtown Milwaukee skyscrapers with a basketball. Sports journalist Peter Gent wrote: "The skyline of Milwaukee looked clear and crisp against the late fall sky. Milwaukee is the Midwest. Clean, healthy, correct, American, its destiny quietly directed by the unseen hands of the brewers and accompanying elite. Social change is slow and calculated, conceived and directed from above. . . . Nine percent of Milwaukee's population is black, very few of them over seven-feet tall" (Gent, 1974, p. 44).

Seattle Supersonics' long-range ("downtown") basketball guard shooter, Fred Brown, was profiled in 1980 with the downtown Seattle skyline in his background. Newspaper readers were told that "Everyone in Seattle—downtown and suburbs—knows Downtown Freddie Brown" and "Seattle Loves Its Downtown" and "Fred Brown's Been There Almost as Long as (the) Space Needle and . . . Could Probably Score From There" (Ostler, 1980, p. III:1).

St. Louis Cardinal Stan Musial, "Like the Stainless Steel Gateway Arch, Musial Stands Tall," according to the *Sporting News* (November 5, 1985). He is "The True Spirit of St. Louis" (more than Lindbergh's airplane?) according to a feature story (Jones, 1984). The writer noted the marble pedestal inscription of him as baseball's "perfect" "knight" and "warrior" on a statue "outside Gate 7 of Busch Memorial Stadium, which is near the St. Louis Sports Hall of Fame, and a couple of long fly balls from the Gateway Arch." Both, the story reads, "are symbols of St. Louis—Musial and the Arch. One soars over the city's river front, a symbol of progress in a downtown area that has seen precious little. . . . And the other, the living monument, is a reminder that there is still a place in the world for grace and good manners." Born in Pennsylvania, but "adopted" by St. Louis in 1942, and later living in suburbia , Musial "has aged better than the city, which finds urban decay gnawing at its innards." He misses the old stadium, which had "character," while his wife comments that he'd have been even more popular if he had played in the larger New York media market, but they were lucky because St. Louis was "'a great place to raise a family" and run his business after retirement from baseball (Jones, 1984).

Players realize that sports fame and fortune are in the bigger cities, and recruits often sign contracts in the shadow of skyscrapers, from the Tower of Learning at the University of Pittsburgh to the signing of draftee Doug Flutie to play for the Generals in the USFL in September 1986 by the team owner Donald Trump, in front of his Manhattan building, the Trump Tower. Other builders of cities and sports teams are often news, as was Philadelphia Eagles owner Jerry Wolman and the development of Chicago's once tallest building, the 100-story John Hancock Tower. Successful Washington Redskins' owner Jack Kent Cooke in 1984 said, "It was a thrill to light the Chrysler Building (for victory), and it's gratifying to own half of downtown Phoenix" (Austin *American-Statesman*, January 13, p. D2).

Sports and skylines merge in media into civic advertisements. Skiers, blimps, and skywriters soar over Olympic host cities, slopes, and stadia. Two Philadelphia Phillies "Alter Chicago Skyline" by beating the Chicago Cubs (*Washington Post*, August 16, 1977, p. D1). CBS showed the Manhattan skyline behind the photo lineups of the Giants in their January 11, 1987, NFL championship game played in the suburban New Jersey Meadowlands. (TV cameras and blimps can visually reduce the distance between outlying stadia and downtowns in a few seconds, compared to hours of traffic in real life, as ABC's Frank Gifford once remarked on *Monday Night Football* from the new Joe Robbie Stadium far from the old Orange Bowl site closer to downtown Miami.)

Tall buildings and statues often are lighted or highlighted for a team victory. The NBA championship trophy was superimposed on downtown Houston skyscrapers in a full, page 1 photo headlined "Champ City" in the *Houston Post* on June 22, 1994. The Rockets beat the Knicks at the Summit, where the newspaper's "extra" was handed out and later reprinted on T-shirts and sold along with a book on the team written by a *Post* reporter. In 1984, Chicago city workers hoisted a 12-foot, 30-pound Cubs' hat atop the Chicago Picasso sculpture in Daley Plaza as the city anticipated a National League championship. In 1986, when the Bears played in the Super Bowl, the plaza was designated "Bears Plaza" for a weekend, and the world's tallest building, Chicago's Sears Tower, was temporarily renamed "Bears Tower." In the 1997 Stanley Cup hockey playoffs, the William Penn statue atop Philadelphia's tallest building was dressed in the Flyers' hockey attire. In the opponent city, Detroit, a statue atop the Wayne County building wore a Red Wing jersey and held a hockey stick. In 1996, the World Series champion, the New York Yankees, paraded up the Manhattan "Canyon of Heroes," where "For one day, New York was like Emerald City. . . . The skyscrapers, the bridges, the parks . . . sharply defined beneath a flawless sky" (Herbert, 1996). "Even if the Giants, Devils, and Nets play in New Jersey . . . if you can see the Empire State Building from the Meadowlands, it's New York, no matter what the politicians think" (Anderson, 1996, p. B8). Such press rhetoric belies the political reality of metropolitan fracture.

Skylines are sacred turf, but criticism around them can surface and arouse citizens' urban experience. A picture of a 1986 World Cup Soccer stadium "looms dimly half a mile away through Mexico City's infamous air pollution" (Austin *American-Statesman*, May 29, p. G7). Readers were reminded by the *Washington Post* (February 3, 1978, p. B1) that its departing Redskin Coach George "Allen Replaces Smog as the No. 1 Topic in the City of Angels" (*Washington Post*, February 3, 1978, p. B1). When the Baltimore Colts owner moved the team to Indianapolis, he was quoted (Sherrod 1979, p. 1C) as saying of Baltimore: "Its skyline is uninspiring. Its buildings are dirty. Its grass is skraggy. Its wind is cold and laden with all sorts of low grade viruses." In contrast, when an eager Denver awaited a possible move of the Oakland Athletics to Denver, a *Denver Post* editorial (December 18, 1980, p. 25) said that such a new team "reinforces what is visible on the city's burgeoning skyline." When ex-Green Bay Packer (idol turned CBS sportscaster) Paul Hornung mockingly referred to a camera shot of mainly snow from atop Lambeau Field in 1975, as "the Green Bay skyline," angry fans lit up TV switchboards to complain (Wolf, 1975). In contrast, 20 years later, when "Titletown USA" (Green Bay) hosted a *Monday Night Football* (September 9, 1996) game, the Goodyear blimp aerial shot showed the 10-story St. Vincent Hospital as the "skyline," and ABC sportscasters (also ex-players) noted that the building, although shorter than the Sears Tower, was "appropriately" named because of the continuing adoration of Packer coach Vince Lombardi in Green Bay. What better civic testimonial to the guarded bond among sports, skylines, and the self in everyday urban life?

MEDIATED SPORTS AS CIVIC AND RELIGIOUS RITUAL

Sports journalists also facilitate the religious ritual of sports with the relentless focus on rules, referees, judges, coaches, and umpires who resolve conflict by rewarding conformity and punishing infractions, with victory as survival, defeat as death. There also is a historic sense of time (past, present, and "Wait until next year") and a mood of sacred place with parables, parades, processionals, uniforms, superstition, jinxes, curses, and prayers in end zones and locker rooms. There is religious homage to the "miracle" of both the Mets and the Braves (in Milwaukee and Atlanta), the Saints in New Orleans, "Touchdown Jesus in South Bend," and the "Hail Mary Pass." "If Jesus were alive today, he'd be going to the Super Bowl," according to the late minister, Norman Vincent Peale.

Throughout the ritual of mediated spectator sport, the religious symbols reflect the recurring issues of everyday life, the rebellion against industrial society, the aesthetic unity of completion, and the transcendence of human limitation (Duncan, 1983). The continuity of sports coverage has a repetitive and ritualistic tone. "[T]he calendar and programs of festivals do change with the development of the community; original sites are preserved even if superseded, but new or expanded rituals arise out of community history as additions to, not replacements, of earlier rites" (Kyle, 1994, p. 280). The latest sports story incorporates the legend, and language of the past, life, and community survive. Most news consists of retold stories, especially news of sports, which binds a community together in a collective conversation that often is missing from the daily routines in large metropolitan areas.

Sports symbolism "enables a community of believers to express their solidarity in a social ceremony" that creates "a communion bond reminiscent of Greek drama. . . . The affective bonds communicated through sports drama are crystallized through language. The groups' emotional bonds are mediated. . . . Language, communication, symbolism, and group life are inseparable pieces of a common plot" (Lipsky, 1979). "As a bonding mechanism, sports cannot be excelled. From the days of the earliest Olympics, when Greek city-states acclaimed their sports heroes with odes and laurels, the athlete has been the incarnation of community values" (Meyer, 1979, p. 17).

Such cities were established by gods as sacred places for symbolic communion. Today's television, often compared to a religious altar, enlarges the symbolic space and the sports heroes who "may be the gods of our age" become "our shared experience by watching . . . a game on television" (Kato, 1974, pp. 59–60). Those "gods" also can capture the headlines as well as cities: "O. J. Conquers Buffalo" (*Los Angeles Times*, December 12, 1974, p. III:1); "The Quarterback (Sonny Jurgensen) Who Captures a City" (*Washington Post*, May 4, 1975, p. D6); "New York is (Vitas) Gerulaitis' Town Once More" (*Los Angeles Times*, September 8, 1981, p. III:1); "Sports teams, bearing the community name (or totem), have become this kind of collective representation, as have players and sports, themselves" (Stone, 1981b, p. 221). Sports journalists "awaken fans to the internal functioning of the team . . . [and] . . . may create the illusion of sharing a personal experience . . . [and] . . . a similar delusion of collective possession" by the community (Stone & Anderson, 1981, pp. 167–168). Sports constitute a source of cohesion, integration, and belongingness. "A sense of community can arise out of identification with urban places, objects, events, and institutions. Once we recognize community as tied up with images, sentiments, and feelings, it is a short step to realize the extent to which many urbanites equate pride of place with pride of local sports teams" (Karp & Yoels, 1990, p. 99).

A SENSE OF PLACE IN MEDIATED SPORTS SITES AND EVENTS

In the decentralized metropolis with many urban nodes, rather than one single center, the mass media help shape space into place. They develop mental sports maps by mixing reality with image in a single place and thereby create and "identify geographic consciousness" (Bale, 1986, p. 39). It is sport that "provides a glue which bonds people to their place" (Rooney & Macdonald, 1982). "Sports-place images are communicated by mass media." Geography and architecture provide the "forum for the local community to celebrate its existence," and cities "most often define sports teams" (Bale, 1989, p. 24). In not only big cities but "At the city limits of many small American towns, the welcoming billboard often proclaims the place's sporting achievements . . . [and] homes of champions. Be it billboard, bumper stickers, or graffiti, the sentiment is essentially the same, namely, pride in place through sport" (Bale, 1989, pp. 16–17).

The image of a team can be designed with a city and region in mind, as was the blue-collar, working-class, clean-cut, family oriented heartland of "Redland" in the four-state Cincinnati, Ohio, area. There "The Reds attempted to project a distinct image, on the field and—to some extent—off the field as well. This attitude also was reflected in the way the Riverfront Stadium was sited, serviced, and maintained" (Walker, 1988, p. 296). St. Petersburg searched for a new baseball franchise team to fill its new Florida Suncoast Dome and to change its city image from "heaven's waiting room" for the retired and aged. It was reported that, "In Florida the quest for the legendary Fountain of Youth has often merged with the state's quest for development or renewal. For many people, the quest for a major league team and the construction of the domed stadium on speculation are just modern-day versions of the same wild-eyed vision" and an attempt to compete against its cross-bay neighbor Tampa "with its cigar factories, phosphate plants and commercial shipping" (Smothers, 1991).

City and team often blend in one place, with the media assisting. For example, the Mexican city of Queretaro (ball game), was one of the sites for the 1986 World Cup soccer game. In Chicago, when the possibility arose that the White Sox might leave Chicago, a *Chicago Sun-Times* editorial (December 6, 1975, p. 31) declared: "The Sox Are Chicago" and are "fused into the collective memory of the city and fused into the city's awareness of itself." It proclaimed that "the Sox are the city the way the Auditorium is the city or the Great Chicago Fire is the city or the Loop is the city or all the parades are the city . . . the Chicago White Sox are in the blood and sinews of this city." When the Los

Angeles Rams planned to move from central Los Angeles to suburban Anaheim, *Los Angeles Times* sports columnist Jim Murray, in his "Farewell to Rams" (July 6, 1978, p. III:1), wrote that "moving the Rams out of the Coliseum is like moving the opera out of La Scala, moving the Mona Lisa out of the Louvre, moving the pigeons out of St. Mark's, moving the kings out of Westminster Abbey, or Grant out of Grant's Tomb. It'll never be the same." Later, the *Times*' Orange County sports editor Marshall Klein (July 9, 1982, p. II:2) described the Orange County fan by borrowing a description from a Rams player, who said, an "Anaheim fan is like a loaf of bread—all white with little substance. He shows up with white shoes and cranberry pants."

In such a manner, sports journalists monitor the proper "fit" of teams with place. Columnist Bob Greene, in the Chicago *Sun-Times* (May 22, 1975, p. 14) said, "The Bulls epitomize the personality of this city . . . old and foul-tempered . . . [they] . . . do not like each other . . . hate their coach . . . hate their owners. If Chicago stands for anything, it stands for a rejection of fantasy notions of a nice, perfect, friendly utopian world. Chicago is real-life, and the Bulls are Chicago . . . the Bulls are a priceless treasure. We need them here." They stayed and won repeatedly and wove in new images to satisfy both the city and the media. When it was reported that the Oakland Raiders were "leaving glitzy Los Angeles for a return to lunch-bucket Oakland" (*Rocky Mountain News*, March 13, 1990, p. 43), one sports columnist (Dick Connor, Denver *Post*, March 14, 1990, p. D1), said, "Raiders Return to Where They Left Character." He said the "real Raiders" belonged in Oakland, "a tough city, in love with a tough team," with "players that grew up in the East Bay where Jack London once roamed, in blue-collar surroundings, among working men and not Perrier sippers." In Los Angeles, he wrote, "They lost their character. . . . They dressed like pirates but played like cricketeers. Time, lads. Tea . . . the color scheme will fit again. So will the team. Silver and black never translated when the Oakland Raiders moved South a decade ago. Fuchsia or magenta or something pale yellow with a touch of washed out red maybe. *That* was a proper Los Angeles Raiders color scheme" (emphasis in original).

When Buffalo first aspired to the Super Bowl in the early 1970s, one sports writer, Jim Murray (*Los Angeles Times*, December 12, 1974), said, as he matched team with place, "Buffalo is a lunch-pail, bowling-shirt, broken-tooth type of town which drinks beer from a can, has hair on its chest, calls the wife 'the old lady', and the team 'Da Bills'. Bad as the town was, the team was worse. The stadium was a municipal ruin. It was a town where they shot McKinley and threw beer at everyone else. It was as direct as a belch, a lunch-counter town which ate with its hat on and chewed toothpicks." When Pittsburgh went to the Super Bowl in 1980, the *Washington Post* "re-discovered" the "shot-and-a-beer town" in an editorial, asserting that "Pittsburgh Lives" (January 18, 1980, p. A16). It said that the city was the only major metropolitan area in the United States that was losing population and was once known as a city of "'hell with the lid off'," with brawling, blue-collar steelworkers and boilermakers. It said the new City of Champions "is no city of Archie Bunkers" but has two Black baseball heroes and deserves recognition "for what this Mill Town has accomplished in downtown renewal and the progress its citizens have made in cleaning up the air."

When Dallas played Denver in the 1978 Super Bowl, syndicated political columnist Joseph Kraft pictured the two teams as mythic symbols of their cities as he suggested that "More than urban sociology, to be sure, explains successful football teams" (Kraft, 1978). He said the cities "represent parts of the country peculiarly in tune with the individualistic ethic" and in command of abundant oil and other natural resources. Kraft wrote that the teams and cities reflected the "values and attributes which make for success," where "economic growth has bred a sense of fellowship." He described their booming real estate and new downtown skyscrapers and millionaires who back professional sports teams, and "an esprit de corps or community spirit." He said loyal fans "create the kind of climate where the television and papers concentrate heavily on the teams" that "crystallize a civic purpose, an aspiration to which the most active part of the citizenry are committed."

TEAM, PLAYER, AND COACH IDENTITY
IN REGIONAL RIVALRY

A distinct image representing a city is projected by journalists most vividly when teams, mayors, and cities are in competition for victory on the field or in the marketplace. Civic wars between the Northeast and the Southwest Sunbelt show "emerging cities using sports imagery as a vehicle for rivalry to attract not only teams, but tourists and industry as media catch and cast the latest boast and bash" (Burd, 1977b). One writer admits, "The Sunbelt may have glamour, while the industrial crescent running from here (Pittsburgh) to the Middle West may be a little gray, workaday, and somewhat worn down at the heels. But don't tell that to a sports fan in the crescent area" (Stevens, 1976, p. 26L). In the collision of the Southwest (Houston Astros) and the Northeast (New York Mets) cultures, it was not just differences in lifestyles and ball parks but "laid-back versus pushy, muggy, saddle-sore versus just sore" (Berkow, 1986, p. 16). In a similar regional rivalry, the Yankees and the Los Angeles Dodgers are presented as reflections of their cities: "The contrast of coasts, climates, and customs is almost complete. The Dodgers are a fair-weather team, tanned and happy with one another. A smile is their insignia. Frank Sinatra and Don Rickles are the clubhouse buddies of their admittedly star-struck manager Tommy Lasorda. The Dodgers are show biz to the core. . . . The Yankees are as gritty and problematic as New York itself" (Boswell, 1977, pp. D1, D2). Links between cities, coaches, and players can be more positive, as when Houston's Rockets played the New York Knicks for the 1994 NBA finals. "The two coaches had once nearly been teammates in a revolving door franchise. The two foreign-born centers were intertwined even before they compared reggae tapes and became friends . . . two proud and successful immigrants (who) never glare or growl at each other" (Vecsey, 1994, p. D1).

The civic ties and related images of coaches may change during their mobile careers, and sports journalists monitor who belongs where. Vince Lombardi "uplifted the self-image of the state" of Wisconsin where its people and Green Bay fans were "almost synonymous terms" and got a "Thanks for the Memory" editorial from the *Milwaukee Journal* (February 6, 1969, p. 24) when he left a disappointed city and state for the Washington Redskins. Similarly, the casual, cowboy-hatted, and country boy Oail A. (Bum) Phillips left the Houston Oilers for New Orleans and was followed by Heisman winner Earl Campbell (of the Houston "Earlers"). "Bum's Not Quite a Saint" inasmuch as "Teams used to come in, crack a few helmets, jerk the Saints around by their fleur-de-lis and whip them like so much bread pudding. . . . Now though . . . (they have) . . . a coach with a crew cut, a chaw, and a certain way of doing business" (Bonk, 1984, p. III:1). However, another writer suggested that "Bum is officially now a Saint," partly because the team owner liked his cowboy boots (Sullivan, 1981, p. E1). When Redskins coach George Allen returned to the Los Angeles Rams, "he looks exactly the same . . . thanks in part to the Grecian Formula he uses to cover the gray in his still-thick frock of black hair" (Green, 1978, p. III:1). In contrast, the departing Ram coach, Chuck Knox, was pictured as being "a little more comfortable around the Buffalo folks than he did mingling with the citizenry of Hollywood," and at Buffalo he's "proclaimed savior by many Bills fans." He "has become more popular than the famous (Niagara) falls" and "got as much newspaper space and TV time as the record snows," but "Some wondered if Knox had finally cracked" by "Leaving Los Angeles' sunshine for Buffalo's blizzards? Leaving a home on the ocean for one on Lake Erie?", the writer asked (Bayless, 1978, p. III:1).

New York, a Yankee town torn by divided sports loyalties, saw its Mets in 1986 facing the Boston Red Sox. "If New York needs the Mets in part to see itself as the poor, misunderstood giant—Lenny in 'Of Mice and Men'—then Queens needs the Mets to see itself as more than a pipsqueak in the shadows of Manhattan" (Freedman, 1986a, p. 20). New York also mistreated the hockey Islanders as "too young, too new . . . (and with) . . . no idea how to be arrogant, egotistical, or demanding" (Herman, 1975). As for baseball in Boston, "The Red Sox are also perhaps the only institution that binds New England together linking Massachusetts with Maine, New Hampshire, Vermont, Rhode Island, and the parts of Connecticut not so foolish as to root for the Yankees. Drive anywhere in New England and the one thing you can be sure to pick up on a summer evening is a Red Sox broadcast" (Butterfield, 1986, p. 21). Television is now reshaping the fan base across governmental and geographical boundaries of traditional cities (Danielson, 1997).

Interstate and intrastate rivalries offer journalists a chance for contrast in city and sport images. Here are some examples: the 1982 World Series between St. Louis and Milwaukee was cast as one between beer towns, as were clashes between the Chicago Cubs and the St. Louis Cardinals in 1977 (Russo, 1977). The North-South rivalry in California between the California Angels and the Oakland Athletics is a pattern that is "natural and traditional in California, politically and culturally as well as in practical matters like water resources. And it is reflected vividly in sports loyalties" (Koppett, 1989a, p. B13). In another, "The good-natured disdain that San Francisco, so sophisticated in their eyes, can express for the Philistines of Tinseland has been focused on the 49er-Ram games for a generation. So has the reciprocal contempt and pity Southlanders feel for those poor fogbound snobs, who fail to comprehend that bright sunshine, a good surf, and a little publicity are all that's needed for the good life" (Koppett, 1989, p. 52).

Regional rivalries often are word wars with these images. Actual soccer wars between cities once were common. The first football game was said to have been the kicking of a ball between two towns with the other town as the goal. In both jest and zest, in 1992 a Philadelphia radio talk show host urged city streets named "Dallas" be changed to "Eagles Street," when the blue-collar, insecure Eagles played the largely white, pretentious Cowboys (Rude, 1992). In the early 1960s, a baseball promoter in Seattle complained that National League officials in the East "act like civilization stops at the Hudson River and that we're still a bunch of rubes out here" (Peterson, 1962, p. 16). In 1986, when the New York Mets won the play-off against the Houston Astros, the *New York Times*, in an editorial, "New York, of the National League" (October 17, p. 226Y), said, "There was special joy in beating the team from Houston, where bumper stickers once said 'Let the Yankees freeze in the dark'." (The local Texas word for Yankees in that slogan was "bastards"). However, when the Houston Rockets beat the New York Knicks (following the Cowboys beating the Buffalo Bills), a *Dallas Morning News* editorial said that the "Rockets' Victory" (June 24, 1994, p. 20A) "further proves the New World [Texas and the Sunbelt] is taking power from the Old World [New York and the Frost Belt]." And in a jab at the *New York Post's* reference to Houston as a "steamy, bug-infested, nondescript prairie town," the Dallas paper said "some big ol New York companies seem to like the pioneering spirit 'prairie towns' offer."

Sports Puts Towns "on the Map"; Makes Cities Feel Good

News of sports, especially victories, boosts internal civic pride and boasts to the external competitive towns and cities. Sports puts places "on the map," whether at Olympic sites or hometowns of Heisman heroes in hinterland hamlets or city slums or at suburban stadia in Arlington, Bloomington, Foxboro, Pontiac, Anaheim, or the Meadowlands. All glory in the gain from the international, national, state, and metropolitan limelight. Otherwise less known places such as Norman, Lincoln, Pebble Beach, Pasadena, Forest Hills, Hialeah, and Green Bay are made famous by sports, as once were Goldfield and Virginia City, Nevada, for boxing matches, such as tiny Shelby, Montana, for the famous 1923 Dempsey–Gibbons fight (McCormick, 1973).

Sport calls forth communal bonds. When Trumbell, Connecticut, won the World's Championship Little League from Taiwan in 1989, "longtime residents said it was the largest such demonstration of communal affection ever in this town" (Cavanaugh, 1989, p. 5). In a rural state such as Nebraska, with no professional sports team, the University of Nebraska Cornhuskers unite the state. A single football game in Lincoln can attract enough people to become the state's "third largest city" (Jackson, 1996). Similarly, in Norman, Oklahoma, "our football gives John Doe Q. Public, wherever he lives, something to identify with—it gives him something to stick out his chest about, and say 'Boy, I'm a Sooner! I'm part of the Big Red' " (Walker, 1974). School teams can put a state or a city on the map. In Las Vegas, the NCAA basketball champions put UNLV on the map in a city more often known for gambling and other vices (Reinhold, 1990). Waco, Texas, once known mostly for Baptists and the Baylor University Bears, celebrated its 1974 Southwest Conference football championship, which "tied the town together . . . [and has] . . . given everyone something in common . . . all of us feel like we have participated in a great victory . . . a thrill . . . [that] . . . gets your mind off inflation, politics, and world hunger" (Waco, 1974).

Winning a game, a site, or a franchise creates civic excitement for teams, towns, mayors, and the media. "HOORAY! HOORAY! HOORAY!" headlined the *Chicago American* on September 23, 1959, when the White Sox beat the Indians in Cleveland to win their first American League pennant in 40 years. The mayor and his wife met the team at 2:08 A.M. at the airport, along with 25,000 other fans of a team "adopted by immigrants" and "part of our life, like our religion," the *American* reported. Air raid sirens were blown (reportedly ordered by the mayor's office), and people rushed into the streets or basement bomb shelters fearing the start of World War III. (By coincidence, Russian Premier Nikita Khrushchev was visiting in Des Moines, putting that city "on the map.") In its largest issue (88 pages) in its 59-year history, the paper announced its "new" name change, along with a front-page, 180-degree panoramic downtown skyline scene of a "New Horizon for a Greater Chicago." It urged readers to "Take A New Look" at the "Breathtaking, pulse quickening, the might, and majesty of our city," which also was at the start of its biggest downtown building boom in 40 years and the start of Mayor Daley's rise to power. Economic growth and success in sports were equated with personal identification with the city.

Bill Veeck, one-time owner of the Indians, and later president of the Sox, (who also met the Chicago victors at the airport), later reflected that, "A pennant-winning team makes an enormous contribution to the morale of a city. Everybody suddenly becomes friendly. There is a feeling of common purpose. . . . There is that feeling of reflected glory in a successful baseball team. . . . The eyes of the whole country are . . . upon us, upon me and you" (Veeck, 1962, p. 104). When the Philadelphia Flyers won the Stanley Cup in hockey in 1974, "nothing in the city's past, not even the canonized epithets of W. C. Fields, had done such violence to the collective psyche of Philadelphia as the monotonously regular inferiority of its professional sports franchises. Once the Stanley Cup had been secured, publications started falling over one another in their haste to congratulate the city on, as *Time* put it, 'the tangible proof that Philadelphia is, at long last, a winner'" (Roberts, 1974, p. 17). The image value of a domed stadium had been promoted in 1966 by the Philadelphia *Evening Bulletin*, when it argued that "a spectacular and advanced facility of this kind should help greatly to enhance the city's general reputation for progressive and imaginative action" (editorial reprinted in the Chicago *Tribune*, June 24, 1966). By 1984, Philadelphia was heralded by the press as "a city of winners" with a "new spirit." "From politicians in their offices around City Hall to shoppers at the Gallery, the city's gleaming new multilevel shopping mall on Market Street and to the bars around Veterans Stadium and the Spectrum in South Philadelphia, where the growing list of sports victories have been won, the spirit is much the same" (Robbins, 1984, p. 8Y).

Sports victories are collective civic victories heralded by the media. The Kansas City *Star* published a 32-page special section on January 18, 1970, when the city's Chiefs won the 1970 Super Bowl. A page 1 editorial called them the "Champs of the World," or "maybe it should be the universe," and the coach "led his warriors in the parade like a Caesar returning to Rome or Alexander the Great to Greece" (*Star*, p. 19H). In similar adoration, the press said, "'Praise the Lord'" for an "Orange Crushmas" of team colors and "good feeling" for the Denver Broncos, in the *Rocky Mountain News* in its "Play-off Extra" (December 24, 1977). It noted that, "never before has the city rallied around any one team or any one thing" (p. 1). "We're No. 1," bragged a March 28, 1978, *Louisville Times* page 1 banner and 16 pages of color photos as the University of Kentucky won the NCAA basketball championship. The celebrants were a "happy, giddy, playful crowd as in King Kong fondling a delicate kitten" (p. 1).

The Detroit Pistons' 1989 NBA championship "is making this working-class city feel positively good about itself," as the team hoped to improve the bad image of the city and its own "Bad Boys" reputatio (Schmidt, 1989). Thousands waited in the airport rain for their return from Los Angeles, and "more than 21,500 people—4,000 more than were inside the Forum in Los Angeles—paid $3 apiece Tuesday night to jam the (Detroit) Palace in order to watch the game on the arena's television system." Those who could not get in listened on their car radios before pouring into the streets and later for the parade (Schmidt, 1989, p. B12). Such positive crowd behavior hints at unity rather than division in the city.

SPORTS VICTORY BRINGS
HOPE FOR RENEWAL, SURVIVAL

Population decline, lost jobs, vacant downtown buildings, and snow had not helped Buffalo's reputation some years ago, but hopefully sports would. "As a notch on the Rust Belt, this city has not always enjoyed a sparking image. . . . But the time has come for Buffalo to smile." A new Bills quarterback, James Kelly, became "an instant symbol of civic pride, a beacon of hope for the future" (Johnson, 1986, p. 12Y). Fans welcomed the "national limelight" and being "back on the map" as the " 'messiah has arrived' " for the " 'religion' " of football in a town where taxi drivers got a new dress code to impress visitors. "Amid the fanfare over the new football star, the lexicon of sports has wended its way into the world of high culture" as the newly praised city symphony director became known as " 'The Jim Kelly of the orchestral world'," after plaudits for a Carnegie Hall appearance said, "We have won the orchestral 'Super Bowl'" (Johnson, 1986, p. 12Y).

The press context for sports goes far beyond the team and game in order to express urban hope. When Atlanta took major league baseball in the mid-1960s away from Milwaukee, one columist argued: "Atlanta deserves a big league baseball team. It is a town that is changing. All over town they are tearing down old buildings and pushing new ones up. The city is pushing out into the country. The suburbs are elegant, and spreading. They are the enlightened city of the South, and they're proud of their decent ways. They have a right to be" (Cannon, 1966). Milwaukee's competitive boosters felt differently (Gendzel, 1995), and when it regained baseball with the Brewers, "We're Big League Again!" proclaimed a page 1 (April 1, 1970) *Milwaukee Journal* editorial, which called the new team "a boon—psychological, to uplift civic spirit and pride of community; promotional, to bring further national recognition and prestige to Milwaukee."

When Milwaukee played St. Louis in the 1982 World Series, it was reported that "the pride of having winning teams has given residents of both cities something good on which to focus. To their residents, they have become giants among cities, winners, and the envy of the nation" (Sheppard, 1982, p. 12Y). The press framed the games as the "World Beeries," the "Six Pack," and the "Suds Series" for cities that had lost industries (Schlitz in Milwaukee, General Motors in St. Louis), had lost a positive national image, and had deteriorating downtowns, especially St. Louis. The teams "managed to do in recent months what professional boosters have been unable to do for the past three years: They have rekindled an upbeat spirit in the midst of troubled economic times" (Sheppard, 1982, p. 12Y). For Milwaukee, it "has taken people's minds off a bad period." "Now people are full of spirit and life," and the series "will put us on the map" and revive memories of the 1957 Series victory over the Yankees, "those New York dandies who were said to have referred to the city as 'bush league'" (Sheppard, 1982). For St. Louis, city boosters compared the Cardinals with downtown redevelopment (a civic boom, "'just like the Cardinals'"), the symphony, museums, and universities. The "two grand old baseball towns" in the Middle American Heartland (removed from the larger coastal media markets) saw their team, fans, and town all as one family (Krause, 1982). (In the spirit of sober stability, the St. Louis Cardinal MVP catcher, a recovering alcoholic, doused himself in victory with nonalcoholic grape juice.) Although Milwaukee lost, the hope of winning next time helps both individuals and cities endure the death of defeat.

It was a "brave new world" for Houston after the Rockets beat the Knicks for the NBA championship in 1994. Parade banners paraphrased Neil Armstrong's reference to Houston as the first word from the moon. More than 50,000 fans celebrated at the Astrodome, although the game was not actually played there. According to the *Houston Post's* lead, page 1 news story on June 24, "We feel better about ourselves. We feel better about our city. We will spend more money and be kinder to our neighbors. Yes, and our children will sit up straight without prompting" (Olafson, 1994, p. A1). New businesses and money were expected to pour into the city, as happened after the 1992 Republican National Convention. The Greater Houston Partnership published a list of "Thirty-four Reasons Why Houston Is an MVP (Most Valuable Place)," No. 1 being the home of the Rockets, while others included growth, diverse population, and corporate and consulate headquarters.

The media "advertisement" of the victory was seen as an antidote to the image of losing the big game in "Clutch City" and of sports stars' fights with local city police in "Trouble Town." "But perhaps the biggest benefit will be the national publicity generated by the hordes of media that are converging on the city . . . millions of dollars worth of exposure, and obviously that's advertising we could not afford to buy," said a convention tourism and marketing official (Stanton, 1994, p. R22). As with the Milwaukee–St. Louis games, "The recognition factor is perhaps the best long-term effect the World Series will have on the two cities" (Sheppard, 1982). A city's media exposure is seen as being as important as economic benefit (Ludden, 1997). Internal civic self-esteem also matters. "FEELING GOOD," read the huge, page 1 headline of the *Houston Post* on July 24, 1984, after the Rockets' victory. A similar, huge, page 1 banner "WE FEEL GOOD," appeared on December 8, 1996, in the Austin *American-Statesman*. It was the day after the University of Texas upset the University of Nebraska to win the first Big 12 football championship. (The winning quarterback was James Brown, an African American whose name is the same as the black soul singer James Brown, whose song lyrics include "I feel good.") Such media-sports hyperbole is not new and has long been used to symbolize both city and state self-conceptions and rivalry between them. In 1875, when the St. Louis Browns beat the Chicago White Stockings for the first time, the *St. Louis Democrat* said, "We have met the enemy, and they are ours." The *St. Louis Republican* editorial proclaimed: "ST. LOUIS IS HAPPY" (Carter, 1975). Cities have grown larger, but civic sentiment is not smaller.

MAYORS, MEDIA, SPORTS, AND THE FRAGMENTED METROPOLIS

Civic bliss is difficult in the fragmented, postmodern metropolis of multiple centers and multiple cultures, but the media metaphor of sports can sometimes simulate civic harmony among factions, especially when the hometown team wins. As New York Mayor Rudolph Giuliani welcomed the victorious Yankees in their 1996 Manhattan parade, media managers Rupert Murdoch and the Atlanta Braves' Ted Turner argued over the turf for CNN and Fox journalistic cable. Frank Sinatra (originally from Hoboken, N.J.) sang (on tape) the city's "sports anthem," "New York, New York," amidst the archaic ticker tape-less parade up the skyscraper Canyon of Heroes as Yankees' owner George Steinbrenner insisted, "This team IS New York," despite talk of moving it out of the city and state. So much for urban reality.

Nevertheless, "historic, majestic, sublime . . . New Yorkers were gleefully lost among the metaphors" in a "sumptuous autumn day of delft skies," as "The ghosts of Ruth, Gehrig, and Mantle have been appeased at last" (McFadden, 1996, p. 1). "And you could hear the sunlit [broadcast] voices of Red Barber and Mel Allen. . . . The team is . . . emblematic of a new New York. The city is renewing itself yet again. It is a safer, less disorderly, a little more relaxed, but as tough as always" (Herbert, 1996, p. A13). Notice how "the symbolic purposes of sport and civic imagery merge with private economic goals and public urban development" (Lipsitz, 1984, pp. 1–18). Also, note how sports is "a central nervous system that connects the body politic" (*Gannett Center Journal*, 1987, p. iv) and is "one of the sinews that holds modern society together" (Rader, 1990, p. 346). Also, "Politically, sport is useful for symbolic purposes, especially in creating a sense of the 'imagined community'" (Wilson, 1994, p. 271). In this respect, New York City's sports and political history illustrates media, sports, and the role of mayors seeking to advertise and promote the city and hold its fragments together.

In 1969, Mayor John Lindsay tied his successful second-term campaign to the successful season of baseball's Mets, when his opposition to the Vietnam War and his liberalism had cost him an endorsement by his Republican Party at a time of urban unrest and division. He called the Mets "his" team, often was televised visiting its locker room, and proclaimed himself "John 'Mets' Lindsay," as he led their victory parade and victoriously announced that the team "brought this town together" (Swartz, 1976). The team made the city and the mayor both look and feel good. The Mets were long "sunk in the dreary hopelessness of the perpetual loser, just as this giant, dirty and all but ungovernable city has been . . . (but victory gave it) . . . some sort of feeling of restored civic communion" (White, 1969). When the Mets won again in 1986 and "metsmerized" the city, Mayor Ed Koch said, " 'The Mets made us a family. . . . The Mets made us a small town with love and affection" (Freedman, 1986b, p. A1). When the Yankees won the series in 1978, Koch had compared their victory to the city's escape from bankruptcy (Yankee parade, 1978, p. C1). Both Lindsay and Koch opposed the move of football's Giants to New Jersey, and Koch said he would not "cross a state line" to watch a "foreign team" when the Giants won the NFL play-off in 1987. However, the *New York Times* urged setting aside "parochial jealousies" for a proud achievement for "the entire New York area" (editorial, January 13, 1987, p. 22Y, "The Giants: Theirs and Ours").

Media and mayors compete for symbolic power in their promotional efforts to unify the fragmented metropolis divided by geography and culture. Both deal in symbols and information, as do sports. In the absence of a single government for the whole metropolitan area, each serves as a kind of "governor" for the total metropolis. They coexist as two "governments" in both conflict and consensus. Client support for the media and mayor extends beyond the central city's borders. It is easier for the media to get readers, viewers, listeners, advertisers, and consumers in the suburbs and hinterland than for a mayor to get political support and votes outside of the politically restricted city (Burd, 1970b). "Their symbiotic common ground is an un-debated and shared civic ideology." Often, this concerns urban vitality and sports (Burd, 1988). Both seek the civic "advertisement" brought by sports. Their conflicts often involve means and methods rather than ends and goals, although the press criticizes a mayor more than it challenges the authority of a coach. Indeed, coaches may be assigned more power by the press. When Green Bay Coach Vince Lombardi arrived in Washington to coach, the *Washington Post* saw him as someone who might inspire solutions to city problems such as crime, poor transportation, and bad schools (Kole, 1969). When Houston's "Bum" Phillips was on his way to New Orleans, "The people of New Orleans are using a football team coached by a crew-cut, tobacco-chewing good ol' boy from East Texas as a rallying point for civic pride" (Hohlfeld, 1983, p. II:1).

For big American cities, sports helps package, promote, and "sell" the "civic ad" for the metropolis, and "more than anyone else, the mayor is the symbol of the city," and in his ceremonial role, "it is the mayor who must somehow hold things together" in a fractured, fragmented, decentralized, pluralistic, urban society (Ruchelman 1969, p. 253). The mayor's relations to the media are crucial to this ceremonial role, and sports naturally nourish an image of consensus with media and the city. For the media, "the (central) city is the only source of symbolism capable of drawing together the fragmented suburban market," and that is a major reason for their focus on downtown development projects. New developments such as sports stadia and the loss or gain of a team often are tied to the reaffirmation of the center of the urban region with its great symbolic "impact on the image of the city" (Kaniss, 1991, pp. 66–67). When the NBA finals were held in his city, Houston Mayor Bob Lanier remarked that most visitors were "'surprised at our skyline and how clean and green Houston is" (Stanton, 1994, p. R22).

Newspapers focus on sports as a geographical and psychological magnet. In the midst of debate on the location of a new Dallas sports arena, a *Dallas Morning News* writer said: "city boundaries may mean little in the midst of metropolitan sprawl, but a community's pride of possession in a sports franchise can make more tolerable the commonplace tribulations of urban life . . . the frequent gathering of thousands of people to cheer on their teams at an arena in their city's heart might help that heart beat a bit more quickly" (Seib, 1996, p. 27A). The "heart" usually means "downtown" in media metaphor.

Mayors As Major Civic Boosters of Sports Teams

Mayors are among the most enthusiastic sports boosters. In 1956, Los Angeles Mayor Norris Poulson went to a Dodgers game and later suggested that a city-owned public housing site be used for its new stadium (Henderson, 1979). Miami Mayor Xavier Suarez argued that a professional baseball team gives a city "a stamp of certification" as a major league city (*The Daily Texan*, June 11, 1991, p. 7). In 1986, San Antonio Mayor Henry Cisneros pushed for a new stadium by saying, "Those of us who lead cities need all the help we can get in bringing people together, and nothing integrates a city better than major league sports" (Cisneros pushes, 1986, p. B2). New Orleans Mayor Moon Landrieu called his city's Superdome "an exercise of optimism, a statement of faith. It is the very building of it that is important, not how much it is used or its economics." In this respect, a city becomes an advertised product or commodity marketed by mayors and the media.

In 1984, Indianapolis Mayor William Hudnut lamented that his city had "no image," but that the newly arriving Colts would be "a cornerstone in a bid for the big time . . . a galvanizing effect . . . a great lift," because "We're major league," and the "rest of the country will be paying attention to us" (Weyler, 1984, p. III:8). In 1986, Chicago Mayor Harold Washington and Jessie Jackson joined an airport pep rally for the Chicago Bears on their way to the Super Bowl. In 1994, Houston Mayor Bob Lanier proclaimed a "Wear Rockets' Red Day" before the NBA finals as a story reported "Rockets Work on City Image" and quoted a player saying, "We know how important it is to the city. We're doing our best to bring pride to the city" (Riggs, 1994, p. C1).

Mayors and media are quick to conclude that sports victories reduce tensions in race, ethnicity, class, and politics. Joe Falls, sports editor of the *Detroit Free Press*, claimed that the Tigers' 1968 World Series victory, in the midst of urban racial unrest, calmed "a city which badly needed time, time to cool off, and the Tigers bought that time" (Falls, 1969, p. 1-B). When the Detroit Pistons planned to move to the suburban Silverdome, protesters complained of a false and an unfair attitude toward Detroit as being too dangerous for white suburbanites to visit (Detroit pickets, 1977, p. G2). *Kansas City Star* sports columnist Joe McGuff said that the Chiefs' 1970 Super Bowl victory "brought people of all classes and political persuasions together in a common bond of pride," and although it would not eliminate crime, hunger, or pollution, "for a few days it made these burdens a little lighter" (McGuff, 1970, p. B2). A *Star* editorial said that the city's people were "caught up together by a sense of community and common hope that made their private concerts and prejudices seem blessedly irrelevant" (January 12, 1970).

As black and white players celebrated the Washington Redskins National Football Conference (NFC) championship in 1972 in the locker room on television, the team chaplain prayed, and the city mayor praised the team for lifting up the depressed city and for loving each other as family and community. Washington journalists agreed that Coach Allen "has been a great coalescent agent for the city," and that the team brought blacks and whites together (Scott, 1972, p. 15). Five years later, political columnist James Reston wrote that the Redskins' and basketball Bullets' victories had unified the District of Columbia with rich Virginia and Maryland suburbs and accomplished more than federal equal opportunity programs (Reston, 1978, p. I:8). As Washington worried about the team plan to move the stadium to a suburban site in 1996, an end-of-the season collapse "left everyone in town both astonished and depressed," according to political columnist David Broder. "It was certainly a strong dose of anti-hubris medicine, a seismic shock that was felt up and down Pennsylvania Avenue" (Broder, 1996, p. 17A).

The arrival of major league teams in the Minneapolis–St. Paul area was said to have helped "create the over-all metropolitan consciousness" that brought the rival twin cities together, according to an editorial in the *Minneapolis Star* (May 10, 1971). Minneapolis Mayor Don Fraser said that the Twins' victory over the Cardinals in the 1987 World Series meant "feeling better about ourselves," and that it was the "best thing" that ever happened to the city (*New York Times*, October 28, 1987, p. 51). In Denver, *Post* editorial page editor Bill Hosokawa said that, in the Broncos, "there is much of Everyman with which all of us common folk can relate" (editorial page, January 8, 1978). The Baltimore Orioles, in 1979, were said to be "the glue of our metropolitan fabric, the catalyst that somehow makes Baltimoreans of us all" (Owens, 1979, p. A19). The role of sports in a metropolitan area was seen in the "unifying effect of the Miami Dolphins" in South Florida and the "inability of the entire South Florida area to coalesce" in replacing the home Orange Bowl (Shuster, 1983, p. 6C). When Los Angeles beat Detroit for its second NBA championship in 1988, it was reported that, "For all the talk that Los Angeles is a city without a center, the city seemed to have found a centering point with the Lakers" (Rhoden, 1988, p. 44Y), although the city has far less water than its previous home of the Lakers in Minnesota, "The Land of 10,000 Lakes." Symbolic and geographic reality merges in sports metaphors.

The press practice of pointing with pride or crying with alarm about publicity on their city is matched by that of frustrated mayors frantically grasping for some political symbolism to help them unite and govern the ungoverned and sprawling metropolis. The cries of civic grief range from onimous to humorous: Seattle Mayor Wes Uhlman called for a court injunction to stop the Pilots from moving to Milwaukee and told the nation on ABC's *Nightline* (October 18, 1982) of the proud and affectionate relationship between the team and his city. Mayor Lindsay in New York fought to prevent the departing football Giants from using the name of New York in New Jersey. Mayor Richard Daley pled for the White Sox to stay in Chicago, because they are "like the Water Tower on the North Side and the Art Institute" (*Chicago Sun-Times*, "Fight to Keep Sox," December 5, 1975, p. 1 banner). Some 15 years later, as pressure grew for a new stadium, the Illinois governor vowed to "bleed and die before I let the 'Sox leave Chicago" (*New York Times*, April 19, 1991, p. A1).

In 1976, St. Paul Mayor Lawrence Cohen blamed the business and industrial community for the demise of the local Fighting Saints hockey team (Businessmen, 1976). When the Evansville, Indiana, basketball team died in a plane crash, the mayor said that it was "the greatest tragedy" in the history of that city. When Wayne Gretzky ("The Great One," No. 99) left the Edmonton Oilers hockey team for the Los Angeles Kings in 1988, Mayor Lawrence Decore said, "It's like ripping the heart out of a city." He compared the departure to losing the River Valley of Edmonton, to which the player and team had brought fairs, tourists, and business. Radio station phone lines in Edmonton were jammed in anguish by fans, and newspaper headlines read "99 Tears," but the hockey star left for Los Angeles (Gretsky trade, 1988, p. 106), then moved to the St. Louis Blues, and then to the New York Rangers, where he was reported to be in a "New York state of mind" (*The Daily Texan*, July 22, 1996, p. 7).

The reaction of mayors to sports defeats can be as frantic as that of sports and media boosters. When the San Francisco Forty Niners lost to the Dallas Cowboys in November 1996 (after backup quarterback Elvis Grbac had replaced injured star Steve Young), San Francisco Mayor Willie Brown said, "'After that bonehead intellectual breakdown in the last game against Dallas, and we lost it 20–17, he [Grbac] can't play in any stadium that I'm gonna assist to be built. . . . This guy Grbac is an embarrassment to humankind'" (Mayor calls, November 13, 1996, p. 10). (The mayor later apologized after he learned that Grbac was under stress over his 9-month-old son having recent surgery for spina bifida.)

In 1992, a Philadelphia radio talk show host suggested that Philadelphia businesses named "Dallas" change their names, and that the Pennsylvania towns of Dallas and Dallastown be renamed, or their mayors would lose re-election (Rude, 1992). The mayor of Buffalo, James D. Griffin, was upset when Howard Cosell, on ABC's *Monday Night Football*, said, "You know, they cloned Cleveland and got Buffalo." In a letter to Cosell, the mayor said, "The people of this community have striven for years to overcome the unfounded, negative misconceptions that have developed about Buffalo." He told the sportscaster that it was "extremely frustrating to hear those years of effort mitigated by an off-handed comment before a national television audience" (Cosell remarks, 1979, p. 2). Cosell's apology was meant to blunt or mend the negative civic image and aid the city's advertising and promotion program.

Beyond the preceding evidence of sports mania, madness, and metaphor by mayors, media, and mass spectators are larger research and policy questions. What are the consequences and wisdom of the sports-media-city symbiosis and the promotion of civic identity through boosterism and the civic ritual of sports "to legitimize political solutions to urban crisis" and to construct "the il-lusion of consensus"? (Schimmel, Ingham, & Howell, 1993, pp. 213, 241). How may this involve the use of exaggerated and unrealistic civic advertising through image making and civic superlatives, the media's self-interest and par-ticipant civic activism, and full and open public debate on the sports enterprise?

What are the psychological benefits and costs of the sports economy and possible regressive imbalance between sports as spectacle and sports as recre-ational and health participation? Is there an excessive and a superficial press and public focus on such feeling and emotion, and on heroic sports role mod-els and morality tales, at the expense and neglect of more rational and substan-tive values related to urban reality?

How do changing communications technologies and the increase in the mediation of sports as an advertised commodity affect the shifting boundaries of sports maps and loyalties? Is there a deterioration of indigenous sports com-munities where teams, coaches, and fans belong, and a decline of symbolic rep-resentation and loss of a sense of sports place? How representative is the sports metaphor of collective consensus in a city, especially for that part of a city that is not, or cannot, be represented symbolically by sports images, either for those within or outside of it?

What are the costs of regional rivalry for sports resources, and what are the merits of sports to explain or affect urban hope, renewal, and survival? And, what are the limits of their value to mayors and others in government who hope that the ritual and ceremony of sports create or reflect a sound consensus in a diverse, divided urban society?

Are spectacle sports distorted by media as being truly reflective of public life and the inner self of everyday life in the metropolis, or are they a projected illusion of individuality, consensus, and a civilized civic bond?

REFERENCES

Altheide, D. L., & Snow, R. P. (1979). *Media logic.* Beverly Hills: Sage.

Anderson, D. (1996, October 28). In New York, New York 90s, championships abound. *New York Times,* p. B8.

Bale, J. (1986). Sport and national identity: A geographical view. *The British Journal of Sports History, 3(1),* 19–41.

Bale, J. (1989). *Sports geography.* London: E & F. N. Spon.

Bayless, S. (1978, July 16). Shuffled off to Buffalo, Knox finds the welcome warm in a cold city/A tale of 2 coaches in best and worst of times. *Los Angeles Times,* pp. III:1, 11–12.

Berkow, I. (1986, October 11). New York and Houston: Collision of cultures. *New York Times,* p. 16.

Bonk, T. (1984, October 11). Bum's not quite a saint. *Los Angeles Times,* pp. III:1, 11.

Boswell, T. (1977, October 12). Happy Dodgers, feisty Yankees reflect their cities. *Washington Post,* pp. D1, D2.

Broder, D. (1996, December 24). All looking good, then 'skins faded. *San Antonio Express-News,* p. 17A.

Burd, G. (1969a). The mass media in urban society. In H. J. Schmandt & W. Bloomberg Jr. (Eds.), *The quality of urban life* (pp. 293–322). Beverly Hills: Sage.

Burd, G. (1969b, September–October). Critic or booster role for press. *Grassroots Editor, 10(5),* 7–8.

Burd, G. (1969c, February 6). *Sports news, economic base, and the civic bond.* Lecture to Alpha Gamma Delta, Marquette University, Milwaukee, WI.

Burd, G. (1970a, January). Protecting the civic profile. *Public Relations Journal, 26(1),* 6–10.

Burd, G. (1970b, May). Mayors, media, and civic co-existence. *Nation's Cities, 8(5),* 49–50.

Burd, G. (1972, April–May). The civic superlative: We're no. 1—The press as civic cheerleader. *Twin Cities Journalism Review, 1(2),* 3–5ff.

Burd, G. (1977a, April). *Urban symbolism and civic identity: Vision and values in architecture and communication.* Paper presented at the meeting of the Western Social Science Association, Denver, CO.

Burd, G. (1977b). The selling of the Sunbelt: Civic boosterism in the media. In D. Perry & A. Watkins Jr. (Eds.), *The rise of the Sunbelt cities* (pp. 129–149). London: Sage.

Burd, G. (1980, Summer). City growth and planning news as civic ideology. *Journal of Communication Inquiry, 6(1),* 55–66.

Burd, G. (1981, February). *Sports as communication and civic spectacle in declining central place.* Paper prepared for Conference on Culture and Communication, San Diego, CA.

Burd, G. (1986, Spring). Reporting an urban 'box score': A journalistic 'sports record' to measure local urban performance. *Journal of Urban Affairs, 8(2),* 85–98.

Burd, G. (1988, March). *Two "governments" in conflict: Mayors vs the media.* Paper presented at the meeting of the Southwest Political Science Association, Houston, TX.

Businessmen tried to save the fighting saints. (1976, March 9). (Editorial, *Mankato Free Press,* reprinted in *Minneapolis Star*).

Butterfield, F. (1986, October 19). In Boston, Red Sox inspire fanaticism—2 cities in combat: It's more than baseball. *New York Times,* pp. 20–21.

Cannon, J. (1966, April 13). Eckert avoids Atlanta debut. *Chicago Daily News,* p. 40.

Carey, J. W. (1989). *Communication as culture: Essays on media and society.* Boston: Unwin Hyman.

Carter, G. L. (1975, July). Baseball in Saint Louis, 1867–1875: A historical case study in civic pride. *Missouri Historical Bulletin,* 31, 253–263.

Cashdan, A., & Jordin, M. (Eds.). (1987). *Studies in communication.* Oxford: Basil Blackwell.

Cavanaugh, J. (1989, August 28). Little leaguers put town on map. *New York Times,* p. 5.

Cisneros pushes indoor stadium for San Antonio. (1986, December 29). *Austin American-Statesman,* p. B2.

Cosell remarks upsetting to Buffalo's mayor. (1979, October 14). *Springfield, MO, News & Leader,* p. 2.

Danielson, M. N. (1997). *Home team: Professional sports and the American metropolis.* Princeton: Princeton University Press.

Detroit pickets protest pistons' move to suburbs. (1977, October 19). *Austin American-Statesman,* p. G2.

Duncan, M.C. (1983). The symbolic dimensions of spectator sport. *Quest, 35(1),* 29–36.

Dunning, E. (1981). Social bonding and the socio-genesis of violence. In A. Tomlinson (Ed.), *The sociological study of sport: Configurational and interpretive studies.* Brighton: Leisure Studies Association.

Falls, J. (1969, April 7). How can tigers match '68 feat? *Detroit Free Press,* p. 1B.

Freedman, S. G. (1986a, October 19). In New York, Met charm stirs hearts—2 cities in combat—It's more than baseball. *New York Times,* pp. 20–21.

Freedman, S. G. (1986b, October 29). It's really over: New York cheers. *New York Times,* pp. A1, A20.

Gannett Center Journal. (1987, Fall). Sports and mass media. (Preface) 1:2, iv–vi.

Garrison, B., & Salwen, M. (1989). Newspaper sports journalists: A profile of the profession. *Journal of Sport and Social Issues, 13(2),* 57–68.

Gendzel, G. (1995, Winter). Competitive boosterism: How Milwaukee lost the Braves. *Business History Review*, 69, 530–566.

Gent, P. (1974, February). Kareem Abdul-Jabbar is still growing. *Sport, 57(2)*, 44–53.

Green, T. (1978, July 16). The Rams may be different team but Allen returns to fold unchanged—A tale of 2 coaches in best and worst of times. *Los Angeles Times*, pp. III:1, 10.

Gretsky has a New York state of mind. (1996, July 22). *The Daily Texan*, p. 7.

Gretsky trade creates furor throughout much of Canada. (1988, August 11). *Rocky Mountain News*, p. 106.

Guttman, A. (1986). *Sports spectators*. New York: Columbia University Press. Review essay, *Urban Affairs Quarterly* (1988). 24(2), 327–332.

Henderson, C. S. (1979). Los Angeles and the Dodger war of 1957–1961. *Proceedings and Newsletter of the North American Society for Sport History*, pp. 26–27.

Herbert, R. (1996, October 28). More than winners. *New York Times*, p. A13.

Herman, R. (1975, May 15). Islanders serve, but stand and wait for days of glory. *New York Times*, pp. 50, 57.

Hohlfeld, N. (1983, November 13). Bum nearing sainthood. *Houston Chronicle*, pp. II:1, 24.

Jackson, Keith (1996, September 17). *ABC-College Football Telecast*. Nebraska vs. Michigan State.

Johnson, D. (1986, September 6). At last, new sports hero puts a smile on Buffalo. *New York Times*, p. 12Y.

Jones, G. L. (1984, March 15). The true spirit of St. Louis is that man named Stan. *Los Angeles Times*, pp. III:1, 8–10.

Kammer, D. J. (1980, May). Sport and culture through architectural criticism. *Proceeedings of the North American Society for Sport History*, pp. 38–39.

Kaniss, P. (1991). *Making local news*. Chicago: University of Chicago Press.

Karp, D. A., & Yoels, W. C. (1990, Fall). Sport and urban life. *Journal of Sport and Social Issues, 14(2)*, 77–102.

Kato, Hidetoshi. (1974, Spring). The city as communion—Changes in urban symbolism. *Journal of Communication, 24(2)*, 52–60.

Kole, J. W. (1969, February 6). Capital won't be same with Lombardi around. *Milwaukee Journal*, pp. II:1.

Koppett, L. (1989, September 27). Rams and 49ers continue their rivalry of traditions. *New York Times*, p. 52Y.

Kraft, J. (1978, January 12). The Super Bowl: A symbolic event. *Washington Post*, p. A27.

Krause, J. (1982, October 15). Milwaukee's champions are champions of city. *Milwaukee Journal*, p. II:11.

Kyle, D. G. (1994, Fall). Book review essay. *Journal of Sport History, 21(3)*, 280.

Lapchick, R. E. (1986). *Fractured focus: Sports as a reflection of society.* Lexington, MA: D. C. Heath-Lexington.

Lipsitz, G. (1984, Summer–Fall). Sports stadia and urban development. *Journal of Sport and Social Issues, 8(2)*, 1–18.

Lipsky, R. (1979). The athleticization of politics: The political implication of sports symbolism. *Journal of Sport and Social Issues, 3(2)*, 28–37.

Ludden, J. (1997, June 2). Profiting in more than one way. *San Antonio Express-News*, pp. 1C, 11C.

Mayor calls Grbac 'embarrassment.' (1996, November 13). *Associated Press/Daily Texan*, p. 10.

McCormick, J. (1973, July 1). Time heals wounds in Shelby. *Associated Press/Austin American-Statesman*, p. 1.

McFadden, R. D. (1996, October 28). It's autumn in New York and triumph is in the air. *New York Times*, pp. A1, B10.

McGuff, J. (1970, January 18). Sporting comment. *Kansas City Star*, p. B1, B2.

Meyer, K. E. (1979, April 28). Love thy city: Marketing the American metropolis. *Saturday Review, 6(9)*, 16–20.

Michener, J. (1976) *Sports in America*. Greenwich, CT: Fawcett.

Northam, J. (1977, May). Sports and boosterism: Seattle's Alaska-Yukon-Pacific exposition, 1909. *Proceedings of fifth annual convention of North American Society for Sport History*, Windsor, Ontario, Canada, p. 48.

Olafson, S. (1994, June 24). Does win mean new image for bayou city? *Houston Post*, p. A1.

Ostler, S. (1980, April 27). Seattle loves its downtown. *Los Angeles Times*, pp. III:1, 10.

Owens, G. (1979, August 7). Baltimore pays. *Washington Post*, p. A19.

Peterson, J. (1962, October 30). Professionals bounce in as Seattle goes bigtime. *The National Observer*, p. 16.

Prebish, C. S. (1993). *Religion and sport: The meeting of sacred and profane* Westport, CT: Greenwood Press.

Rader, B. G. (1990). America in Sports: From the age of folk games to the age of televised sports (2nd ed.). Englewood Cliffs, NJ: Prentice Hall.

Real, M. (1977). The Super Bowl: Mythic spectacle. In Michael R. Real (Ed.), *Mass mediated culture* (pp. 31–43). Englewood Cliffs, NJ: Prentice Hall.

Real, M. (1990). Sport and the spectacle. In J. Downing, A. Mohammadi, & A. S. Mohammadi (Eds.), *Questioning the media: A critical introduction* (pp. 345–356.) Newbury Park, CA: Sage.

Redding, S. (1975, March 2). That other dome. *Houston Chronicle/Texas Magazine*, p. 12.

Reinhold, R. (1990, April 4). Campus put on the map by a team. *New York Times*, p. A8.

Reston, J. (1978, May 16). Politics could learn something from sports. *Houston Chronicle*, p. I:8.

Rhoden, W. C. (1988, June 23). After victory, L. A. loses its cool. *New York Times*, p. 44Y.

Riess, S. A. (1989). *City games: The evolution of American urban society and the rise of sports.* Urbana: University of Illinois Press.

Riggs, R. (1994, June 7). Rockets work on city image. *The Austin American-Statesman*, p. C1.

Robbins, W. (1984, November 19). Sports prowess brings a new spirit to Philadelphia. *New York Times*, p. 8Y.

Roberts, M. (1974, November 23). The vicarious heroism of the sports spectator. *The New Republic*, p. 17.

Rooney, J., & Macdonald, J. (1982). Sport and games. In J. Rooney, W. Zelinsky, & D. Louder (Eds.), *This remarkable continent: An atlas for U. S. and Canadian society and culture* (pp. 50–63). College Station: Texas A & M.

Rosentraub, M. S. (1996). Does the emperor have new clothes? *Journal of Urban Affairs, 18(1),* 23–31.

Ruchelman, L. I. (1969). *Big city mayors: The crisis in urban politics.* Bloomington: Indiana University Press.

Rude, J. (1992, September 28). Philly in a frenzy. *Dallas Morning News*, pp. B1, B5.

Russo, N. (1977, April 22). A tale of two cities. *St. Louis Post-Dispatch*, sec. 20, pp. 1, 6.

Sage, G. H. (1981). Sport and religion. In R. F. Gunther, L. Luschen, & G. H. Sage (Eds.), *Handbook of social science of sport* (pp. 147–159). Champaign, IL: Stipes.

Schimmel, K. S., Ingham, A. G., & Howell, J. W. (1993). Professional team sport and the American city: Urban politics and franchise relocations. In A. G. Ingham & J. W. Loy (Eds.), *Sport in social development—Traditions, transitions, and transformations* (pp. 211–244). Champaign, IL: Human Kinetics.

Schmidt, W. E. (1989, June 15). Detroit hopes Pistons help image. *New York Times*, p. B12.

Scott, J. (1972, December 16). The Redskins and reporters. *Editor and Publisher*, pp. 15, 33.

Seib, P. (1996, May 27). Sports teams are important for cities. *Dallas Morning News*, p. 27A.

Shaikin, B. (1988). *Sport and politics: The Olympics and the Los Angeles games.* Westport, CT: Praeger.

Sheppard, N., Jr. (1982, October 17). World Series proving to be a shot in the arm of Milwaukee and St. Louis. *New York Times*, p. 12Y.

Sherrod, B. (1979, September 27). Colts' move isn't just matter of packing up. *Dallas Times-Herald*, p. 1C.

Shuster, R. (1983, February 11). South Florida split over sports complex issue. *USA Today*, p. 6C.

Smothers, R. (1991, June 15). No hits, no runs, one error: The dome. *New York Times*, p. 6Y.

Stanton, R. (1994, June 8). Rockets' success to bring city national exposure, but athletes already know Houston's reputation. *Houston Post*, p. R22.

Stevens, W. (1976, November 28). Sports arouse exultation in the industrial crescent. *New York Times*, p. 26L.

Stone, G. P. (1981). Sport as a community representation. In R. F. Gunther, L. Luschen, & G. H. Sage (Eds.), *Handbook of social science of sport* (pp. 214–245). Champaign, IL: Stipes.

Stone, G. P., & Anderson, D. F. (1981). Sport: A search for community. In S. L. Greendorfer (Ed.), *Sociology of sport: Diverse perspectives* (pp. 164–172). West Point: Leisure Press.

Sullivan, B. (1981, January 23). Bum is officially now a saint. *Austin American-Statesman*, p. E1.

Swartz. S. H. (1976, December). Yes Virginia, everybody loves a winner: Sports, the media, and politics. Unpublished paper, J391, University of Texas, Austin.

Tucker, D. (1996, December 26). For sale: NCAA's headquarters site. *San Antonio Express-News*, p. 8C.

U. S. Congress, Senate, Committee on the Judiciary. (1983) *Hearings* on professional sports antitrust immunity (as quoted in Wilson, 1994, p. 161).

Vecsey, G. (1994, June 23). Finals show links of cities, coaches. *San Antonio Express News*-New York Times Service, pp. D1, D4.

Veeck, B. (1962). *Veeck—As in wreck.* New York: Putnam's Sons.

Waco, Texas, *Herald-Tribune.* (1974, December). Editorial: The Baylor bears a civic asset.

Walker, R. H. (1988, Summer). The Reds: Inventing the Midwest. *The Antioch Review, 46(3),* 284–302.

Walker, W. (1974, January 16). The football phenomenon and its place on campus (Oklahoma athletic director quoted). *New York Times*, p. 91C.

Weyler, J. (1984, July 31). Indianapolis Colts: So far, Hoosiers are having love affair with new team. *Los Angeles Times*, pp. III:1, 3, 8.

White, W. S. (1969, October 10). Mets make Lindsay and N.Y. look good. *Detroit News*, p. 27.

Whitson, D., & Macintosh, D. (1993). Becoming a world-class city: Hallmark events and sports franchises in the growth strategies of western Canadian cities. *Sociology of Sport Journal, 10,* 221–240.

Wilson, J. (1994). *Playing by the rules: Sport, society, and the state.* Detroit, MI: Wayne State University Press.

Wohl, R. R., & Strauss, A. L. (1958, March). Symbolic representation and the urban milieu. *American Journal of Sociology, 63,* 523–532.

Wolf, B. (1975, December 7). Why should packer fans object to Hornung's humor? *Milwaukee Journal*, p. 1 (sports).

Yankee parade tops since '45. (1978, October 20). *St. Louis Post-Dispatch*, pp. C1, C4.

4

Urban(e) Statuary Times

Synthia Sydnor Slowikowski

Many fragments:

- *Torso.* "Only he who can view his own past as an abortion sprung from compulsion and need can use it to full advantage in every present. For what one has lived is at best comparable to a beautiful statue that has had all its limbs broken off in transit, and that now yields nothing but the precious block out of which the image of one's future must be hewn" (Walter Benjamin, from Bullock & Jennings, 1996, p. 467).
- In the film *Pumping Iron II*, Bev vows at the beginning of her weight training that she will come to look like a Greek statue.
- Some of the "enemies" in *Mortal Kombat*, the video game, turn to statues of ice, stone, or bronze when they are "hit" on the urban streets.
- "One-half pound of dry wallpaper paste; adding a few ounces of glycerin and one-third of a pound of bronze powder, care being exercised *not to inhale* the bronze powder while mixing . . . this is a striking makeup, but surfaces under the arms and between the thighs must be free of makeup to ward off the danger of suffocation and possible collapse of the model."[1]
- In his famous *Reflections on the Imitation of Greek Works in Painting and Sculpture*, Johann Joachim Winckelmann wrote, "the more tranquil the state of the body, the more capable it is of portraying the true character of the soul" (Winckelmann, 1987, p. 35).
- Michael Jordan poses among male, ancient, Greek-like athlete statues wearing underwear in a 1996 advertisement for the Hanes Company.

I use these fragments above and throughout this chapter in order to sculpt urban statuary into sites of fascination (e.g., Schechner, 1989, 1993a, 1993b)[2] for scholars of sport, glossing over what we usually say sociologically or anthropologically about statues. I treat statues in my staccato writing, as voids, or empty spaces. Borrowing from Giorgio Agamben's *The Coming Community*, statues[3] are pure singularities that communicate only in the empty space of the example . . . they are expropriated of all identity, so as to appropriate belonging itself. . . . Tricksters or fakes, assistants or 'toons, they are the exemplars of the coming community. (Agamben, 1994, section 10, p. 1)

Statues of athletes are cliché, they are assistants and 'toons, exemplars of the coming community, so as to be blanks with no clear meaning except to refer to the world as it is. And as the world is, great athlete forms—say, for instance, the bronze statue of Carl Lewis wearing five gold medals that stands in the foyer of the Santa Monica Track Club—are screens (e.g., Parker & Kosofsky Sedgewick, 1995) that tune onlookers to perform hegemonic formations of nation, family, work, and so on. We know that such hegemonic formations evoke emotions such as nostalgia, joy, and sadness. These affects are not innocent—in our times, emotions are commodities or signifiers of experience. We also know that statues of the West (e.g., Bieber, 1971; Grant, 1991) are part of an invented Greek heritage.[4] Our cultural spaces of sport are fused with these affects—witness the onlookers who cry when they see the statue of Rocky (the boxer played by actor Sylvester Stallone in the *Rocky* films) at the top of the stairs at the Philadelphia Art Museum, or those physical educators who make pilgrimages to the site of the ancient Olympic Games and pay homage to the charioteer statue.

Agamben says that:

the root of all pure joy and sadness is that the world is as it is. Joy or sadness that arises because the world is not what it seems or what we want it to be is impure or provisional. . . . In the highest degree of their purity . . . sadness and joy refer not to negative or positive qualities, but to a pure *being-thus* without any attributes. (Agamben, 1994, appendix 90.1)

It is this *being-thus* that I attach to interpretations about urban statuary within the context of sport and physical culture.

- Discobolus[5]: a sculpture, bronze, or marble of a man in the act of throwing a discus, an ongoing representation of an ongoing representation of the first-century B.C. Roman rendition of a fifth-century B.C. Greek work by Myron (Ridgeway, 1984, pp. 65, 68, 83–84; Furtwangler, 1964; Bieber, 1971, pp. 1–2; Juenther, 1929; Vermuele, 1981, p. 7; Mensch, 1943–1945), the world's first simulacra (Baudrillard, 1983); sometimes his head looks down, sometimes his head looks back (Haskell & Penny, 1981, p. 152).
- Leni Riefenstahl's Olympia begins with a series of close-ups of faces from Greek statues—Medusa, Aphrodite, Apollo, Achilles, and Paris,

dissolving to Myron's discobolus. As the camera rotates past the statue, it comes to life throwing the discus (Downing, 1992, pp. 48–49).

- There is a photograph, circa 1902, of the early founders of American physical education. At least 12 men sit together at a table, at the center of which looks like a 12-inch reproduction of Myron's discobolus. The men stare magisterially at the statue. I look closer at the photograph and see that the statue holds body fat measurement calipers instead of a discus.
- "Discus Athletic: Work Clothes for Athletes." The clothing company's logo is a black-and-white rendition of a discobolus.
- In *Travels in Hyperreality*, Umberto Eco describes a Sarasota Bay art museum: "A pleasant Italian garden. This garden is peopled with statues: It's like going to a party and finding old friends: Here is the Discobolus . . . hello Apollo, how've you been? My God, always the same crowd" (Eco, 1976, p. 36).

Walter Benjamin was concerned with things like the discobolus (although he never specifically mentioned it), with how the "uniqueness of a work of art is inseparable from its being imbedded in the fabric of tradition" (Benjamin, 1968, p. 223). He forged an approach that we reckon with today when he read tradition as "thoroughly alive and extremely changeable" (1968, p. 223). Benjamin explored how new methods of production are interwoven with the old, and "'dialectical images' still arise from which it is possible to deduce various collective ideas of wish fulfillment" (Bronner, 1994, p. 143).

But Benjamin claimed that with the increasingly pronounced effect of technology upon art, the ability of an audience to fasten upon the utopian residues of art became weak. He perceived premodern objects and artwork to have an "aura" that allowed the object to "look at us in return" (Bronner, 1994, p. 142). As technology made possible new ways of mechanical reproduction, there was a loss of aura, the utopian presence of the past was weakened, and the "quality of presence always depreciated" (Benjamin, 1968, pp. 220–222). For Benjamin, when technical reproduction put the copy of the original into situations that would be out of reach for the original itself, the original "authority" of the object was lost. Yet it seems that statues, particularly the discobolus, still have authority, or even aura, in our times.

I have focused thus far on the discus statue motif. Using such foundational thought as Benjamin, let me move beyond the discobolus to the broader topic of urban statuary. What is the urban statue? Here are some definitional efforts: Statue: a three-dimensional representation of a person, an animal, or a mythical being that is produced by sculpturing, modeling, or casting. There are problems with such definitional efforts: the Barbie doll, a little statue (Lord, 1994), certainly populates our urban landscape (according to Mattel, 1 million Barbie dolls are sold every hour); moreover, Barbie has been an urban athlete: she has the gear and wardrobe for gymnastics, ice skating, roller blading, skiing, swimming, running, golfing, bowling, soccer, and tennis.[6] Doll: a small-scale figure of a human being . . . a small statue . . . silk-screened T-shirts; jewelry; the plastic figurine of Michael Jordan; a victory trophy; the bad guys who get turned to statues in *Mortal Kombat;* a baby rattle; a skyscraper; the discobolus . . . all statues. Each in its own way recalls European Western "archaeological fetishism for white statues" (Eco, 1986, p. 34). But here we are concerned with "sport in the city." I must limit my phantasmagoric[7] walk among statues to those that are associated with sport, with city. City: the earth, populated, and all that that population has made. Sport: to move. To move is to be alive. But the statue? The statue is an in-between thing, a liminal thing; it is human, yet it is not; it lives and moves, yet it is still. Perhaps the statue does retain the aura Benjamin thought lost in contemporary art. Kenneth Gross, in *The Dream of the Moving Statue*, describes this aura:

> These things cannot happen: A statue cannot move or speak; it cannot open its eyes, nod, or call out, cannot tell a story, dance or do work; it cannot turn on the viewer, or run away, banishing its solidarity and repose, shedding its silence. A statue is almost by definition a thing that stands still, and what we call its movement is at best a resonant figure of speech. Yet these things happen; we imagine them happening. Our language requires that they happen. The fantasy of a statue that comes to life is as central a fable as we have. Time and again, we find texts in which the statue that stands immobile in temple or square descends from its pedestal, or speaks out of its silence . . . it is one of our oldest images of the work of magic, one of our most primitive metafictions. (Gross, 1992, p. xi)

The urban statue that depicts a sporting human or humans—for example, that of Michael Jordan, which stands in front of Chicago's United Center (this statue is now the number 1 tourist destination in Chicago)—behaves in the fantasy that Gross describes of the moving statue, the *tableau vivant*.[8] A statue such as Jordan's comes to life imaginatively, televisually, and through commodification (e.g., Andrews, 1996a, 1996b). At United Center, the statue freeze-frames for us the human sport endeavor, it "museualizes" (Huyssen, 1995, p. 14) or captions and publicly displays Jordan's simulacrum as a special collection, a unique museum, "the ultimate" person engaged in sport, our hero, our victor. This collection that is curated, preserved, remembered, and displayed in the late twentieth century acts as a vehicle of remembrance: Jordan as moving statue stands as a souvenir for us to remember what it is to be human, how our form can be divine; the athlete statue shows us how far we can go; in an orderly parcel, standing in Chicago, hanging in miniature on a Christmas tree, or encased in a snow globe—all that we want to say that is good and noble about humanity is on display. Here I loosely follow philosophers such as Mirceau Eliade and

Martin Heidegger. Eliade wrote of the power of images such as rock, vegetation, and fire: "such images bring men together, however, more effectively and more genuinely than any analytical language. Indeed, if an ultimate solidarity of the whole human race does exist, it can be felt and activated only at the level of images" (Eliade, 1952, p. 17).

But now I have romanticized the statue, the sporting statue. I want to be cynical. Like Susan Sontag (1990) and others point out, I should associate the statue and the acts of gazing, voyeurism, touching, and stilling that are linked to cultural practices of display or looking to be in and of themselves pornographic and violent. The body displayed as a statue, most often in poses reminiscent of classical Greek statuary, made of white stone,[9] still,[10] naked-yet-not naked,[11] is a body spectators can gawk at or even desire. Voyeurism of "Greek" flesh is acceptable, a practice of "high" culture. Although they may be hung in Nike Town and may be depicted on mountain bikes, we are voyeurs to bodies from the past (a past that has been invented, selected, reified, narrated, collected, labeled, protected, pillaged, duplicated, reenacted, copied, and remembered[12] as "ancient Greek" or from "some past"), for statues are always from the past. And as Lowenthal says in his work, *The Past Is a Foreign Country,* "the past is a world into which time travelers may pry without embarrassment or fear of rebuff" (1985, p. 296). The "remoteness" of the past enables people to engage with it creatively, to frame it however they want.[13]

The surrealism of urban sport statuary makes it acceptable, and the eroticism of the physical is subtle, for such statues are nostalgically contextualized aesthetically to be patriotic, to hail from "our" (such as forwarded by Percy Shelly's infamous words, "we are all Greeks") noble past, to pay homage to a team or national hero, and to be historical or commemorative, whatever that is.

Art critic Joanna Frueh uses the phrase "fear of flesh that moves" to describe models of feminine perfection, writing that "the flesh that moves disgusts the self that is designed out of Western thought" (Frueh, 1991, p. 71).[14] This flesh suggests infirmity or unfitness, lack of muscularity. But in sporting statues, the body is gilded/pasted/frozen into distinct boundaries: again, the paradox surfaces of the flesh that comes to life yet never moves.[15]

I have so far looked upon statues in the same way that we have made sense of museums: as organs of remembrance (Huyssen, 1995, p. 25); as vehicles of hegemony; and in a poststructuralist, apocalyptic way as voiced by Baudrillard (1983), Eco (1976), Boon (1991), and Stewart (1984), among others. That is, statues are practices of "stockpiling." "Our entire linear and accumulative culture would collapse if we could not stockpile the past in plain view. We need an invisible past, a visible continuum, a visible myth of origin to reassure us as to our ends" (Boudrillard, 1983, p. 19).

I have exposed the statue as something that serves to legitimate particular ideals in physical or sport culture, or culture at large. The statue poses as an authentic[16] experience/event for the visitor, the purchaser of the postcard of the statue, the owner of a Barbie doll, the viewer of Olympic Games statuary *tableaux vivant*, or whatever, and at the same time articulates certain hegemonic ideals. Of course, to argue for the importance of things like statues in conveying and sustaining social memory (Connerton, 1989, p. 109), capitalism, or other cultural formations is nothing new. We know that living bodies, and statues too, as signs are highly adaptable vehicles for the expression of socially constructed categories, such as the category of "the past," the "American," "the normal," "the strong," "the anti-Semitic," and "the fetish."

What can I say that is significant about the urban statue? I can claim that it is a prop-artifact-backdrop that rips liminal spaces for us. The thought of Henri Bergson from the 1890s might be revisited. He reminds us that "space, by definition is outside us; yet the separation between a thing and its environment cannot be absolutely definite and clear-cut; there is a passage by insensible gradations from one to the other" (Bergson, 1991, pp. 202, 209).

I am interested in these gradations, in the liminal, in the paradox of the statue that does not come to life yet at the same time offers the viewer (or the artist creator-designer) the pantomime of a person most alive—an athlete: a man about to throw a discus, Mike flying, Carl Lewis just beribboned with gold medals. Liminal means borderlands, threshold, in-betweenness. Victor Turner from Van Gennep (1960, pp. 138–139, 170–171) called the liminal *betwixt and between* (Turner, 1967, p. 106, also pp. 93-111). Liminality is "a realm" where there is a certain freedom to juggle with the factors of existence. The liminal can apply not only to rites of passage of individuals or groups but to the liminal spaces, the "not here, not there," which are in theory, in writing, in statuary, in culture at large, in our post modern times, all at the same time.

The liminal characterizes the coming community that Agamben (1994) creates for the future, Agamben's words being those that I quoted earlier in this chapter. The coming community is similar to Homi Bhabha's (1994) idea of the Third Space.[17] Bhabha suggests in his work, *The Location of Culture* (1994), that theory, being, and history exist in a timeless space of unmeaning called the Third Space, which is beyond control. According to Bhabha:

> This is the space in which the question of modernity *emerges as a form of interrogation:* what do I belong to in this present? In what terms do I identify with the "we," the intersubjective realm of society? This process cannot be represented in the binary relation of archaism/ modernity, inside/outside, past/present, because these questions block off the forward drive or teleology modernity. . . . What is crucial to [a vision of the future] is the belief that we must not merely change the *narratives* of our histories, but transform our sense of what it means to live, to be, in other times and different spaces, both human and historical. (Bhabha, 1994, pp. 245, 256, emphasis in original)

Perhaps statues, which are as old as the history of human community, are among many transformative, liminal features of times of new meaning and cultural creativity. I insinuated earlier that statues might rip liminal cultural spaces, that they are props that float viewers and creators into liminal narratives. But I do not mean that statues are special, particular cultural spaces more so than any other cultural "thing" has special cultural properties: *all* of our terrain, all cultural formations and artifacts, and all practices, sport, and otherwise are *third spaces*, spaces where we are *whatever*, where *whatever* can happen. (A caveat: later I argue that the specific cultural space of celebrity has distinct cultural properties related to third spaces and liminality.) This *whatever* is the word of Agamben (Agamben, 1994, 2.1; "Translator's Notes," 106.5–107.5). The coming community of Agamben is made up of liminal passages, inside/outside spaces around which the symbolic discourse of human history comes to be constituted, around which celebrity (and in Agamben's words) "assistants, and 'toons" are glorified. Here is a description of the coming community from the on-line journal *Postmodern Culture:*

> The basis of the coming community, the singular being, is *whatever being*—not in the sense of "I don't care who you are," but rather, "I care for you *such as you are*. As *such* you are freed from belonging either to the emptiness of the universal or to the ineffability of the individual . . . human identity is not mediated by its belonging to some set or class (being old, being American, being gay). Nor does it consist in the simple negation of the "negative community." . . . Such a singularly exposed being wants to belong—which is to say, it belongs to want, or for lack of a less semantically burdened and empty word, to love: The singularity exposed as such is whatever you *want* that is lovable. . . . In [this] work, philosophy becomes once again, perhaps, a kind of homesickness, a longing to belong. To a permanent disorientation. To oscillation. To whatever. (Chang, 1994, ls. 48–50, 60, emphasis in original)

If statues are spaces of *unmeaning*, then they are a liminal realm where there is a certain freedom to juggle with the factors of existence. In this freedom, third spaces are becoming places where the old rules may no longer apply, where identities are fluid, where meanings are negotiated, where what Agamben calls *whatever* can happen, *whatever* can be loved. From Agamben, *"whatever* refers precisely to that which is neither particular nor general, neither individual nor generic" (Agamben, 1994, translator's notes, 1). The epistemological and ontological standpoints, offered by *whatever* and shown to us in things such as urban statuary, transport us into liminal spaces and spaces of freedom. But, as I warned earlier, I think especially the standpoints offered by the imaginary of celebrity transport us to the liminality of *whatever.*

By celebrity, I refer to fame, achieved recognition, notoriety, and the act of being extolled, filmed, or talked about in the media, *in real time, imagined or remembered*—those qualities normally associated with movie stars, sports heroes, television personalities, characters, politicians, Hollywood, the tabloids, being in/on television, in the movies, in the public eye, a recognized maker of culture. I refer to the pervasive nature of celebrity and its pursuit—most of how we and those around us pursue it in little, everyday ways. Evidence our children—children everywhere—who want to be game-show hosts, famous athletes, fashion models, movie stars, opera singers, or members of the dream team. Evidence also our acquaintances whose lives are defined around moments when they played guitar for a few seconds on stage with a famous band, saw a movie star in a restaurant, were interviewed on a news show, or made a pilgrimage to the Olympic Games. I point to the dentist who dreams of being a world-class weight lifter, the housewife who takes acting lessons, the small-town farmwife who urges a movie made about her adultery with a fireman, the millions who fantasize that they are Michael Jordan on the court as they shoot baskets in the schoolyard, the thousands on deathbeds who produce videos about their ends, writers everywhere who dream of making it, everyone everywhere who harbors a fantasy of being famous, of being the object of a gaze, of a lens, of Andy Warhol's scant minutes of fame ("in the future, everyone will be famous for fifteen minutes"). As a writer in *Utne Reader,* reciting the routines of his life, put it, "Two questions constantly occur to me: 'What would this look like filmed? What would the sound track be?'" (Shields, 1994, p. 170).

In the spaces of celebrity, we are Agamben's *whatever.* These third spaces of celebrity, media, the *whatever* of celebrity, the *whatever* of sport, and the *whatever* reproduced by urban sport statuary are examples of the pure *being-thus* that Agamben highlights (1994, 50.0). Celebrity and *being-thus* are third spaces at the end of the twentieth century where for a few seconds one may be free, happy, and unjudged as black, white, rich, or poor. These *being-thus* spaces, sometimes signified by statuary, are culture itself.

I gaze at statues again. It seems that statues have an extraordinary role in our culture, perhaps because they are props to *whatever,* to *being-thus;* they serve not as ways for us to remember but as performances that dehistoricize/create/prolong liminality. Possibly, statues serve to do precisely the opposite of what we say they do: they deform,[18] not form. In the everyday sense of the use of the statue, the statue is commissioned to save a moment, a memory, a person. But performitively, the statue tears a liminal space into everyday space, prolonging the nature of the threshold whose moments are liquid and undefinable, and whose memories are always in the act of becoming. Thresholds are exciting (e.g. Turkle, 1995; McCorduck, 1996, pp. 106–110, 158–165), dangerous, and wondrous.

On this idea as it engagingly applies to break dancing, see Baudrillard's *Cool Memories II.* "You have to be a perfect dancer to dance immobility, like those solitary breakdancers on the sidewalks of Venice (California). . . . Their bodies only move at long intervals, like the hand of a clock stopping for a minute on every second, spending an hour on each position. . . . This immobility is not an inertia, but a paroxysm which boils movement down into its opposite" (Baudrillard, 1996, p. 44).

NOTES

1. Olds (1949, p. 127). This is a recipe for Living Statuary. See note 11 for a description of this ritual.

2. Schechner's work (1989, 1993a, 1993b) is my foundation for this chapter.

3. Agamben never refers to statues—I have appropriated his words to apply to statues.

4. The philosophical basis of Greek revivalism, of carrying on the Greek heritage in modernism, was the idea, from thinkers such as Winckelmann, that "the only way for us to become great . . . is to imitate the ancients, especially the Greeks" (Winckelmann, 1987, p. 5; see also Clarke, 1989, p. 112). This invented tradition is continually performed by our bodies. For example, early body builders made their bodies into Greek statuary to make viewing these bodies palatable. The early body builders' skin had to be veiled. They could not move, except in certain poses that had been Greek statuary poses. American Eugene Sandow is known for "his pioneering live display of human muscularity for its own sake which he introduced in 1982 (Dutton & Laura, 1990, p. 142; see also Chapman, 1987, p. 62). Sandow posed in glass booths, behind gauze curtains, and dusted his body with white powder (Chapman, 1987, p. 62) to look like a statue. A pose called the "Sweeping muscular back," taken up by Michelangelo from the statue of the Apollo Belvedere's torso, was used by Sandow and later body builders. The three-quarters back shot perfected by Arnold Schwarzeneger also was a clear derivative of the discobolus' (statue of a man throwing a discus) back. Later artistic classical statuary influences are many. See also, for example, Robert Mapplethorpe's *Thomas* 1986, *Michael* 1987, and *Apollo* photographs (Mapplethorpe, 1988; Marshall, 1988), which echo Greek statuary. The aesthetics of statuary (e.g., McKenzie, 1932; Vance, 1989, pp. 297–351) influenced the culture of the Western body. So, too, the invention of the camera also affected the art studio tradition of early body building, which in turn had authority over how participants were photographed, which continued statuary emulation. In this tradition, photographic studies of athletes were portrayed with props from classical athlete statuary such as leopard skins, shields, spears, sandals, and fig leafs.

5. Greek sculptor Myron of Eleutherae was born in the earlier part of the fifth century B.C. He was known for his statues of Apollo, Dionysus, Athene, a satyr, and a work called Nike on a Bull. But Myron's fame in antiquity (and today) rested with his discobolus creation, in part, it seems, because Myron experimented in this work with the novel body position of a man about to throw a discus. Although Myron has been immortalized for his discus thrower, the discobolus was a common artistic subject in antiquity before Myron. Myron worked entirely in bronze, but the discobolus survived only in several Roman marble copies, of which there is a great variety in detail. Many ancient authors all refer to Myron. Lucian (*Philopseudes* 18) speaks of the discobolus

"who is stooping to throw, turning his face towards his hand which holds the discus, and bending one leg, as if, after he threw, he would stand erect again." Philostratus (*Imagines* 1.24.2; see also Philostratus, *On statues* 1.24) followed Myron's discobolus in order to give evidence of the best technique for discus throwing. Quintilian (*Institution oratio* 2.13.8) described the pleasure to be derived from novelty and difficulty in the treatment of works of art such as Myron's discobolus. There also was ongoing criticism by early authors surrounding Myron's treatment of the discus thrower's hair, and the fact that the "quiet impassive expression of the head clashes with the violent movement of the body" (Furtwangler, 1964, p. 173).

6. When refugees evacuated Bosnia, they took with them not religious statue icons but Barbie dolls.

7. *Phantasmagoria* was a term that Marx used to "refer to the deceptive appearances of commodities as 'fetishes' in the marketplace" (Buck-Morss, 1993, pp. 81, 212). For Benjamin, the phantasmagoria was Paris (Benjamin, 1973, p. 165; see also Buck-Morss, 1993, pp. 66, 81, from Konvolut V, p. 1056 [fo, 3]): a "magic lantern show of optical illusions, rapidly changing size and blending into one another" (Buck-Morss, 1993, Konvolut V, pp. 698-707, 1049). Benjamin wrote of Paris:

> As a social formation, Paris is a counterimage to that which Vesuvious is as a geographic one: A threatening, dangerous mass, an ever-active June of the Revolution. But just as the slopes of Vesuvious, thanks to the layers of lava covering them, have become a paradisical orchard, so here, out of the lava of the Revolution, there bloom art, fashion, and festive existence as nowhere else. (Buck-Morss, 1993, pp. 66, 81, from Konvolut V, p. 1056 [fo, 3] as quoted by Buck-Morss, 1993, p. 66)
>
> All that the phantasmagoria was was of purely representational value—it was made of everything desirable that held the crowd enthralled; with Baudelaire's flâneur, Benjamin marveled at walking among, yet above the crowd; he was awed by the activity of window shopping, at "charging time with power like a battery, at [empathizing] himself into the soul of the commodity." (Buck-Morss, 1993, p. 105, from Konvolut V, p. 162 [D2a, 4])
>
> Benjamin called the phantasmagoria revolutionary. He wrote, "in reality, there is not one moment that does not bring within its own revolutionary possibility—it wants only to be defined as a specific one, namely as the chance for a totally new resolution in view of a totally new task." (Benjamin, Notes to "Thesis on History, I, p. 1231, as quoted by Buck-Morss, 1993, p. 339)

8. There are centuries of *tableaux vivant* tradition. The first tableau was the opening for doorways and windows, long before the easel and canvas painting—this is the idea of Paul Virilio (1991, p. 90), who notes that to understand the first tableau, we would have to try to return to the visual unconscious, to the nature of opening and closing. In the nineteenth century, Lady Emma Hamilton struck attitudes at parties in imitation from classical history and mythology that included statuary; in Belgium, in the early twentieth century, M. Verdonck organized the Ganda Gent gymnastic group to perform large Flemish-nationalist tableaux vivant; and tableaux vivant whose actors

went without body make-up were common in Germany (e.g. Tolleneer, 1992; Sontag, 1992; Sturzebecker, 1996; Annan, 1992, pp. 3–6).

9. To thinkers such as Heidegger, "stone" represented "authentic experience" and "mythical time" (Heidegger, 1971, pp. 21–22).

10. On "stillness" of statues, Renaissance writers such as Winckelmann (1987) pointed out that the general and most distinctive characteristics of Greek masterpieces are, finally, a noble simplicity and quiet grandeur, both in posture and expression. Just as the depths of the sea always remain calm, however the surface may rage, so does the expression of the figures of the Greeks reveal a great and composed soul, even in the midst of passion (p. 33).

11. For example, physical educator Leslie Judd wrote of Living Statuary (a boys' activity in American physical education from the 1930s to the 1970s, which was a performance of famous Greek statues such as the Dying Gladiator and the Discobolus. The performances were creative ventures with "original" Greek images. There were tableaux in physical education shows, for example, of Greek athletes saluting the American flag; of Greek statuary moving to the musical score, "The Impossible Dream"; of Greek statues moving World War II plane propellers): "It is very important that the entire body be covered with make-up in order to remove the appearance and feeling of nudity. . . . A net curtain before the poseurs and the audience creates a fine illusion and promotes the sense of unreality so necessary to this type of performance" (Gruber, 1947, pp. 5, 8).

12. Historians now insist upon the invention of traditions. Yet it seems that few spectators, participants, athletes, and/or kinesiologists protest or even notice this vigorous cultivation of certain motifs, such as classical statuary forms, within the boundaries of physical culture, physical education, and so on. Can these communities be disillusioned, unsettled, by this Greek heritage that it has disquietly appropriated over the past 200 years? One aim I have here is to make a rupture in the appropriation of ancient Greece by physical culture and sports professions.

13. I am not trying to produce a theory of difference with the statue as my keystone, nor is it my purpose to ingenuously map out the convergence of race, sexuality, aesthetics, elitism, ethnoterroism, complicity of Western rationality, and so on onto the athlete-statue phantasmagoria. These themes frequent my work, but I seek no exacting interpretations of the statue.

14. Also, historically, obscenity legislation has taken the criteria of stasis for its definition of an acceptable display of the naked body. For example, a 1968 New York State law "states that persons could appear on stage naked without moving—that is, if they became statues. Movement or physical contact between nude persons was criminal" (Schneemann, 1979, p. 169).

15. On this idea as it engagingly applies to break dancing, see Baudrillard (1996), *Cool memories II:* "You have to be a perfect dancer to dance immobility, like those solitary breakdancers on the sidewalks of Venice (California). . . . Their bodies only move at long intervals, like the hand of a clock stopping for a minute on every second, spending an hour on each position. . . . This immobility is not an inertia, but a paroxysm which boils movement down into its opposite" (p. 44).

16. On authenticity, see Bruner, 1993; Bruner, 1994, pp. 397–415; Bruner & Kirshenblatt-Gimblett, 1994, pp. 435–470. These pieces, however, go far beyond the trope of "musealization" as quest for authenticity and instead highlight the creative, unique experiences that individuals and groups may encounter in their travels for authenticity.

17. I have modified Bhabha's Third Space, a singular, capitalized entity, into third spaces, lowercase plural, in my work.

18. On the idea of "deforming," see Benjamin, "Imagination" (Bullock & Jennings, 1996, pp. 280–282).

REFERENCES

Agamben, G. (1994). *The coming community* (Michael Hardt, Trans.). Minneapolis: University of Minnesota Press.

Andrews, D. L. (1996a). The fact(s) of Michael Jordan's Blackness: Excavating a floating racial signifier. *Sociology of Sport Journal, 13(3)*, 125–128.

Andrews, D. L. (1996b). (Guest Ed.). Deconstructing Michael Jordan: Reconstructing postindustrial America [Special issue]. *Sociology of Sport Journal, 13(4)*, 315–318.

Annan, G. (1992, August 13). A moral tale. [Review of the book, Susan Sontag, *The Volcano Lover: A Romance*]. *New York Review of Books*, pp. 3–6.

Baudrillard, J. (1983). *Simulations* (Paul Foss, Paul Patton & Philip Beitchman, Trans.). New York: Semiotext(e).

Baudrillard, J. (1996). *Cool memories II: 1987–1990* (Chris Turner, Trans.). Durham: Duke University Press.

Benjamin, W. (1968). The work of art in the age of mechanical reproduction. In H. Arendt (Ed.), *Illuminations* (pp. 217–251, H. Zohn, Trans.). New York: Schocken Books. (Original work published 1936).

Benjamin, W. (1973). *Charles Baudelaire: A lyric poet in the era of high capitalism* (Quintin Hoare, Trans.). London: Verso.

Bergson, H. (1991). *Matter and memory* (pp. 202, 209, N. M. Paul & W. S. Palmer, Trans.). New York: Zone Books. (Original work published 1896).

Bhabha, H. K. (1994). *The location of culture.* London and New York: Routledge.

Bieber, M. (1971). *Ancient copies: Contributions to the history of Greek and Roman art.* New York: New York University Press.

Boon, J. (1991). Why museums make me sad. In I. Karp & S. D. Levine (Eds.), *Exhibiting Cultures: The Poetics and Politics of Museum Display* (pp. 255–278). Washington and London: Smithsonian Institute.

Bronner, S. E. (1994). *Of critical theory and its theorists.* Oxford: Blackwell.

Bruner, E. M. (1993). Epilogue: Creative persona and the problem of authenticity. In S. Lavie, K. Narayan, & R. Rosaldo (Eds.), *Creativity/Anthropology* (pp. 321–334). Ithaca and London: Cornell University Press.

Bruner, E. M. (1994, June). Abraham Lincoln as authentic reproduction: A critique of postmodernism. *American Anthropologist, 96(2),* 397–415.

Bruner, E. M., & Kirshenblatt-Gimblett, B. (1994, May). Maasai on the lawn: Tourist realism in East Africa. *Cultural Anthropology, 9(2),* 435–470.

Buck-Morss, S. (1993). *The dialectics of seeing: Walter Benjamin and the Arcades Project.* Cambridge, MA, and London: MIT Press, 1993.

Bullock, M., & Jennings, M.W. (Eds.). (1996). *Walter Benjamin: Selected writings. Volume 1 1913–1926.* Cambridge, MA: Belknap Press of Harvard University Press.

Chang, H. (1994). [Review of the book, Girgio Agamben, *The coming community*]. *Postmodern Culture 4,* n. 1, 1994: ls. 48–50, 60. (pmc@unity.ncsu.edu).

Chapman, D. (1987). The first great strongman. *Muscle and Fitness,* 62.

Clarke, G.W. (Ed.). (1989). *Rediscovering Hellenism: The Hellenic inheritance and the English imagination.* Cambridge: Cambridge University Press.

Connerton, P. (1989). *How societies remember.* Cambridge: Cambridge University Press.

Downing, T. (1992). *Olympia.* London: BFI Publishing.

Dutton, K. R., & Laura, R. S. (1990). The birth of bodybuilding. *Muscle and Fitness 51,* 142.

Eco, U. (1986). *Travels in hyperreality* (William Weaver, Trans.). San Diego and New York: Harcourt Brace Jovanovich.

Eliade, M. (1952). *Images and symbols: Studies in religious symbolism* (p. 17). New York: Sheed and Ward.

Frueh, J. (1991). The fear of flesh that moves. *High Performance 55,* 71.

Furtwangler, A. (1964). *Masterpieces of Greek sculpture* (p. 168). Chicago: Argonaut.

Grant, M. (1991). *The founders of the Western world: A history of Greece and Rome* (p. 2). New York: Charles Scribner's Sons.

Gross, K. (1992). *The dream of the moving statue.* New York: Cornell University Press.

Gruber, F. C. (1947). *Living statues: A manual for Boy's Clubs.*

Haskell, F., & Penny, N. (1981). *Taste and the antique: The lure of classical sculpture 1500–1900.* New Haven and London: Yale University Press.

Heidegger, M. (1971). The origin of the work of art. In M. Heidegger (Ed.), *Poetry, language, thought* (pp. 21–22). New York: Harper & Row.

Huyssen, A. (1995). *Twilight memories: Making time in a culture of amnesia.* New York and London: Routledge.

Juenther, J. (1929). Das Problem Des Myronische Diskobols. *Osterreichische Jahreshefte 24,* 123–161.

Lord, M. G. (1994). *Forever Barbie: The unauthorized biography of a real doll.* New York: William Morrow and Co.

Lowenthal, D. (1985). *The past is a foreign country.* Cambridge: Cambridge University Press.

Lucian. *Philopseudes.*

Mapplethorpe, R. (1988). *Ten by ten.* Munich: Schirmer/Mosel.

Marshall, R. (Ed.). (1988). *Robert Mapplethorpe.* Boston, Tornonto, and London: Whitney Musuem of American Art, Bulfinch Press, and Little Brown and Co.

McCorduck, P. (1996, April). Sex, lies and avators. *Wired, 4(4),* 106–110, 158–165.

McKenzie, R. T. (1932). The athlete in sculpture. *Antike und Abeland 33*, 115-125.

Mensch, M. L. (1943–1945). A Myronic statue of an athlete reconsidered. *Marsyas*, 1–14.

Olds, L.W. (1949). Living statuary. *Health, Physical Education, and Recreation, 20*, 127–128.

Philostratus. *Imagines.*

Philostratus. *On Statues.*

Parker, A., & Kosofsky Sedgwick, E. (Eds.). (1995). *Performativity and performance.* New York and London: Routledge.

Quintillian. *Institution Oratio.*

Ridgeway, B. S. (1984). *Roman copies of Greek sculpture: The problem of the originals.* Ann Arbor: University of Michigan Press.

Schechner, R. (1989). *Between theater and anthropology.* Philadelphia: University of Pennsylvania Press.

Schechner, R. (1993a). *The future of ritual: Writings on culture and performance.* London and New York: Routledge.

Schechner, R. (1993b). Ritual, violence, creativity. In S. Lavie, K. Narayan, & R. Rosaldo (Eds.), *Creativity/Anthropology* (pp. 296–320). Ithaca and London: Cornell University Press.

Schneemann, C. (1979). *More than meat joy: Complete performance works and selected writings.* New York: Documentext.

Shields, D. (1994, March–April). Information sickness. *Utne Reader,* 170. (Originally published in *Zyzzyva,* Spring 1993).

Sontag S. (1990). *On photography.* New York: Anchor Books.

Sontag, S. (1992). *The volcano lover.* New York: Farrar, Straus, and Giroux.

Stewart, S. (1984). *On longing: Narratives of the miniature, the gigantic, the souvenir, the collection.* Baltimore and London: Johns Hopkins University Press.

Sturzebecker, R. (1996). *Gymnastic circuses, dance festivals, athletic exhibitions: West Chester University, 1871–1991.* West Chester, PA: Russell Sturzebecker.

Tolleneer, J. (1992). *Gymnastics in Belgium in the interwar period: The Catholic way.*Unpublished paper.

Turkle, S. (1995). *Life on the screen.* New York: Simon and Schuster.

Turner, V. (1967). *The forest of symbols: Aspects of Ndembu ritual* (pp. 93–111). Ithaca, NY: Cornell University Press.

Van Gennep, A. (1960). *The rites of passage* (M. B. Vizedom & G. L. Caffee, Trans.). Chicago: University of Chicago Press. (Original work published 1909).

Vance, W. L. (1989). *America's Rome.* New Haven and London: Yale University Press.

Vermuele, C. C. (1981). *Greek and Roman sculpture in America.* Berkeley: University of California Press, 1981.

Virilio, P. (1991). *The lost dimension* (Daniel Moshenburg, Trans.). New York: Semiotext(e).

Winckelmann, J. J. (1987). *Reflections on the imitation of Greek works in painting and sculpture* (E. Heyer & R. C. Norton, Trans.). La Salle, IL: Open Court Press. (Original work published 1755).

5

No Christmas Dinner

The Effect of Major Sporting Events on Local Homelessness

Robin M. Mathy

An athletic event is a microcosm of a society's social structures. At its most fundamental level, athletic competition reflects the essential dichotomy of self and other. *Some* others are opponents. *Other* others are teammates, coaches and staff, officials, cheerleaders, and fans. Somewhere beyond the periphery are the marginalized folks who for various reasons do not compete, and who do not directly or indirectly contribute, officiate, or gain access to the events. The homeless[1] are a marginalized group in society's social structures, generally denied full access to economic, political, and social participation—and competition. They seldom receive responsible roles in deliberating or officiating their plight. Limited by their stigmatized roles and circumscribed resources, they obtain little access to direct and indirect participation (and competition) in the economic, political, and social mainstream. They get little attention unless they become obtrusive—or, perhaps, problematic to the dominant economic and political social structure.

An important exception is the attention afforded the homeless by academic social scientists, who are to the study of homelessness what sports journalists are to athletics. To use a sports metaphor, I wrote this chapter from the vantage point of a local sports journalist. I had the opportunity to watch, with a mixture of awe and disdain, as events unfolded and subsided when the virtually concurrent collegiate and professional national championships in U.S. football occurred in Tempe, Arizona, in 1996. The Fiesta Bowl of early January 1996 determined the unofficial National Football Championship of the National Collegiate Athletic Administration (NCAA).[2] Super Bowl XXX in late January 1996 decided the National Football League Championship. These are arguably the major sporting events in the United States.

Most of the ethnographic research for this chapter was conducted between the fall of 1995 and the summer of 1996. The particular suburb in which these athletic events occurred was the long-standing research site of the author. Therefore, much is known about the structural antecedents and cultural consequences of the homeless in the particular suburban enclave in which these events took place (Mathy, 1990). The names and identifying information of participants and some specific locations are generalized and intentionally vague to prevent officials from thwarting the survival adaptations of the homeless individuals who participated in this study, as many of them live in constant apprehension of detection. Many are reluctant to reveal essential information until significant efforts at building rapport lead to trust. This meant living as a homeless person among homeless people during this study and sharing their biographies, resources, and activities without divulging more information about them than they wanted to reveal to "outsiders." They were primarily afraid that the hiding places of their few belongings would be co-opted, and expressed trepidation over being discovered while sleeping in relatively vulnerable locations.

Some of the better known and more deliberated causes of homelessness include the scarcity of affordable permanent housing for low-income people, economic disruptions leading to sporadic layoffs and unemployment, finite or nonexistent financial reserves for personal problems, chemical dependency usurping limited financial resources, mental illness, and intrapersonal instability. However, until now, the effects of major athletic events have received little attention. This research demonstrates that these events impede the ability of the homeless to extract themselves from their precarious plights. Thus this chapter relates to virtually all major metropolitan areas with homeless individuals, precisely because these locales are the primary sites for major athletic events as well as large concentrations of the homeless.

SITE OF THE STUDY

Tempe, Arizona, is a relatively small suburb southeast of Phoenix, the capital of Arizona, and a major metropolitan area with a population of approximately 2 million people dispersed throughout Maricopa County, the third largest county in the United States. The domicile ecology is flat and widely dispersed. Although there are a dozen (predominantly business-oriented) high-rises in central Phoenix, only a few exist elsewhere within Maricopa County. Public transportation is extremely limited, and travel by privately owned vehicles is the vastly dominant mode of transportation. Public transportation is limited in duration and frequency. Cessation of inter-city transportation coincides with the end of weekday regular business hours, with regularly scheduled bus service curtailed on Saturday and entirely unavailable on Sunday. This greatly impedes access of the poor and homeless to social and shelter services in Phoenix or suburbs at some distance from where they find themselves, forcing them to make accommodations in the suburban enclaves in which they are struggling to survive. Limited transportation also poses catastrophic hardships for the poor and homeless attempting to travel to work in other areas, especially when the work is performed during evening and nighttime hours. This generally precludes poor and homeless individuals without private transportation from obtaining slightly better paying employment with shift differential incentives. In general, the limited public transportation acts as a mechanism of social control to "keep off the streets" the homeless, the poor, and the disabled. Ownership of private transportation, with all of its attendant costs, including fuel, state-mandatory insurance, extremely high costs of automobile registration, and maintenance expense, is an important passport to social, economic, and political freedom in Maricopa County.

Much of Tempe's economy is dependent upon the student population of 45,000 at Arizona State University (ASU). Tempe does not have a homeless shelter. However, many homeless individuals in Tempe are very adept and creative at utilizing the resources on the university campus in lieu of a formal shelter. The influx of individuals using the campus increases when homeless individuals are thwarted from the main streets in Tempe and coincides with times when major sporting or civic events dominate the area. The university's administration is hostile to the homeless. In fact, one leading expert on homelessness, who resides in central Phoenix, has stated that the administration has posed the greatest opposition to establishing affordable housing near the site of a new branch campus in another suburb (L. Stark, personal communication, 1996).

The homeless population in Tempe includes a large number of students and working poor (many of whom also are students) who utilize resources on the campus of Arizona State University. At any one time, the number of homeless students fluctuates between 100 to 200. Some are short-term homeless who have been evicted from their apartments for various infractions. Others are short-term homeless who are determined to stay in school despite having lost their jobs, their parents' financial support, or their financial aid. Many of these individuals sleep in their automobiles in remote locations, remaining anchored to Tempe by their commitment to complete their education or to find near the university employment that is compatible with their class schedules.

One subpopulation of homeless individuals in Tempe frequents the coffee shops along Mill Avenue, the main commercial street in the downtown area. This subpopulation consists primarily of adolescents and young adults living a relatively bohemian lifestyle. They tend to come from relatively affluent families. Although they enjoy the intellectual and artistic social milieu provided by the nearby university, they generally are uncommitted to both stable employment and education. The core of this group maintains its popularity by supporting newcomers with financial scraps and places to "crash" (sleep). They occupy a flourishing niche of illicit drug traffic, which in turn is supported by the needs and desires of faculty, staff, and students at the university. Marijuana and amphetamines are the predominant supply. According to Rod Keeling, executive director for the Tempe Community Council, police sweeps by plainclothes officers for panhandling and other nuisance offenses often have netted arrests for crack cocaine (R. Keeling, personal communication, 1996). Although the Tempe Police do not have current statistics, the information officer for the City of Tempe Police readily acknowledged arrests for possession of drugs (primarily marijuana and crack cocaine) and drug paraphernalia by youths along Mill Avenue. Some newcomers occasionally are seen venturing onto and around campus with an illicit delivery, although this tends to be rare. More frequently, students can be seen negotiating a transaction with them on Mill Avenue. Virtually all of these transactions are relatively small and discreet, despite the fact that they usually occur within a block or two of Tempe's police station, patrolling police (including plainclothes officers), and numerous security personnel.

Another subpopulation of homeless in Tempe has taken up longer term residence along the railroad tracks that run through the suburb. Many of these individuals seem to have significant problems with alcohol dependence, although few admit to being alcoholic. Nonetheless, a significant proportion of their limited financial resources is spent on alcohol consumption. They aggregate primarily in parks to socialize, and they congregate at key entertainment locales on campus designated for the exclusive use of students, staff, and faculty.

The homeless group that frequents the coffee shops tends not to utilize the resources of the university, preferring instead to attend to hygiene in whatever private household they awake. However, the City of Tempe Police and the Tempe Community Council noted that public urination constitutes another major cause of arrests for the bohemian youth. The homeless individuals in the other major groups, however, surreptitiously utilize resources on the university's campus for food preparation, hygiene, and inexpensive entertainment. In general, access to showers in recreation complexes is fairly easy, and public-use microwaves can be found in many locations frequented by students acquiring meals. One building has an abundance of televisions, accessible most days of the school term from 6:30 A.M. until midnight. Many of the homeless of various groups know each other and interact closely as they enjoy the free entertainment.

Many homeless individuals sleep on campus during the day, their homelessness concealed by the large numbers of students napping in student lounges and libraries. Hopper (1991) has noted similar use of public space in airports. Skills at utilitarian adaptation and "passing" (Goffman, 1964) as nonhomeless, nonstigmatized persons are impressive and not unlike those of individuals who use airport terminals. In fact, many are so adept at "passing" that they defy detection, and only great familiarity with the research site of the university and suburb, as well as long-standing access to friendship and support networks, leads one to ascertain an individual's homeless status.

Some mention must be made of a typology of homeless that one tends not to see in Tempe. These are families and women with children. Most individuals in this homeless typology tend to find shelter fairly quickly (Anonymous, Autumn House, personal communication, 1996). For example, Autumn House and most domestic violence shelters will try to accommodate homeless women with children whether or not domestic violence has been an articulated issue.

PURPOSE OF THE STUDY

This chapter examines the ways in which the Fiesta Bowl and the Super Bowl affected homelessness, in general, and homeless individuals, in particular, utilizing ethnographic data and field notes from several months prior to many months after these events. Of particular concern were the overt and covert attempts to remove the homeless during prestigious major sporting events, as well as the incidental effects upon homeless individuals as a result of these events. Cities bid and vie with each other to attract these potentially lucrative sporting events. Increased business revenues lead to increased tax revenues, so one would expect overt cooperation between business and government to thwart homeless individuals from remaining in the area during the time of the events. Insofar as government exercises a monopoly on the legitimate use of force, one would expect police action aimed at deterring homeless individuals from remaining in the area. However, intentional actions often have unintentional and unforeseen consequences. It was the aim of this study to examine these unintentional cultural and social structural consequences. Examination of these consequences, in turn, leads to a better understanding of the social dynamics of homelessness.

OBSERVATIONS FROM THE STUDY

Officials with the City of Tempe were candid about their use of the city police to deter homeless individuals from remaining in the area during the Fiesta Bowl and Super Bowl XXX. However, their overt efforts had little effect. Police sweeps, including those by plainclothes officers, were easily detected by homeless individuals and communicated readily to others. There was no noted increase in arrests for vagrancy for loitering, although there was a temporal increase in arrests for drug-related offenses. However, individuals whom I knew to be homeless were only rarely approached by police during these sweeps, whereas high school and university students sporting a "grunge look" (extremely casual, almost disheveled appearance) were approached by police much more frequently. Ironically, perhaps, despite the best efforts of the police and the candidly stated intention of city officials, the increase in arrests for drug-related offenses occurred among students and their friends, not homeless individuals. Even homeless individuals of the bohemian lifestyle typology were less likely to be affected, having gained greater proficiency at watching for police as well as "ditching" (getting rid of) drugs and related paraphernalia.

Another relatively obvious way of deterring homelessness is to provide incentives for homeless individuals to go elsewhere. During the preparation for the Fiesta Bowl and Super Bowl XXX, local print and television news media reported that homeless individuals were receiving offers from officials for free bus tickets to go to San Diego, Tucson, or Albuquerque, other large cities in the Southwestern United States. The reports seemed questionable to me, however, precisely because other cities would likely oppose the intentional bussing of homeless individuals to their cities by another municipality, whether or not they had a major sporting event. Despite the rumor, no reporter had spoken with an individual who had actually been offered a bus ticket to go elsewhere. In each case, the homeless person being interviewed had heard of the offer through someone else and knew of no one personally who had actually gone elsewhere. In fact, the best evidence that the rumor was untrue is the fact that a number of homeless people who desperately wanted transportation to Tucson and San Diego were unable to obtain assistance from the city, local businesses, officials affiliated with the athletic events, or even local social service agencies.

Although overt efforts by business and government in Tempe to thwart homelessness were relatively inconsequential, the Fiesta Bowl and Super Bowl XXX had indirect but major negative structural impacts on homeless individuals surviving in Tempe. The most apparent consequence was the increase, in some cases by several hundred percent, of the price of temporary accommodations such as motels. Housing accommodations were being advertised in the area for as much as several hundred dollars a night. In addition, the costs of motel rooms increased, and most hotel and motel rooms throughout the Phoenix metropolitan area were reserved weeks and even months in advance. The lack of a formal shelter in Tempe forced increasing numbers of Tempe's homeless, especially students and university employees, to utilize as temporary shelter the public space on the university campus. Many of these individuals would have used the short-term accommodations of local hotels and motels as transitional housing, however, the lack of inexpensive short-term accommodations in concert with the lack of a homeless shelter in Tempe dramatically increased the numbers of homeless. Many of these homeless individuals were anchored to Tempe because of temporary employment associated with the sporting events and the aforementioned inadequate bus transportation. The increased housing costs also delayed the ability of the longer term homeless to "move up" from absolute homelessness to short-term motel housing en route to renting an apartment.

In addition, the ranks of the homeless in Tempe swelled, precisely because a large number of migratory homeless people traveled to Tempe to "catch the atmosphere" of the event, even though they knew that gaining entrance to the event was impossible. As Rod Keeling noted, "Oh, yeah, we're in *The Slacker Handbook!* Tempe is one of the top places in the country to be a slacker" (personal communication, 1996). This influx of "slackers" also radically depleted the scarce resources allocated to local homeless persons by social service agencies in Tempe.

Some primary participants in this ethnography were homeless individuals who used the public space of the state university to survive. One couple (Cindie, age 38, and Perry, age 28) "camped" along the railroad tracks in Tempe. They had "been together" for a year and a half and became homeless for the first time in August 1995. Cindie had been laid off, and Perry had lost a seasonal landscaping job after an injury. Although neither ever had been in a homeless shelter, Cindie had been in a domestic violence shelter in another suburb for "a couple weeks" after an incident of domestic violence with Perry. Perry had been arrested once for domestic violence. Although both denied problems with alcoholism and chemical addiction, they frequently appeared intoxicated or "high." At the conclusion of the study, in fact, both were undergoing inpatient chemical dependency treatment.

During this study, they had gained and lost numerous opportunities for more permanent housing. When talking about where they had lived (by the railroad tracks), Cindie and Perry stated, "We're like a little community down there. Everybody knows each other and watches out for each other." Independently, they stated that there are "quite a few homeless down there." This was corroborated by independent visits, and it should be noted that the number of homeless in that area increased during the sporting events. The property along the railroad tracks afforded relatively secluded areas, and it was an area ignored by the police. Nonetheless, they were careful to avoid detection because, as Perry stated, "The police sometimes hassle you when you're on private property." Cindie's and Perry's "campsite" generally was well secluded, just beyond the fence of a secondary school, in a cluster of oleander bushes, adjacent to the railroad tracks quite a distance from any city streets. The City of Tempe Police acknowledge that they rarely go back there, because they have so many streets to cover—unless they are called for some reason.

Cindie and Perry obtained most of their clothing at the "Free Store" on University Avenue, west of Mill Avenue. They stated with pride, "That's where we get 99% of our clothes!" The exclamation suggests pride in their success at finding attractive clothing at no cost. Some of their food was obtained at the Salvation Army, on University Avenue, east of Mill Avenue. Many meals were acquired by "eating out at all-you-can-eat specials." Some of their food came from a nearby independent grocery store, when inexpensive, cooked meat was discounted 50 to 75% in the evening, making affordable an otherwise scarce source of protein. They also went "dumpster diving" at fast-food restaurants along Broadway Road. They found important as well as delightful their ability to acquire an occasional inexpensive, hot meal. This can be seen in the following field note.

> We were hungry and decided to go to Mickey D's [McDonald's] for some breakfast. The food from breakfast hadn't been dumped yet, so [we] were told to come back at 10:35 A.M. We came back, and Perry got in the dumpster. There was *a lot* of food—and still hot! Biscuits and muffins! Perry was handing me the food out when a manager (lady) came out and said "Can I help you?" I said, "We're hungry." She said, "Well, you'll have to get out of there!" Then she said, "You can get sick from eating that food." And I said, "We can get sick from not eating, too." (Cindie, January 16, 1996)

Rod Keeling, who said he would be a "mall manager" if Mill Avenue were a mall, said that trash collections are now scheduled to coincide with the closing of regular business hours at the 65 restaurants in the area. He indicated that their specific intent is to discourage dumpster diving by homeless individuals (personal communication, 1996). He also said that they have actively discouraged churches from doing outreach to give food to the homeless, for fear that the practice would increase the number of homeless individuals who survive in the area.

Both Cindie and Perry obtained work sporadically at a day labor agency (American Work Force). For a brief period, Cindie held a steady job at a T-shirt imprinting store. However, she became ill after a rainstorm, from which their "campsite" provided little shelter. She was unable to report to American Work Force for several days and lost her job. Both wanted to work to save money to get into a motel with weekly rates. Cindie stated, "If we both work three weeks, we can get a place—after Super Bowl. Super Bowl has raised the cost of weekly rental places." Perry remarked dryly, "There's no homeless shelter in Tempe. It's because this is a college town. No Christmas dinner. No transportation to get to shelters or Christmas dinner." Moreover, "according to Madeline" (Salvation Army), "they're getting less donations because of the Super Bowl."

Intermittently, Perry has tried to restart a (purportedly) once-thriving lawn-mowing business, although these efforts were thwarted because his lawn mower and other equipment had been stolen several times. Perry became familiar with the public accommodations at the university, because he formerly was employed as a food worker in the kitchens of residential halls. He claims that he cannot be rehired, because he "walked out" without giving notice of his intent to leave. He went to college for two and a half years, studying culinary arts. Cindie has two years of college, having studied biology.

Both Cindie and Perry reported that, before the Super Bowl, "Police are really getting down on homeless people. We were stopped by two female cops because we were 'suspicious characters'." Both reported several times before and during the Fiesta Bowl and Super Bowl that "Police are busting homeless in parks." This too pushed many homeless to utilize more greatly the public accommodations available on the university campus. Periodically the university's police officers and the Tempe Police made sweeps of the Memorial Union (MU) lounges designated for "currently registered students, faculty, and staff only," although the homeless who use the MU have informed each other that the "key" they use is possession of a backpack or book bag. Virtually all of the homeless who use the space for a period of weeks have backpacks with them. As Monica said, "I just keep all my stuff in there. They don't know what's in it—that there ain't no books in there. All they know is I got a backpack. As long as I got me a backpack there's no reason for them to check, is there?"

Cindie and Perry continued to try to extract themselves from homelessness, but the lack of public transportation and a homeless shelter in Tempe has thwarted their efforts. Although the lack of affordable housing certainly was a factor prior to and during the Fiesta and Super Bowls, other factors and events had thwarted their efforts to obtain affordable housing since then. Among these reasons, repeated illnesses precluded them from working consistently. Ironically, the lack of appropriate permanent shelter was a causal factor in their fatigue and illness, contributing to a "catch-22" in which they could not save money to get shelter because they could not save enough money from day labor, and they could not consistently work at day labor because they were frequently so fatigued and ill.

Monica is a 32-year-old woman who intermittently has been an ASU undergraduate student. She obtained her money from student loans. During the study, she found a one-bedroom apartment to share with another female student. However, for several months she had lived in the unoccupied dorm room in Sonora Hall with a quadriplegic friend. Monica had been extremely evasive about talking about her living situation, merely stating, "I have a place." While coincidentally visiting her friend one evening, Monica "came home." Monica had been secretive because she had been an unregistered guest, constituting grounds for her friends' expulsion from university housing.

Chuck, in his mid-40s, used the resources of the MU primarily for entertainment. For hygiene, he went to a resort on Baseline Road and "blended in." He ate once a day, during the week making the rounds at "happy hours" at various bars, where he would purchase a beverage, which entitled him to consume the food being served. "Except on weekends. Then I go to McDonald's or to the buffet upstairs" in the MU, he stated. Chuck lived in his van with three cats. Initially, he came to enjoy the atmosphere of the Super Bowl and Fiesta Bowl, but he liked the mild winter climate and thus stayed. Chuck was very informative about survival adaptations at ASU as well as other universities across the country. Like many homeless, Chuck worked as much as he could. However, as a self-employed and an uninsured professional house painter, injuries and economic recessions made it hard for him to maintain an apartment or other rental property. His van served as a safe place to sleep at night, as well as a secure place to store the equipment necessary for his livelihood.

Madeline was diagnosed with a serious mental illness, and she received only Social Security. She essentially lived in the MU, carrying with her all of her belongings in a large bag. As with others who were homeless, she tended to hygiene in recreation and exercise facilities on campus. She stored her belongings in day-use-only lockers in the MU. As she put it, "It ain't ideal, but it works."

A disabled graduate student in her thirties stated:

> I've been homeless for the past eight months. Although I had a subsidized apartment, it proved to be too far away from school to be accessible without a private vehicle. Public transportation could not get me to or from campus when I needed to access the library or computing commons. I have learned to adapt to my situation and essentially consider the Memorial Union "home." In a sense, it's a fictive home. I often rationalize it provides about the same thing as a dorm room: a place to sleep. I was able to rent a storage facility near campus for $48 a month and a locker in P. E. East for $10 a semester. I keep most of my belongings in the storage locker and shuttle some back and forth between the two. The savings of $200 to $250 a month may not seem like much, but it has enabled me to travel to two conferences where I was able to make connections which have led to opportunities elsewhere. (Michelle, field notes, August 1, 1996)

Other individuals, including students, survive like those described above by making use of the public spaces on the university campus. When major sporting events occur in Tempe, their numbers increase. As with Cindie and Perry, this is largely because these events diminish the availability of hotels and motels, delaying the opportunity for individuals to transition out of their homeless plight. In part, this also reflects the increase in motel and hotel rates when demand for their spaces increases. This invariably coincides with major sporting and civic events.

Few individuals will acknowledge that they are homeless. Chuck, for example, did not consider himself homeless, nor did Madeline. In part, this reflects what Marilyn French (1985) has referred to as "normative dualism," an essential dichotomy of self and other that leads to social comparisons. Homelessness is a stigmatized social status that even the homeless (as defined above) are wont to accept. To use French's paradigm, nonhomeless and homeless are a dichotomy for which one is morally superior to the other. Given this dichotomy, the homeless label is shunned. Ironically, many of the homeless individuals who use the public spaces on campus point to others as examples of what they are not, even as their adaptive strategies are virtually identical. Monica often would exclaim with disdain, "They're not even students!" Others would exclaim, "They don't even work!" Fundamentally, "homeless" described the situations of others, and whatever regular place one had found to sleep—whether under a tree, along the railroad tracks, or Memorial Union—became defined to self as "mine," although public and neither rented nor owned. As Michelle stated:

> I have experienced the angst of finding someone else asleep in my bed. Others can be seen sleeping on precisely the same couches at approximately the same times, day after day. Sleeping in a public place is an art not easily mastered. One must learn to endure crinkling newspapers, turning pages, slamming books, conversation, and other annoyances which are significantly better controlled when one has a place of their own. (Michelle, field notes, August 1, 1996)

Some graduate students consider their tiny offices a "place of their own." The exact numbers are unknown and probably indeterminable. In speaking with evening and night custodians for several buildings on campus, it became clear that they are aware of the situation, although as one put it, "It's hard to know whether they're working or sleeping in there. And it's none of my business. I figure if they have keys, they're entitled." When asked where (graduate) students were most frequently encountered at night, they knew little about buildings other than those in which they worked. However, one young woman, a custodian in the Social Sciences building, stated, "We know they're here. We just look the other way. You have to be pretty desperate to sleep in your office, don't you think?" In all, most custodians indicated that they know students are occasionally homeless, sleeping in their office, but seldom say anything. "We're supposed to," said another custodian in Social Sciences, "but we don't. What goes around, comes around—you know?"

Learning to be homeless is an art of passing and a ritual of subtle deceptions. It is, as well, an art of self-denial. Others are homeless, and few who meet the official definition of homeless own the self-identity of "homeless." Given the shunning of the homeless and the self-definition of homeless, it is not especially surprising that many myths exist about the homeless. In essence, homelessness is about other people. (There are exceptions, of course). Hence, when *The Arizona Republic* reported that homeless individuals were being given one-way tickets out of Tempe during the Fiesta and Super Bowls, many people who met the definition of homeless could point to others who had been offered tickets, although they themselves had not. In the end, however, the Bowl Organizing Committees, the City of Tempe, the Tempe Chamber of

Commerce, the Downtown Tempe Community, and the Tempe Community Council, as well as all of the local social service agencies, adamantly denied giving anyone a bus ticket to leave town. Rod Keeling of Tempe Community Council acknowledged that they have given four one-way bus tickets during the several years he has been executive director, and all were for "bonafide" homeless people who had been well screened, had a place to go, with work when they got there.

Myths tend to reflect the dominant values of a society. In this case, the media myth of a one-way bus ticket out of town served to inform the homeless that they were unwelcome (Benedict, Shaw, & Rivlin, 1988)—and to sell newspapers. However, this had dubious efficacy, precisely because the "homeless" as perceived by others so rarely exist as such to themselves. In a random survey of over 1,000 residents, Lee, Lewis, and Jones (1992) found that the single greatest predictor of negativity toward the homeless was the proximity of the homeless to where one lived. Thus it is not surprising that the homeless prefer to identify themselves as something other than a member of this ostracized, stigmatized group. Even the most hard-core homeless in Tempe tend to identify the "great outdoors" as their home, beckoning to a vast expanse of sky overhead to indicate the roof over their head (Mathy, 1990).

Summary and Conclusions

Homelessness in Tempe represents a precarious social dance between the interests of business and government, who are determined to discourage the homeless from making Tempe their home, and religious and charity groups, who are determined to assist individuals in need. Although most citizens of Tempe probably do not recognize the individuals who meet the definition of homeless in this university-dominated suburb, they are quick to identify those they do see as a significant social problem. Although citizens readily identify homelessness as a problem and are eager to address homelessness as a social problem, they work hard not to have it "in their own back yards" (Benedict, Shaw, & Rivlin, 1988).

In part, the social dance of homelessness in Tempe reflects the economic competition of businesses with each other, with the City of Tempe in competition with other cities to attract business and profit-making sporting events, and with residents determined to "keep out" the "negative elements." The homeless are caught midstep in the social dance, excluded from much of the economic, political, and social activities that lead dialectically to more active economic, political, and social participation. As Monica stated, "It's spite—pure and simple. They resent having to pay for a place to live and sleep when you don't." In many cases, it seems worthwhile to use the accommodations of a public space for an indefinite period to regain a voice and participation in economic, political, and social activities. It is precisely active involvement in these activities that leads to continued involvement—and a future.

In addition to businesses competing with each other, and the City of Tempe competing with other cities for profit-venture sporting events to increase sales tax coffers, the economic, political, and social interests often are in dynamic opposition. Even as the economic interests are attempting to thwart homelessness on Tempe streets, various member organizations of the Tempe Interfaith Council found homeless individuals sleeping on their lawns. Even as the religious groups strove to give food to the homeless, they found themselves channeled by political interests into doing so in a way that "discourages homelessness." While it certainly did that, it also made life extremely difficult for individuals who were already discouraged and depressed, with little choice but to endure.

Although business and government agencies cooperate with each other to thwart the homeless from the Tempe area, religious and charitable organizations have no unified approach. The rules of faith vary regarding what each organization can and must do. For example, Rabbi Lee at Hillel Jewish Student Center indicated that under Jewish Law, they are compelled to give food to anyone who requests it, and they cannot "check bonafides" (whether or not someone really needs it), although Jewish Law does permit them to "check bonafides" if someone requests money. Personal styles vary as well. Paul Petersen, campus minister for the Lutheran Campus Ministry, compassionately collects food regularly and takes it to the Lutheran Social Ministry. Although the ministry frequently finds homeless people sleeping on their lawn "or on our roof," he indicated that he just lets them sleep. Other staff at other churches, however, have called the police in similar situations. In essence, obtaining assistance from charitable organizations is extremely varied. What a homeless person can obtain depends a great deal on various and inconsistent factors. Charitable and social service organizations in Tempe are at an extreme disadvantage in helping the discouraged homeless, precisely because the economic and political interests in Tempe are much better organized and mobilized to thwart the homeless from remaining in the area.

In sum, during major sporting events, the use of public accommodations such as universities, as well as airports and other transportation terminals, is likely to increase. Overt attempts to thwart homelessness are generally ineffective. Homeless individuals are adept at finding secluded places to sleep during the day as well as at night. They are so adept at passing as nonhomeless persons that police and authorities unfamiliar with their realities are unlikely to ascertain their homeless status. Moreover, many (if not most) homeless individuals can hardly admit their homelessness to themselves, let alone others, mitigating against overt outreach to "the" homeless. Nonetheless, given the well-coordinated response to homelessness by political and economic interests, it seems important for social service interests to identify, coordinate, and meet the unintended consequences of the major sporting events on local homelessness. Addressing the needs of homeless individuals will expedite their recovery from their homeless plight. At a minimum, adequate mass transportation and alternative, affordable, short-term housing are essential. In the absence of adequate social preparation for the effects of major sporting events on local homelessness, the effected individuals will continue to remain in the area—with no Christmas dinner.

NOTES

1. Pursuant to the McKinney Act (Public Health Law 100-628, November 7, 1988), "A homeless person is an individual who lacks a fixed, regular, and adequate residence or an individual who has a primary night-time residence that is either: a supervised or publicly operated shelter designed to provide temporary or transitional living accommodation; a public or private place not designed for, or ordinarily used as, a regular sleeping accommodation for human beings."

2. Currently the largest, most dominant university football programs in the United States do not have a play-off system. The championship is determined by polls of sportswriters or coaches.

REFERENCES

Benedict, A., Shaw, J. S., & Rivlin, G. (1988). Attitudes toward the homeless in two New York City metropolitan sample. *Journal of Voluntary Action Research 17*, 90–98.

French, M. (1985). *Beyond power: On women, men, and morals.* New York: Summit Books.

Goffman, E. (1964). *Stigma: Notes on the management of a spoiled identity.* Englewood Cliffs, NJ: Prentice Hall.

Hopper, K. (1991). Symptoms, survival, and the redefinition of public space: A feasibility study of homeless people at a metropolitan airport. *Urban Anthropology 20*, 155–176.

Lee, B. A., Lewis, D. W., & Jones, S. H. (1992). Are the homeless to blame? A test of two theories. *Sociological Quarterly 33*, 535–552.

Mathy, R. M. (1990, March). Welcome to the wide world of reality: Structural antecedents and cultural consequences of self-esteem in a suburban homeless community. Paper presented at the Southwestern Anthropological Association Meetings, Long Beach, CA.

6

Rounders or Robin Hoods?

Questioning the Role of the Ticket Scalper As Entertainment Outlaw or Free Market Capitalist

Michael F. Atkinson

The study of the professional criminal dominated early interactionist ethnography (particularly the Chicago school), and certainly there are key pieces to cite in research on ticket scalping. The study of drug dealers and drug use (Adler, 1985; Fields, 1984); the motorcycle subculture (Wolf, 1991); the "unethical" business of used cars (Browne, 1973); the white-collar criminal (Clinard, 1969); the professional gambler (Lesieur, 1977); and the professional shark, thief, hustler, or confidence artist (Cressey, 1932, 1953; Ditton, 1977; Goffman, 1952; Inciardi, 1975; Klockars, 1962; Letkemann, 1973; Maurer, 1974; Polsky, 1967; Prus & Irini, 1980; Prus & Sharper, 1991; Rock, 1973; Shaw, 1930; Stebbins, 1971; Sutherland, 1937; Whyte, 1943; Wrighter, 1972) all provide insight into the processes involved in "doing" ticket scalping activity.

None of these works, and to the best of my research no sociological research conducted prior to this study, investigated the everyday life of the urban ticket scalper. With this glaring omission in the sociological discourse at hand, I originally had intended to design and carry out ethnographic research solely on the everyday life and culture of the urban ticket scalper. However, I became increasingly aware that a research program designed as such limited the potential scope of findings and failed to adequately provide the data with any significant cultural context. The research has since blossomed into an encompassing critique of the ticket sales industry in both legal and illegal forms. This critique is grounded upon several core questions, including the ones I explore in this chapter.

Building upon symbolic interactionist (Mead, 1934; Blumer, 1969) and cultural studies (Williams, 1977; Hall, 1980, 1981; Grossberg, 1987; Fiske, 1989; Willis, 1978) theory, this chapter addresses the issues related to how ticket scalpers acquire their goods of exchange in relation to the structured inequalities of distribution contained within the "legal" ticket vending processes. In this chapter I question whether or not the ticket scalper shakes the foundations of morality, ethics, justice, and equality in the urban entertainment industry. Is the scalper's role constructed from a web of context unseen (or at least unconsidered) by those criticizing ticket scalping? Whose opinion, voice, or perspective should we turn to for the "correct" meaning of the question, what "is" ticket scalping?

Here I take the first steps down the path leading to an awareness of the ticket scalping process. Centrally, this research engages in a questioning of the role of the urban ticket scalper by critically examining how ticket scalpers acquire their commodities as part of a public service or as outlawed (Hobsbawn, 1969) capitalist enterprise. Seen as an ongoing process of negotiation, influence, interaction, and interpretation, acquiring the goods necessary for the ticket scalping process provides several analytical, pivotal points of debate as to whether the scalper is an entertainment pariah or is astigmatized (Goffman, 1963), free market capitalist.

Method

Data for this chapter have been collected as part of ongoing research into ticket scalping. Being fortunate enough to have an existing contact in the field, entry into the subculture in an "observer as participant role" occurred swiftly. I met with three key informants, referenced by my contact, and asked if it would be possible to observe what "they do" as part of a sociological research project. With little hesitation on their part, in the preliminary stages of research I simply hung out (Willis, 1978, p. 196) with the scalpers at venues and buildings used for live event entertainment in the greater metropolitan area, unobtrusively observing from a distance.

After two months of strict observation and minimal conversation with the scalpers, I asked if I could follow them to the local "hangouts" they frequent after working hours. At these restaurants, bars, pool halls, and coffee houses I became involved in group discussions with the ticket scalpers and listened to their banter on the ticket industry. After feeling comfortable with the scalpers in a group context, I inquired about possibilities for one-on-one interviews with each scalper. The sample of ticket scalpers drawn is still accumulating in a snowball fashion, and 34 interviews have been conducted with ticket scalpers (n = 17) in Toronto and Hamilton, Ontario. These interviews are unstructured and open ended, ranging from 1 to 4 hours in duration.

HISTORICAL DEFINITIONS
AND LEGAL CONSIDERATIONS

The very term "scalper" is derogatory in connotation. The racist implications of the term relegate the "scalper" to an outlaw status through a pejorative labeling process (Lemert, 1972). The modern usage of the term has roots embedded in over 200 years of economic activity. "Scalp money" (circa 1712) referred to the money or reward paid out for bringing in the scalps of men or game animals. By 1869, the term had taken on another popular meaning, this time referring to a process involved in the buying and selling of stock. A "scalper" bought stocks secretly from inside sources or friends and sold these stocks to other friends at a slightly higher (albeit still less than market value) price to accumulate profit.

Around this time scalpers began to be considered "professional" speculators who widely "scalped" the stock market for small profits. Shortly following this transfer of meaning, the term mutated again, this time taking great strides toward the current usage. "Ticket scalpers" in the early 1900s became known as persons who bought up the unused or return portions of railway tickets and then resold them (for a profit) to other railway patrons. Then, "scalping" became a term commonly associated with reselling tickets to popular entertainment spectators for more than face value.

By 1980, the law reached in and provided a definition of scalping for the popular culture. Statutory law in Ontario regulating the scalping process is officially titled the *Ticket Speculation Act*. Under this act, the official hegemonic position and definition of the ticket scalping process (referred to, in relation to historical application of the term, as "ticket speculating") are provided according to the canons of enforceable law. The statute commences by broadly defining what a "ticket" is and ends by cleverly including that a ticket can be considered an entrance document "to an amusement of any kind" (Ticket Speculation Act, 1990, sect. 1).

According to the statute, one is guilty of "ticket speculation" when a ticket is sold for more than face value, when one attempts to sell for more than face value, or even when one shows intention to commit this act. Furthermore, a ticket speculator can include anyone who offers to purchase a ticket at a higher-than-face-value price or shows intention to purchase at a higher price (Ticket Speculation Act, 1990, sect. 2). As a result of any of these infractions the perpetrator can face a maximum fine of $5,000. Lastly, the act establishes the legality of box office sales by venue owners, corporate ticket promoters, or brokers (Ticket Speculation Act, 1990, sect. 3).

The study of the scalping process begins, then, with a grasp of how scalping has been historically (and is now) defined. Since we are socialized to trust the law to clarify social issues of ambiguous ethics or morality, society looks to law for definitions of activity as being appropriate or not. Based on the legal definition, the contemporary meaning of "scalping" is used in this research to denote *an outlaw who illegally sells prepurchased or stolen tickets at an inflated or above face value price to third party consumers.* This chapter challenges the concurrently broad and narrow legal definition of ticket speculating by investigating the issues and techniques of ticket acquisition as a part of the larger scalping process.

OUTLAW OR CAPITALIST?
PRELIMINARY CONSIDERATIONS

Five general issues exposed in the analysis of how ticket scalpers acquire their goods of exchange receive critical assessment in this chapter. First, the investigation of how goods are acquired and used for illegal purposes teaches us much about how goods are legally distributed, and how this legal distribution can be in itself inept, corrupt, monopolistic, and stifling for the popular consumer. Second, the acquisition process relates how spectators actively utilize scalpers as primary ticket sources and in some cases become part-time scalpers in their own right. Third, since the acquisition of tickets to be scalped often is accomplished on urban streets, in front of public buildings, and through sources of public media, we witness how various forms of public space can be "criminalized" in the "doing" of entertainment. Fourth, I question whether or not the enforcement (or lack thereof) of statute or criminal law against outlaw activity associated with the entertainment industry (such as ticket scalping) reflects a lack of seriousness taken by many segments of society toward sport-related social policy. Fifth, the examination of how ticket scalpers acquire tickets outlines the rudimentary link between the process of ticket scalping and the popular culture.

THE MAIN PLAYERS

Although I am reluctant to establish a typology of ticket scalpers, a distinction between ticket scalpers is a useful, conceptual tactic at this point in the analysis. Ticket scalpers are a peculiar group to pigeonhole or distinguish into neat, conceptual categories. They are, like most social groups involved in some form of collective or joint action (Blumer, 1969), extremely diverse while exhibiting common characteristics and traits. The typology provided here is a "loose typology" employed to provide an analytical line between the *types of scalping* and not necessarily the *types of people* involved in ticket scalping.

Much to my surprise, the age of scalpers studied ranged from 14 to 42, with the average age being between 22 and 26. I originally had perceived scalpers that would be much older, with an average age range of between 30 and 35, and while there were several scalpers contacted within this age range, the younger scalper predominated the field. Furthermore, all were male, and all except three (two Asian and one Afro-Canadian) in the sample were "white."

A common characteristic of ticket scalpers is that they all, with several notable exceptions, possess "legitimate" jobs. Some are taxi-cab drivers, some are tattoo artists, some are retail store clerks, others work in construction or at factories, and some are students.

Akin to Stebbins's (1988) remarks on those who pursue careers in forms of tolerable deviance, the other jobs that ticket scalpers have generally are flexible, in that the hours are not necessarily fixed, nor do they encompass night or weekend shifts. The scalper must be willing to be mobile and not constricted by a rigid time clock, or he or she misses prime opportunities to scalp. The occupations are part time, but they provide the ticket scalper with two necessary social elements: income and identity. Scalpers need the income from a "straight" or legitimate job to support them during the lean months or during the "off season" when they are not scalping. Income also provides the ticket scalper with a necessary occupation to claim on a tax form.

The social element provided by having a legitimate career lies in the maintenance of the scalper's social identity. To the outside culture of those not "in the know" of ticket scalping or ticket scalpers, the scalper is known through her or his job as a taxi driver, a store clerk, or a student, not a ticket scalping outlaw. There is an element of positive identity maintenance in holding a regular job, or holding a master status that is not a "ticket scalper." The person's identity is not stigmatized by the scalper identity as most of those whom the scalper knows view the scalper as a regular, hard-working, law-abiding member of the culture.

I have divided the typology of ticket scalpers into two broad categories, with the line of distinction being drawn along the scalper's level of involvement in the scalping process. The two major categories involved *professional* versus *temporary ticket scalpers.*

PROFESSIONAL TICKET SCALPERS

At any given time, any person can transgress the fine line between outlaw and law-abiding citizen (as outlined in the Ticket Speculation Act, 1990) and engage in scalping activity. This does not necessarily make a person a "ticket scalper." Becoming a ticket scalper involves immersing oneself in the scalping practice and becoming knowledgeable about the ticket industry in general. Lumping persons who have committed the act of ticket scalping, according to the law, into one category overlooks the essential, interactive, subcultural element of becoming a member of a culture or a life world of others.

The *professional ticket scalper* is a person who makes a focused and deliberate effort to make monetary profits over time through the act of ticket scalping. Professional ticket scalpers are organized hustlers with extensive contacts in the community to all forms of outlawism and business. They know drug dealers, pimps, prostitutes, petty thieves, gamblers, concierges, taxi drivers, stadium workers, ticket brokers, box office ticket workers, and any other number of people surrounding the tourism or entertainment business. They use these contacts as extensive friendship networks by exchanging favors for favors to accomplish scalping activity.

Professional ticket scalpers' legitimate jobs play a large role in this process of establishing contacts. Professional ticket scalpers establish many relationships as ticket scalpers, but they also encounter scores of other valuable contacts through their other forms of "legitimate" employment. Since they are each involved in their own respective mosaic of subcultural involvement (Prus, 1996, pp. 85–87), they encounter people from all professions who become potential friends, ticket suppliers, customers, or "inside men."

Professional ticket scalpers follow events across the country and across the world, traveling wherever and whenever there is a potential profit to be made. While they do not often operate at only one venue or handle only one type of entertainment, they usually are renowned for being experts at acquiring the best seats or tickets for a certain type of event or venue. Professional ticket scalpers invest heavily in their scalping activities, buying hundreds or thousands of tickets a year and incurring extensive travel costs, and mobile communication costs, such as cellular phones and pagers (along with the costs incurred for any involvement with the law: legal fees, bail, and fines).

Professional ticket scalpers have extensive careers (Becker, 1963) in the scalping subculture. They associate with other ticket scalpers, know the legal "drill," and are friendly with tolerant police officers. Professional ticket scalpers often are involved with other forms of illegal commodity distribution, such as drugs, prostitution, or other petty criminal activity, thus they are hustlers in an overall sense. I prefer using the term *rounders* (Prus & Irini, 1980) to describe them, as professional ticket scalpers typically are competent in "rounding up" whatever a person needs, whether a ticket, drugs, a prostitute, a gambling game, an after-hours party, or anything else a person needs a "middleman" to find. Even though professional ticket scalpers are rounders, hustlers, and grifters, they take pride in their ability to do expert scalping activity and feel somewhat accepted (or at least tolerated) by a large segment of society.

To summarize the main points made, professional ticket scalpers acquire a scalping perspective, are involved in many forms of scalping activity, internalize and exhibit a scalping identity, establish extensive relationships and networks to accomplish scalping, and make intensive commitments to the scalping profession or the scalping way of life.

Temporary Ticket Scalpers

On the other side of the scalping coin, temporary ticket scalpers, either "straight" or "fringe rounders" (Prus & Irini, 1980), are much less organized, directed, or integrated into the scalping community. Their scalping activity is haphazard and unskilled, and they make little, if any, money from the scalping process. In fact, most temporary ticket scalpers are looking to utilize ticket scalping as a source of securing only a small amount of money. For instance, a person, a "straight" or a "square," according to the professional scalpers, may have purchased a block of tickets and by some circumstance, one or more of the tickets may become unclaimed or will be unused. Instead of wasting the money laid down for these tickets, people frequently will scalp the tickets at the venue or at some other location to avoid an unrecoverable loss from an unused ticket. Not only can these people be considered temporary ticket scalpers, they are more accurately described as "one-time scalpers."

In opposition to the "straight" or "square" one-time scalper, the temporary ticket scalper category also includes "fringe rounders." The fringe rounder as a temporary scalper may know one scalper or a few scalpers and may use this contact to aid their own brief stint into scalping. They may need to make some money quickly, may want to experience a brief taste of what the scalper's life involves, or may even want to feel the thrill of being an outlaw. Fringe rounders often are "hangers-on" or "wanna-bes" who have the contact with scalpers but who are not heavily involved in the subculture. Frequently they are young and look up to or admire professional ticket scalpers, or they may be fascinated with hustling or outlawism in general without wanting to completely immerse themselves into a dangerous, stigmatized life world.

This initial or fringe involvement in ticket scalping can be assessed as an integral process of becoming a professional ticket scalper. Following Prus's (1984, 1996) model of career involvement, initial interaction with ticket scalpers provides a context for temporary scalpers to be recruited, to develop seekership for, or experience closure into, longer-term involvements in the scalping subculture. They may be recruited by other ticket scalpers who actively bring them into the subculture, may seek out longer involvements from a fascination with the scalpers or the scalping life world, or may face unemployment or financial strife and experience a closure into the scalping scene (realizing the potential to make money scalping and to have contacts in the subculture).

GETTING THE FRUIT

Techniques for acquiring tickets, or "cardboard," "juice," "ducats," "fruit," "jewels," or "goods," vary between ticket scalpers, and most certainly between professional and temporary ticket scalpers. However, there are several primary sources that all scalpers rely upon for tickets. Acquiring tickets becomes the first step in the scalping process that is examined in this chapter. It is the starting point for the actual accomplishment of scalping activity and poses significant barriers to success for all scalpers. In the analysis of how scalpers acquire tickets for resale, the issues of ticket availability, public usage of scalpers, the criminalization of space in entertainment, the seriousness of sport-related social policy, and scalping as a form of popular activity are all introduced.

Scalpers ordinarily acquire their tickets through five routes:

1. at a box office, authorized retail ticket distributor, or venue
2. on the street or "on site" from the public or other scalpers
3. through the mass media
4. from people "on the inside" at ticket companies, box offices, or venues
5. from promotional companies, contests, or tour companies

Another defining characteristic demarcating the line between a professional or a temporary ticket scalper is the extent to which they employ a variety of sources to acquire their tickets. Professional ticket scalpers, putting their extensive connections to use in order to get "hooked up," are forever seeking out new sources of tickets. Temporary ticket scalpers, on the other hand, as will be documented, rely on two dominant routes for their scalping activity.

ROUNDING UP ACTION:
THE PROFESSIONAL SCALPER

The most basic route in acquiring tickets for the professional scalper is through the box office or venue distributor. Like any other entertainment patron, the ticket scalper can secure a block of tickets through legal retailers by simply standing in line or hiring others to stand in line. Typically the scalpers prey on those who are around the street scene or in contact with their outlaw community to do their bidding. Scalpers hire the homeless, their unemployed friends or, most commonly, street kids, who can all be easily found and exploited in light of their own economic situations.

> I don't mind standing in line if it comes down [to] that. Christ, it's not my first choice or anything but when it's third and long and I need a score, there's always the line up. The big problem is when some kid working decides he's seen you around too often and he lets his fat ass boss know about me. Then the whip comes down and they won't sell to you so you go somewhere else . . . that's a pain in the ass. (professional scalper, male)

> Man I've been in this racket long enough to know better than to wait in line like a mule at the feed trough. That's a rookie's role, you know? I waited in line when I was green about the deal, when I was happy to eat up the scraps they gave me at the ticket window . . . that was years

ago . . . now I hire a couple of kids from the neighborhood to do it for me, they pick up some cheap seats that people always look for. I give 'em a piece of the action and a little pay to boot. . . . Believe me, it's better than seeing them washing windows down on Bay street and having yuppies spit at them. (professional scalper, male)

So what if I pay somebody to stand in line for me? It's bullshit anyway, making people herd together to fight over the worst no count seats anyway man. People don't want to stand in line and neither do I, I mean if I had to wait for every ticket . . . man no way. I'm up working at night, or out late, or even have to work the next day, I'm not spending any time in a line when I can pay somebody else to do it for me, somebody who does it and calls it ice cream. (professional scalper, male)

Professional ticket scalpers become Fagins of sort, but this role is not easily or objectively appreciated at first glance. While some may argue that their recruitment of others to stand in line and gather tickets is corruptive and encourages youth participation in a life of crime, the pay that they provide for this service often is one, if not the only, source of consistent income for these groups.

Yeah I hear that fuckin' argument from the cops sometimes. Look it's simple to me, nobody helps the bums around here except us, as far as I can see it. Everyday I see more street people in Toronto and the politicians don't help them, people driving by in their cars don't want to. I don't see how it's exploitive when we pay them to work, you know? I mean these guys thank me man, they thank me for the money. I get calls all the time from some of the old timers who are just beggin for a job. (professional scalper, male)

The relative ease by which professional ticket scalpers can infiltrate and abuse the legal means of acquiring tickets is recognized by people on the inside of companies. To combat this abuse, innovative ticket distribution techniques are introduced. To prevent or at least to curb scalping activity, venues have introduced wristband distribution policies, purchase limits, electronic identification systems for tickets, and randomized number drawing. All have an initial effect, but the professional ticket scalpers improvise, adapt, and overcome the system with the end result being a newfound means of acquiring tickets.

Stupid, I think ticket caps are stupid. Only an idiot can't get around a ticket cap. Ooooooh, so I can only buy up four or five tickets. If I've got ten people standing in line, what's the point? (professional scalper, male)

The random numbers scam, o.k., this is how it goes down. Oh yeah, keep in mind they do this, not around here yet, but it's because of us. First the outlet releases like two or three hundred numbers, from one to whatever. Then a couple of days later they post a "random" list of all the numbers and according [to] the order of numbers, that's the order of how people line up to get their tickets, right. So a couple of things are going on. They want it to be a surprise, right, nobody, well almost nobody [laughs], knows how the numbers are going to be drawn. So that way we're not supposed to be tempted to line up people to buy up tickets, but we have just as many people, even more actually, lining up to get the numbers. And the outlet seems to think decreasing the ticket limit to like two or three works well with this, and it does actually, so we have to hire some more people to line up. (professional scalper, male)

Wristbands, ticket maxes, they're easy man. What's a bitch is this new thing being introduced, I can't remember what they call it, but the gist of it is this. Each ticket gets printed with a numerical identification scan code that is used at the entrance wicket that the goon working at the gate scans and all kinds of info about the ticket like where it was sold, who bought it, and all that comes up on the computer. They're trying to nab us at the door, or at least the guy who buys from us. Kinda sounds like busting the Johns that go to the whores on Church, right? . . . It's a roundabout way of getting to us, trying to piss off our customers and make them scared to buy from a broker like me, and in the end we get banged because our client base gets wiped out . . . that's the plan anyway. But somewhere there's a bunch of the boys working a plan of their own, and in a couple of months we'll hear through the grapevine how to beat the program they lay down on us. (professional scalper, male)

While rounding up action includes using legal sources illegally, the professional ticket scalper's second main route for acquiring tickets is on site through the public. Interestingly enough, an overlapping of roles occurs in these instances. Professional ticket scalpers not only stand in front of venues screaming profusely "who needs tickets?" at the crowd of patrons, they also inquire "who's selling?" Enter the temporary ticket scalper. Professionals pick up a single ticket or pairs of tickets from "straight temporary scalpers" or just common spectators who possess an extra ticket or two.

I don't see the problem with buying up a square or two if some Joe Schmoe wants to sell me his nickel and dime seat. If he can't find someone to use it I sure as hell can. (professional scalper, male)

I'm like a recycler in the age of recycling. Waste, you got waste, give it to me, I'll take care of it for you. I got no problem buying whatever people are selling. (professional scalper, male)

I use my pre-game time to grab up as much paper [tickets] as possible. The best hustlers, I mean the best, can show up a couple of hours before the gig and walk away after with a fist full of quid. . . . Yeah I think the measure of a good broker is how successful you are in coming up with something from nothing, especially when the pinch is on [the police are about] or when a headline show comes to town and all of my sources dry up quick. (professional scalper, male)

Spectators also may travel to the event fully intending to view the spectacle but are frequently enticed by the presence and influence of scalpers to sell their choice seats for large amounts of money.

I can't count how many times I weaseled people out of tickets. Seek and ye shall find brother, or ask and they will sell if the price is right. . . . People are so goddamn stupid though. Here comes a guy, right. I ask him if he wants to sell, and he starts thinking about it. I only ask a guy by himself or with one other person, cause if he's with a family, no chance, no way. O.K. yeah, so this guy coughs it up thinking I'm giving him a lot of coin and he's a real shrewd guy. Yeah he's the man. But two seconds later he realizes he wants to see the show still, or his old lady bitches cause their date is fucked up, and it's back to me or somebody else, and so from one guy at least two deals go down. A third when I turn over his original tickets. Then it's all good. (professional scalper, male)

Another consistent source of tickets acquired through the public is from season ticket holders. Similar to any other ticket holder's desire to sell, season ticket holders use scalpers to reclaim money spent on tickets that will be otherwise unused. However, the mostly corporate-owned season tickets often are given to employees who, rather than for personal entertainment (written off as an expense by the company as corporate entertainment), use the seats to make some quick money by selling the commodities to scalpers.

Jesus, don't even get me started about those pimps! Man I've got about ten guys who roll up on me regularly with season tickets for sale. Some of them have Leafs' tickets, and some Raptors' but it all means da bigga bucks for moi . . . primo stuff man, the best. I make the biggest margins off season tickets, cause they're the best seats I can get so the price [sticks up thumb]. None of them give a shit about the game, they don't even care who's in town. O.K., yeah, o.k., naw, that's not exactly true. These guys aren't dumb man, they know just enough to sell the tickets to the hottest games in town, and that's when they start to care about sports, when Wayne [Gretzky] or Mike [Jordan] is in town. (professional scalper, male)

The fringe rounders also sell to professional ticket scalpers to gain entry into the professional circle, or to impress the professionals with their acquisition skills. Most of the professionals sell to one another as part of the everyday process of ticket scalping. Scalpers return favors to one another by selling, at a highly reduced rate, "fruit" that they may acquire, or they give a fellow professional a ticket or two needed to fulfill a group purchase request.

There's no problem in asking another guy for a seat or two if you're having a tough day. It evens out man. The guys in the crew are pretty tight, and passing around singles means nothing but good business. I always remember who's hooked me up with seats, and whenever I can't handle an order, I send em over to a bro' like a referral business. (professional scalper, male).

Sometimes if I need a single or a pair I call over to one of my partners and they wheel up with what I need and they get a cut of the action. I don't like asking too much cause the cut isn't as much as it would be if they went solo on the sale. But it's my deal, my people, so my cut is the biggest. . . . Awww I feel shitty every once in a while, but we're all in the same business, all looking to make money, and the only way to get along is to help each other out and keep competition to a minimum . . . that's not how it works most of the time though, man. Too many guys only look out for old number 1, but those dudes don't last. (professional scalper, male)

The professional scalper need not venture out into the uncertain public arena to do ticket scalping. The mass media provide an impersonal, detached, and faceless context for doing scalping activity. Professional ticket scalpers utilize newspapers, radio, magazines, and, most recently, the Internet to acquire vast amounts of tickets. With a lack of internal or external regulations imposed on the use of public media to round up ticket action, the professional ticket scalpers' unbridled usage of the media is relatively unchecked.

The best investment I make is the twenty bucks it costs me to drop an ad in the paper. With a couple of words and a pager number I can advertise to thousands of people what tickets I have or tickets I need. I find the process ridiculous though, man. The trick is to make the ad

sound like I'm a guy in town who needs a seat for himself, but in reality it's me looking to score a seat. . . . It's a tightrope walk around the
law, because it doesn't take a genius to figure out the scam, but the
cops or the paper don't get pissed unless the ad is way blatant. . . . Respect the boundaries, man, and things go along smooth. (professional
scalper, male)

I've never had any ad I wanted to put in the paper hassled or rejected,
and in four years in the broker business, I've probably bought up at
least 500 tickets through the paper. (professional scalper, male)

The professional ticket scalper diversifies his or her pool of potential
sources most extensively through the media. By advertising a need for tickets in
the community, the professional ticket scalper can contact wide populations of
ticket holders and reach "would-be" temporary scalpers. Similar to advertisements for prostitution and escort servicing, the wording of these solicitations is
vague enough not to be blatant, but encoded enough to convene a message
understood by ticket sellers and buyers.

I don't like putting anything in writing, but the guys who do tone it
down, you know, keep the ad low profile. My best advice would be to
use as few words as possible. O.K., like "tickets needed," and what
games or shows, then a cell or beeper number, and that's all. (professional scalper, male)

Stressing the importance of having a series of contact networks throughout the community, professional ticket scalpers rely heavily on people on the inside to acquire tickets. The professionals have "people on the inside" who
actively set aside blocks of tickets for them, selling the tickets to the scalpers at
a fee per ticket amount, or an overall cut of the profits. The people on the inside realize the potential profits to be made from scalping, and compared to the
meager money made from the straight work that they do, scalping profits seem
considerable. According to ticket scalpers, corporations such as Ticketmaster
are renowned for being havens for inside men, typically at lower levels of
employment, such as store teller or box office worker.

I can't give you any names or name any places, but let's just say I have
partners in just about every legit store in this province. For just a few
bucks more than it costs to hire a little punk kid to stand in line and
wait for tickets I have people hold back tickets for me. Kinda makes
their $7 an hour job feel a hell of a lot better . . . we meet these guys
around, man, or maybe even on the job, they approach a lot. I check
the person out before agreeing to anything, cause your ass can get

stung by an undercover cop pretending to be a worker and shit. (professional scalper, male)

I think these guys, well, without them, you're screwed. They tell me everything I want to know about upcoming events, even what promoters to contact and where the best tickets are going. . . . They come down on the employees at Ticketmaster every so often if they suspect any shenanigans, and the beauty about it is we don't get burned, they do. I'll just move on to greener pastures or another source. . . . No way, I don't feel "bad" when they get canned. Nobody forced them to give me tickets or let me into the front of the line. They're motivated by profits like everybody else. That's the drug of the industry, man, seeing how much money is and can be made. Once you try it you're hooked, and once people like me know about you being on it you'll have 100 guys calling you up asking for favors and all that. (professional scalper, male)

The venue workers aid the scalpers in the same fashion, doling out information on upcoming events and giving them the inside track on how to beat programs designed to stifle scalping activity. The inside box office worker, venue employee, security guard, or retail teller are the ones who give the scalpers an advantage on all programs initiated to curb their involvement in the process, such as ticket randomization, plastic bracelets, or electronic security scans of tickets.

Like I was telling you before, I can beat any scam they throw down the pipe, cause I know people who help me out. Like, for instance, ummm, o.k. yeah, like those wristband programs. . . . Hey what's the point if the guy who's passing them out is a buddy of mine or another dealer? He gives me 10 or 12 of them under the table before the public even knows about them, and I get a few people to wear 'em and pick up the tickets. Big fuckin' deal. (professional scalper, male)

I love it when they pull the random ticket drawing for the lineups. What a joke, I mean, honestly, man, who was the retard who thought that would work? If I can get sheets of tickets, even the card stock the tickets are printed on straight from the people at Ticketmaster, what makes anybody think we can't fix it so that some of the boys are in on the randomization process, right? . . . If a person or a company comes up with a plan to stomp us out, they have to first clean up their own act, because I know guys personally who live and breathe off the business given out by people who work for companies like Ticketmaster or store clerks at some bush league retail outlet. These guys are supposed to be the responsible ones. They're in charge not me, and if they want to start the money machine rolling, I'm more than willing to be a part of it. (professional scalper, male)

Lastly, and perhaps the most controversial and well-known abuse of the ticket distribution system, professional ticket scalpers receive large blocks of tickets from event promoters who hold back (from Ticketmaster or other direct ticket distributors) thousands of tickets per event to be distributed to whomever they please. Promoters sell the tickets to the professional scalpers, becoming professional scalpers in their own right, and they receive kickbacks from the sale of the tickets. Claiming that these tickets are to be used for family, friends, contests, players' or performers' personal use, or other V. I. P. use, promoters distribute many of the withheld tickets into the hands of the professional ticket scalpers.

I heard from a guy who used to work as a promoter that they hold back anywhere up to 75% of the best seats. . . . Imagine any building o.k., and the bottom half being the best seats, the top being the worst, right. Yeah, so most of that whole bottom half of the building people never even have a chance at getting . . . like when it's announced a show sold out in a half an hour, that's bullshit. The few fucking seats they decide to sell to all the chumps are the pieces of burger bun the pigeons fight over in the parking lot. You don't even have a prayer in hell at getting a good ticket to any decent show if you do it legit. So it's not hard to sell out when only like half of all the seats go on a straight sale. (professional scalper, male)

When I first got started I was amazed when one of the guys waltzed down with a gold mine in his hands. Oh man, like the best seats, and I would look at him like a god, and all the time it was killing me how he did it every time. . . . When I got to know him, he introduced me to this promoter buddy of his, and then everything fell into place. . . . The promoter runs the show from start to finish. They call the shots, and if you try to buck their system, you get shot. You may as well have a license to print money when you become a promoter, you get so much jack in this business. Think about it, man, they decide where the tickets go. . . . Any of like "the best" tickets I've ever held I got from promoters. (professional scalper, male)

Arguably, there is no better or more direct supply of the premium tickets than the promoter who effectively administers the distribution of seating. Like the people at the lower levels of the inside racket, the promoters, the upper echelon of the inside scalping business, are in a position to make enormous amounts of money from selling to professional scalpers for profit.

> Every once and a while I lie in bed at night and wonder if what I'm doing is right and all that. I have a conscience, and that's not the best asset in this business. But then I start thinking about pricks like the promoters who don't have to work their asses off like me. A promoter has everybody standing in line to kiss their ass. . . . If I'm a promoter and I handle hundreds of thousands of tickets a year, I make thousands of bucks under the table from private sales. If I call myself a ticket agent or ticket broker, then the promoter can claim he doesn't deal with scalpers. (professional scalper, male)

Another supposedly legitimate business operation feeding the professional scalpers' insatiable hunger for tickets is the tour company or entertainment promotional tour business. These businesses, selling event tickets as part of a weekend or an overnight deal, including transportation (usually bus or air) and accommodations, receive tickets that have been held back from the promoter. The promoter legally sells tickets to companies that are supposed to sell the tickets for a fixed rate to customers, but too often these tickets end up in the hands of scalpers. The tour company, like others in the system, has recognized the potential profits to be made by giving scalpers access to tickets.

> Here's a tip for you, bro'. Tour companies get tickets from promoters and have to pay an arm and a leg for them, so when we get workers at tour companies who do favors for a guy like me, we have to pay two arms and a leg for a ticket. So Johnny lunch pail has to pay two arms and two legs for the ticket. . . . Anyone who complains about the prices of tickets, whether they pick them up from me or the other guy, has to realize so many hands get greased along the path, the end price has to be high so everyone gets covered. (professional scalper, male)

Who, then, in the first analysis of how professional ticket scalpers acquire their tickets, is not a professional scalper of the ticket industry? On every level of activity, from every outlet to every position involved in the public distribution of tickets, there are people who pursue their own economic self-interests by selling tickets to "scalpers" for profit. The entire system is nothing more than ticket scalping, with scalpers existing in every niche of the industry, some legal and others illegal. The "on the street" hustlers we refer to as the professional ticket scalpers are only one group of professional ticket scalpers in this business. The inside industry thrives on the existence of the street hustler, and this breeding factor of low-level outlawism is too often ignored by critics of the street criminal.

Scalping by Default

The fringe rounder, as a temporary ticket scalper, generally acquires tickets from similar sources as the professional ticket scalper, but with less frequency or success. This is due, in large part, to the lack of personnel networks established within the ticket distribution community. Therefore, without repeating the last section of the analysis, what will be addressed briefly is how people acquire tickets leading to a process referred to as "scalping by default."

Scalping by default typically involves the scalping of tickets unwanted or unusable by a person or persons. A common practice of "straight" temporary ticket scalpers, scalping by default implies a perspective adopted indicating a desire to avoid the loss of money incurred in a wasted ticket. Instead of throwing a ticket away, or simply giving a ticket to someone without monetary compensation, people can resell their tickets at the venue site for profit. Knowledge of this practice arises from the general knowledge of the existence of a scalping business, and scalpers in general.

> I've bought so many tickets from scalpers that I felt like I knew how to do it myself, so when my brother couldn't go with me to a Jays game I went down to Skydome and just stood there with the two tickets in my hand and in about five minutes the tickets were gone. . . . I didn't feel like watching the game by myself so why not sell 'em. (temporary scalper, male)

> Scalping, no way, I don't think of myself as a scalper. I mean, if I have extras [tickets] I know how to get rid of them, but I don't scalp for a living, that's wrong . . . well, yeah, I do buy from them [scalpers] all the time though. (temporary scalper, male)

In these cases, the sources for acquiring tickets are normally through the box office (ticket company), or through a promotional contest. At the last minute, people may encounter a situation in which an extra ticket exists, one that may have been claimed by someone else who is no longer capable or willing to use the ticket. The scalping by default action does not carry with it the same internalization of the outlaw identity, as the process is interpreted by most (scalpers, spectators, customers, etc.) as a one-time event not to be repeated. Furthermore, since the person is not a professional scalper and merely seeks to cover the losses (with some profit) potentially incurred by wasted tickets, one rarely perceives the act in any way as being "wrong."

This being noted, the scalping by default mentality receives little sympathy in the eyes of the police. The police recently have frowned upon the practice, for they argue that these forms of ticket scalping provide the professional ticket scalpers (as previously suggested) with a means of acquiring more tickets, and it sends out the public message that ticket scalping, in certain forms, is accept-able. According to the letter of the law, any and all forms of ticket scalping (in Ontario) are, in essence, illegal, and the police have begun to actively pursue the "one-time," "default," or "straight" temporary ticket scalper with the same rigor and enthusiasm as the professional ticket scalper.

> The problem with citizens letting their tickets go in the public auction of ticket scalping is in the creation of a garden of sources for the ticket scalpers. They [scalpers] can pick out and take advantage of an "every-day" sports fan who wants to get rid of their tickets. What we want is for people to refrain from selling to the scalpers. Faced with the grim reality of either selling or losing money, we realize most people sell if they can muster up the courage. Unfortunately, citizens are learning the hard way the police cannot tolerate any form of ticket scalping . . . they'll face the same penalties the pros do. (police officer, male)

ACQUIRING TICKETS IN PERSPECTIVE

The process of acquiring tickets indicates how all types of ticket scalpers are involved in a system that supports and fails to regulate (when regulation is desired) the ticket scalping process. Whether we are contemplating the role of the professional ticket scalper or the temporary ticket scalper, how scalpers get their hands on tickets is a starting point for a critical evaluation of the scalping industry.

For example, where does the average spectator fit into this process? If we strictly remain with the issue of ticket acquisition, the average spectator is the most adversely affected by the process. As an estimated "street figure," up to 75% of the best seats for an event is never competed for by the general public (sold as season tickets first, or being held back by promoters, allocated to scalpers, or some other inside source). More and more, the public is taken out of the arena of competition for tickets through legal sources. The public is in-creasingly pushed toward the heavens of the venue, facing proverbial nose-bleeds from high-altitude spectating, and having little or no chance at ever securing prime seats for an event.

With the impossibility of taking a day off from work to wait in line or wasting time trying to get through the phone lines to buy tickets to an event, is the scalpers' acquisition and sale of the best seats a direct public service? Does all of the scalpers' networking and connecting needed to acquire tickets serve the public's lack of interest in doing the same networking and legwork? Do these scalping middlemen, by flushing out ticket sources and digging up the commodities for an all too willing and now more reliant popular culture, actu-ally do a disservice to the public? The scalping market only exists as long as there is a market willing to bear the brunt of the costs of the commodities. Most critics of ticket scalping fail to recognize or admit that the public actively exchanges the ease of buying a choice ticket five minutes before an event for an inflated price requested by the scalper.

From the analysis of ticket acquisition, we also can see how the popular culture is heavily involved in the scalping process. The events chosen and the people involved are mostly what have been referred to as "low" or "popular." Rock concerts and sports events are prime spectacles for the scalping industry, and the scalpers (and their customers) are not typically members of the social elite. From this, the popular role in the criminalization of public space is a crucial point of analysis. The popular subversion of public venues, institutions of business, mass media, and community street space for scalping purposes climatizes the urban landscape toward outlawism. The ticket scalping process runs uninhibited in the inner city, as the popular influence on urban life and perspectives on urban entertainment are consequential.

With this being mentioned, the proverbial social jury is still out on the issue of ticket scalping. With a mosaic of social interpretation surrounding the practice of scalping, no one group or social authority seems to exhibit the strongest voice on the ethics or morality of the process. As long as the public continues to actively play a role in the scalping process, and as long as professional and temporary ticket scalpers are able to locate and acquire a myriad of ticket sources, there will be ticket scalping. Recognizing the internal corruption contained within the so-called legitimate ticket distribution system, combined with an apparent lack of concern on the part of the citizenry or the police force, one should wonder if there will ever be an end to any form of ticket scalping.

REFERENCES

Adler, P. (1985). *Wheeling and dealing*. New York: Columbia University Press.

Becker, H. (1963). *Outsiders*. New York: Free Press.

Blumer, H. (1969). *Symbolic interactionism: Perspective and method*. Berkeley: University of California Press.

Browne, J. (1973). *The used car game: The sociology of the bargain*. Lexington, Va.: Lexington Books.

Clinard, M. (1969). *The black market: A study of white collar crime*. New York: Holt, Reinhart and Winston.

Cressey, D. (1932). *The taxi-dance hall*. Chicago: University of Chicago Press.

Cressey, D. (1953). *Other people's money*. New York: Free Press.

Ditton, J. (1977). *Part time crime: An ethnography of fiddling and pilferage*. London: Macmillan.

Fields, A. B. (1984). Slinging weed: The social organization of streetcorner marijuana sales. *Urban Life 13*, 247–270.

Fiske, J. (1989). *Understanding popular culture*. Boston: Unwin Hyman.

Goffman, E. (1952). On cooling out the mark. *Psychiatry 14*, 451–463.

Goffman, E. (1963). *Stigma*. Englewood Cliffs, N.J.: Spectrum.

Grossberg, L. (1987). History, politics and postmodernism: Stuart Hall and cultural studies. *Journal of communication inquiry 10(2)*, 61–77.

Hall, S. (1980). Encoding/Decoding. In S. Hall, D. Hobson, A. Lowe, & P. Willis (Eds.), *Culture, media, language: Working papers in cultural studies 1972–79* (pp. 128–139). London: Hutchinson.

Hall, S. (1981). Notes on deconstructing the popular. In R. Samuel (Ed.), *People's history and socialist theory* (pp. 227–239). London: Routledge.

Hobsbawm, E. (1969). *Bandits*. New York: Delacorte.

Inciardi, J. (1975). *Careers in crime*. Chicago: Rand McNally.

Klockars, C. B. (1962). *The professional fence*. New York: Free Press.

Lemert, E. (1972). *Human deviance, social problems, and social control*. Englewood Cliffs, N.J.: Prentice Hall.

Lesieur, H. (1977). *The chase*. New York: Anchor.

Letkemann, P. (1973). *Crime as work*. Englewood Cliffs, N.J.: Prentice Hall.

Maurer, D. (1974). *The American confidence man*. Springfield, MA: Thomas.

Mead, G. H. (1934). *Mind, self, and society*. Chicago: University of Chicago Press.

Polsky, N. (1967). *Hustlers, beats, and others*. Chicago: Aldine.

Prus, R. (1984). Career contingencies: Examining patterns of involvement. In N. Theberge & P. Donnelly (Eds.), *Sport and the sociological imagination* (pp. 297–317). Fort Worth: Texas Christian University Press.

Prus, R. (1994). Consumers as targets: Autonomy, accountability, and anticipation of the influence process. *Qualitative Sociology 17*, 243–262.

Prus, R. (1996). *Subcultural mosaics and intersubjective realities*. Albany: State University of New York Press.

Prus, R., and Irini, S. (1980). *Hookers, rounders, and desk clerks: The social organization of the hotel community*. Salem, WI: Sheffield.

Prus, R., and Sharper, C. R. D. (1991). *Road hustler: Hustlers, magic, and the thief subculture*. New York: Kaufman and Geenberg.

Rock, P. (1973). *Making people pay*. London: Routledge and Kegan Paul.

Shaw, C. (1930). *The jack-roller*. Chicago: University of Chicago Press.

Stebbins, R. (1971) *Commitment to deviance: The non-professional criminal in the community*. Westport: Greenwood Press.

Stebbins, R. (1988). *Deviance: Tolerable differences*. Toronto: McGraw-Hill.

Sutherland, E. (1937). *The professional thief.* Chicago: University of Chicago Press.

Ticket Speculation Act. (1990). *Revised statues of Ontario.* Volume 11, chap. s.5–w.12. Ottawa: Queen's Printer.

Whyte, W. (1943). *Street corner society.* Chicago: University of Chicago Press.

Williams, R. (1977). *Marxism and literature.* Oxford: Oxford University Press.

Willis, P. (1978). *Profane culture.* London: Routledge and Kegan Paul.

Wolf, D. (1991). *The rebels: A brotherhood of outlaw bikers.* Toronto: University of Toronto Press.

Wrighter, C. (1972). *I can sell you anything.* New York: Ballantine.

7

Horse Racing in Chicago, 1883–1894

The Interplay of Class, Politics, and Organized Crime

Steven A. Riess

This chapter will examine how horse racing provided a nexus between urban machine politics and organized crime in Chicago, the second largest city in the nation, and the site where organized crime reputedly first emerged in the United States. The rise of organized crime in the late nineteenth century reflected the growing political clout of urban political machines and the growing demands of citizens in increasingly anonymous urban enclaves to secure illegal services. Organized crime refers to crime syndicates that are protected by political connections. This is a symbiotic relationship in which the criminal gangs are protected from the criminal justice system by political cronies who forewarn them of occasional police raids and guarantee lenient treatment by friendly judges in the unlikely event of an arrest. The politicians gain sources of campaign financing, party workers, and bribes. The primary activities of organized crime in the late nineteenth century were in gambling and prostitution, victimless crimes in which the participants were willing clients. These were moral violations that large segments of the population felt should not be criminalized, and there was rarely a great deal of pressure upon the police to enforce such violations.[1]

In Chicago, the man who is credited with organizing the first crime syndicate was Michael Cassius McDonald, born near Chicago in 1839. He was a swindler at age 16, selling fruit, candy, newspapers, and fake prize packages to railroad passengers for John R. Walsh, a politically connected publisher. Two years later, he became a gambler on the Mississippi, returning in 1861 to Chicago, where he became a well-known gambler. He became prominent along Gamblers' Row, where he was a partner in several gambling houses and became known as the leading dice and cards man in the city. McDonald then went into the liquor business, where he became connected with powerful

German brewers. In 1873, he opened "The Store," a deluxe downtown gambling emporium at 176 Clark Street, across the street from the county building. The first floor housed a cigar store and saloon that became the center of the local male bachelor subculture. The second floor housed McDonald's elegantly furnished gambling operation, which got a lot of business from traveling businessmen as well as local sports. McDonald and his fellow gamblers formed a syndicate or trust that compelled newcomers to the trade to pay them a percentage of their profits to stay in business. Among the other leading gamblers were the Hankins brothers and Harry Varnell. The Hankins had an elegant gambling hall on Clark Street that purportedly made $20,000 a month in the 1880s. Another important ex-rival, Varnell, had a downtown gambling operation with over 90 employees, and it was open 24 hours. Varnell had a brief political career, serving in 1880 as warden of the Cook County insane asylum, which he transformed into a clubhouse for politicians where several county commissioners lived. His political clout enabled him to run his gambling business with little interference from the authorities.[2]

From the mid-1880s, the McDonald–Hankins–Varnell bookmaking syndicate dominated Chicago and Indiana racetracks. They maintained a slush fund to support their political interests. One pool operator reportedly made $190,000 in 1889 alone. A few bookmakers, friends of McDonald's, were permitted to operate outside of the alliance, most notably Big Jim O'Leary and Silver Bill Riley. O'Leary was the son of a woman whose cow many thought had started the Chicago Fire. At the turn of the century, he was the preeminent handbook operator on Chicago's South Side. Riley's poolroom reportedly was the first gambling enterprise in the 1880s to focus exclusively on horse racing.[3]

According to the *Chicago Herald*, Mike McDonald was a political boss "who never held office, but he ruled the city with an iron hand. He named the men who were to be candidates for election, he elected them, and after they were in office they were merely his puppets."[4]

McDonald first became prominent in politics in 1873, when he helped found the People's Party, a coalition of Democrats and others interested in protecting personal freedoms that were under attack by moralists in post–fire Chicago. The coalition succeeded in electing Mayor Henry Colvin, who promoted a wide-open city. For the next several years, McDonald had several friends on the county board. Nonetheless, in 1876, a reform Republican mayor was elected in reaction to the wide-open city. Mayor Monroe Heath made matters hot for the gamblers, with frequent raids, despite the presence of their friend, Mike Hickey, who was general superintendent of police. Underworld figures relied on McDonald and his trust to provide protection, advance information about rates, secure favorable witnesses, and avoid heavy sentences in the police courts. McDonald was recognized as the man to see for bailouts from jail, to arrange payoffs to policemen, or to influence a judge to release arrested gamblers or assess them token fines.[5]

The gamblers' interests became more settled with the mayoralty of Carter H. Harrison I, a blue blood who supported the concept of personal freedom. During Harrison's tenure as mayor (1879–1887), the gamblers were largely left alone. He believed that Chicagoans should be allowed to enjoy their vices, as long as they did not harm anyone else. Harrison refused to enforce anti-poolroom laws, because that would cause worse evils, and the gamblers would move to hotels, clubhouses, and saloons. The *Tribune* felt that he was wrong, albeit honest and outspoken: "He told no lies and made no excuses. He behaved like a man, defending a bad cause with courage and ability."[6]

Historians debate the extent to which McDonald influenced Harrison, who was an old friend. In 1882, when McDonald was indicted on gambling charges, the mayor appeared on his behalf as a character witness, testifying that he had often called on him. McDonald would appear with candidates at athletic halls and public meetings, and he helped raise campaign funds by requiring each gambler to put up $500. McDonald claimed at one time that his support was worth 5,000 votes.[7]

According to Mayor Harrison's biographer, McDonald was a constant supporter who "figured in nearly every convention which nominated him, and was one of the leading spirits in one of them." In the 1893 campaign, Harrison denounced McDonald for his political activity, likely for political purposes. McDonald or someone else collected funds from gamblers for Harrison's contest. The *Inter-Ocean* claimed that $300,000 to $500,000 had been amassed. Harrison told campaign manager Adolf Kraus that a bag with $25,000 had to be returned to the gamblers. Harrison told him why he had taken the money. "Why a gambler votes with his money. If I refuse their money, they withhold their votes. I accept their money, get their votes, and after election return their money. I want their votes, not their money."[8]

After around 1885, McDonald reputedly sought more legitimate endeavors to gain social acceptance for himself and his children. In addition, he eventually became involved in downtown real estate, construction, and traction interests, most notably Charles T. Yerkes's Lake Street el, and, for two years, the *Chicago Globe* newspaper. According to Chicago police historian Richard Lindberg, his syndicate reputedly fell apart around 1889, when there were important police scandals. Organized gambling in Chicago became less centralized, and gamblers began to cut their own deals. However, as the history of Chicago's racetracks indicates, the reported demise of the McDonald syndicate was premature.[9]

ORGANIZED CRIME AND HORSE RACE GAMBLING

By the end of the Civil War, gambling on horses in Chicago surpassed the traditional riverboat games such as stud poker, faro, and craps. At first, horse race gambling in Chicago primarily took place on racetracks, where auction pool operators dominated the business. In this form of betting, the man taking bets set up a pool and "auctioned off" each horse to the highest bidder. The bettor whose horse won the race took the pool, less a commission to the bet taker. The city had a couple of second-rate tracks, but the big boom in the turf came in 1884 with the opening of Washington Park Racetrack, perhaps the finest in the Midwest, which was operated by the prestigious Washington Park Jockey Club. The track originally was located south of the city limits in the town of Lake, which was annexed in 1889 by a growing Chicago. The jockey club's members were the leading citizens of the city, and the opening of the track became the major event of the summer social season. The American Derby, the signature race of the Chicago meet, became one of the preeminent sporting events in the United States.[10]

During this era, the auction pool betting system, which was largely limited to well-heeled bettors, gave way to bookmaking, in which individuals set odds on all of the horses in a race. In 1887, for example, Washington Park had 36 bookmakers' stalls, 4 parimutuel machines, and 2 auction pools. The sport was under a lot of pressure from anti-gambling forces that felt that betting was ruining families and encouraging embezzlement. An anti-pool law was passed, but it permitted gambling at the tracks. But even worse than betting on the tracks was the illegal gambling away from the facilities, which reflected that the gamblers' main concern was betting, not enjoying the sport.[11]

The leading Western tracks were organized into the American Turf Congress, whose goals included prohibiting the telegraph transmission of results to hinder off-track poolrooms that were taking a lot of business away from the tracks. Downtown Chicago was the primary locus for off-track Midwestern betting parlors in the mid-1880s. After Carter Harrison left office, his successor, Republican Mayor John Roche, came into office in 1887 with the goal of elevating public morality and stopping gambling. He ordered the police to close six of the more notorious downtown poolrooms, and they remained shut during his term.[12]

Prior to the 1889 election, the gamblers offered both political parties a deal, trading permission to gamble in return for votes and campaign contributions. They worked hard for Democrat DeWitt Cregier and contributed about $6,000 to him. According to the *Tribune*, the gamblers were instrumental in getting him elected:

> This is an open secret to everybody at all versed in the unwritten history of the campaign. Cregier was a defeated man until within a week of the election. His Campaign Committee was destitute . . . and there was no prospect of getting enough to pay the expenses of printing the tickets and peddling the same. Cregier was apparently irreconcilably opposed to the reopening of the gambling houses which had on their walls the accumulated cobwebs of two years

while Mr. Roche was mayor. Friends came to his rescue and induced him to promise that the gamblers should be permitted to resume business at their old stands.

Michael C. McDonald, the eminent philanthropist and rare diplomat, had left Chicago in disgust, and was at this time in Philadelphia looking after some railroad interests. He was summoned to Chicago . . . Mr McDonald exercised the talents which have made him famous and wealthy.[13]

Under the regime, gaming houses that were closed for two years now re-opened, and they remained so, except for a day or two to help out the Cregier administration's bad public image. The *Tribune* asserted, "While there is not and cannot be any written proof of a bargain, there is sufficient circumstantial evidence to show that one was made between the gamblers and some one who held Cregier in the hollow of his hand. During his term, while he kept some of his promises to the gamblers, he did encounter pressure to close up the lesser faro games. Overall, the Cregier years were not as good for gamblers as Harrison's four terms.[14]

Downtown poolrooms flourished in the 1890s and hurt local tracks, even if most only posted out-of-town events. The selling of pools on foreign events was a specialty of gambler Joseph Ullman, who often ran afoul of the Hankins–McDonald syndicate. They demanded 60% of his profits for protection, while Ullman refused to go over 40%. In 1890, the *Tribune* urged the Cregier administration to shut them up. Typically some pool operators would be fined; they would appeal, and often the violation would be forgotten. Journalists wondered if the mayor and police were afraid to act.[15]

The grand jury, in the summer of 1890, was concerned that the mayor, police chief, and staff were not suppressing gambling. A gambling war was emerging, in which political influence played a significant role. The press reported that Edward Corrigan, owner of the West Side Racetrack, was persecuting downtown poolroom men to make them operate at his track where they would have to pay him fees. The mayor and the city police sided against Corrigan on the pool selling issue. Corrigan meanwhile used his Pinkertons to protect the West Side Track against outside interference. On July 28, for instance, Pinkertons tried to kick off the track some intruding constables and city police. A truce was supposed to be arranged in the gambling war, but Corrigan got warrants against the downtown bookies. In response, the poolroom men orchestrated a raid on Joseph Ullman's racetrack poolroom. The truce ended after the last race, when fighting broke out.[16]

The *Tribune* was very down on the city for "its open siding with the downtown poolrooms in the war." It also took to task the state's anti-pool law that did not apply to racetrack pools. It permitted pool selling on the grounds of an incorporated racing association one day prior to the opening of a meet and while races were in progress. The *Tribune* hoped to see both sides of the fight eat each other up:

> One must be protected because the gamblers are interested in it, and the gamblers control the Mayor, who controls the police, who put their heavy hands on one set of scoundrels while protecting, encouraging, and supporting the other—for a consideration.
>
> The down-town pool-rooms are backed by that syndicate of gamblers which made and runs the present City administration. The Law Department gave an accommodating opinion that the state law might be unconstitutional, and was risky to enforce. Yet it was apparently constitutional to break up the foreign books at the track. This is the most shameless confession yet of the ownership of the City Administration by the gaming trust. The people have seen the police force restrained from raiding protected halls. They have seen it making raids on those which were not protected. But they never before have seen it ordered out publicly to fight the battles of these gamblers, and to assist them, in conjunction with an auxiliary force of constables and private detectives, in suppressing their adversaries while defending the trust.
>
> It is the lowest depth of degradation which has been reached yet by any City Administration. But if the gamblers demand still stronger evidence of servility they will doubtless be forthcoming. And it is to this the "moral scratchers" have brought the city—its patrolmen obeying openly the orders of Hankins and McDonald, the real Chiefs of Police.[17]

On July 30, Corrigan secured an injunction against Mayor Cregier and the police chief to prevent interference with his track. There had been no interruptions in 1889, but since opening up nine days before, Chicago officials had threatened Corrigan and his associates with arrests. Corrigan indicated that poolrooms were operating in the city contrary to law but were "kept open pursuant to an agreement and understanding made between the owners and operators . . . and DeWitt C. Cregier, Mayor of Chicago, Frederick H. Marsh, Superintendent of Police of Chicago, and sundry other persons connected with said defendees, wherein and whereby said pool-sellers in the city of Chicago contribute a certain percentage of their profits . . . for so-called police protection" on a weekly basis. The mayor was irate and denounced the charges. Corrigan asked the poolroom men to observe the same policy for his track as Washington Park, but they refused. "We have done enough for Cregier in shutting down during the Washington Park races, so that he might keep faith with some of his political backers. We do not propose to close down for you, even if the Mayor should ask us." Then Corrigan threatened to enforce antipoolroom laws. Hankins and McDonald responded with threatened raids. "We can turn

Hayes loose on you." The *Tribune* noted: "They evidently spoke with authority. They are putting their threat into practice. They control the police force. That is clear. Cannot Mayor Cregier see that they do?"[18]

The *Tribune* found it embarrassing for the city's chief executive to encounter such charges, using "hackneyed and stereotyped line of defense once cleverly employed by Mr. Harrison, but stupidly persisted in too long." The mayor's claims of having effected the closing of poolrooms were ingenuous. Indeed, "It is hard to get to City Hall without running into a poolroom."

The original contract made with the gamblers was that their place should not be unmolested. Nothing was said of pool selling. Therefore, when the trust demanded protection for the poolrooms, the mayor should have refused permission. But he yielded abjectly, trying to hide his surrender by securing a judgment from the law department that the law could not be enforced. Then when rival poolrooms not in the trust began operations, the gamblers insisted that the city police close them, which was done. "So the lawful poolsellers are suppressed and the unlawful poolsellers are protected by the police." Whatever the outcome of Corrigan's accusations may be, these facts are enough to condemn the administration that has surrendered unconditionally and is the mere puppet and tool of a handful of gamblers.[19]

Cregier's motivation for closing the poolrooms during the Washington Park meet is unclear. According to one story, some of his main backers were interested in the Washington Park races and threatened to blow Cregier "out of the water" unless the rooms were closed up. Pat Sheedy's was raided for the first time, possibly because it became known that he had paid attorney Richardson to help prosecute Corrigan and Ullman. The *Tribune* continued to take Cregier to task for allowing six downtown rooms to operate that Mayor Roche had closed, and it criticized City Prosecutor May (a former attorney for the gamblers) as practically being an attorney for the Gambling Trust.[20]

The *Tribune* unfavorably compared Cregier to his immediate predecessors. Harrison had been wrong in his actions, but he had stood up for a man for his point of view. Then came Roche, who had carried out his plan to curtail gambling. Cregier, on the other hand, had decried gambling as a great evil that should be stopped, but he had not, either because his orders were not obeyed or respected. Consequently, the *Tribune* claimed, the public saw him as insincere or incompetent.[21]

A number of lawsuits followed the Corrigan–Cregier dispute and, as a result, in mid-August, the local poolrooms were closed. Two months later, Judge Tuley ruled that pool selling was illegal, and that the state and city laws permitting it at the tracks were void, because gambling everywhere was the same. This contradicted prior courts that had held that pool selling was not gaming within the meaning of the general statute on gambling.[22] The *Tribune* applauded Tuley's righteous action that promised to wipe out the privileged class of gamblers, putting pool sellers and bookmakers on the same level:

It would cut temptations from the path of young men and make busi-ness-men more secure in the honesty of their employees. It will re-move the shameful spectacle of gamblers protected by police authority. It will place gambling of every kind where it can be reached by the law. It also opens up a golden opportunity for his Honor, Mayor Cregier, as it gives him the power to suppress gambling of every description and save him from the trouble of regulating it.[23]

Corrigan's West Side lease expired in the fall of 1890. He dismantled the buildings at the West Side Track and made plans to remove his operations to the southwestern border of the city. On February 12, 1891, state Senator Sol Van Pragg, a Chicago poolroom operator, introduced legislature aimed at ha-rassing Corrigan. The bill proposed limiting racing meets to 30 days, and tax-ing the tracks 5% of their gross receipts.[24]

Mayor Cregier was up for reelection that spring against the reform Re-publican candidate Hempstead Washburne. Cregier sought financial support from the gamblers, who knew that Washburne was sure to oppose them. The Gamblers' Trust and its allies purportedly amassed a $25,000 fund to support Cregier's retention. The trust was monopolizing Chicago faro banks, and other forms of gambling, including policy, were wide open under the Democratic regime. However, despite the aid from organized crime, Cregier was defeated by the reform-minded Washburne.[25]

In April 1891, Mayor Washburne came into office and turned the screws on gambling. Police were instructed to warn gambling rooms to close up or ex-pect to get raided and have their property confiscated. They virtually all com-plied, if not willingly. Some bookmakers left Chicago for Southern tracks, while others announced the start of handbook betting with 150 workers immediately available, since they had lost their old jobs.[26]

On May 20, Corrigan's Chicago Racing Association opened for business just outside of the city limits at the border of the village of Hawthorne and the town of Cicero. His partners in the new Hawthorne Racetrack included former West Park Commissioner John Brenock, a man with some political clout. Hawthorne opened in the spring, charging 75 cents to $1 admission, but it closed early in the summer, when Washington Park held its meet.[27]

After Corrigan had left the West Side, two North Siders leased the site where the old racecourse still stood, with a 10-year option. A new $300,000 West Side track known as Garfield Park was planned at Madison and 40th Street. It was named for the beautiful suburban park adjacent to the track. This was a "bookmakers' track," run by the Hankins syndicate, with Demo-cratic politician Washington Hesing, publisher of the *Staats-Zeitung*, serving as track president. The stockholders included Mike McDonald ($20,000), B. J. Johnson ($15,000), George V. Hankins ($35,000), Al Hankins ($10,000), Jeff Hankins ($10,000), William J. Wightman, Harry Varnell,

Harry Romaine, Sidney McHie, and John Condon, a fixer for the McDonald syndicate, and a man who had run his own gambling hall in the late 1880s. They budgeted $150,000 for a 20,000-seat grandstand, with a fine clubhouse, sheds for 800 horses, and running tracks that measured 3/4 of a mile and 1 mile. But when the track opened, the grandstand built in 1878 was still employed. Nonetheless, one thing Garfield Park had going for it was its location. It was situated much closer to the center of the city's population and was more accessible than either Washington Park or Hawthorne. The other thing going for the track was the political clout of McDonald, the Hankins, and Varnell.[28]

Moral reformers opposed the establishment of Garfield Park on the West Side. They found support from the West Chicago Park Commissioners, who sought an injunction on June 20 to block construction. The commissioners claimed that the Park Act gave them the power to forbid horse racing, gambling, or any offensive activities within 400 feet of the parks and the West Side boulevards, as well as a 50-foot easement for a building line around the park. They further argued that the track would harm the usefulness and benefits of the park and neighborhood, bringing in "vast crowds of objectionable persons and necessitate an increase in the park police force." Neighborhood property owners living within 400 feet of the site also filed for an injunction, complaining that virtually all of the track owners were pool sellers or bookies, including many notorious keepers of common gambling houses. They pointed out that the new track was not intended to improve the breed, to develop speed, or for sport, but purely to promote gambling. Local landlords pointed out that Corrigan's racetrack had been a nuisance, with foul odors and noise, and the attraction to their neighborhood "of thieves, confidence men, loafers, tramps, beggars, and adventurers, . . .

> Women and children could not venture from their house for fear of violence or insult at the hands of this mob. Dog fights and prize fights were other attractions offered. Property has depreciated to such an extent since the new track was talked of that there is no sale for lots and people who can are moving out of the neighborhood.

Property owners expected nothing better and a lot worse from the new promoters. It would attract "all classes of low people, thieves, prize-fighters, abandoned women, tramps, and other disreputable characters."[29]

The efforts of the park commissioners, moral reformers, and neighbors failed to block the sporting venture, and Garfield Park was leased to the bookmaking syndicate for $60,000 over three years. The track was in a very accessible site, just 16 minutes from Union Depot by special Wisconsin Central trains, and there had been racing there since 1878. The cheaper streetcars took 35 minutes from downtown.[30]

Garfield Park track operated in direct competition with Corrigan's new Hawthorne course. Neither track drew the best horses that raced at Washington Park, and purses were about the same at both tracks. Garfield quickly developed a reputation for dubious integrity, as bookmakers regularly bet against horses they owned. They competed for the more plebeian audiences, with Garfield usually coming out ahead, averaging over 7,000 each day, and drawing as many as 22,000 one afternoon. Admission cost 75 cents to $1, but each scheduled a number of free dates. Garfield's ticket sales were modest, often no more than $200, partly because so many people got in on passes. However, it made up for small admission fees with large profits from the betting.[31]

Hawthorne operated until early September. Its meet was described by the *Spirit of the Times*, a leading sporting weekly of the day, as a "heroic struggle against peculiarly adverse circumstances." Corrigan and his partners were said to be losing a lot of money each day, despite Hawthorne's integrity and good training facilities, hurt by the expensive and infrequent public transit. What saved them was that Corrigan's horses made $25,000 during the meet, and their bookmaking on foreign races brought in $55,000. The *Spirit* also blamed politics for many problems:

> Then again, the Tweed and Tammany rings of New York in their palmiest days were babies in comparison to the clique of Chicago, who have strained every source known to the order to down Mr. Corrigan. Every dive, barroom, and thug ugly of the Garden City were in league against him, in fact so bitter has been this element that most of the public resorts boycotted his racing cards, so that patrons were obliged to wait the morning papers to see the entries at Hawthorne. Almost every respectable racing stable of the West stuck to him until the flag was furled, and few men in Chicago to-day have more friends among horsemen than Edward Corrigan.[32]

In the fall, Mayor Washburne put a lot of pressure on the city council to curtail the operations of Garfield Park. On December 3, 1891, the council passed an ordinance to prevent Garfield from reopening in the spring. McDonald and the racetrack crowd looked to their allies on the city council for support against the mayor.

Garfield's proprietors reputedly made a fortune during the three-month meet, even though the track had provided only $43,280 in stakes and purses. The foreign book alone took in $600,000, with total profits at $1 million. The owners planned winter meet encountered strong public opposition, led by the local press. The police, under orders from the park commissioner, intervened at the end of the planned three-month season on December 12, claiming the mile track infringed on the protected boulevards around Garfield Park. (Actually, the racing occurred at the 3/4 mile track that was legally far enough away.) The *Inter-Ocean*, a paper that normally supported racing, as well as some other papers, stopped printing results from Garfield Park, stating that "the racing at Garfield Park is not honest and it is cruel." The city council continued to put pressure on the bookmakers. An ordinance was drawn up to run streets through the track, although it never passed. Another was approved to ban bookmaking and pool selling within tracks inside the city limits, although its constitutionality was uncertain, since it contradicted the state law that permitted betting on all regular tracks.[33]

In the spring of 1892, the press, particularly the *Chicago Times*, vigorously criticized Chicago racing, particularly McDonald and the Garfield Park crowd. The *Chicago Times* proclaimed: "Mike McDonald is an unscrupulous, disreputable, vicious gambler, a disgrace and menace to the city. He should be driven from the city and the racetracks closed up forever." The strong critique by the *Times* surprised many observers, because it was owned by former Mayor Harrison, McDonald's old friend.[34]

Mayor Washburne indicated that he intended to close Garfield, which had optimistically enlarged its grandstand to seat 17,000. Management tried to get a three-month license but, like the other tracks in the area, it was only granted a 30-day permit. The owners encountered considerable pressure from the mayor, and they failed to secure an injunction to prevent Washburne from interfering with the pools, foreign books, and local books. Instead of charging the normal $1 admission, patrons were let in free. There were 97 bookmakers at the track on opening day, attended by 6,000 fans. With nearly 100 police on hand, only the handbooks were in business, and there were no foreign pools. The spectators were frightened by the police presence, and there was little betting One bookmaker put up his slate after the fifth race and was arrested in a test case. Consequently, the track closed for several days.[35]

Washburne thereafter stepped up his fight against Garfield Park. Alderman John Cooke, an administrative spokesman in the city council, presented an ordinance on July 18 to close up the racetrack, because "This is a residential district and the residents complain that the betting pools cause disreputable men and women to loiter in the neighborhood." The track's interests were protected by machine politicians such as Bathhouse John Coughlin, the colorful First Ward alderman and Democratic committeeman that the bookmakers helped elect in early 1892 to protect their interests. Coughlin himself was a racing fan who owned a small stable of thoroughbreds and had a box at Garfield Park. He developed into one of the most notorious political bosses in Chicago history, who took full advantage of the grafting opportunities of his wide-open Levee district. Bathhouse John staunchly stood up for Garfield Park:

> You can't do that. . . . You can't shut up a man's property. . . . It's unfair.
> . . . It's . . . un-American, that's what! Why gentlemen, think of the

money racing brings to Chicago, the millions of dollars. You can't get an order like this through the council, and I tell you, Me? Maar, I'm going to vote against it, and I know every man here will do the same.

The proposal to close the track and make permanent the anti-Garfield Park law was sent to the judiciary committee. One week later, the committee reported that the plan was unfair, and it suggested closing all of the other tracks, although the only track in the city limits was Washington Park.[36]

Varnell failed to get the city collector to issue him a 90-day license, and his colleagues then sought an injunction to require the city to give them the license. Their efforts were rejected by Judge James Horton, who denounced all horse racetrack gambling, particular at Garfield Park.[37]

The council passed a bill in late July before its summer recess to circumvent the mayor's licensing powers in the racing business. Councilman Johnny Powers of the Nineteenth Ward, chairman of the finance committee, and the "Prince of Boodlers," recommended a plan to permit a racing association to hold meets between May 1 and November 1 for a $200-a-day license fee. "We must have races in Chicago," said Alderman Powers. "It is a sport center, and the great majority of people favor racing." The Powers bill was approved by 38 aldermen and sent to the mayor for his approval. Washburne, as expected, immediately vetoed the bill, criticizing the measure for leaving the authorities with insufficient control to close a racetrack, should it become a menace to public order. McDonald, that afternoon, tried to get a license for the track, but because of the veto, he was out of luck.[38]

The council recessed for the summer, which halted any additional action on the racing license issue. The track owners were certain that Washburne would not take action until the council reconvened in September, so they reopened Garfield Park in early August.[39]

When Garfield Park reopened, local citizens organized to protest. Bishop Fallows claimed that most of the embezzling in Chicago was a consequence of betting losses, and another commentator judged the gambling at Garfield worse than the infamous Louisiana Lottery. The meet attracted about 40 bookmakers, compared to only about 11 at Hawthorne, and there was a lot of betting. Of course, "The four hundred are not out in force at Garfield."[40]

On Friday, September 2, the racing situation came to a head. Acting on a petition from local businessmen and clergymen, Police Chief R. W. McClaughry ordered a raid on Garfield Park for operating without a license and for permitting gambling. The track was surrounded after the first race by Inspector Lyman Lewis, leading 100 officers and 13 paddy wagons. Nine Pinkerton guards were ordered away from the front gates and placed into some of the wagons. Thirty-three people were arrested, including track manager M. Lewis Clark, his secretary, the race starter, nine Pinkertons, and the 13 jockeys who raced in the opening event. Coughlin and Varnell bailed them out, charging that Corrigan and ex-Mayor Harrison, who they believed was part owner of Hawthorne, were behind the raid. Mayor Washburne later testified in court that Corrigan's partner and secretary, James E. Burke, had told Chief Mc-Claughry early in the summer that Hawthorne would pay big money to the Republican Party if Garfield was closed up, and that the chief had passed the offer to the mayor, which Washburne rejected out of hand. The chief admitted that he had known Burke for 15 years, but he denied that Burke had offered $50,000 to close up the competition. He did admit taking advice from Burke, whose brother, a bishop, had frequently visited McClaughry at home. Burke retorted, "Why I'm a good Democrat. What would I be doin', givin' dough to the Republicans?"[41]

The press applauded the raid. The *Tribune* described the track as a vile resort of the lowest type, a nest of thieves, burglars, confidence men, and lewd folk: "It has been a veritable charnell-house for morals, a den in which were killed off all the good and noble sentiments that were originally entertained by its frequenters, and for them substitute vile ambitions, a test for wicked enjoyments, and an admiration for the ethics of the thief and libertine."[42]

On Saturday, despite the raid the day before, and the presence of 150 police officers, 8,000 attended the races. The start was delayed for 3 hours with Inspector Lewis in front of the starter's stand. As soon as George Hankins finally rang the starter's bell, the police moved in, arresting Hankins, Varnell, and as many employees as they could catch. McDonald blamed the raid on Corrigan, who he claimed was tight with Chief McClaughry and the Republicans, and he urged all racing fans to vote Democratic in the next election.[43]

The track was closed on Sunday for the Sabbath. On Monday, September 5, Pinkerton guards closed and bolted the front gates once the crowds were in to keep out the police. Two races were staged without interference, but then around 3:30 P.M., five wagon loads with several hundred police officers arrived, having received reports that gambling was going on inside the track. They stormed and smashed the gates with axes, raced into the track, and surrounded the betting ring with paddy wagons. They arresting 25 gamblers, 25 jockeys, Col. Clark, George Hankins, Varnell, and Michael Coughlin (Bathhouse's older brother). In all, 800 people were detained, and 125 were locked up. This was one of the largest raids in the city's history. McDonald made bond for the track officials.[44] On the following day, attendance was down to 1,500. Shortly after 3 P.M., the police moved into the park and fired their pistols into the air. Among the men in the crowd was noted horseman and former Texas sheriff Jim Brown, well known as a tough guy, who sat up on a barn roof where his horses were stabled, twirling his .44 (which had 12 notches for men he had killed) and shouting that no one was going to stop the races. Brown fled, but when he was cut off by Officer John Powell, he shot and killed the policeman. Brown tried to escape but ran into Officer

William Jones, whom he also tried to shoot, but his gun jammed. Jones shot and killed Brown.[45]

This bloody event precipitated the end of Garfield Park, confirming Chief McClaughry's determination to close the track. "If police offices cannot enter the park in the discharge of their duty without being killed, it is time the park was closed." Reformers ranging from the daily press, clergymen, and women's clubs all called for the end of Garfield Park.[46]

Garfield's last breath came on September 12, when the city council considered Washburne's license veto. Prior to that vote, a test vote was taken on a bizarre resolution proposed by Alderman Henry Eller and backed by Coughlin, which praised the courage of ex-sheriff Brown and demanded an investigation of the police and the reported bribe offers from Ed Corrigan and Jimmy Burke. The resolution failed, and the veto was upheld by a vote of 60 to 3. Newspaper headlines screamed, "The Reign Is Ended."[47]

The closing of Garfield did not mean the demise of Chicago racing, or of the bookmakers and organized crime. Several of the Garfield Park investors, including John Condon, Harry Varnell, and Paddy Ryan, simply moved their business in November to Roby, Indiana, 1 mile across the state border. Roby was accessible by water transport and a half-hour train ride from Chicago. The new track's president was Chicago Alderman Ernest Hummell. The Garfield crowd invested money in the local Democratic campaign chest to ensure noninterference and to gain influence in the state legislature.[48]

Horse race gambling was an issue in the next mayoral campaign. The Democratic candidates were former Mayor Cregier, Washington Hesing, denounced by the *Times* as "the candidate of the Garfield Park gang and the management of their racetrack, and *Times'* publisher Carter H. Harrison, who was running for a fifth term. He did not oppose pool selling on the tracks and admitted making wagers and buying pools. Harrison did not believe that gambling could be eliminated, and he sought to regulate it when it was too obnoxious (betting on foreign races, late closing hours, juveniles at the track, free liquor given as enticements, etc.). He was targeted by the press for having failed to squash the gambling interests in his prior terms.

Harrison felt that the elite Washington Park merited special consideration, because it ran short, one-month meets, was less accessible, and was owned and operated by prominent moral men:

> I should judge that the class of patrons of Washington Park can much better afford to lose their money than those who go to Garfield. At the former track I have seen the majority of the crowd to be respectable people, while at the latter they are very disreputable. At Washington Park it is a great sight to see a well-dressed society lady betting on her favorite horse and clapping her pretty hands when he comes in first. At Garfield, this cannot be seen, for the demi-monde prevails.[49]

Harrison won the nomination and then the general election over Republican Samuel Allerton, a wealthy meatpacker. He got to preside over the Columbian Exposition, but his term was cut short in 1894 by an assassin.

In the short run, racing did very well in Chicago after the closing of Garfield Park. Racing enjoyed a banner year in 1893, benefiting from the excitement and tourism surrounding the World's Fair. Hawthorne was open for 260 dates, while at Washington Park stakes and purses amounted to $378,000, twice more than in 1892. The American Derby was attended by 47,000 spectators and was won by Boundless, who earned a record $50,000 for his victory. Nonetheless, the track encountered a lot of negative press, particularly from the crusading *Chicago Daily News*, which considered Derby Day to have been a disgrace, with many respectable women seated "in the presence of scores of harlots, most of whom are drunk and all of whom are loudly dressed and otherwise act their infamous callings." The *Daily News* commenced a vigorous crusade against Washington Park, complaining about minors betting, the presence of loose women, the integrity of certain races, and declining property values near the track.[50]

In the fall of 1894, reformers mounted a strong campaign to close Washington Park, Hawthorne, and the new west suburban Harlem Racetrack, established by George Hankins, John Condon, and other former associates of Mike McDonald's. The fight to end racing and curb the gambling menace was promoted by such reform groups as the newly formed Civic Federation.[51] At a rally called by the South Side Anti-Track Association, one speaker took to task the elite Washington Park track:

> The chief difference between [the] Washington Park racetrack and the Garfield track is in the character of its members. The Washington Park track includes the same bad elements, the gambling, the evil association, the disreputable elements are all there, but there is a sprinkling of respectability who use these races as a cover to their vices. Yearly at its meetings are dumped on a respectable and quiet residence community a mass of humanity, gamblers and disreputables, and the offscourgings of the earth. . . . It is a well-known fact that this racetrack has greatly degenerated in morality and is becoming decidedly "tough."
>
> This club becomes the common meeting-ground between supposed respectability and total depravity. Women of loose character swarm the grounds and hold sway where the young men of the city are here led into gambling and evil associations, and the air of semi-respectability given it by its list of prominent members and their attendance, example, and sanction is a large factor in leading them on.[52]

In mid-September, the Civic Federation commenced a crusade against Chicago gambling. Daily raids were made against gambling houses and poolrooms. Hawthorne was raided, and the reformers also went after Washington Park, whose president, George Wheeler, had been arrested during the summer for running a gambling facility.[53]

The tracks had a checkered career over the next few years. A number of new tracks were built in the suburbs, but the elite Washington Park was closed in 1895, most of 1896, and again in 1899 because of pressure from moral reformers, particularly the Civic Federation. Members were concerned about the growing presence of a less desirable element, possible adverse legislation in Springfield, the need for funds to placate hostile legislators, and possible grand jury indictments.[54] Eventually, in 1905, all of the tracks were closed, and they remained virtually shut until the 1920s.

Bookmaking, on the other hand, thrived, from the downtown poolrooms to the hundreds of handbooks found in most working-class neighborhoods. Handbook backers, who took bets of $1 and up, did not seem worried about the racetrack woes, getting their information on out-of-town races from Western Union. Chicago became a national center for off-track betting, second only to New York.[55]

CONCLUSION

Horse racing in Chicago and in other parts of the United States provided a key nexus for organized crime and machine politics. This often meant ownership of racetracks, participation in racing stables, and management of legal wagering, and always control of illegal, off-track gambling. Machine politicians needed financing and votes from the underworld, while the gangsters needed protection for illegal gambling networks and speedy information on the results of races. These findings are similar to that previously discovered for New York and New Jersey, where urban machine politics and crime were integral elements of late-nineteenth-century and early-twentieth-century horse racing. In metropolitan New York, the most prestigious tracks were not owned by professional politicians or the underworld, but the legality of horse racing was tied to the political clout of well-to-do horsemen allied with Tammany Boss Richard Croker, himself a famed owner of outstanding thoroughbreds. More importantly, there was an extensive off-track betting business controlled by the Gambling Trust, prominent figures in Tammany Hall, which included Big Tim Sullivan, number 2 man in the machine, and Frank Farrell, the leading gambling impresario in New York. In New Jersey, racing in the late nineteenth century was intimately tied to the Democratic political machines in Hudson and Gloucester counties, home of the notorious Guttenberg and Gloucester racetracks. These outlaw tracks were owned and operated by prominent Jersey pols. Similarly, in St. Louis, Cincinnati, and New Orleans, urban political machines and syndicate crime played a prominent role in the turf. Yet the alliance was not omnipotent, as outlaw tracks in New Jersey and Illinois were closed despite the owners' political influence, and racecourses in most major racing areas were slammed shut for varying periods of time.[56]

NOTES

1. On the history of organized crime, see, e.g., Johnson, D. (1979). *Policing the urban underworld: The impact of crime on the development of the police, 1800–87.* Philadelphia: Temple University Press; Johnson, D. (1977). A sinful business: The origins of gambling syndicate in the United States, 1840–1887. In D. H. Bayley (Ed.), *Police and society* pp. 17–47. Beverly Hills: Sage Publications. 1977.

2. Lindberg, R. (1991). *To serve and collect: Chicago politics and police corruption from the lager beer riots to the Summerdale scandal* (pp. 90–95). New York: Praeger. Asbury, H. (1940). *Gem of the prairie: An informal history of the Chicago underworld* (pp. 142–144). New York: A. A. Knopf. Asbury, H. (1938). *Suckers' progress* (296–302) New York: Dodd, Mead. Wendt, L., & Kogan, H. (1940). *Lords of the levee: The story of bathhouse John and Hinky Dink* (p. 28) Garden City, N.Y.: Doubleday. Pierce, B. L. (1957). *A History of Chicago, 1871–1893* (p. 305) Chicago: University of Chicago Press.
On the Hankins brothers, see, e.g., *Chicago Tribune*, 16 (6–4), 17 (4–4), 23 (8–1) July 1890.

3. Longstreet, S. (1973). *Chicago 1860–1919.* (p. 209). New York: David McKay Co. Asbury, *Sucker's Progress*, 299; Pierce, 476–477.

4. Quoted in Longstreet, S. (1973). *Chicago, 1860–1919* (p. 201). New York: McKay.

5. Ibid., 42–44.

6. *Chicago Tribune*, 9 (1–3), 10 (1–5, 12–2) Aug. 1890.

7. Johnson, C. O. (1928). *Carter Henry Harrison I* (p. 139). Chicago: University of Chicago Press; *Chicago Inter-Ocean*, 28; Lindberg, 94–95; Asbury, *Gem of the prairie*, 146–147.

8. Johnson, 187–188, 188 (quote); Kogan & Wendt, 67.

9. Lindberg, 96–98; Asbury, *Gem of the prairie*, 158.

10 . *Spirit of the Times*, 106 (22 Dec. 1883): 625; (5 Jan. 1884): 689; (12 Jan. 1884): 720; 107 (28 June 1884): 680, 684; (5 July 1884): 710, 711; (12 July 1884): 736, 108 (3 Jan. 1885): 713; Clark, H. (1941). *The elegant eighties: When Chicago was young* (p. 205). Chicago: A. C. McClurg.
On the history of American horse racing, see Robertson, W. H. P. (1964). *The history of thoroughbred racing in America.* Englewood Cliffs, N. J.: Prentice-Hall; Parmer, C. B. (1939). *For gold and glory: The history of thoroughbred racing in America.* New York: Carrick and Evans.

11. *Chicago Times*, 28 (2–3) June 1887. See also *Chicago Tribune*, 16 April 1887 (1–5).

12. *Chicago Tribune*, 9 (1–3), 10 (1–5, 12–2) Aug. 1890.

13. *Chicago Tribune*, 3 Apr. 1891 (1–7).

14. Ibid., 13 Aug. 1890 (4–2), 3 Apr. 1891 (1–7).

15. *Chicago Times*, 3 (12–1,2), 11(3–5) Nov. 1889; *Chicago Tribune*, 4 May 1890 (12–3); *Spirit* 118 (31 May 1890): 830; (7 June 1890): 865; 119 (26 July 1890): 1; *Clipper* 37 (9 Aug. 1890): 347; (8 Nov. 1890): 554.

16. *Chicago Tribune*, 25 (2–4), 29 (1–5) July 1890.

17. Ibid., 30 July 1809 (4–4).

18. *Chicago Tribune*, 31 July 1890 (1–3, 4–2).

19. *Chicago Tribune*, 31 July (1–3, 4–2) 1890.

20. Ibid., 1 Aug. (1–3, 4–3), 31 July (1–3) 1890 (on May). The six rooms were owned by Al Hankins, Sid McHie, Corrigan, J. H. Levy, Shepard and Argo, and Pat Sheedy. On Mayor Roche's early efforts against Chicago gamblers, see ibid., 16 June 1887 (1–5).

21. Ibid., 9 (1–3), 10 (1–5, 12–2) Aug. 1890.

22. *Chicago Tribune*, 14 (8–1), 15 (7–5) Aug.; 31 (8–1) Oct.; 1 (4–3) Nov. 1890.

23. Ibid., 30 Nov. 1890 (4–5).

24. Ibid., 24 (6–3) Jan., 13 Feb. 1891 (7–3).

25. Ibid., 3 Apr. 1891 (1–7).

26. Ibid., 29 Apr. 1891 (1–1); *Spirit* 120 (16 May 1891): 743.

27. *Chicago Tribune*, 19 June 1891 (1–5); *Chicago Times*, 20 (3–6), 23 (6–4), 24 (2–3), 26 (4–5) July, 3 (2–5,), 7 (8–1), 23 (1–5) Aug. 1891.

28. *Chicago Tribune*, 5 (6–3), 27 June 1891.

29. *Chicago Tribune*, 21 (5–5), 27 (3–5) (quote) June 1891; *Chicago Times*, 4 (4–2), 8 (9–4), 11 (5–4) July 1891.

30. *Chicago Times*, 4 (4–2), 8 (9–4), 11 (5–4) , 13 (3–5), 14 (6–7), 15 (6–7), 17 (7–1), 19 (5–3) July 1891.

31. *Chicago Times*, 20 (3–6), 23 (6–4), 24 (2–3), 26 (4–5) July, 3 (2–5), 7 (8–1), 23 (1–5) Aug. 1891; *Spirit* 121 (9 Sept. 1891): 330; 123 (2 July 1892): 995.

32. *Spirit* (9 Sept. 1891): 329, 330 (quote).

33. *New York Times*, 10 Dec. 1891 (5–5); *Spirit*, 121 (5 Dec. 1891): 717; (12 Dec. 1891): 787; (19 Dec. 1891): 818; (26 Dec. 1891): 857; (16 Jan 1892): 996. On street closing, see *Spirit* 121 (6 Feb 1892): 86.

34. Kogan & Wendt, *Lords of the Levee*, 15, 21, 27–28, 50 (quote).

35. *Chicago Tribune*, 16 (1–2), 20 (7–3), 24 (6–1), 25 (3–1) July 1892; *Brooklyn Eagle*, 25 July 1892 (2–4).

36. Kogan and Wendt, 15, 21, 27–33, 50 (quotes), 52. Coughlin's older brother had worked as a teenager at the tracks, where he was befriended by many touts and jockeys and had become a good handicapper. He was responsible for getting Bathhouse interested in the turf.

37. Ibid.

38. Kogan & Wendt, 51; *Chicago Tribune*, 27 (4–4), 30 (8–1) July 1892.

39. Kogan & Wendt, 51–52; "Mayor's Veto of Ordinance Licensing the Tracks," July 28, 1892, filed September 12, 1892, #3901. Proceedings Files of the City Council of Chicago, Illinois Regional Archives Department, Northeastern Illinois University.

40. Ibid., 1 (7–4), 3, 9 (6–3), 11? (1–5), 12 (7–3), 18 (6–3) Aug. 1892; *Clipper* (6 Aug. 1892): 349; (13 Aug. 1892): 365; *Spirit* 122 (3 Sept. 1892): 223.

41. *Chicago Tribune*, 3 Sept. 1892 (1–7, 9–1); Kogan & Wendt, 54, (quote); *New York Times*, 7 Sept. 1892 (1–5).

42. *Chicago Tribune*, 4 Sept. 1892 (28–2); *New York Times*, 3 Sept. 1892 (3–3).

43. Kogan & Wendt, 54.

44. *Chicago Tribune*, 6 Sept. 1892; *New York Times*, 6 Sept. 1892 (3–6).

45. Kogan & Wendt, 55–56.

46. *New York Times*, 7 Sept. 1892 (1–5); Kogan & Wendt, 56.

47. *Chicago Tribune*, 12 October 92 (7–7).

48. *Chicago Tribune*, 1 (2–4), 7 (4–3) Aug., 22 (6–5) Sept. 1892; *Brooklyn Eagle*, 1 Aug. 1892 (2–4); *Spirit* 124 (12 Nov. 1892): 607.

49. *Chicago Daily News*, 17 Feb. 1893 (8-1); *Chicago Tribune*, 5 Apr. 1893 (1–2); Johnson, C. O. (1928). *Carter H. Harrison I: Political leader* (pp. 188, 257–258). Chicago: University of Chicago Press.

50. *Spirit* 126 (22 July 1893): ?; (29 July 1893): 36; *Chicago Daily News*, 26 (1–1, 4–2), 27 (1–1), 28 (1–1, 6–3), 29 (1–1), 30 (1–1) June; 1 (1–1), 6 (3–1), 18 July 1893 (3–4).

51. *Chicago Daily News*, 16 Apr. 1894 (1–1,2); Kogan & Wendt, 109–110.

52. *Chicago Daily News*, 8 (1–1), 10 (1–3) 1894.

53. *Spirit* 128 (29 Sept. 1894): 358; *Chicago Daily News*, 28 Sept. 1894 (1–4).

54. *Chicago Daily News*, 15 (1–5?), 20 (2–1) Oct., 2 (8–1), 3 (6–2) Nov. 1894; *Spirit* 128 (20 Oct. 1894): 466, 480.

55. *Spirit* 132 (19 Dec. 1896): 670.

56. Riess, S. A. (1988). *City games: The evolution of American urban society and the rise of sports* (pp. 185–187). Urbana: _____; Riess, S. A. (1988). Sports and machine politics in New York City, 1890–1920. In A. Mohl (Ed.), *The making of urban America* (pp. 105–110). Wilmington, DE: Scholarly Resources; Riess, "The turf in the garden state: The politics of New Jersey horse racing, 1870–1894." Southern Historical Association, Louisville, KY, November 12, 1994.

8

Athletics in the Ward and Beyond

Neighborhoods, Jews, and Sport in Toronto, 1900–1939

Danny Rosenberg

Influxes of Central and Eastern European immigrant Jews who settled in Toronto between 1880 and 1914 dramatically altered the composition of Jewish life in Canada's second largest city (Abella, 1990; Elazar & Waller, 1990; Belkin, 1966). The immigrants' world in Toronto at this time was mostly centered in the crammed neighborhood of St. John's Ward between Yonge Street and University Avenue and College and Queen Streets. The Ward was known for its appalling living conditions, where a lack of water was commonplace, sanitation was poor, and many buildings were structurally defective. But the Ward provided familiar surroundings and cushioned the cultural shock faced by immigrant families on their way to becoming Canadianized. Their New World ghetto was comprised of familiar sights, sounds, and smells, as well as conflicting ideologies, dissenting political views, and various forms of religious practice (Tulchinsky, 1992). From this ethnically rich environment emerged a new Jewish community that eventually migrated to other neighborhoods and locales in the city's downtown core. This generation of immigrants also refined organizational life during the interwar years and produced the many institutions that now dominate the Toronto Jewish community (Speisman, 1979).

Of the numerous cultural activities and institutions Jewish immigrants were involved in, historians have either neglected or superficially treated sport as a relevant practice among Toronto's Jews. Despite this lack of attention by scholars, we know that many Jews took up athletics before and after the Great War, and some even rose to national and international prominence (Luftspring & Swarbrick, 1975; Rosenberg, 1993). Therefore, not all immigrants in Toronto, and certainly not their children, accepted long-held beliefs that Jewish culture and tradition emphasized a life dedicated to intellectual pursuits, or the myths that Jews are weak and physically incompetent (Postal, Silver, &

Silver, 1965). Many new arrivals were eager to embrace the customs and cultural activities now open to them, and many were drawn to sport.

The sport experiences of Toronto's Jews during the first four decades of the twentieth century raise numerous questions related to acculturation, assimilation, ethnicity, social mobility, generational tensions, and identity formation. They also shed light on issues related to class, economic status, family values, and communal affiliation. As Levine (1992) argues, for many (North) American Jews, sport was appropriated as a middle ground—a complex urban experience shaped by interactions between Jews as well as between Jews and ethnic and majority cultures that involved sensitive adaptations and transformations. Sport became a significant social domain, both in practice and as symbol, for immigrants and their children to define themselves as Canadians and as Jews. In a polyethnic society and an institutionally complete city such as Toronto, which was far more free and open than they had ever experienced in Eastern Europe, sport and leisure activities expressed cultural values that could both coexist and challenge or even undermine Old World attitudes and values. For newcomers and their offspring in Toronto who took up an interest in sport in the first half of the twentieth century, identity and ethnicity were necessarily problematized, negotiated, and redefined (Harney, 1985). In short, then, sport confirmed a meaningful Jewish identity while it also promoted more widespread social acceptance. But this transformation would take considerable time and was not without conflict.

Part of the difficulties that immigrant Jews faced in Toronto was related to their restricted living space and to their relatively small internal urban migration patterns. Between 1900 and 1940, the majority of Jews lived in the Ward. They then migrated just west to the Kensington Market area along Spadina Avenue, and then further west and north around Bathurst Street (Driedger, 1991; White, 1993). In each of these downtown regions, public space for sports was confined mainly to playgrounds, school yards, and small, inner-city parks. For most Jewish youth, play areas and facilities were within walking distance of home. By the 1920s and 1930s, cheap mass transit and an improved quality of life permitted some Jews to travel to large suburban parks such as High Park in the city's west end and to public beaches in the city's east and west ends. While insufficient to adequately accommodate the rapid growth of immigrants in Toronto, local playgrounds and parks remained the most important public spaces for engaging in sport (cf., Riess, 1991). The "urban ethnic mosaic" in Toronto was more or less well defined in the first decades of the twentieth century, even though in the three areas described above Italians, blacks, and Chinese could be found in these predominantly Jewish neighborhoods (McGahan, 1986). Jewish youngsters therefore intermingled with their own kind on the playing field, and they also developed important relationships with Gentile immigrant children. Because spatial segregation was not entirely complete between ethnic groups, and sport participation was confined to a limited number of public areas, issues of identity, assimilation, and acculturation via sport were made more complex. This chapter, then, will trace some of the challenges that Toronto Jews faced in sport in relation to urban neighborhood life, to the institutions they affiliated with, and to their involvement at different levels of play in the first four decades of the twentieth century.

In the last half of the nineteenth century, Jewish residents comprised a tiny fraction of Toronto's population and were relatively ineffectual in the life of the city (Shapiro, 1984; Sack, 1965). Starting in the 1880s, Jews began to emigrate to Canada to flee the pogroms and virulent, rabid anti-Semitism they experienced in Russia and Eastern Europe. By 1901, over 3,000 Jews resided in Toronto, which had a population of over 200,000. And for the first time, Eastern Europeans numerically exceeded the older, established Jewish community of English and German nationals (Speisman, 1985).

Toronto had been and would continue to be for several more decades in the twentieth century staunchly conservative, British, and mostly Protestant, though certainly not a homogeneous society. At the turn of the century, over 90% of the population listed their ethnic origins as either British or Irish, and this proportion would remain over 80% until after World War II (Piva, 1979). Of all the non-British Isles minority groups in Toronto at this time, the Jewish community would eventually become the largest single religio-ethnic minority in the city. In 1907, there were between 8,000 and 10,000 Jews. Two years later, there were approximately 15,000 Jews. By 1911, the number exceeded 18,000, a decade later it almost doubled, and through the 1930s, there were over 50,000 Jews (Speisman, 1979).

In addition to this phenomenal rate of growth, most of Toronto's Jews in the first two decades of the twentieth century invariably resided in one small area known as St. John's Ward, or simply the Ward. Throughout the nineteenth century and first half of the twentieth century, the Ward had been mostly an eyesore, especially for a city whose image earned it the name "Toronto the good, the city of churches." The local poorhouse, the red-light district, "[l]ittle frame cottages, junk wagons, pit privies, lean-tos in back lanes, open drains, the sweet smell of rotting plaster and manure, sweatshops, malnourished children, families crowded together—all were descriptive of The Ward" (Kluckner, 1988, p. 134). Before and after World War I, numerous reports from the City Health Department were prepared to document the appalling living conditions in the Ward. Most attempts at reform failed miserably (Bureau of Municipal Research, 1918). Yet in this slumlike enclave, one also could find hospitals, a private school, factories, public schools, theatres, a YWCA, a playground, the city's armories, a registry office, numerous churches and synagogues, and city hall (Dennis, 1995).

Despite the impoverished residential conditions, along with several notable institutions and businesses, the Ward became known as a Jewish neighborhood until the end of World War I, "a community within a community"

(Gillis & Whitehead, 1971). Jews owned shops, cafes, theatres, restaurants, and bookstores. They were bakers, butchers, grocers, tailors, shoemakers, blacksmiths, carpenters, peddlers, rag pickers, and factory workers (Harney & Troper, 1975). There were synagogues and shteibls for Russians, Romanians, Poles, Lithuanians, Ukranians, and several others, and each group practiced its religious rites according to traditions from the old country. In the Ward of this period, one could find a Yiddish press, Jewish religious and secular schools, Zionist organizations, social clubs, mutual benefit societies, a Jewish day nursery, and a free dispensary. As Speisman (1985) vividly observes, "by 1911, the Ward had achieved the apex of its development as a Jewish area and had generated enough inertia to maintain itself as a self-contained community, even as many of its residents were economically capable of leaving of it. The presence of Jewish institutions, retail shops, and other amenities, coupled with the secure Yiddish-speaking atmosphere, was a powerful cohesive (p. 118).

Of all the various cultural practices that Toronto's adult Jews engaged in during this period, the majority did not participate in sport and athletics. On one level, this is understandable. Necessity demanded that newcomers secure inexpensive housing and find steady employment. For many, religious demands precluded working on Saturdays (Driedger, 1996). Many, therefore, eked out a meager living as independent businessmen, usually as peddlers, scrap collectors, and rag pickers (Speisman, 1985). Athletics was neither a priority for, nor did it arouse even a mild interest among, most adult immigrant Jews.

On another level, one would expect sport to have some impact on the Jewish community, because it was in close proximity to sporting elements in Toronto, and the city had a well established sporting heritage (Kidd, 1996; Metcalfe, 1987). Clubs began to form in the early 1800s, and by the end of the nineteenth century, all major sports of the period were well represented. Toronto had a professional baseball team in the International League in the 1890s, professional rowing had existed since mid-century, and horse racing had always been popular (Middleton, 1934). Amateur sport prevailed in such activities as cricket, lacrosse, ice hockey, skating, curling, yachting, canoeing, ice boating, golf, tobogganing, swimming, track and field, basketball, rugby, and football. Many of these sports were organized into clubs, and they were offered at public schools, colleges, including the University of Toronto, and local YMCAs and YWCAs. Arguably, Canada's first individual sports hero was Toronto's Ned Hanlan, who dominated international singles sculls rowing for almost a decade in the 1870s and 1880s (West, 1967). The city newspapers covered major sporting events, reported on league play, and highlighted some of the best known local athletes and teams that were ranked nationally and internationally. Finally, Toronto offered citizens numerous parks, playgrounds, beaches, and recreational facilities to enjoy leisure outings (Glazebrook, 1971). It would take some time before the majority of Jewish immigrants recognized the many sporting and leisure opportunities available in Toronto. On the other hand, many of their children were quickly immersed in athletic pursuits, and some at the highest levels.

The first organized sports for Jewish youth appeared as an outgrowth of various social and cultural clubs and societies that emerged in the early part of the twentieth century. Organizations such as the Judean Literary and Debating Society, established in 1901, attempted to bridge the gap between members of the old and new Jewish communities, those outside the Ward, and those within it. At about the same time and to combat deliquency in the Ward, the Young Men's Hebrew Progressive Club offered some rudimentary athletics. Perhaps the first exclusive sports entity was the Judean Athletic Club, formed in 1908. Six years later, the Hebrew Literary and Athletic Club was organized. Both clubs offered young people the opportunity to play baseball, rugby, basketball, and hockey. In 1909, Jewish newsboys organized their own rugby team and were frequently successful against Irish teams (Speisman, 1979). Unfortunately, many Jewish youth found these clubs and their athletic programs less desirable than those offered by other local institutions. Speisman (1979) writes, "by 1912 the *Jewish Times* was complaining that all across the continent Jews were forming YMHAs on the model of the YMCA, while in Toronto although 'hundreds of Jewish young men are at present members of non-Jewish athletic associations' for want of Jewish facilities, no one would take the initiative in founding a Jewish Y. Many became members of the YMCA, despite reports that its membership fees partially financed proselytizing among the Jews. The *Times* maintained that a Jewish Y would not only combat delinquency and the missions, but would also attract those for whom the synagogue had no appeal" (p. 183).

These types of complaints led the YMHA Benevolent Society to spearhead a campaign to organize an athletic centre and club meeting rooms, to be called the YMHA Institute. Unfortunately, in-fighting broke out among several groups; each tried to define the functions of the proposed building. Since the new multipurpose facility was to have served athletic, social, educational, and Zionist groups, securing the cooperation of all interested parties was essential. Not only were there ideological and pragmatic conflicts over this issue, but the wealthiest members in the Jewish community, whose support was absolutely necessary, were not ready to underwrite this venture. All of these difficulties eventually led to a collapse of support for the project in 1913. Several young people's groups then formed a loose organization called the Hebrew Association of Young Men's and Young Women's Clubs. This body would be the nucleus of Toronto's YM-YWHA, which would not be established until the early to mid-1920s (Speisman, 1979).

In addition to Jewish clubs and societies where youth could engage in sporting activities, various playgrounds in the city provided athletic and recreational opportunities. In the northern portion of the Ward, the Elizabeth Street playground had reasonably good facilities for recreation, but there was a lack of space to meet the district's needs. The Bureau for Municipal Research, reporting specifically on this playground in 1918, complained, "Children can at all times be found playing in the streets, lanes and less healthful surroundings and with a greater liability to accident than if there was adequate playground accommodation . . . we find the youths of the district, instead of seeking healthful exercise, continuing to haunt the main thoroughfares where there is the lure of the picture shows, and other cheap amusements, with the consequent loss of physical stamina and vigor, not to mention moral effect," (pp. 61, 63). Virtually every playground fielded a baseball or softball team as well as several other sports such as basketball and soccer. Playground leagues were created, and citywide competitions were held between various ethnic neighborhoods. In addition to the YMCA, where Jews participated in athletics, playgrounds offered another sport setting where Jewish youth interacted with Gentiles. Playground sport was fierce and intense, since ethnic pride was as much at stake as was winning the contest. Members of so-called Jewish teams forged lifelong bonds and friendships and endured together not only the physical challenges created by opponents but sometimes their anti-Semitic slurs. Perhaps the most famous neighborhood club in Toronto originated from the Elizabeth Street playground, and for much of its early history, many Jewish athletes filled the rosters of its numerous teams.

The Lizzies teams came into existence in 1913, and by 1917, they began earning championship titles in baseball and basketball under legendary coach and playground supervisor Bob Abate. For 49 years, Abate was a mentor to downtown athletes of all ethnic persuasions, and he is revered by many to this day (Lizzies Old Timers Association, 1993). With the support of Toronto's long-time director of playgrounds, Sy Armstrong, Abate not only guided the lives of thousands of young downtown athletes in sport but helped launch the careers of many of his players, both in and out of sport. Goody Rosen of the Brooklyn Dodgers and Alex Levinsky of the Toronto Maple Leafs were two of Abate's most famous players to reach the professional ranks. Dr. Jack Cooper recalled how Abate helped him gain admission to the University of Toronto's dental school by securing a letter from Sy Armstrong (personal communication, June 19, 1997). Inner-city neighborhood playground teams such as the Lizzies were therefore integral to the lives of many ethnic youth on many different levels. They also were the sites where Jewish youth became acquainted with non-Jews in clearly defined terms while developing a strong sense of identity among themselves. However, this process of identity formation was not always so unambiguous.

While the Ward was home to most of Toronto's Jewish population prior to World War I, other immigrant groups, such as the Italians, Chinese, Poles, Finns, and Ukrainians, also inhabited the neighborhood, but in much smaller numbers (Harney & Troper, 1975). Non-Jewish immigrant children thus played in the same playgrounds and sometimes on the same teams as Jewish youth. Because they shared common living space and immigrant status, many of these children recognized few differences among their peers, as opposed to Anglo-Canadian youth, who mostly had a disdain for non-British immigrants. Playground sport promoted these mixed sentiments and attitudes under informal and formal conditions, and among all age groups, from children to young adults. Evidence of these conditions can be gleaned from the extensive photograph collection compiled by the City of Toronto Parks Department for this era. Two notable sets of photos depict the Elizabeth Street playground in August 1913 and a City Park Senior Baseball Championship game between Osler and the Judeans in September 1915. These photos vividly portray the range of sports and activities in the playgrounds available to Jewish youth and the sites of interaction with the larger Anglo-Canadian community and Gentile immigrant children. In the following, Harney and Troper (1975) describe part of Toronto's sports scene prior to the 1920s, as well as the generational tensions such involvement created for Jewish parents and youngsters:

> Baseball and basketball were the games of the public schools, playgrounds, and the settlement houses. Boxing, while it went on at the YMCA and elsewhere, lived in a twilight between the practice of manliness and the hint of corruption in downtown gyms and clubs. Jewish parents had to make a transition from seeing the kid on the sandlot as a good-for-nothing who should have been helping his father in the shop or practising on his violin to acknowledging the importance of sports to their children. (p. 198)

Perhaps one institution that legitimized the aforementioned transition and was beyond the control and influence of Jewish parents was education. The public school system and, to some extent, universities supplied another means for Jewish youngsters to learn about and experience sport, which also became a focal point of acculturation. Although military drill and rote exercises comprised much of the physical training programs in schools at the turn of the century, a number of sports were soon accepted as both curricular and extracurricular activities. Basketball, football, track and field, baseball, soccer, rugby, and other sports could all be found in the public school system. Since most Jewish youngsters attended public schools on a full-time basis, rather than Jewish religious or secular schools, they likely experienced sport as a classroom subject or on school teams. In this setting, greater integrative forces were at work, since Jews and Gentiles not only played together, but they also learned and studied together.

In the first two decades of the twentieth century, then, there were two main points of entry for Jews to experience sport. In some instances, specific Jewish sport organizations were created to fulfill a need for athletics, as well as to combat delinquency and proselytizing. In other circumstances, public and nonprofit institutions such as the YMCA, schools, and playgrounds provided Jews with an opportunity to engage in athletics. Each of these settings produced different effects upon the level and degree of maintaining one's Jewish identity. Associations created by Jewish adults of the older community for immigrant Jewish youth were directly trying to combat forces of assimilation and establish strong communal ties among their charges. Neighborhood playgrounds, schools, and non-Jewish institutions were more complex sites of interaction where Jewish identity usually was either strengthened or compromised.

In each of these social spheres, however, sport definitely transformed immigrant Jewish life. It called into question one's religious and cultural values, introduced and extolled new ideals such as competition and physical prowess, demanded that one experience novel forms of interaction with the non-Jewish community, and created tension within families who were mostly trying to survive and make ends meet. If these were the general conditions of sport and Jewish life in Toronto in the first two decades of the twentieth century, the 1920s and 1930s provided numerous opportunities for highly talented Jewish athletes to emerge and enjoy success in sport. In the following, the important contributions of two prominent Jewish stars, one from each decade, will be discussed.

While the Ward was the first area of refuge in Toronto for most Eastern European immigrant Jews, those who could began moving to other neighborhoods to the west and northwest of the Ward (Harney & Troper, 1975). This inner-city migration was especially prevalent after World War I and thus expanded the area where playgrounds and school yards would have an impact on Jewish youth. In the ethnically mixed neighborhoods between Spadina Avenue and Grace Street and College and Bloor Streets, which housed many Jewish families, some top Jewish athletes and teams competed in industrial and senior leagues in hockey, basketball, and baseball. As a result of these new concentrated areas, many Jewish athletes also were featured on some of the best school teams in the city, especially Harbourd, Central Tech, and Jarvis Collegiates. By the mid-1920s, the reconstituted YM-YWHA opened a new athletic facility on Brunswick Avenue near College Street, and this became the home of many city and provincial championship teams and athletes in a number of sports. Other talented individuals were able to join various elite amateur clubs or rise to become premier stars in amateur and professional sports. In Toronto, during the 1920s, no one exemplified these opportunities and trends more than Fanny "Bobbie" Rosenfeld.

Rosenfeld was born in Russia in 1903, and her family emigrated to Canada one year later. They lived in Barrie, Ontario, about 60 miles north of Toronto, and this is where Rosenfeld learned and refined her athletic skills. When her family moved to Toronto in 1922, she joined industrial teams in women's hockey, softball, and basketball. That same year, her softball team competed near Barrie in a sporting carnival. Her teammates coaxed her into a 100-yard dash event, which she won, unknowingly defeating the reigning

Canadian champion. The sports director of the Canadian National Exhibition happened to be there, and assured her that she would no longer be an obscure sports figure.

This event marked Rosenfeld's entry into high-level competitive women's sport. She worked for Patterson's Chocolate Factory as a stenographer, but the company also served as her sponsor in almost all of her sporting endeavors. She also joined the prestigious Toronto Ladies Athletic Club and participated in upper-class activities such as golf and tennis. She won the Toronto ladies singles tennis title in 1924. Although Rosenfeld played a myriad of sports, both team and individual, winter and summer, she gained her greatest fame in track and field. In 1925, she held the world record for the 100-yard dash with teammate Rosa Grosse. In the same year, at the Ontario ladies track and field championships, she won the points title for Patterson's Athletic Club as its only entrant. Her remarkable feats that day included first place in the discus, the shotput, the 220-yard dash, the low hurdles, and the long jump. She finished second in the javelin and 100-yard dash. Rosenfeld also competed in international competitions, mainly against U. S. teams.

While engaged in track and field pursuits, Rosenfeld played on championship teams in basketball, hockey, and lacrosse, and she also speed skated. Her YWHA women's basketball team, for example, won the eastern Canadian title, only to be defeated for the national championship by the legendary Edmonton Grads. The highlight of her athletic career, however, came when she was a member of Canada's Olympic women's track and field team, which competed in the Amsterdam Summer Games of 1928. Rosenfeld won a gold medal as leadoff runner in the 4×100 meter relay, a silver medal in the disputed 100-meter race, and placed fifth in the controversial 800-meter event. After her athletic career ended, she was a sports reporter for the *Globe & Mail* between 1936 and 1957, and she wrote a popular sports column. In 1950, Rosenfeld was named Canada's woman athlete of the first half-century (Rosenberg, 1993). Further sport opportunities existed in the 1930s, as Jewish athletes and teams became some of the most prominent, both locally and nationally. For example, the Yolles-Herzl softball team won the Jewish Senior League and Toronto championship title in 1930. Bill Engel, from nearby Oshawa, was a well-known sprinter who competed at the Maccabi Games, held in Prague, Czechoslovakia, in 1933. Harry Sniderman was a local sensation in several sports in the early 1930s and sometimes was featured in the *The Jewish Standard*, Toronto's Anglo-Jewish newspaper. Jack Sillen competed out of the YMHA and became an Ontario amateur wrestling champion in 1936. In professional sport, Alex Levinsky, a grandson of a founder of one of the city's earliest synagogues in Toronto, was a star forward for the Toronto Maple Leafs (Abella, 1990). These are just a few of the people who attained a noticable measure of success in sport. Perhaps the most famous individual Jewish athlete of this decade, however, was Canadian boxing champion Sammy Luftspring.

Luftspring was born in the Ward in 1916 to religiously devout Polish immigrant parents. Although his father was a shoemaker by trade, the family operated a home bootlegging and drinking establishment, a risky, illegal but steady business during Toronto's prohibition years. In 1920, the family moved west of the Ward to the Kensington Market district in the Spadina-College area, where Luftspring was introduced to a number of sports, including boxing. At age 9, his father took him to his first smoker at the Leonard Athletic Club to watch the main event between Harry Katz and future Brooklyn Dodger great Goody Rosen. Of Katz's victory, Luftspring would write, "He was king, that's the only way I can describe it. A Jewish king who had won his crown with the force of his fists. And I wanted so much to take his place that I could taste it. That was it, for me. That was the night I decided on my life goal. I, too, would take a shot at becoming a king" (Luftspring & Swarbrick, 1975, p. 34).

One year later, Luftspring began his upward climb to become welterweight boxing champion of the world by fighting in local clubs and arenas. He trained at the Leonard Athletic Club, the Central YMCA, and the Elm Grove Athletic Club, and he officially registered as an amateur in 1932. He made his big-time debut at Maple Leaf Gardens on April 24 of that year, and for the next four years, he fought in and out of Toronto in the lighter divisions under the management of his uncle. By 1936, he was considered by most to be the best welterweight in Canada and a likely representative in that division for the upcoming Berlin Olympics. After a heartfelt appeal from his parents, Luftspring declined the invitation to attend the Olympic trials in Montreal, along with fellow Olympic contender Ben ("Baby Yak") Yackubowitz. In their letter to the *Toronto Globe* on July 7, 1936, they wrote:

> It is a matter of keen disappointment to us to turn down the opportunity of trying for the great honor and privilege of making a place on the Canadian team. However, we have gone into the question very carefully with our families and friends in the community, and find that we cannot act differently from what we have decided. . . . We are making a personal sacrifice in refusing the chance, and we are sure that all true Canadian sportsmen will appreciate that we would have been very low to hurt the feelings of our fellow-Jews by going to a land that would exterminate them if it could. (Luftspring & Swarbrick, 1975, p. 85)

With these prophetic words, Luftspring and Baby Yack accepted an invitation from *The Daily Worker,* a communist newspaper, to attend the International Workers' Olympics, the antifascist games in Barcelona, Spain. The entire Jewish community, it seemed, including the Canadian Jewish Congress, supported this cause by raising funds and giving the two dissident boxers and their chaperone, Harry Sniderman, a parade-like send-off at Union Station. Despite these efforts, and just as the Torontonians arrived at the Spanish border that

July, the Barcelona Games never came off, due to the start of the Spanish Civil War. Upon his return from this unsuccessful trip, Luftspring turned professional and ended an amateur career of well over 100 bouts.

After winning his first seven professional matches, Luftspring fought for the welterweight championship of Canada against Gordon Wallace of Vancouver in April 1937. He lost the bout in a split decision and was heavily criticized by the Toronto press for the remainder of the year. In early 1938, he left Toronto to seek his fortune in New York, boxing's Mecca, under the management of Madison Square Garden matchmaker Al Weill. Later that year, in October, he returned to Canada to capture the national title from his old nemesis and fellow Torontonian, Frank Genovese. By 1939, Luftspring was ranked around third in the world in the welterweight division, and he was just a few fights away from a world title match. Unfortunately, all of his hopes and aspirations came to an abrupt end in May 1940. In a final tune-up bout against Steve Belloise, before seeking the world championship, Luftspring was accidently caught by a thumb to his left eye that later could not be saved (Luftspring & Swarbrick, 1975).

So ended the career of Sluggin' Sammy Luftspring, the most famous Jewish boxer that Canada has ever produced. He was a great hero for many in the Toronto Jewish community during the 1930s, because he proudly and publicly adhered to traditional Jewish values while he achieved success in a tough and dangerous sport. In addition to great Toronto athletes such as Rosenfeld and Luftspring, with whom many Jews could closely identify and take pride in, there was a shocking event in the early 1930s that brought Jews of every persuasion together. Surprisingly enough, an athletic competition set the stage for one of the ugliest episodes in Toronto history.

Organized anti-Semitism had not been an issue in Toronto until Hitler's rise to power in Germany in 1933. Although discrimination in employment and housing had existed and exclusionary practices were in force in some social and sporting circles, these were mainly episodic incidents. During 1933, however, more daring and open displays of anti-Semitism began to appear. This was most notable in the beach areas just east of the city, where downtown Jews often would picnic. In the summer, local thugs from one of these beaches formed the Balmy Beach Swastika Club. Their goal was to keep "obnoxious visitors" from the beach, but most simply wanted a pretext to vent their anti-Semitic sentiments. In July, there were some minor clashes between Jews and non-Jews. The club prominently displayed a swastika, Jewish women were harrassed on neighboring streets, and youth members would drive by Jewish homes, throw garbage on their lawns, and shout Nazi slogans. The Swastika Club downplayed these activities, and the police essentially ignored the matter, much to the horror of Jewish citizens (Driedger, 1996; Speisman, 1979).

Events came to a head in early August, when the club held a dance in a building posted with swastikas. About 50 Jewish youth tried to take matters into their own hands by storming the dance, but somehow the club had been tipped off and took the signs down, and the police had been called in before any violence erupted. City officials finally condemned the activities of the Swastika Club and banned the public display of swastikas. Newspapers basically reacted by saying that such episodes would blow over, and that there was no large-scale anti-Semitic movement in Toronto. Jews were told by their leaders not to pursue the matter and to avoid any further altercations. Two weeks later, however, serious violence erupted (Levitt & Shaffir, 1987).

On August 16, at Christie Pits, a playground in the northwest area of the downtown core, thousands were watching the first game in a championship baseball series between Jewish and non-Jewish teams. A small group at the very edge of the crowd unfurled and paraded a huge white sheet with a swastika on it, shouting "Heil Hitler" (White, 1993). Later, after the game, they painted a large swastika on one of the park buildings and admitted that they wanted to exclude Jews from the park. A few days later, while thousands attended the final game in the series, the same group brought out the same sheet. This time a gang of Gentile youths carrying baseball bats and lead pipes ran into the crowd assaulting people.

In light of the beach incidents earlier, when news of the attack reached the Jewish neighborhood, Jewish toughs assembled at the YMHA and quickly were brought to the Pits by truck. For 6 hours a full-scale race riot raged in the streets of Toronto. Fights broke out, serious injuries were incurred, Jewish shops were vandalized, and many Jews did not leave their homes for fear of being attacked. The police were slow to react and contained the riot by not letting people into the areas where skirmishes were still occurring (Speisman, 1979). Following the riot at Christie Pits, blatant anti-Semitic provocations disappeared, and Jews became more vigilant and organized in matters relating to their rights as citizens.

While all of the diverse influences and consequences of immigrant Jewish participation in sport, as situated first in the Ward neighborhood and later in other areas of Toronto in the first half of the twentieth century, have not been fully recounted here, as well as a lack of detailed discussion of other sport institutions that Jews either created or were associated with, several salient patterns of involvement can be drawn thus far. First, Jewish immigrant adults were least involved in sporting pursuits, though established members of the older community did found several exclusive Jewish sports clubs. There was a clear acknowledgment then that sport could sustain Jewish links among youth who were exposed to the strong missionary movement in Toronto and who often engaged in delinquent acitivities. Due to internal strife among several Jewish societies and clubs, attempts to create a central organization, a YMHA, would not be realized until the early to mid-1920s.

Second, during this period where no Jewish Y existed, Jewish youth and young adults satisfied their athletic interests in other ways. Many favored the

YMCA, much to the dismay of community leaders and the Jewish press. Others relied on playground teams and leagues, and most engaged in sport through various levels of education. In these settings, Jews interacted more closely with their non-Jewish neighbors, and this may have had a double effect in terms of negotiating their identities. On the one hand, Jews were exposed to and likely shared common struggles and hardships faced by other ethnic groups in a new environment. On the other hand, they still felt a sense of security and familiarity among those around them who had similar origins, language, faith, and family structures. In these constant and dynamic adjustments to urban life through sports, Jews had to develop several streams of trust relationships, had to learn about living in a polyethnic society, and had to deal with differing attitudes about group coherence within their own enthnocultural sphere (Harney, 1985).

As for the third group of Jewish athletes who became elite performers nationally and internationally, most were heroes in the eyes of the Toronto Jewish community. These athletic stars moved farthest from the spatial and temporal boundaries of their ethnic neighborhoods, yet virtually none denied their Jewishness. Some, like Rosenfeld, practiced what urban historian Robert Harney (1985) calls "weekend ethnicity—returning to the immigrant areas for religious services, food supply, haircut, or family visits only on the weekend" (p. 18). Issues related to group coherence and Jewish identity challenged these athletes most. By having to move in Gentile circles to fulfill their athletic aspirations, many faced defining personal decisions. In the case of Rosenfeld, her family strongly objected to her proposed marriage to a non-Jewish athlete. Luftspring also was influenced by his family when he publicly expressed his political views and refused to go to the Canadian Olympic trials. Some elite Jewish athletes in Toronto therefore experienced public and private levels of tension between their retention of traditional values and Jewish identity and their giving in to forces of assimilation.

Urban neighborhood life for Eastern European Jewish immigrants and their children in Toronto changed dramatically over the first four decades of the twentieth century. The Jewish community existed in three relatively close neighborhoods, beginning in the heart of the downtown core and moving westward and to the north. As newly formed organizations and institutions were established to deal with employment, health, housing, religious, and political and artistic needs and interests, athletics also entered into the mix of cultural activities that Jews took up. But the manifest and subtle purposes that sport served in the Jewish community were varied. Sport values were viewed as foreign and a threat, yet they also were utilized to affirm and inculcate positive sentiments. With no deep historical roots, interest in sports competed with religious practices and beliefs, family kinships, career aspirations, and retaining one's Jewish identity and status in the community. On the other hand, athletics strengthened personal and collective Jewish bonds by forming Jewish teams, leagues, clubs, and a YM-YWHA and by venerating local Jewish athletic heroes. Many individual Jewish youngsters likely experienced these strains created by sport, as did this author, who grew up in Toronto two generations later. Having a love of sport, being Jewish, and living in a polyethnic city produced a confluence of ideals, symbols, meanings, and perceptions, not only about one's own religio-ethnic identity but also about one's place among others.

REFERENCES

Abella, I. (1990). *A coat of many colours: Two centuries of Jewish life in Canada.* Toronto: Lester & Orpen Dennys.

Belkin, S. (1966). *Through narrow gates: A review of Jewish immigration, colonization, and immigrant aid work in Canada (1840–1940).* Montreal: Canadian Jewish Congress and the Jewish Colonization Association.

Bureau of Municipal Research. (1918, December). *What is the 'the Ward' going to do with Toronto?* Toronto: Bureau of Municipal Research [City of Toronto Archives, SC3 E8 Box 1 File 5].

Dennis, M. (1995, October). Private landlords and redevelopment: The Ward in Toronto, 1890–1920. *Urban History Review/Revue d'histoire urbaine, 24(1),* 21–35.

Driedger, L. (1991). *The urban factor.* Toronto: Oxford University Press.

Driedger, L. (1996). *Multi-ethnic Canada: Identities and inequalities.* Toronto: Oxford University Press.

Elazar, D. J., & Waller, H. M. (1990). *Maintaining consensus: The Canadian Jewish polity in the postwar world.* Lanham, MD: University Press of America.

Gillis, A. R., & Whitehead, P. C. (1971). Halifax Jews: A community within a community. In J. L. Elliott (Ed.), *Immigrant groups* (pp. 84–94). Scarborough, ON: Prentice Hall of Canada.

Glazebrook, G. P. deT. (1971). *The story of Toronto.* Toronto: University of Toronto Press.

Harney, R. F. (1985). Ethnicity and neighbourhoods. In R. F. Harney (Ed.), *Gathering place: Peoples and neighbourhoods of Toronto, 1834–1945* (pp. 1–24). Toronto: Multicultural History Society of Ontario.

Harney, R. F., & Troper, H. (1975). *Immigrants: A portrait of the urban experience, 1890–1930.* Toronto: Van Nostrand Reinhold.

Kidd, B. (1996). *The struggle for Canadian sport.* Toronto: University of Toronto Press.

Kluckner, M. (1988). *Toronto the way it was.* Vancouver, BC: Whitecap Books.

Levine, P. (1992). *From Ellis Island to Ebbets Field: Sport and the American Jewish experience.* New York: Oxford University Press.

Levitt, C. H., & Shaffir, W. (1987). *The riot at Christie Pits.* Toronto: Lester & Orpen Dennys.

Lizzies Old Timers Association. (1993). *10th anniversary program guide*. Toronto: Department of Parks and Recreation.

Luftspring, S., & Swarbrick, B. (1975). *Call me Sammy*. Scarborough, ON: Prentice Hall of Canada.

McGahan, P. (1986). *Urban sociology in Canada* (2nd ed.). Toronto: Butterworths.

Metcalfe, A. (1987). *Canada learns to play: The emergence of organized sport, 1807–1914*. Toronto: McClelland and Stewart.

Middleton, J. E. (1934). *Toronto's 100 years*. Toronto: The Centennial Committee.

Pira, M. (1979). *Condition of the working class in Toronto, 1900–21*. Ottawa: University of Ottawa Press.

Postal, B., Silver, J., & Silver, R. (1965). *Encyclopedia of Jews in Sport*. New York: Bloch.

Riess, S. A. (1991). *City games: The evolution of American urban society and the rise of sports*. Urbana and Chicago: University of Illinois Press.

Rosenberg, D. (1993, May). *Fanny "Bobbie" Rosenfeld: Canada's female athlete of the first half-century*. Paper presented at the meeting of the North American Society for Sport History, Albequerque, NM.

Sack, B. G. (1965). *History of the Jews in Canada* (R. Novek, Trans.). Montreal: Harvest House.

Shapiro, S. M. (1984, Spring–Summer). The rise of the Toronto Jewish community, the reminiscences of S. M. Shapiro. *Polyphony, 6(1)*, 59–63.

Speisman, S. A. (1979). *The Jews of Toronto: A history to 1937*. Toronto: McClelland & Stewart.

Speisman, S. A. (1985). St. John's shtetl: The Ward in 1911. In R. F. Harney (Ed.), *Gathering place: Peoples and neighbourhoods of Toronto, 1834–1945* (pp. 107–120). Toronto: Multicultural History Society of Ontario.

Tulchinsky, G. (1992). *Taking root: The origins of the Canadian Jewish community*. Toronto: Lester & Orpen Dennys.

West, B. (1967). *Toronto*. Toronto: Doubleday Canada.

White, R. (1993). *Too good to be true: Toronto in the 1920s*. Toronto: Dundurn Press.

9

Urban Sanctuary

Youth Culture in a Recreation Drop-in Center

Brian Wilson and Phil White

> Downtown Toronto was engulfed by a mob of young marauders who
> stormed along Yonge St. last night in an orgy of looting, vandalism and
> violence. As hundreds of rioters—of all colours—surged north on Yonge,
> police were pelted with rocks and eggs, hundreds of windows smashed and
> stores looted.
> —Duffy, Hall, & DeMara, "Metro police, mob clash on Yonge St."

This uprising, coined the "Yonge Street riots" of 1992, developed both from
an organized, peaceful protest of the acquittal of four Los Angeles police officers in the trial of the Rodney King case and a death by shooting of a black
man at the hands of Metro Toronto police. Most police sources, media accounts, and sociologists of youth suggested that the incident was not only connected to racial issues but also to restlessness and anger among youth of all
races (Mathews, 1993; Walker, 1992). More than a mass-mediated moral
panic, the "Yonge Street Riots" were widely interpreted as symptomatic of
broader perceptions, that for many young Canadians, life in the 1990s was a
struggle (Mathews, 1993).

In the spring and summer of 1996, concerns about youth violence were
amplified in southern Ontario by a series of news stories reporting "acts of violence" in schools, in shopping malls, and on the streets (Hahn, 1996; Nolan,
1996). For example, the following introductory statement is typical of recent
articles on youth violence:

> Reports of violence have filled the news recently and juvenile crime is
> on the rise. The number of adolescents charged with various types of
> assault, robbery, stabbing of other teens, manslaughter, and shootings
> have more than doubled since 1986. (Farah, 1996, p. A9)

153

Evidence supporting these claims of escalation is ambiguous and largely anecdotal (Mathews, 1993, pp. 9–10; see also Tanner, 1996, p. 120). Statistics on youth crime during the period 1992–1993 taken from the Canadian Center for Justice Statistics "showed a 9 percent increase in violent crime over the previous year," although careful scrutiny shows that two thirds of this increase in crimes "was due to greater reporting of minor assaults, such as fights and scuffles" (Visano, 1996, p. 152, cited in the *Ottawa Citizen*, December 10, 1994). Despite this ambiguity, there have been frequent demands to revamp the "Young Offenders Act" in Canada in order to better "crack down" on youth crime.[1] Debates surrounding the effectiveness and cost of these "get tough," "zero tolerance" initiatives have raged (Visano, 1996). It is generally recognized that an alternative focus is necessary.

One area of debate has centered on the potential benefits of organized leisure for "at risk" youth.[2] Youth recreation drop-in programs promoting the "wellness" of youth have existed for years. Their efficacy, however, has coincidentally come under study as a result of these heightened concerns about youth violence, and the perceived need for prevention measures. Recent research focused on the positive impacts of youth recreation drop-in centers shows that these programs often provide youth with positive role models, give youth "something constructive to do," offer a sense of community, promote self-confidence and self-esteem, and enhance cultural awareness (Reid & Tremblay, 1994; see also Martinek, 1997; Offord & Knox, 1994). These applied studies suggest how youth "preventative" programs can be most effectively delivered to benefit youth "at risk" for violence or other deviant behaviors.

These studies do *not* address the creative ways that youth negotiate these surroundings and how youth culture operates in these recreation drop-in center environments. Although the "restless," "oppressed" youth "at risk" of the 1990s were perhaps better served by a recreation drop-in center than a gang, the dynamic of a youth "at risk" group in a relatively structured youth center environment is still highly charged. In this context, it makes sense that a relatively stable youth culture within youth-serving agencies would be central to its functionality. As Fine and Mechling (1993) suggest:

> [I]t is not enough that adults create an organization and program that provide strong identity structures for the young participant. Within a successful organization there grows an independent, *robust peer culture* [italics in original]. One of the paradoxes of organizational cultures is that the health of the organization depends equally on its official culture and its unofficial culture, which at times may be antagonistic to its official culture. The best laid plans of adults go awry if the group never coalesces to create and sustain a small group culture. (p. 143)

In this chapter, we report on findings from a study of youth culture in a successful recreation drop-in center. Drawing on symbolic interactionist approaches, we focus on the distinct characteristics of a youth peer culture, attending to the ways that "knowledge, beliefs, behaviors, and customs" are created, maintained, and referred to as the basis for interaction (Fine & Mechling, 1993). What follows is an overview of symbolic interactionist approaches to the study of organizations and lived experiences, and a discussion of interactionist and neo-Marxist approaches to youth subcultural activity. The methodological rationale and the key study findings are then provided, and a preliminary interpretation of the relationship between youth culture and youth "at risk" prevention initiatives in Canada is developed.

SYMBOLIC INTERACTIONISM AND THE STUDY OF YOUTH

> Symbolic interaction rests in the last analysis on three simple premises. The first premise is that human beings act toward things on the basis of the meanings they have for them. . . . The second premise is that the meaning of such things is derived from, or arises out of, the social interaction that one has with one's fellows. The third premise is that these meanings are handled in, and modified through, an interpretive process used by the person in dealing with the things he encounters. (Blumer, 1969, p. 2)

The study of group life in organizational settings (such as a youth drop-in center) is central to the symbolic interactionist perspective. In studying these social settings, certain conceptual themes help orient researcher interpetations. These include: (a) "organizational socialization"—the learning of relevant rituals, symbols, and ideologies for neophyte organization participants, and the organizational commitments by different participants; (b) the subjective meanings in organizations—the power struggles among organizational groups; (c) the "negotiated orders" within organizations—the pluralistic and sometimes contradictory aspects of the organization that may inspire resistant behaviors; (d) the individual's conception of "self" in the organizational setting—formed identities through interaction and participation; and (e) the informal aspects of the organization—the subtle and not so subtle patterns of interaction that exist, along with formal structures (see Lauer & Handel, 1983).

An interactionist approach to the study of youth (sub)cultural activity has been proposed by Prus (1996a) in a recent work focusing on setting a research agenda for the study of "adolescence as lived experience." Prus proposes a revised version of "generic" interactionist approaches to the study of group life—approaches emphasizing the "perspectives, activities, identities relationships, and commitments" that distinguish each subcommunity, subculture, or group within the broader community (p. 17). This position is consistent with Prus's focus on the trans-situational aspects of life worlds, or "generic social processes," which are defined as follows:

> *generic social processes* [italics in original] refer to the trans-situational elements of interaction; to the abstracted formulations of social behavior. Denoting parallel sequences of activity across diverse contexts, generic social processes highlight the emergent interpretive features of association. They focus our attention on the activities involved in "doing" or accomplishing group life. When researchers are mindful of generic, or trans-situational concepts, every piece of ethnographic research in any realm of human behavior can be used to generate insight into any other realm of human behavior. (Prus, 1994b, p. 395; see also Berger & Luckman, 1971; Garfinkel, 1967; Lofland, 1976; Prus, 1987, 1996b)

In this context, the study of youth is rooted in the notion that "the processes involved in the adolescent 'struggle for existence' are exceedingly parallel to those characterizing other people in other settings," despite some inevitable content variations between adolescent life worlds and the community at large (Prus, 1996a, p. 24).

Although Prus's approach is a useful and an encompassing analytic method for attaining rich, process-oriented understandings of subcultural groups, the perspective does not address the possibility that the "cultural" is a "site for struggle and conflict" (McRobbie, 1991, p. 36). As Donnelly and Young (1988) argue in their research on sport subcultures:

> such focused views of specific processes within subcultures should not lead researchers to consider subcultures in isolation from their structural, historical, and geographic contexts. Without such contextualization, subcultural research will remain an interesting appendage to more mainstream patterns of social development. (p. 238)

Research conducted in the 1970s at England's Center for Contemporary Cultural Studies in Birmingham effectively extended the study of youth subculture to encompass issues of class conflict and hegemony. In this context, the term *culture* encompassed more than just the "peculiar and distinctive 'way of life' of the group or class, the meanings, values and ideas embodied in institutions, in social relations, in systems of belief, in mores and customs, in the uses of objects and material life" (Clarke, 1976, p. 10). As McRobbie (1991, p. 36) suggested in her ethnographic study of working-class girls in a youth club, "culture" has more profound meanings related to class struggle:

> Culture is about the pre-structured but essentially expressive capacities of the group in question. The forms which this expressivity takes

are "maps of meaning" which summarize and encapsulate social and material life experiences. But these cultural artifacts or configurations are not created out of nothing. Individuals are born into what are already constructed sets of social meanings which can then be worked on, developed and even transformed. The cultural is always a site of struggle and conflict. Here hegemony may be lost or won; it is an arena for class struggle.

Willis's (1977) research on working-class males provided a similar analysis of class, gender, and youth.[3] His approach, while interactionist in its focus on the intricacies of the day-to-day activities for 12 working-class youths, provided a rich *critical* understanding of the symbolic meanings of these youths' activities. Willis argued that the group's "masculinist" attitudes and activities (e.g., sexist humor, vandalism, horseplay) were fatalistic attempts to resist their oppressive social conditions. This approach was similar to McRobbie's in attempting to clarify the ways that the symbolic relations and resistances embodied in youth subcultures potentially reinforce class hegemony. Updated versions of this thesis, while less focused on class struggle and more concerned with resistance "at the more mundane, micrological level of everyday practices" (McRobbie, 1994, p. 162; see also Willis, 1990), still transcend the narrower processual understandings central to interactionist approaches. Although our focus in this chapter is on providing a dense description of interaction processes within a social setting, we recognize that the issues raised by McRobbie and Willis are central to a comprehensive account of youth culture.[4] We address this latter issue in our further work on this topic (see Wilson & White, 1997).

Our focus here, then, is on detailed processual elements of youth interaction. As a point of departure, we use Fine's (1987) notion of "idioculture" to theorize the ways youth groups are created, sustained, and useful:

> Every group has its own lore or culture, which I term *idioculture* [italics in original]. Idioculture consists of a system of knowledge, beliefs, behaviors, and customs shared by members of an interacting group to which members can refer and that serve as the basis for further interaction. Members recognize that they share experiences, and these experiences can be referred to with the expectation that they will be understood by other members, thus being used to construct a social reality for its participants. This approach stresses the localized nature of culture, implying that it need not be part of a demographically distinct subgroup, but rather be a particularistic development of any group. (pp. 125–126)

Fine and Mechling (1993) have integrated this notion of idioculture with organizational theory in their work on youth-serving agencies—an approach that provides useful insights into factors predicting success in a youth-serving agency. This perspective distinguishes between the informal (e.g., youth peer culture—the idioculture) and the formal (adult leadership models, identity models) aspects of youth-serving organizations:

> whereas adult leaders have a great deal of control over the design and operation of the identity structures of a successful youth organization, adults will find that they have less control over the creation and sustenance of the idioculture of the group. Idiocultures provide young people (especially adolescents) with important, symbolic means of resistance against the dominance of the adult leaders' definitions of the organization. Along with a supportive culture, young people invent and share some elements of the idioculture as ways of taking power in an organization. These symbolic traditions of resistance may strengthen the organization, giving the young people the sense that they are equal participants in and, accordingly, have an equal stake in the culture of the group. No doubt, the adult leaders will be uncomfortable with elements of the idioculture invented or appropriated by young clients. Adults should tolerate these expressions of idioculture as much as possible, recalling that youth groups are competing against deviant gangs with their rich lore and tradition. (p. 137)

Embedded in the processes of the informal organization and the youth idioculture are issues of masculinity. In this regard, both Willis's ethnographic study *Learning to Labour*, described earlier, and Connell's (1991) research on Australian working-class males discuss ways that "masculinist" attitudes and activities are used to deal with oppression and alienation. Connell's research has particular relevance to the study, because his insights into the significance of different masculine rituals in contexts where male youth have minimal expectations of stable employment have parallels for males attending drop-in centers in Canada. Connell explains:

> [T]he labour market (rather than the labour process) and the state play a major part in the in framing the development of a "protest" masculinity, a stressed version of hegemonic masculinity, sustained as a collective practice in milieux such as bike clubs. But dramatic rejections of masculinity, as well as a low-keyed "complicit" masculinity, emerge from the same social context by different class/gender praxes. (p. 141)

Drawing on these conceptions of masculinity construction, we theorize and empirically study a culture of youth "at risk" in an urban drop-in center, focusing on *the ways masculinity operates within a "preventative" environment, the cultural and symbolic meaning of interactions within and between individuals and subgroups in the center (e.g., the ways that youth are "self-policing"), and the ways authority figures (who traditionally pose a symbolic "threat" to working-class males) are understood and approached by these youth.*

METHODOLOGY

To gain insight into the culture of youth in a low-income, recreation drop-in center, we used ethnographic techniques similar to those used to gain in-depth understandings of cultural groups (Humphreys, 1975; Liebow, 1967; Whyte, 1943), such as youth subcultures in Britain (Corrigan, 1979; Hall & Jefferson, 1976; McRobbie, 1977; Willis, 1977). Using predominantly observations and informal interviews with youth, our study of the "social setting" and "organization" of the youth center also draws on Lofland's and Lofland's (1984) approaches to the study of group meanings (rules, typifications), relationships (hierarchies, cliques), and roles (organizational, social, formal) through qualitative observation. This research is part of a larger, ongoing project that includes interviews with staff members and group interviews with youth, in addition to the informal interviews with youth and observational data provided here (see Wilson & White, 1997).

The research setting of an inner-city recreation drop-in center in southern Ontario was selected during a related study of youth "prevention" programs, which was part of a broader investigation of youth violence. The center's history as a well-attended, nonviolent facility located in a "relatively violent" urban area made it an optimal location to study a successful youth idioculture. Permission to spend time in the center to observe and interview participants was obtained from the supervisor of the facility, who subsequently informed other staff members about the project.

The center is adjacent to a major shopping mall located in a low-income, urban area.[5] The center has approximately 3,000 youth members, ages 4 to 24, although people of any age are welcome. Membership fees are inexpensive, in order to cater to low-income youth, ranging from $3 per year for youth under 12 to $6 per year for youth under 17 to $35 per year for older age groups. For youths unable to afford a membership, special "payment plans" allow them to pay when they can. The high membership rates from this low-income area are, in part, due to the low cost.

The center is equipped with a gymnasium, approximately the size of a regulation basketball court (with some space along one side for other activities, for bleachers, and for "hanging out"), a swimming pool, a weight room, a games room (with video games, pool table and ping pong table), a meeting room with VCRs, a crafts room, and a computer room. The center employs five full-time staff members, five part-time staff members, and several secondary school and college student volunteers. In addition to supervising the facilities, staff members organize programs and trips.

Although these facilities are open to all members most of the day (including adults and seniors), time slots in the evening—a "high traffic" time, particularly during school months—were assigned by age group. Only youth ages 13 years and under were allowed to use the gym from 6 P.M. to 8 P.M. The 8 P.M. to 10 P.M. slot was reserved for youth 13 and over.[6] These age divisions led to quite distinct groups of youth attending the center at different times in the evening, although the number of youth present at any given time varied considerably, depending on the time of year (variability was evident over the four months of observation at the center, from late summer to early winter). The number of participants in the gymnasium at any given time ranged from 8 to 50. There were, on average, 6 youths playing in the games room and 5 youths in the weight room (the time restrictions for age groups did not apply to the weight room) at any particular time. Although there was a group of youths considered "regulars," who came to the center three or more times each week, there also were a larger number considered "semi-regulars," who came to the center approximately one to two times each week.

Participant observation and *observation* usually took place in and around the gymnasium area, the center of activity during the 8 P.M. to 10 P.M. time slot. This allowed for a better focus on the "teen" group. Over the course of data collection, observations usually were made from the bleachers in the gymnasium, where basketball and ball hockey, played predominantly by males, were the most common activities. Often females would either sit or hit a volleyball back and forth on the side of the gymnasium. Although the females were involved in the center's activities in a general sense, they appeared marginal to the gymnasium idioculture during the 13 and older time slot.[7]

During data collection, a good rapport was developed between the researcher and some of the more outgoing youth. As the researcher spent time "hanging around," the youth seemed increasingly disinhibited about being observed (most did not appear to notice). The youth seemed unconcerned about what they did while being observed. In most cases, it seemed that the youth also were unconcerned about whether a staff member was present—the staff member's presence did not appear to influence their behavior. Seldom did I see a youth look around before doing something "mildly" deviant, like swear at or challenge another youth.

One youth in particular, who is well known and well liked in the center, took the time to "show off" the center to the researcher. He conducted a "guided tour" of the facility, during which he pointed out the trophies won by the teams representing the center.[8] He also led the researcher through a haunted house that was made by members at the center for the community to enjoy on Halloween. This youth, a 13-year-old white male, was a primary informant who provided key insights into the culture of the center.

Observation techniques were variable due to the diversity of the clientele and the flexibility of the social scenario at the center . Sometimes the researcher became a participant-observer when he was invited to join teams short of basketball players. The researcher also became involved in shooting games at other times when there were not enough players to make a basketball game. Participation in the Halloween haunted house also allowed the researcher to observe and experience an event that required youth subgroups to actively contribute to the center and work together beyond their day-to-day activities. Generally, observation sessions lasted 1 to 2 hours and were followed by writing field notes. Over the course of data collection, observations were made of approximately 80 members, with various informal discussions occurring with 10 of them. In total, the researcher visited the center 18 times over four months.

Although youth were not told "up front" what the researcher was doing at the center, the study was explained to those who asked (which happened on occasion), or to those with whom the researcher established a strong rapport. When the purpose of the research was explained to the youth, some offered insights into why they liked the center, while others were indifferent. These conversations usually took place when the researcher sat on the bleachers during long periods of observation. Members asked fewer questions when the gym was busy, which was fortunate, because these times usually provided the richest observational data. Conversely, conversations with the youth were more frequent during "dead" times (most common in the late summer and early fall). While observations were made throughout the center, most of the richest material was obtained in the gym, watching and listening to the subgroups interact. During busier times in the gym, observations were made when the bleacher area also was occupied by members who were watching the games or resting in between games, in addition to a small group of females who watched the males play. There also was an older group of youth (17 and older, for the most part) who worked out in the weight room and who sometimes joined in the games after their workout or sat in the bleachers to spectate.

The primary researcher, a 27-year-old adult white male, collected all of the empirical research at the center, with the second researcher, a 44-year-old white male, acting as a second coder. The researchers discussed findings and interpretations of data shortly after each fieldwork session. This process of conferring in the analytic process was intended to clarify and expose subjectivities and field note report and quotation bias.[9]

RESULTS AND ANALYSIS

The gym today was full, with many different groups of youth in different parts of the gym. There were about 30 youth in total. At one end of the basketball court there was the "cool" crowd of basketball

players (8 players, all male), the older (ages 13 to 16) and better players playing on one hoop. At the other end was the younger group of
basketball players playing on the other hoop (6 players, all male).
Across the middle of the court, the hockey players were shooting at a
net at the side of the gym. There were 5 males playing hockey. They
were playing rougher and "horsing around" as they usually did. This
did not affect the other games being played, except in a couple of instances. No conflict resulted. There were also youth shooting on the
side baskets. One of the center's staff was shooting baskets on a side
rim with a couple of younger kids. On another hoop, there were some
of the older youth (they were approximately 20 years old, again, all
male) who had been lifting weights and were shooting baskets. On the
bleachers there were some male basketball players resting and watching. There were 5 females (about 12 to 13 years old) talking and sometimes stepping out to the side of the court to hit a volleyball around.
(field notes, December 16, 1996)

An extraordinary diverse culture of youth coexisted in the youth center.
Over the course of the research, clear areas of cultural convergence emerged
that demonstrated how these groups successfully "got along" and at times "came
together." Although we have identified and emphasized three dominant areas
(see below) that relate to the "informal" organization of the center, they incor-
porate a multitude of interwoven processes and social practices characterizing
this group.

The *first* area of convergence was the informal "rules" that allowed this diverse youth culture to cohere. These included shared perspectives on acceptable
behavior, perspectives related to both inter- and intra-group relationships in the
center. The *second* area was the "informal" hierarchy that existed in the center,
within which negotiated identities and relationships could be sustained. The
third area included the different reasons youth "use" the center, the varying investments youth have in the center, and the extent to which youth have been
socialized into the center's idioculture.

Together, these intricate and sometimes contradictory perspectives, activities, identities, relationships, and commitments make up the idioculture of youth
that supports and characterizes life in this youth recreation drop-in center.

The "Conflict" Rules:
Diverse Youth Sharing Social Space

Although each coexisting group in the center had norm and codes governing
intra-group behavior, a set of unofficial rules understood by most of these
youth (regardless of group affiliation) allowed members to avoid or deal with

conflict. These rules generally were respected, despite the distinct play patterns characterizing each group:

> The hockey players often were rougher and more aggressive in their play and interactions than any of the other subgroups. [For example], the hockey players like shooting the ball at each other. Sometimes they do this when the other player isn't looking so it will "sting" the player when it hits them unexpectedly. They do this in a joking way, usually laughing about it. One incident happened today where the hockey player who was hit, picked up the ball (the player seemed sort of "pissed off" and embarrassed that his friends had "got him"), and from about 20 feet away threw the ball as hard as he could at the head of the player who shot it at him (he did not hit him). This kind of behavior just doesn't happen in the basketball group. The hockey players seem pretty careful not to "hit" anybody other than those in their own group, especially the other "major" group, the basketball players. Although some of the subgroups seem to get along well, the hockey players and some of the basketball players seem more like they just tolerate each other, never talking to each other, despite constant "contact." Usually they make special efforts to make sure the ball doesn't hit somebody. Apologies are not usually offered when the ball does get away. There was one instance where the hockey ball went into the basketball game. The hockey player stepped in trying to avoid any contact with the basketball players. He didn't apologize for having the ball go into the game. It was almost expected that [the] ball is going to go into their game every now and again. However, nobody became angry. Everybody seemed tolerant, and more than anything, more concerned with playing ball than arguing with each other or fighting. (field notes, December 16, 1996)

Occasionally the groups were less successful in sharing this social space, prompting individuals and groups involved to diffuse tension:

> [T]he one area of anticipated potential conflict was between the hockey players and the basketball players. Except for that they played in the same gym, [they] did not seem to have much in common. The hockey players seemed quite a bit older, most had longer hair and visible tattoos, and were all white. The basketball players had short hair or shaved heads, were a little bit younger, between 13 [and] 16, and were black and white playing together [older basketball players started coming in more often during the winter months]. When one of the kids was coming across the hockey side, the ball went near him and almost hit him in the leg (this was a youth who the staff at the center said had a history of problems, although he was "pretty good" now).

He turned toward the guy who he thought shot the ball and said, "fuck off." The youth stood and waited for a reaction from the other youth. The other youth gave him a look like "come on" or "get real." The youth who shot the ball then lifted up his hand and pointed his thumb to the other side of the gym. The other youth walked away, back to his friends on the other side of the gym. Nobody said anything, although it seemed like the guy who walked away looked kind of foolish. None of his friends gave him any positive feedback, or any feedback at all for that matter. (field notes, October 17, 1996)

In contrast to the macho norms of street gangs, in the cultural context of the center, the need to "save face" was rarely resolved through physically violent confrontation (the staff referred to a few instances that had occurred in the past, although no physical violence occurred during research sessions). If a problem did arise, it usually was not allowed to escalate to violence, at least partially because most members largely policed themselves, although the ameliorating influence of the adult leaders cannot be discounted.[10]

When conflicts did arise, usually they were precipitated by one group clearly deviating from the norms of the idioculture. For example, in one instance, a group allowed its activity to interfere with the action of another group. A group of younger youth (around ages 11 to 12—this observation was during an open gym time during Christmas holidays, when no age restrictions were in place) was having fun throwing a soccer ball at each other. The group's ball kept going onto the basketball court, where an older group was playing their own game. This disruption provoked a verbal "keep the fuckin' ball down in your end, you moron" from one of the older and more outspoken basketball players, which was sufficient to prevent the problem from recurring that day (field notes, December 30, 1996).

Generally, the gym remained relatively free of conflict, as long as each group did not allow its activity to "spill over" because a member was "being stupid." Members, in general, appeared to respect the rights of other members who were "doing something" in the center. They, pointedly, did not give positive feedback to anyone who was "fooling around" or "looking for" conflict. One youth explained to me why there was not much "trouble" in the center:

Kids who come in here, even if they do bad stuff other places, won't do it here. Here, everybody's doing something. Playing ball, swimming, lifting weights, whatever. They might smoke out front, but they won't break windows or anything. (interview, male youth "Rob," 13-year-old, September 26, 1996)

Any incidents that I saw in the gym where an individual was "acting up" and causing problems (which in all cases were youth who were "regulars" at the center) were mediated by the individual's friends, according to their group's subcultural rules.

> During a shoot-around session, one of the youth shot the hockey ball at the goalie when the goalie was turned around looking behind the net. The ball (a hard, orange hockey ball) hit the goalie in the back, where there was no padding. The youth who was [the] goalie became very angry at this, took off his goalie mask, and threw it at the youth that shot the ball. The goalie went over to the bench and nobody said anything. The youth that shot the ball didn't apologize, but he did go over to the goalie and said, "put your mask back on, let's play." By talking to him first and by "asking" to play again, the goalie appeared to cool off (and was ready to play again). This was a great example of an intra-group incident that was kept under control only because nobody made "too big a deal" out of the initial confrontation or allowed it to elevate. There was no pressure put on the goalie to "save face" because of the "cheap shot" or for the other player to retaliate for the mask throwing. (field notes, October 17, 1996)

Underlying these informal procedures for conflict prevention and resolution was the functional need to be "tolerant" and "respectful," although interactions between groups appeared to require more "tact" than interactions within groups. According to the informal rules, it was *un*acceptable for members to: (a) "fool around" if it would affect those who were "doing something"; (b) allow their own activity to impose spatially on other groups—there was a need to accommodate the fact that there was limited space in which to play; and (c) be confrontational.

These processes were congruent with Fine's (1987, p. 133) notion of *functional culture*, which draws on interactionist claims that "group culture is functional, and much culture production is directly related to group problem-solving" (see also Becker & Geer, 1960; Spector, 1973). This conception embodies the cultural rules (e.g., the "conflict rules" or "tolerance code" mentioned above) that are incorporated into a group's idioculture, and the successful integration of these rules to facilitate the "survival and successful operation of the group."

ORDER ON THE (BASKETBALL) COURT: STATUS, POWER, AND ACCEPTANCE IN THE CENTER

Because of a hierarchy within the idioculture, certain groups had a greater license to "do what they want" within the gym. The factors determining this *hierarchy* appeared to be age, athletic ability, charisma, perceived "toughness," and "activity group" membership. Basketball and hockey players were numerically dominant "activity groups," although the weight lifters also comprised a smaller but recognized and "respected" group that did not get "pushed around."

> A "pecking order" in the gym was evident in who played in the big games and who was left to shoot on the side baskets (usually the older kids, the better players, and the odd, charismatic younger kid were part of the "in" games). Weight lifters also seemed to feel comfortable walking into the gym and participating in any activity without worrying about the whole social hierarchy that exists in the gym. This in large part could be attributed to their age, since most of them are 18 years old and older. Although the weight lifters rarely "interfere" with the games, usually playing noncompetitive games on the side baskets, they make their presence known at other times. One weight lifter, a white male who appeared to be about 22 years old, would sometimes walk out of the weight room to the gym, pick up a hockey stick, and take a slap shot at the ball, although there was obviously a group of youth that were playing amongst themselves. Nobody seemed to mind, but part of that seemed to be because of his physicality. He wasn't part of the hockey culture and when he would join in, their subcultural "rules" did not seem to apply to him (meaning, for example, that they would not shoot the ball at him as a joke, which they often do to each other). (field notes, October 7, 1996)

Interestingly, the hierarchies and the subgroups that characterize this idioculture did not appear to have any distinct racial divisions. The youth in the center were from various racial backgrounds, and although all of the black youths who played in the center were basketball players (none of the black youth were part of the hockey games during my visits to the center), there was no racial division or tension within the racially mixed "basketball crowd." The group played together harmoniously and appeared to be friends.

An interaction with a black and white youth during an interview also provided some insight:

> [In response to the question "How long have you guys been going to the center." The question was posed to two male youth—both are regulars at the center—a black youth and a white youth, who were sitting with me on the bleachers. Both youth are 13 years old]:
> Rick, the black youth, said "about 8 years."
> Rob, the white youth, said, "ya, I've been here for about 8 years too."
> This questions lead the youths to talk about how long they had known each other. Although they couldn't remember exactly, they thought that it must be at least 5 years. (field notes, October 1, 1996)

Many of the members had known each other much of their young lives. At the center, an environment existed that allowed them to get to know each other without race being a "sticking point." The older youth who had been going to the center and playing basketball together for several years appeared to have long-standing friendships that transcend race because of their familiarity with and understanding of one another. The development of this "code of tolerance" (intergroup and racial tolerance) was likely created by an interaction between the agency of the members and the ability of the staff to "keep youth coming" from a very young age, thus allowing youth from different backgrounds to get to know each other in preadolescence.

In this sense, the youth *acquired these cultural perspectives* through both immediate feedback ("keep that fuckin' ball down at that end"), and through a "growing up" process that involved feedback from the apparently inseparable combination of "role-model" staff and "high-status" peers—both important groups in the center's hierarchy.

An observation of a high-status youth on a night's events demonstrates this idea:

> An older-looking male black basketball player (looked about 20 to 22) showed up to the center today. All of the regulars seemed to know him. He seemed very friendly, well liked. He also was an exciting basketball player, one of the few players who could dunk the ball. People gave him space on one of the glass backboards to shoot around. He shot around and joked around with "Rob," a main informant. The new player eventually took charge of organizing the game. Nobody "acted up" in the game—it seemed as though nobody wanted to look bad in front of him [according to a staff member]. "Chad" was a long-time member of the center and nobody wanted to look bad in front of him. Also, he just seemed more adept at organizing a good game. (field notes, October 14, 1996)

Construction of "dominant" cultural attitudes toward intergroup cohesion is consistent with Prus's (1994b, p. 397) processual understanding of *acquiring groups perspectives*, where definitions of reality are encountered and defined by others (the older, "high-status" youth and the "in" staff) who promote and defend group perspectives. Similarly, Fine (1987, p. 135) suggests that potential cultural items, rules, and behaviors "are more likely to be accepted into a group's idioculture when proposed by a high-status member." This was evident when Chad, the older, charismatic, skilled basketball player "introduced" a more organized, competitive style of basketball play.

Connell's notion of "variable masculinities" also is evident within this hierarchy. For example, the "hockey player" male subculture's intragroup rivalries and physical jokes were "offset" by a general respect for the center, authority, and other groups. In this sense, this potential culture of "violence" is tempered by the center's "tolerance code," so that appears to be more a culture of "toughness."

"REGULARS," "SEMI-REGULARS," AND "THOSE GUYS": YOUTH COMMITMENTS AND IDENTITIES

While some members were more committed to the center than others, the "regulars" appeared in certain circumstances to demonstrate an "ownership" of the center, indicating a willingness to protect and to be empowered by their "second home." Older regulars were the most invested in the center, because they: (a) were most influential in the center's social hierarchies; and (b) appeared to have the most well-developed sense of what the center's role has been in their lives. Having said this, the staff recognized that there are many former members (usually older youth) who are doing "other things" now—whether work, school activities, or deviant activities. They also noted that the younger youth, who are less reflective about the place of the center in their lives, have the most benefit from the center environment.

This feeling of ownership was most evident during a special event in which many of the youth were involved—the haunted house that was put on in the center for the community. Most of the regulars from all of the different groups volunteered for involvement in this project, helping to set up the displays, dressing up as monsters, and being tour guides for the children and parents. A few incidents on Halloween night demonstrated the importance that this event had for "the center" and for many of these youth:

> At the back of the center there were a couple of doors that had been open. A few kids who weren't from the center "snuck in" without paying. The youth volunteers, much more than the staff, were livid. Different youth, on their own initiative, would go out and do a patrol. This was very important to them, and obviously they didn't want anybody ripping off the center, or wrecking what they had created. "Tim," one of the volunteer youth, said, "Don't let those kids in, they haven't paid. We have to make sure they don't get in." Another volunteer staff member chased a couple of the kids out back and yelled, "If you sneak in, you will be banned from here for life, that's it." (field notes, October 30, 1996)

Other incidents observed where "outsiders" caused problems (such as youth hanging on the basketball rims, or youth sneaking into the center) usually were handled by the staff, who were particularly cognizant of who "belonged" in the center, who the potential troublemakers were, and what "tricks" the youth would play:

Two males had come in the gym. "John," the gym supervisor, went right over to them and told them to leave [John was an experienced staff member who had talked at other times about knowing who "belonged" to the center, and who did not]. Although the youth playing in the gym at the time were aware of what was going on, they didn't seem too concerned. The youth seem to have considerable faith in the staff to take care of these situations. For example, the youth (male and female) often wanted to hang around the staff, talking to them about anything from what happened at school that day to what happened when they were in the mall when it was closing. One youth said that he thought "the staff were great role models." This might be part of the security that they have in the center and why they don't want to do anything to cause problems themselves. Of course, not every youth (especially those that don't come that often and have less "stake" in the center) is this "into it." (field notes, September 26, 1996)

The staff member in charge of the gym also indicated that sometimes when youth "who are not in a group" come into the center, he will let them stay as long as they say who they are and they give the staff member their parents' telephone number. In this sense, the youth trust and rely on the staff to be "gatekeepers" to the center.

The general attitude toward new members and outsiders appeared mixed. On the one hand, when new youth came to the center, especially groups from other areas who came to play basketball, there were initial tensions. However, these appeared to have more to do with the "playing basketball against new competition" and taking up valuable gym space than it did with other youth threatening their "stake" in the center. An observation from a "crowded" night in the center and another incident where three males who were new to the center came in and started playing basketball demonstrate this idea:

The gym was packed tonight. In one end of the gym, there was a basketball practice for the older youth. In the other end, there were about 15 males of all ages who were rotating in and out of a basketball game. It was very crowded. "Rob" walked back to the bleachers after a game had ended and said, "Who *are* all those guys. I hate it when this happens. I don't even want to play when it's like this." I asked Rob why he hates it, and he said that he doesn't like the style of play [the games were "crowded" and rougher because they were playing 5 on 5 in a half court area]. Rob's friend, "Tom," came over and sat down, and they proceeded to talk about why it "sucked" playing tonight. There seemed to be some resentment toward "those guys" (the new members or occasionals) taking up valuable court space and changing the relaxed pace of many half-court games (usually it was the full-court games that were the roughest and most competitive among the regulars—half-court games were usually more relaxed). (field notes, February 11, 1996)

"Jim" watched the new group of basketball players when they came into the gym. He watched a couple of their shots until one of the players, who did not appear to be very skilled, took a bad shot, and "Jim" laughed, saying "no game" [meaning the player is not a good basketball player]. "Jim" went out and joined in a game with these youth, where he dominated. He was pretty cocky about it (really making one player look bad by scoring on him consistently). Everybody seemed to be enjoying the game, and there were no confrontational moments. "Jim" seemed to enjoy having new people to "show off" to, although it didn't appear that he was not trying to make these guys specifically feel unwelcome. (field notes, Thursday, September 26, 1996)

In this sense, "new members" seemed to be both a source of tension and a welcome "change in scenery" for the regulars.

Gaining acceptance into the center on a superficial level (e.g., playing in games and using the facilities without feeling threatened or uncomfortable) did not appear to be a problem for most youth. New members were welcomed as a way to add "new life" to the center, although the "regulars" took pride in their longer-standing status within the center (e.g., they know where everything is, and they know all of the leaders by first name) and were empowered by this. Certainly regulars at the top of the informal hierarchy "take possession" of the center to the extent that even new staff were initially considered outsiders.

In this way, the "new members" (and most staff) were used by the "regulars" to help alleviate boredom as well as to reinforce their identity as regulars by "showing off" in their "home" environment. As interlopers, new members formed a subgroup in the center's overall community. They were temporarily excluded from what Fine (1987, p. 131) has referred to as *known culture:* "the pool of background information" shared by members of the group. New members knew in a superficial way who the staff were but did not know who the "influential" groups or individuals were, and may not have been aware of the "code of tolerance." In most cases, however, neophytes successfully negotiated their probationary status by remaining "low key." Before acceptance, they also were excluded from what Fine (1987, p. 132) has called *usable culture,* meaning the cultural elements (such as language) that "are common to all members of a group, but may not be publicly shared because of sacred or taboo implications." These youth did not know, as the staff members suggested, "how far they can bend the rules," or "what they can get away with"— essentially the differences between the official and unofficial culture. Their uncertainties about the appropriateness of "goofing off" or "swearing" (a part of gym culture not rigorously discouraged by staff) were manifested by the hesitancy in their behavior.

Evidently, then, there were many levels of "knowledge, beliefs, behaviors, and customs" (Fine, 1987) making up the idioculture of the center. The nature of the *relationships* within the center, between regulars and outsiders and the youth and the leaders and between regulars of high and low status was central to the functioning and maintenance of the group. Similarly, the *identities* created within the center (e.g., the extent to which youth were empowered by and/or assumed some ownership of the center) and the *commitments* to the center (e.g., the extent to which youth "protected" the center, actively put faith in the leaders, and subscribed to the center's official and unofficial rules) were central to this culture of youth.

Conclusions and Recommendations

This chapter explored the intricacies of youth interaction in an inner-city recreation drop-in center. Although we examined the youth idioculture at this center without reference to "formal" leadership models and identity structures, we suggest that this is a false separation. Clearly, by "giving" them the freedom and responsibility to spend time in a relatively unstructured environment, the leaders at the center have made successful efforts to empower these youth. In turn, the youth have colonized this social space and have established an "unofficial" peer culture that maintains order and relative "peace" within the center—a culture that, for many youth, contrasts their lived experiences outside of the center in this relatively violent inner-city setting. The conflicts that often occur between different ages, different style/interest groups, and different races in other settings are less evident in the center, largely because of the integration of the cultures in this small space, the production and reproduction of a stable idioculture, and mutually nurturing relationships with adult leaders. The tradition of friendships and acquired understanding among the different youth members who have known each other through the center from a very young age also was an integral feature of this community. Although traditional "masculinist" tendencies characteristic of many youth cultures existed in this setting, the values supporting these rituals were not consistent with the rebellious views toward authority (at least the leaders in the center) noted in other research.

For many of these youth, membership at the center gave them a stake and an identity in this inner-city context. Participation in the center's culture allowed them to gain skills relevant outside of the center. For example, they learned to "negotiate different roles in different places," including home, school, the street, and possibly a workplace (McLaughlin, 1993, p. 38). In essence, an environment is created where these youth can develop a secure sense of self and can effectively develop several identities. Similarly, youth seeking (satisfactory) employment-related experiences, experiences denied to many inner-city youth, were well served by the center, which provided valuable volunteer opportunities and educational incentives. The valued act of "giving back" to the center (e.g., volunteering at the Haunted House) worked subtly to advance these youths' skill sets. These cultural elements operated along with more conventional strategies employed by staff to break down barriers that prevented many youth from participating in recreation programs—barriers such as high costs for membership, poor facility location or lack of transportation to facility, lack of program awareness, and lack of adequate leadership. The benefits for these youth augmented those outlined by Reid et al. (1994) in their examination of recreation initiatives for "at risk" youth in Canada, such as increased cultural awareness and enhanced self-esteem and self-confidence.

Overall, these findings highlight the connection between this neighborhood-based organization, the local, inner-city setting, and the larger context of urban Southern Ontario. McLaughlin (1993) explains the intricate relationship between the structures that influence urban youth socialization in these various settings:

> The civic, community, and neighborhood settings in which urban youth grow up furnish different signals and supports for their social identity, worth, and possible futures. Young people construct their identities within these embedded, diverse, and complex environments, a reflection of such elements as local political economy, peer relations, family circumstances, civic supports, churches, schools, and neighborhood based organizations. . . . The institutions from which inner-city youth derive support and hope are institutions that are enmeshed in the lived realities—not imagined conditions or construed circumstances—of urban youth.
>
> Neighborhood-based organizations that enable youth to construct a positive sense of self and to envisage a hopeful future have roots deep in the local setting and have caring adults who provide bridges to mainstream society (p. 36)

Providing this bridge is key to the lasting positive impacts of these "sanctuaries."

Despite these successes, it is important to remember that many youth "at risk" in the studied area never join the center, or previously joined the center but no longer attend. Other youth have at times left the center and then have reestablished contact at a later date. As Prus (1996b, p. 153) argues, "each involvement is best envisioned against a backdrop of multiple, shifting, and potentially *incompatible involvements* [italics added] in other settings." To develop more depth of understanding of these processes, further research is required that transcends the interactions within this social setting and explores the intricacies of everyday life for these youth outside of the center. By locating youth involvements in the context of existing leadership models, and by understanding how attending (or abstaining from) a drop-in center is related to youth activity outside of the center, a broadened theoretical awareness of the youth group process and a substantive understanding of the benefits and failures of youth recreation drop-in programming can be attained. Furthermore, the "moral panics" the surrounded youth behavior in the 1990s can be better informed with "down-to-earth" research about the lived experiences of youth cultures.

NOTES

1. In 1994, Canada's Justice Minister, Allan Rock, tabled Bill C-37 to amend the Young Offenders Act to lower the age limit for those who face adult punishment for committing "serious criminal acts" (first-degree murder, manslaughter, kidnapping, armed robbery, rape, and aggravated assault) from 18 to 16 years old. This change would mean, among other things, that 16- and 17-year-olds charged with murder would now be tried in adult court rather than youth court, where the penalty is life imprisonment instead of 10 years (Visano, 1996, p. 77; see also Schissel, 1993).

2. A number of factors "predispose" youth "at risk" to deviant behavior, according to Collingwood (1997), McKay (1994), Laub & Sampson (1988), Cernkovich & Giordano (1987), Agnew (1991), Dishion, Loeber, Stouthamer-Loeber, & Patterson (1984), and others. These include: low socioeconomic status, lack of family support, group or "gang" peer interactions, poor academic performance, and living in a high-crime area. Although the definition of "youth" in these studies is inconsistent, Reid et al. (1994, p. 11) suggest that the "majority of empirical research has concentrated on youth attending high school, ages 14–18 years."

3. In fact, McRobbie's research was intended to be a feminist response to Willis's *Learning to Labour*.

4. We also do not address the development of research on youth culture in Canada. Suffice it to say here that this area has received limited attention to date. Some youth analysts argue that there has been a relative lack of "serious subcultural delinquency or visible deviant youth culture" in Canada until recently because of a traditionally strong economy and high employment rates (Tanner, 1996, p. 143; see also Glenday, 1996). For a critical discussion of existing research (including Baron, 1989a, 1989b; Davies, 1994a, 1994b; Hagan & McCarthy, 1992; Mathews, 1993; O'Bireck, 1996; Solomon, 1992; Tanner, 1990; Wilson & Sparks, 1996), see Tanner (1996) and Wilson & White (1997).

5. Census Canada showed the following income distributions for males, females, and families, and the following education distribution for the area surrounding the drop-in center (approximately 1 square mile). An examination of other adjacent areas showed similar statistics:

Income: Males and Females 15 and Over *with an Income*:

Income less than $9,999:
Males: 15.3%
Females: 35.1%
Family: 8.9%

Income between $10,000 and $19,999:
Males: 33.3%
Females: 46.9%
Family: 13.0%

Income between $20,000 and $29,999:
Males: 16.3 %
Females: 10.1%
Family: 24.6%

Income between $30,000 and $39,999:
Males: 18.6%
Females: 6.0%
Family: 12.3%

Income between $40,000 and $49,999:
Males: 13.1%
Females: 0.0%
Family: 18.8%

Income $50,000 and over:
Males: 1.6%
Females: 0.0%
Family: 22.4%

Median income:
Males: $21,356
Female: $11,940
Family: $31,926

Education: Total Population (of the area) 15–24 By School Attendance
Not attending school: 58.3%
Attending school full time: 40.3%
Attending school part time: 2.8%

Education: Total Population (of the area) 15 Years and Over By Highest Level of Schooling
Less than grade 9: 22.3%
Grades 9–13 without secondary school certificate: 33.2%
Grades 9–13 with secondary school certificate: 15.0%
Trades certificate or diploma: 5.1%
Other nonuniversity education only:
Without certificate: 6.6%
With certificate: 10.2%
University
Without degree: 4.6%
Without certificate: 3.2%
With certificate: 1.5%
With degree: 2.9%

6. 13-year-olds are given the option of playing with the older group or the younger group.

7. Although one female staff volunteer usually participated with the males in basketball games, few other females ventured onto the main court for the youth-organized games. The male-female imbalance was acknowledged, although not "endorsed," by the staff. All programs in the center are advertised for males and females. Females were involved in most other areas of the center, particularly around the swimming pool.

8. The center often would sponsor members to attend youth basketball tournaments or other open youth competitions. These events usually were subsidized through fund-raising efforts by the youth or through external support.

9. For a discussion of "coding" procedures in qualitative data analysis, see Krippendorf (1980).

10. The youth generally were compliant with the direct requests of staff, and some staff were more likely to elicit "good behavior" than others. However, the less overt conflict between youth was necessarily handled within the peer group.

References

Agnew, R. (1991). The interactive effects of peer variables on delinquency. *Criminology, 29(1)*, 47–72.

Baron, S. (1989a). Resistance and its consequences: The street culture of punks. *Youth and Society, 21(2)*, 207–237.

Baron, S. (1989b). The Canadian west coast punk subculture: A field study. *Canadian Journal of Sociology, 14(3)*, 289–316.

Becker, H., & Geer, B. (1960). Latent culture: A note on the theory of latent social roles. *Administrative Science Quarterly, 5*, 304–313.

Berger, P., & Luckman, T. (1971). *The social construction of reality.* New York: Doubleday.

Blumer, H. (1969). *Symbolic interactionism: Perspective and method.* Englewood Cliffs, NJ: Prentice Hall.

Cernkovich, S., & Giordano, P. (1987). Family relationships and delinquency. *Criminology, 25(2)*, 295–321.

Clarke, J. (1976). Style. In S. Hall & T. Jefferson (Eds.), *Resistance through rituals: Youth sub-cultures in post-war Britain* (pp. 175–191). London: Hutchison.

Collingwood, T. (1997). Providing physical fitness programs to at-risk youth. *Quest, 49(1)*, 67–84.

Connell, R. (1991). Live fast and die young: The construction of masculinity among young working-class men on the margin of the labour market. *Australian and New Zealand Journal of Sociology, 27(2)*, 141–171.

Corrigan, P. (1979). *Schooling the smash street kids.* London: Macmillan.

Davies, S. (1994a). In search of resistance and rebellion among high school drop-outs. *Canadian Journal of Sociology, 19(3)*, 331–350.

Davies, S. (1994b). Class dismissed? Student opposition in Ontario high schools. *Canadian Review of Sociology and Anthropology, 31(4)*, 422–445.

Dishion, T., Loeber, R., Stouthamer-Loeber, M., & Patterson, G. (1984). Skill deficits and male adolescent delinquency. *Journal of Abnormal Psychology, 12(1)*, 37–54.

Donnelly, P., & Young, K. (1988). The construction and confirmation of identity in sport subcultures. *Sociology of Sport Journal, 5*, 223–240.

Duffy, A., Hall, J., & DeMara, B. (1992, May 5). Metro police, mob clash on Yonge St. *Toronto Star*, p. A1.

Farah, E. (1996, July 17). Getting to the roots of teenage acts of violence. *The Spectator* (Hamilton, Ontario), p. A9.

Fine, G. (1987). *With the boys: Little league baseball and preadolescent culture*. Chicago: University of Chicago Press.

Fine, G., & Mechling, J. (1993). Child saving and children's cultures at century's end. In S. Heath & M. McLaughlin (Eds.), *Identity and inner-city youth* (pp. 120–146). New York: Teacher's College Press.

Garfinkel, H. (1967). *Studies in ethnomethodology*. Englewood Cliffs, NJ: Prentice Hall.

Glenday, D. (1996). Mean streets and hard time: Youth unemployment and crime in Canada. In G. O'Bireck (Ed.), *Not a kid anymore: Canadian youth, crime, and subcultures* (pp. 147–174). Toronto: Nelson Canada.

Hagan, J., & McCarthy, B. (1982). Street life and delinquency. *British Journal of Sociology, 43(4)*, 533–561.

Hahn, C. (1996, June 5). Murder at Lime Ridge: Jackson wants changes to Young Offenders Act. *Hamilton Mountain News*, pp. 1, 4.

Hall, S., & Jefferson, T. (Eds.). (1976). *Resistance through rituals: Youth sub-cultures in post-war Britain*. London: Hutchison.

Humphreys, L. (1975). *Tearoom trade: Impersonal sex in public places*. Chicago: Aldine.

Krippendorf, K. (1980). *Content analysis: An introduction to its methodology*. Beverly Hills: Sage.

Laub, J., & Sampson, R. (1988). Unravelling families and delinquency: A reanalysis of the Gluecks' data. *Criminology, 26(3)*, 355–380.

Lauer, R., & Handel, W. (1983). *Social psychology: The theory and application of symbolic interactionism*. Englewood Cliffs, NJ: Prentice Hall.

Liebow, E. (1967). *Tally's Corner: The study of Negro streetcorner men*. Boston: Little, Brown and Co.

Lofland, J. (1976). *Doing social life: The qualitative study of human interaction in natural settings*. New York: John Wiley & Sons.

Lofland, J., & Lofland, L. (1984). *Analyzing social settings*. Belmont, CA: Wadsworth.

Martinek, T. (Ed.). (1997). Serving underserved youth through physical activity. Special issue of *Quest, 49(1)*, 3–7.

Mathews, F. (1993). *Youth gangs on youth gangs*. Ottawa: Solicitor General Canada.

McKay, S. (1994). *A review of the effectiveness of recreation prevention and intervention efforts with at-risk and juvenile delinquent populations*. Unpublished master's thesis, Texas A&M University.

McLaughlin, M. (1993). Embedded identities: Enabling balance in urban contexts. In S. Heath and M. McLaughlin (Eds.), *Identity and inner-city youth* (pp. 36–68). New York: Teacher's College Press.

McRobbie, A. (1977). *Working-class girls and the culture of femininity*. Unpublished master's thesis, Centre for Contemporary Cultural Studies, University of Birmingham, UK.

McRobbie, A. (1991). The culture of working-class girls. In A. McRobbie (Author), *Feminism and youth culture* (pp. 35–60). Boston: Unwin Hyman.

McRobbie, A. (1994). Youth culture and femininity. In A. McRobbie (Author), *Postmodernism and popular culture* (pp. 155–176). New York: Routledge.

Nolan, D. (1996, June 11). Student, 19, stabbed, beaten near school. *The Spectator* (Hamilton, Ontario), p. A1.

O'Bireck, G. (Ed.). (1996). *Not a kid anymore: Canadian youth, crime, and subcultures*. Toronto: Nelson Canada.

Offord, D., & Knox, M. (1994). *Yours, mine, and ours. Ontario's children and youth*. Phase 1: Premiere's Council on Health and Well-Being and Social Justice. Ontario: Queen's Printer.

Prus, R. (1987). Generic social processes: Maximizing conceptual development in ethnographic research. *Journal of Contemporary Ethnography, 16*, 250–293.

Prus, R. (1994a). Approaching the study of human group life: symbolic interaction and ethnographic inquiry. In M. Dietz, R. Prus, & W. Shaffir (Eds.), *Doing everyday life* (pp. 10–29). Mississauga, ON: Copp Clark Longman.

Prus, R. (1994b). Generic social processes: Intersubjectivity and transcontextuality in social science. In M. Dietz, R. Prus, & W. Shaffir (Eds.), *Doing everyday life* (pp. 393–412). Mississauga, ON: Copp Clark Longman.

Prus, R. (1996a). Adolescent life-worlds and deviant involvement. In G. O'Bireck (Ed.), *Not a kid anymore: Canadian youth, crime, and subcultures* (pp. 7–70). Toronto: Nelson Canada.

Prus, R. (1996b). *Symbolic interaction and ethnographic research: Intersubjectivity and the study of human lived experience*. Albany: State University of New York Press.

Reid, I., & Tremblay, M. (1994). *Canadian youth: Does activity reduce risk?* Ottawa: The Fitness Directorate of Health Canada and the Canadian Parks/Recreation Association.

Schissel, B. (1993). *Social dimensions of Canadian youth justice*. Toronto: Oxford University Press.

Solomon, P. (1992). *Black resistance in high school: Forging a separatist culture.* Albany: State University of New York Press.

Spector, M. (1973). Secrecy in job seeking among government attorneys: Two contingencies in the theory of subcultures. *Urban Life and Culture, 2,* 211–229.

Tanner, J. (1990). Reluctant rebels: A case study of Edmonton high-school drop-outs. *Canadian Review of Sociology and Anthropology, 21(1),* 79–94.

Tanner, J. (1996). *Teenage troubles: Youth and deviance in Canada.* Toronto: Nelson Canada.

Visano, L. (1996). What do "they" know? Delinquency as mediated texts. In G. O'Bireck (Ed.), *Not a kid anymore: Canadian youth, crime, and subcultures* (pp. 71–106). Toronto: Nelson Canada.

Walker, W. (1992, May 5). Ottawa plans to tighten law on police use of deadly force. *Toronto Star,* p. A2.

Whyte, W. (1943). *Street corner society.* Chicago: University of Chicago Press.

Willis, P. (1977). *Learning to labour: How working-class kids get working class jobs.* New York: Columbia University Press.

Willis, P. (1990). *Common culture.* San Francisco: Westview.

Wilson, B., & Sparks, R. (1996). "It's gotta be the shoes": Youth, race and sneaker commercials. *Sociology of Sport Journal, 13(4),* 398–427.

Wilson, B., & White, P. (1997). *The culture of "at risk" youth in a recreation/drop-in center: An ethnographic study.* Unpublished paper, McMaster University, Hamilton, Ontario.

10

Researching Youth Sports Programs in a Metropolitan Setting

Essentials of, Barriers to, and Policy for Achieving a Comprehensive Program

Michael A. Clark

Although practically everyone agrees on the importance of youth sports programming in the life of a community, people seldom give thought to planning and organizing such efforts. Rather, whether looking at small towns or urban centers, one finds that tradition, cost, facilities, and similar considerations have a greater influence on what is available than does a conscious effort to create a well-rounded program. Consequently, team sports such as baseball, softball, basketball, and football have tended to dominate. Swimming programs often stress instruction or "drown-proofing." And new activities, such as soccer and floor hockey, often are added only after much discussion and not a little political infighting. Nontraditional sports or creative programs receive little consideration, as do questions about the suitability, appropriateness, or benefits of program elements. Moreover, the interests, needs, and concerns of the youthful participants generally receive little consideration, except as they are interpreted by various adult parties to the decision-making process.[1] Given all of this, it is little wonder that in most communities youth sports efforts appear to have little coherent direction.

Recognizing this, researchers from the Institute for the Study of Youth Sports at Michigan State University focused their attention on the sports activities available to youth in the three-city Detroit metropolitan area made up of Detroit and the two communities completely surrounded by it, Hamtramck and Highland Park. The two-year-long project was sponsored by the Skillman Foundation, a Detroit-based philanthropic organization concerned with youth development. The goal was to collect information about the number and variety of available programs, associated costs and fees, numbers of participants, and basic demographic information about the youth involved. The study also was expected to outline a comprehensive sports program to describe barriers to expanding programming and participation and to propose relevant public policy.

Methods

The initial year's effort focused on connecting with various elements of the community while developing and testing strategies for collecting information. This resulted in a procedure emphasizing personal contacts with providers preceding questionnaires, follow-ups, and eventually a brief telephone survey. In addition, school administrators and parent organizations were asked to provide information about community activities and leaders. Finally, leaders were invited to participate in focus groups; these sessions provided checks on information about community programs and also allowed the opportunity to critically assess them. The involvement of two consultants, lifelong residents of the area with extensive experience in education and recreation, was critical to our implementing this strategy.

The various resources supplied basic information about program sponsors, most importantly, a contact person and a telephone number. Once this information was available, a member of the research team entered each program into a comprehensive database that others used to make formal contacts. This process began with a telephone call to confirm that the program existed, and that the contact person was still involved. A brief explanation of the project followed, and the person was asked whether he or she might be sent a formal questionnaire regarding the program. This instrument requested a variety of information, including:

- a confirmed name and a telephone number for the contact person, along with a mailing address;
- the name, address, and telephone number of the sponsoring group;
- the type of program offered;
- the time of day and season when the program was offered;
- the number, age, and gender of participants;
- the equipment needed;
- the provisions made for providing equipment when participants did not have their own; and
- the cost of the program.

Even conducting telephone surveys did not produce complete results.[2] Business and religious organizations proved to be the most elusive, but even when ongoing programs were sponsored by identifiable groups, solid questionnaire data proved elusive. For example, many of the numbers appeared to be estimates, and relatively few of the sponsors provided detailed information on the ages and gender of the youth involved. Questions relating to costs typically elicited responses describing out-of-pocket cost to participants or team sponsors; clearly, these figures did not include the maintenance of facilities, salaries of personnel, and fees for officials or capital outlay. These realizations convinced researchers that only a partial picture of the situation was emerging.

FINDINGS

Three distinct categories of program providers provided essentially all of the information considered: (1) private, not-for-profit providers—PAL, CYO, neighborhood groups, Boys and Girls Clubs and Scouting organizations; (2) public recreation departments; and (3) educational institutions, both public and private. (A fourth category of providers was noted—for-profit groups and individuals, such as bowling establishments, martial arts academies, and tennis clubs. However, members of this group were so reluctant to provide information that they effectively eliminated themselves.)

Table 10.1 outlines general information about each type of program sponsor. Note that information about the gender of participants was not provided by all sponsors, thus "Total Participants" far outnumber "Males/Females."

These figures suggest that private, not-for-profit providers supported programs in the most sports and reached more athletes than the schools or recreation departments. School-based sports had the highest average number of athletes; they were very efficient in using their resources. On the other hand, recreation departments sponsored the most programs but attracted relatively fewer youth.

TABLE 10.1
General Information Reported by Youth Sports Sponsors
in Each of Three Categories of Providers

Type of Sponsor	Number of Programs	Sports Sponsored	Total Participants	Participants by Gender
Private, not-for-profit	76	19	21,384	Males, 8,228 Females, 4,229
Recreation departments	100	14	6,257	Males, 525 Females, 186
Educational institutions	36	13	9,323	Males, 5,199 Females, 3,456
Totals	212	46	36,964	Males, 13,952 Females, 7,871

TABLE 10.2
Youth Sports Sponsored in the Three-City Area

Baseball	Flag football	Ice skating	Tennis
Basketball	Floor hockey	Martial arts	Track and field
Bowling	Football	Skiing	Volleyball
Boxing	Golf	Soccer	Wrestling
Cheerleading	Gymnastics	Softball	
Cross country	Hockey	Swimming	

As shown in table 10.2, 22 different sports were offered by the various providers. However, sponsors in all categories focused primarily on team sports, which accounted for 69% of programs (146 of 212) and 80% of participants (29,633 of 36,964). Moreover, just four sports accounted for 71% of reported involvement: basketball (10,887 athletes), baseball (7,343), football (4,583), and softball (3,504). Soccer was essentially nonexistent, with only 358 athletes in the combined reporting of all three groups. Volleyball was slightly better represented by its 1,029 athletes. Sports such as golf, tennis, and skiing involved few young people. Still, the emphasis clearly was on traditional, competitive pursuits.[3]

Generally, sports were offered during their traditional seasons. In other words, baseball and softball were played in the late spring and summer; football during the fall, and floor hockey in the winter. However, basketball was played throughout the year, and soccer had both fall and spring seasons. Additionally, a few sports (most notably gymnastics and ice hockey) had relatively long seasons, often requiring 6 to 11 months of involvement by participants. Most of the sports were played on weekday evenings; relatively little weekend play was reported.

The ages of the young people involved in the various programs ranged widely. One sponsor of baseball and softball opened the program to children as young as 4 years of age; several others allowed 5-year-old children to participate. Six years was the most common age for beginning involvement in sports. However, most youth were active between the ages of 9 and 16. Relatively few programs involved older adolescents, and even fewer programs were intended specifically for them. Based on the incomplete data provided, it was estimated that approximately 10% of participants were 16 years of age or older.[4]

Together, the various sponsors reached nearly 37,000 youth. It is difficult to say exactly what percentage of potential participants this represented, for several reasons. First, this total likely counted some athletes more than once, because they played several sports or were on more than one team in a single sport. Second, it was possible that a number of programs, even some relatively large ones, were not located by efforts to identify program providers. Some sponsors supplied incomplete or estimated data. Finally, some failed to respond to repeated requests for information. While these points made it difficult to accurately gauge the involvement of youth in organized sports programs in the three cities, they did not make it impossible to formulate a rough estimate of participation rates: census data indicated that approximately 184,000 youth between the ages of 6 and 16 lived in Detroit, Hamtramck, and Highland Park. Knowing this, a simple calculation suggests that only 20% of the youth likely were involved in organized sports.[5]

Sponsors of only 84 of 212 programs (39%) reported data on the gender of participants. However, this information accounted for about 59% of athletes (21,823 of 36,969 reported). Educational institutions were doing the best job of providing athletic opportunities for females, however, even in those programs, girls represented only 40% of participants (3,456 of 8,655). Overall, males outnumbered females nearly 2 to 1.[6] The actual percentage of total participation may be still lower, because two of the largest programs failing to report information were nonscholastic-sponsored football and martial arts, activities traditionally dominated by males. Since the census figures indicated that females represented nearly 52% of the youthful population in these communities, young women clearly were underrepresented in the sports programs of Detroit, Hamtramck, and Highland Park. Youth with special needs were even more disadvantaged, as there was no evidence of their significant involvement in any of the programs.

The costs to participants in athletic programs seemed minimal. Recreational programs seldom reported charging more than $5 for participants, and other providers reported fees in the range of $20 to $25 per season. Some sponsors of team sports, most notably baseball and softball, indicated fees for teams as being around $100. However, program providers in sports such as gymnastics, martial arts, hockey, and ice skating reported fees as high as $250 per participant. Many sponsors, including the recreation departments, indicated that there was a provision for covering these direct costs to athletes who were unable to pay participation fees. Additionally, program providers typically reported that equipment could be supplied to those youth wanting to be involved but who could not afford equipment and uniforms.

Program administrators in all categories reported anecdotally that budgets had been shrinking, even as they were pressured to increase offerings. In some instances, this caused the reduction or elimination of programs. In other cases, providers looked for additional funds from outside or nontraditional sources. However, these efforts had been only marginally successful.[7]

ESSENTIALS OF A COMPREHENSIVE YOUTH SPORTS PROGRAM

Describing a youth sports program as "comprehensive" implies several things: (1) the program serves all youth; (2) a variety of experiences are available; (3)

the various needs—social, emotional and developmental—of the young participants are being met; and (4) sponsors work together to offer a coherent, overall program. More specifically:

- all youth are encouraged to be active;
- a variety of programs are available throughout the year;
- youth are encouraged to take part in a variety of activities;
- adequate opportunities are given to learn skills and develop them
  through practice;
- recreational as well as competitive experiences are provided;
- coaches and administrators, educated in the needs of youth and youth
  sports programs, provide positive leadership;
- practice, play, and travel are conducted in safe environments;
- program providers coordinate their efforts; and
- real and imagined barriers to participation are overcome.

This list of desirable program characteristics has found support in a variety
of sources. Most succinctly, they derived from recommendations spelled out in
three sources: (1) the Guidelines for School and Community Health Programs to
Promote Physical Activity among Youth from the National Center for Chronic
Disease Prevention and Health Promotion; (2) the Parent/Guardian's Checklist
for Quality Sports and Physical Activity Programs for Children and Youth from
the National Association for Sport and Physical Education; and (3) Participation
and Attrition Patterns in American Agency-Sponsored and Interscholastic
Sports from the Institute for the Study of Youth Sports.[8] However, numerous
other commentators have supported most, if not all, of the proposed elements.[9]

Assessing the recreational sports programming in the Detroit metropolitan area, researchers concluded that there was not a comprehensive program in
place. First, it was clear that not all youth were active: Barely 20% of the 6- to
16-year-old residents were being reached; male participants outnumbered females nearly 2 to 1; older youth accounted for less than 10% of participants;
and special needs youth appeared completely uninvolved.

Similarly, although 22 different sports were available, the overwhelming
majority of involvement was in just four of them—baseball, basketball, football, and softball. Moreover, only basketball was played at times other than the
expected ones during the year. Finally, focus group contacts with females and
older adolescents revealed that current programming did not meet their needs.
Specifically, these youth expressed two concerns: (1) desired activities such as
aerobics and weight training either were nonexistent or of limited availability;
and (2) existing programs emphasized competitive play at the expense of purely
recreational enjoyment.

The reasons for these existing conditions were seemingly well known to
the various groups involved. Focus group participants from all sectors gener-

ally agreed in describing the many barriers, some real and others perceived, to the creation and maintenance of a comprehensive youth sports program in the three-city area.

ACTUAL AND PERCEIVED BARRIERS
TO DEVELOPING A COMPREHENSIVE
YOUTH SPORTS PROGRAM

Some of the barriers to achieving this goal clearly were real, in that they resulted from structural consequences of how programs developed. Efforts by the three types of providers simply grew over time; there was no coordination of efforts. Thus programs often competed for both resources and participants. In many cases, a certain hostility was displayed toward "competitors," especially between the Detroit Public Schools and the city's Recreation Department. Moreover, when it came to the potential clients—the community's youth—the approach often taken had been, "build it and they will come." Providers did not survey the young people, and community members had not been involved in making decisions. As a result, programs reflected the sponsors' interests and needs, causing significant numbers of facilities and programs to not be located near the youth population. While these obstacles might have been overcome by vigorous promotion, relatively few providers had a strategy for advertising themselves and their efforts. Finally, all categories of program providers found it difficult to maintain appropriate levels of funding for programs, facilities, and maintenance. The result was program sponsors who focused on traditional patterns: the easiest groups to serve, team sports with large numbers and community support, and activities requiring little specialized equipment or facilities. Together, these represented important structural barriers to creating a comprehensive program.

Perceived barriers to participation were identified in focus groups and interviews involving program administrators, community residents, and youths themselves. In session after session, numerous anecdotes and personal observations were simply variations on the following problems:

- limited program choices and/or unavailability of desired programs;
- lack of knowledge of programs in other parts of the community;
- inadequate care for the safety of all people associated with the program;
- the need to transport participants to practices and competitions;
- lack of qualified adult leaders;
- lack of facilities;
- poor maintenance or inadequacy of existing facilities;
- need for facilities meeting the specialized needs of some youth;
- inadequate funding of programs, especially new or experimental ones;

- need to provide equipment; and
- requiring participants to pay fees.[10]

Though there may be arguments over how serious an obstacle any one of these actually was, they often were cited enough by diverse groups to represent a serious challenge to program sponsors and community leaders.

Specific Policy Recommendations

Recommendations made as a result of these considerations focus on two distinctly different areas of potential change: the broad institutional and political arena, and the conduct of specific programs. Among those falling into the first category are[11]:

- The facilitation of improvements in programming through the reorganization of the metropolitan area into smaller, more compact units. These groupings should respect local governmental as well as traditional neighborhood boundaries. However, the emphasis should be on 8 to 10 regions serving as local foci for considering issues related to sports programming within the context of the entire three-city area.
- The creation of Regional Program Advisory Committees. These committees, made up of neighborhood leaders volunteering their services, are to be the conduit for "grassroots" input on planning programs and services within each region. Each of these committees has associated with it a youth council that will provide the community's young people with formal involvement in the decision-making process.
- The creation of an area-wide Commission on Youth Sports and Recreation to be responsible for overall planning and allocation of resources. Although this body likely needs an executive director and a small office staff, the primary work has to be done by the members who are drawn from among program providers and regional Advisory Committee members. This group also must have an advisory youth council associated with it.
- The collection, by this commission, of firm information on budgets, programs and participation rates for all programs. Only by sharing such hard data about their efforts, can youth sports programmers develop the spirit of cooperation and coordination required to make meaningful, long-range plans for a diverse community.
- The development, by the commission and allied advisory committees, of plans to broadly publicize existing programs while conducting a needs assessment among current clients. In addition, a review of the present geographical location of programs and services with the view toward a more equitable reallocation and redistribution of activities

should be included. The results of these efforts, along with any identified gaps in programs, should be made available to all program providers as a guide for future program development.

- The establishment of a communication network, using the new computerized system of the Detroit Recreation Department as the central terminal, to connect all program providers with appropriate information. Various databases should be available on this network; among these might be listings of program offerings, facility availability, outside funding sources, and so forth.
- The assistance of those who provide programs in youth sports and recreation with the development of a volunteer advocacy program. Key goals should be recruiting and screening volunteers, recognizing the contributions of volunteers, and sharing information regarding their education and retention.
- The establishment of a Public Information Center to increase general awareness and knowledge about youth sports. This service should provide program information to potential clients while allowing for public feedback and comments. While traditional media likely will be a key element in this effort, either a local computer network or a site on the World Wide Web should be created as an additional means of efficiently reaching large numbers of providers and clients.
- The incorporation of the resources, offerings, and expertise of service clubs, special-interest groups, religious groups, and businesses into the offerings of youth sports and recreation.
- The establishment of in-service programs for educating, orienting, supervising, and evaluating current staff, both professional and volunteer.[12]
- The organization of in-service programs for sponsors to assist them in becoming more skilled in attracting outside funding. The first such effort should be an ongoing workshop in writing proposals for grants from private and governmental sources.
- The assessment of all sites and facilities with regard to the criteria of the National Standards for Accreditation of Park and Recreation Agencies. This will require not only a survey of sites but also the commitment of significant funds for maintenance, repair, replacement, and the upgrading of facilities—including making them accessible to special-need's users.[13]
- The focusing of efforts to improve and completely utilize facilities in neighborhoods with established volunteer programs. This has the additional benefit of reinforcing the efforts of current volunteers and might serve as a means of encouraging people to remain active.
- The creation of city-wide "shoe banks" and resale shops for used equipment so potential athletes are not deterred by the cost of sporting goods.

Among specific programming recommendations are[14]:

- the review by sponsors of the role of various activities in their offerings. Both current participants and nonparticipants should be involved in this assessment;
- the spreading of recreational sports programs throughout the year. Administrators similarly should seek unconventional ways of promoting youth sports and consider alternative seasons. For example, volleyball could be played outside in the sand during the summer season; soccer might be conducted inside during the winter months;
- the development of plans for doubling the number of participants in the next 5 years, as the 20% overall participation rate of youth in sports programs is unacceptable;
- the setting of a goal to increase the proportion of female participants to 50%. Staffing—making certain that appropriately prepared female administrators and coaches are available in adequate numbers to work with this important population—is a complementary requirement;
- the provision of opportunities for special-needs' youth. At the very least, this should involve creating a catalogue of activities and facilities appropriate to this population's needs and making this information available to community residents. Providers should work together to identify and train staff, including coaches, in working with these athletes; and
- the recruiting and educating of 3,700 new coaches in the next 5 years, while retaining essentially all qualified current coaches. This means almost complete dependence on volunteers and will require a shift in thinking for some administrators. However, only by involving the general public as volunteers can the outlined goals be reached.[15]

The preceding proposals imply radical changes in organized youth sports efforts in the three communities. The proposed modifications are intended to provide the framework and motivation for such change. Moreover, they attempt to do so at a minimal cost, as many of the suggestions involve little more than the reallocation of resources or the more efficient utilization of existing elements. But most needed are flexibility and creativity. These seem to be the key ingredients in any effort to improve the recreational sports programming—and ultimately the quality of life—for youth in the three-city metropolitan area.

SOME IMPLICATIONS AND CHALLENGES

While much of the preceding dealt with conditions in a particular metropolitan community, there remains much that is of potential use to others. Researchers should note particularly the following points. First, personal contact and employing researchers with an intimate knowledge of the community are essential—even to getting questionnaires completed by well-known sponsors. Several potential groups of sponsors can be elusive, and they are best reached by investigators with an awareness of how the community functions. These people will know about block clubs, service groups, religious organizations, and even individuals who may provide activities for youth but without a fixed office or permanent administrator. Even when considering public agencies such as recreation departments and school systems, someone with "inside contacts" is critical to getting things done in a timely manner and in gathering such "privileged" information as hard financial data or firm enrollment figures.

But more importantly, researchers with a presence in the community have a better chance of gathering data on an important group of providers that seems extremely reluctant to provide information about its efforts. Businesses and other "for-profit" elements—bowling lanes, martial arts studios, private coaches, and the like—apparently feel that data about their efforts is a trade secret, and that they will be placed at a disadvantage by revealing such information. Promises of confidentiality do not seem to reassure these people; only a trusted community resident might be able to convince them to cooperate.

Even for a well-known, respected researcher, certain material can be difficult to attain. For example, basic demographic data—especially information on gender, ethnicity, and the involvement of physically challenged individuals—simply may not be kept. Thus, seemingly not knowing how many participants actually are involved, sponsors guess when asked for numbers. In some cases, sponsors may feel that they have nothing to gain and much to lose by supplying such data. (For example, they might fear criticism for not having enough programs for young women or a suit for not having accessible facilities.) Again, a community member may be better able to gather the information.

People working for changes in a community's youth sports programming should concern themselves with several critical issues, most notably, institutional inertia. The various elements of the community involved in providing activities tend to have their own interests and direction. Certain sports are conducted in a particular way at predictable times of the year, and administrators seem reluctant to consider alternatives. Nontraditional programming, the accommodation of special-needs' populations, community outreach, deemphasizing competitive play, and involving youth in programming decisions are all potentially unsettling to sponsors. However, if they are to maintain their role as primary program providers, current sponsors—especially public agencies—will have to change. Most importantly, they will need to find ways of dealing effectively with two challenging and intertwined developments: an increasing demand for services at a time when budgets are either stagnant or shrinking, and a dramatic increase in private, for-profit program offerings.

Youth sports activities traditionally have been dominated by public entities and service or charitable groups. The analysis of efforts in the Detroit metropolitan area reinforces this conclusion. However, as previously noted, serious budgetary problems face program administrators. Even while having to lay off personnel, minimize maintenance efforts, and close buildings, supervisors are hearing demands for increasing and diversifying offerings. This pinchers attack on programming has caused some sponsors to consider novel ways of financing, staffing, and maintaining facilities and activities.[16]

At the same time, private providers—especially for-profit ones—have appeared. Previously, this type of youth sports programming was focused in bowling establishments, roller and ice rinks, martial arts studios, and a few centers offering instruction in gymnastics, swimming, tennis, or golf. More recently, however, promoters have come to view the growing demand for services as a potential market. Among the consequences have been:

- the creation of youth leagues—both "travel" and "house"—at ice rinks and tennis centers;
- the promotion of youth golf leagues and tournaments;
- the expansion of swimming and diving into competitive leagues;
- the offering of aerobics, weight training and general conditioning classes at previously all-adult health clubs;
- the building of facilities for in-line skating, indoor soccer, and basketball, with attendant leagues and tournaments;
- the development of well-maintained, lighted private fields for baseball, softball, soccer, and football;
- the promotion of new sports and competitions in various cycling activities, skateboarding, and beach volleyball; and
- the taking of competition to ever-higher levels involving state, regional, and national events, with attendant travel.

Whether these represent healthy changes in youth sports is debatable and beyond the focus of this chapter. Rather, what is important is the realization that these developments have affected youth sports. So far, the impact seemingly has been concentrated in smaller, suburban communities; however, more metropolitan centers cannot escape being involved.[17]

The consequences for urban programmers are problematic, but two points are clear. One, youth sports involvement may become another means of separating the "haves" and the "have-nots." Those youth whose parents or guardians can afford to pay for the use of facilities and instruction will have even more choices than they currently enjoy. These private playing fields and their diverse offerings will provide opportunities unavailable elsewhere, with money being the critical factor. To some extent, this always has been the case in some sports; however, the likelihood is that this trend will accelerate and move into activities previously unaffected. Thus interest, skill, physical development, or motivation may become increasingly less important in determining who plays and who is successful. Rather, the availability of private resources becomes the deciding factor.[18] Two, urban activity sponsors will be able to compete for participants only by providing quality instruction, safe environments, and new programming. In other words, the previously outlined changes must occur. To accomplish these ends, providers will have to be particularly careful about how they apply their resources, both financial and human. By having volunteers serve as middle-level administrators and coaches, program sponsors can effectively stretch their dollars. However, this creates a tension between the quantity and quality of people available.[19] Essentially, if volunteer programs are to meet the challenge, then providers face a series of problems seemingly unrelated to their goal of offering a range of sporting activities to youth. Chief among these are the selection, education, and retention of personnel, all crucial determinants of the quality of the youth sports experience.[20] As a result, program sponsors will need to put into place a formal educational program that prepares volunteers to coach athletes and to administer programs. This effort, combined with recognition of outstanding performance, can be an effective means of retaining quality personnel.

CONCLUSIONS

Researching youth sports programs in a major metropolitan area was a challenging but rewarding activity. After developing a strategy involving community residents as consultants and personal contacts with providers, a large quantity of data was collected. This information focused on recreation departments, educational institutions, and private, nonprofit groups; for-profit and religious sponsors provided essentially no hard data. A wide variety of sports was available to youth, but actual participation was focused in four sports: baseball, softball, basketball, and football. Sports programming, available throughout the year, involved youth of all ages and both genders. However, barely 20% of the communities' youth were active. Males outnumbered females 2 to1, and adolescents over age 16 represented less than 10% of active participants.

It was felt that these findings implied that the cities did not have in place a comprehensive sports program. Focus groups involving activity sponsors, community members, parents or guardians, and youth revealed a variety of barriers to realizing a comprehensive program. Some of these were real, structural obstacles that necessitated institutional change. Others were perceptual and could only be dealt with by providers opening lines of communication with all interested parties and becoming more concerned with public relations. Finally, it was noted that the privatization of recreational sports and budgetary constraints provided a sense of urgency but made it more difficult to overcome the barriers cited.

In any case, it was concluded that as urban program providers work to meet these challenges, they will have to become more dependent upon community volunteers. The quality of these people will determine the effectiveness of programming, and the educational preparation of volunteers is essential to their success and retention. By working to identify community members to work in programs, preparing them with a formal educational program, and rewarding them for being successful, urban recreational sports sponsors can begin to effectively meet the challenge of providing a comprehensive experience to their clients.

Notes

1. Rauner, Stanton, & Wynn (1994); Rossman (1995).

2. These efforts notwithstanding, providers often did not supply complete information, were late in returning data, or simply failed to communicate with the researchers. (Businesses provided essentially no information, while the only religious organizations responding were the Archdiocese of Detroit and its affiliated Catholic Youth Organization.) Further, many of the smaller programs were identified only through word of mouth. Thus many of them may not have come to the researchers' attention.

3. In subsequent discussions, researchers assessing programs in St. Louis, Milwaukee, and San Francisco suggested that much the same thing was happening in their communities—a large majority of involvement was focused on a mere handful of sports.

4. Aaron, Kriska, Dearwater, et al. (1993) noted a similar decrease in participation levels for older youth.

5. Similarly low rates of involvement were observed in several other studies, most notably the following: Pate, Long, & Heath (1994); Sallis (1993); Simons-Morton, O'Hara, Parcel, Huang, Baranowski, & Wilson (1990).

6. Three reports, by Kelder, Perry, Peters, Lytle, & Klepp (1995), one by Robinson & Killen (1995) and another by Lang (1981), supported the view that young women tended to be less involved in sports.

7. Rauner, Stanton, & Wynn (1994) found that much the same situation existed in Chicago.

8. National Center for Chronic Disease Prevention and Health Promotion (1996); National Association for Sport and Physical Education n.d.; Ewing & Seefeldt (1993).

9. Klieber (1981); Lewis & Appenzeller (1981); Baumgarten (1984).

10. These barriers were not unique to the cities studied, as other researchers have noted similar, and even identical, problems. For example, Rauner, Stanton, & Wynn (1994) cited essentially similar conditions in Chicago. Ewing & Seefeldt (1993), Ewing, Seefeldt, & Walk (1993), and Lang (1981) noted similar commentary in national samples. A study of youth by the Arizona Outdoor Recreation Coordinating Commission (1994) elicited similar responses. Finally, Petlichkoff (1992) and Weinberg (1981) reported youth indicating similar reasons for not participating in activities.

11. Kolbe (1993), the American Heart Association (1995), and the Center for Disease Control (1996) have recommended similar institutional changes aimed at improving participation in physical activity.

12. Kimiecik (1988) and NASPE (1995) both stressed the importance of coaches' education as a means of improving the youth sports experience while attracting and retaining needed personnel—especially volunteers.

13. National Recreation and Park Association (1983).

14. Both NASPE (1994) and the Carnegie Council on Adolescent Development (1994) made similar statements about both structural and programmatic changes that need to be made to attract more youth.

15. Smith (1983) and NASPE (1995) dealt with the issues surrounding the recruitment and education of such large numbers of new coaches.

16. Knott (1997).

17. Ibid.

18. Clearly the increased cost of sports equipment, now approaching $800 to outfit a hockey or football player and $175 to purchase a single baseball bat, exacerbates the problem of limited financial resources in the public and not-for-profit sectors.

19. Smith (1983).

20. Ewing & Seefeldt (1993); Kimiecik (1988).

REFERENCES

Aaron, D. J., Kriska, A. M., Dearwater, S. R., et al. (1993). The epidemiology of leisure physical exercise in an adolescent population. *Medical Science in Sports and Exercise, 25(7),* 847–853.

American Heart Association. (1995). *Strategic plan for promoting physical activity.* Dallas: American Heart Association.

Arizona Outdoor Recreation Coordinating Commission. (1994). *Arizona outdoor recreation demand: A youth perspective.* Washington, DC: U. S. Department of the Interior.

Baumgarten, S. (1984). It can be done! A model youth sports program. *Journal of Physical Education, Recreation, and Dance, 55,* 55–58.

Carnegie Council on Adolescent Development. (1994). *A matter of time: Risk and opportunity in the out-of-school hours: Recommendations for strengthening community programs for youth.* New York: Carnegie Corporation of New York.

Center for Disease Control. (1996). *Promoting physical activity: A guide for community action.* Atlanta: U. S. Department of Health and Human Services, Public Health Service.

Ewing, M. E., & Seefeldt, V. D. (1993). *Participation and attrition patterns in American agency-sponsored and interscholastic sports.* East Lansing, MI: Institute for the Study of Youth Sports.

Ewing, M. E., Seefeldt, V. D., & Walk, S. (1993). *Overview of youth sports programs in the United States.* Washington, DC: Carnegie Council on Adolescent Development.

Kelder, S. H., Perry, C. L., Peters, R. J., Jr., Lytle, L. L., & Klepp, K-I. (1995). Gender differences in the class of 1989 study: The school component of the Minnesota heart health program. *Journal of Health Education, 26(2),* S36–S44.

Kimiecik, J. C. (1988). Who needs coaches' education? US coaches do. *The Physician and Sports Medicine, 16(11),* 124–136.

Klieber, D. A. (1981). Searching for enjoyment in children's sports. *The Physical Educator, 38,* 77–84.

Knott, L. (1997). Area athletes are mining for diamonds. *Lansing State Journal, 143(52),* 1A, 5A.

Kolbe, L. J. (1993). An essential strategy to improve the health and education of Americans. *Preventative Medicine, 22,* 544–560.

Lang, M. (1981, March). NAGWS surveys attitudes, seeks solutions. *Update.*

Lewis, G., & Appenzeller, H. (Eds.) (1981). *Youth sports: A search for direction.* Greensboro, NC: Sport Studies Foundation.

National Association for Sport and Physical Education. (n.d.). *Parent/Guardian's checklist for quality sports and physical activity programs for children and youth.* Reston, VA: NASPE.

National Association for Sport and Physical Education. (1994). *Sport and physical education advocacy kit.* Reston, VA: NASPE.

National Association for Sport and Physical Education. (1995). *Quality sports, quality coaches: National standards for athletic coaches.* Reston, VA: NASPE.

National Center for Chronic Disease Prevention and Health Promotion. (1996). *Guidelines for school and community health programs to promote physical activity among youth.* Atlanta: U. S. Department of Health and Human Services, Public Health Service.

National Recreation and Park Association (NRPA). (1983). *Recreation, park, and open space standards and guidelines.* Alexandria, VA: NRPA.

Pate, R. R., Long, B. J., & Heath, G. (1994). Descriptive epidemiology of physical activity in adolescents. *Pediatric Exercise Science, 6,* 434–447.

Petlichkoff, L. M. (1992). Youth sport participation and withdrawal: Is it simply a matter of fun? *Pediatric Exercise Science, 4,* 105–110.

Rauner, D. M., Stanton, L., & Wynn, J. (1994). *Sports and recreation for Chicago youth.* Chicago: Chapin Hall Center for Children at the University of Chicago.

Robinson, T. N., & Killen, J. D. (1995). Ethnic and gender differences in the relationships between television viewing and obesity, physical activity, and dietary fat intake. *Journal of Health Education, 26(2),* S91–S98.

Rossman, J. R. (1995). *Recreation programming, designing leisure experiences.* Champaign, IL: Sagamore.

Sallis, J. F. (1993). Epidemiology of physical activity and fitness in children and adolescents. *Critical Review in Food Science and Nutrition, 33(4/5),* 403–408.

Simons-Morton, B. G., O'Hara, N. M., Parcel, G. S., Huang, I. W., Baranowski, T., & Wilson, B. (1990). Children's frequency of participation in moderate to vigorous physical activities. *Research Quarterly for Exercise and Sport, 61(4),* 307–314.

Smith, R. (1983). Keeping the quality in coaching of the quantity of coaches? *Sports Coach, 7(1),* 2–5.

Weinberg, R. S. (1981, May). Why kids play or do not play organized sports. *The Physical Educator, 38,* 71–76.

11

Soccer, Race, and Suburban Space

David L. Andrews, Robert Pitter,
Detlev Zwick, and Darren Ambrose

For one month in the summer of 1994, the football world's gaze was trained upon a nation that embodies commercial capitalism in its most advanced, manipulative, and often outlandish forms. True to form, the 1994 World Cup in the United States was, in a more concerted fashion than any of its predecessors, devoured by the marketing impulses and schemes of corporate capitalism (Redhead, 1994; Wagg, 1995). In their visually pleasing photographic compilation, *This Is Soccer: Images of World Cup USA '94*, Cheeseman, Alway, Lyons, & Cornwall (1994) brought together a series of images that expressed their interpretation of the tournament's essence as it unfolded on American soil. As could perhaps be expected from a *When Saturday Comes* publication, the images and accompanying textual vignettes painted an irreverent, ironic, and amusing narrative. Nevertheless, the book's undoubted humor belied a pointed condemnation of the crass *Americanization* of the World Cup, and thereby the wider commercial exploitation of football itself. Images of a smirking Bill Clinton juggling a football, patrons at Michael Jordan's restaurant in Chicago watching the USA versus Switzerland game on a video wall, an Adidas poster for "The Alexei Lalas Experience," and, most poetically, the figure of a Bulgarian player laying prone beneath a horizontally laid billboard poster of an ice-cold bottle of Coca-Cola all conjoined to illustrate that the "World Cup (*in its hypercommercial American reincarnation*) fitted the United States like fingers in a snug glove" (Barclay, 1994, p. 6, italics added). However, if the crass commercialism of the event is what made the World Cup USA '94 a distinctly American spectacle then, as I believe Redhead (1994) was intimating, we are resigned to the fact that every subsequent tournament is to be held *in America*.

Note: This chapter is from "Soccer's racial frontier: Sport and the segregated suburbanization of contemporary America. In. G. Armstrong & R. Giulianotti (Eds.), *Entering the field: New perspectives on world football* (pp. 261–281), by D. L. Andrews, R. Pitter, D. Zwick, and D. Ambrose, 1997, Oxford: Berg. Copyright 1997 by Berg. Reprinted with permission.

From the edifice of World Cup '94, it is possible to discern the essence of a thriving transnational postindustrial culture, which commandeers and reworks major sporting events as global spectacles designed to seduce and thereby exploit the global marketplace (Wagg, 1995). Nevertheless, the tournament demonstrated little of the peculiar place occupied by football—henceforth referred to in the American vernacular as "soccer"—within contemporary American culture. In a very real sense, soccer is at one and the same time a distinctly un-American and explicitly American cultural practice. The game has long been associated with the waves of immigrants—initially drawn in greatest numbers from Europe and latterly Central and South America—who came to America over the last 120 years (see Mormino, 1982; Sugden, 1994). For many of these "hyphenated Americans" (Anonymous, 1993, p. 100), especially those arriving in the decades spanning the turn of the twentieth century, soccer had not long (if at all) been identifiable aspects of everyday existence in their respective nations of origin. Nevertheless, once confronted with the homogenizing impulses of *new* world culture, many (but certainly not all) American immigrants enthusiastically appropriated soccer as an expression of national cultural Otherness. Through this association, soccer became identified as the "sport of urban immigrants" (Post, 1994, p. 61). Thus within the American popular imaginary, soccer was ascribed a multiaccentual un-American identity, whether English, Scottish, German, Polish, Italian, Spanish, Columbian, or Mexican.

In recent decades, soccer's culturally differentiating un-American identity has comfortably coexisted with the game's emergence as perhaps *the* sporting practice and symbol of fin-de-millennium suburban America. Indeed, such is soccer's material and symbolic incursion into the *middle* American lifestyle that Post's identification of the game as a "mini-passion of suburban America" (1994, p. 61) represents a considerable understatement. While not envisioned as part of the suburban American Dream (see Jackson, 1985), soccer, like the detached family home, the reliance on the automobile, the shopping mall, and a preoccupation with material consumption, has become a core constituent of suburban American reality. If Norman Rockwell were still alive and creating his romanticized depictions of embodied Americana, there is little doubt that he would have chosen to represent the ubiquitous Umbro- and Adidas-clad, almost invariably white, suburban male and female youth soccer player on one of his *Saturday Evening Post* covers.

Without wishing to deny the cultural significance of American soccer in its residual *multiethnic* manifestation(s) (see Hayes-Bautista & Rodriguez, 1994; Malone, 1994), this project concentrates on youth soccer's emergence and influence as a sporting symbol of America's suburban crabgrass frontier (Jackson, 1985). According to Hersh, "soccer in the U. S. is essentially a white, middle-class, suburban sport, just the opposite of the game's demographics in most of the world" (1990, p. C1). Strangely, although widely acknowledged and discussed by the popular media (see Armijo, 1995; Gardner, 1993; Waldrop, 1994), soccer's prominent location within the cultural landscape of contemporary suburban America has yet to be the focus of a thorough, intellectual examination. Spatial constraints prohibit such a goal being realized herein, however, this chapter is intended as a preliminary contribution toward critically addressing the cultural phenomenon of soccer within suburban America.[1]

In Bourdieu's words, this chapter offers a substantive explication of how "people acquire the 'taste' for sport, and for one (*soccer*) rather than another" (1978, p. 820, italics added). In order to facilitate such a project, and as Grossberg pointed out, "Understanding a practice involves theoretically and historically (re)constructing its context" (1992, p. 55). Yet this core element of critical cultural analysis does not merely involve locating a cultural practice *within* its context. Rather, it implores us to map out the conjunctural relationships through which *"identities, practices, and effects generally, constitute the very context within which they are practices, identities or effects"* (Slack, 1996, p. 125, italics in original). Uppermost in terms of contextualizing any aspect of contemporary American culture is the need to discern the intersecting manifestations of class and race, which profundly influence the experiencing of everyday existence. As Thomas Dumm correctly noted, "Class cannot be a substitute for race" (1993, p. 191). Hence, given the racial complexion of the American class formation (see Omi & Winant, 1994; Wilson, 1980, 1987, 1993), any analysis of soccer's widespread appropriation by the children of a predominantly white suburban middle class has to acknowledge and interrogate soccer as a point of intersection between class and race. Hence, this chapter locates soccer within the on-going classed and raced process of American suburbanization.[2] Such a project is designed to interrogate the extent to which soccer contributes to what Frankenberg described as "the symbolic construction of whiteness" (1993). The first step in this examination would appear to be an empirically based exposition of soccer's position within the American suburban environment.

SOCCURBIA, USA: MEMPHIS, TENNESSEE

From the 1930s onward, there have been numerous attempts to establish a professional soccer league in the United States, all of which subsequently failed. Although these aspiring professional leagues sought to capitalize on soccer's popularity within certain ethnic minority groups, more pertinent to their success was the attraction of the expanding disposable leisure incomes of America's swelling suburban market. Their inability to do so determined the economic viability, and hence the longevity, of these ephemeral professional soccer ventures. The most prominent of these leagues, and therefore the one that had the most visible and public demise, was the North American Soccer League (NASL). Founded in 1968, the NASL's popularity peaked in the mid to late 1970s, with the signings of Pele, Franz Beckenbauer, and a host of foreign soccer mercenaries. While 77,691 witnessed the New York Cosmos winning the NASL play-off game in 1976, average attendance for the 1977 NASL season approached a respectable 15,000 for each game. Such was the optimism that enveloped soccer's future as a popular American spectator sport, that Phil Woosnam, then commissioner of the NASL, said "Every sport seems to have a five-year explosive period. . . . And all signals indicate now we have just had our first year of that period" (quoted in Anonymous, 1977, p. 100). By the mid-1980s, such optimism had proved to be misguided, and in 1985, the NASL folded, the victim of overspending, overexpansion, and an accelerated rate of player turnover (Toch, 1994).

Despite its ignominious demise, the NASL left a "significant American legacy" (Hersh, 1990, p. C1) through its comprehensive network of grassroots youth soccer programs. Designed to stimulate mass youth interest in the NASL soccer product, these promotional programs profoundly contributed to the growing interest in soccer as a participant sport within the crucial suburban market. By the mid-1980s, "All that NASL missionary work, all those clinics, were beginning to bear fruit" (Gardner, 1993, p. 225). Between 1981 and 1991, participation in high school soccer rose from 190,495 to 350,102, an increase of 83.78%. This staggering growth was even more remarkable given the fact that high school basketball (−2.07%), baseball (−2.07%), and basketball (−7.56%) experienced declines in participation during the same period (Pesky, 1993b). At the collegiate level, there are now more National Collegiate Athletic Association (NCAA) men's soccer than football programs (Pesky, 1993a). As well as the promotional machinations of the NASL, soccer's popularity—especially among the female population—was stimulated by the passing of Title IX of the Education Amendments Act of 1972. This legislation sought to address gender equity issues in public education by providing equivalent funding for male and female programs in federally financed institutions. Although the practical implementation of Title IX was delayed for 6 years by political wrangling, the act proved to have a dramatic effect on female athletic participation in general. In high schools alone, this rose from 294,000 (4% of the female school age population) in 1972 to 1.8 million (26% of the female school age population) in 1987 (Messner & Sabo, 1990). As a direct result of Title IX's implementation, soccer gained increased popularity as a female sport, in part because it represented a socially acceptable outdoor team game to counter the expansive and expensive presence of all-male football programs. As well as surging in popularity within the nation's high schools, female soccer also expanded in universities, where the number of women's programs exploded from 80 in 1982 to 446 in 1995 (Schrof, 1995).

By 1995, soccer had been firmly established as the second most popular team sport for Americans under 12 years of age, with 7.7 million annual participants, a figure that dissected basketball (9.7 million) and softball (5.3 million), activities more commonly associated with American youth culture (Anonymous, 1995). As one commentator wryly noted, "Generation X may not be soccer-crazy, but Generations Y and Z have got the bug" (Anonymous, 1994, p. 100). The game's soaring suburban popularity even spurred Hank Steinbrecher, executive director and general secretary of the United States Soccer Federation, to proclaim that one fifth of the U. S. population were somehow embroiled in American soccer culture. Of these reported 45 million "Soccer Americans," 18 million comprised individuals who played the game (70% of which were under age 18), and 27 million represented the all-important "involved family members" (Steinbrecher, 1996).

Given the gender breakdown of soccer participants, which approximately equates to 60% male and 40% female, the game is widely touted as a "non-gender discriminatory sport unlike any other" (Steinbrecher, 1996; see also Schrof, 1995). Such claims of inclusion cannot be made with regard to soccer's racial complexion. A 1994 National Family Opinion Survey for the Soccer Industry Council of America described 75.6% (83%) of Americans who played soccer at least once a year as being "white," and 5.2% (12.5%) "African American" (Harpe, 1995, p. C3). Figures in parentheses refer to the racial breakdown of U. S. population as a whole. Evidently, explanations for the racial breakdown of American soccer participants can be gleaned from the fact that the game's remarkable emergence over the last 20 years has been concentrated within very definite socio-spatial locations, and among clearly defined socioeconomic sectors of the American populace. According to Hank Steinbrecher:

> What has happened is that soccer was viewed by the general populous (*sic*) as ethnic, urban, and very blue collar. What we find, however, is that while there is still a base of ethnic and urban supporters, the reality is that soccer today is mom and dad, two kids, two lawn chairs, Saturday afternoon with the family dog, watching the kids play, $40,000 income, mini van. (Quoted in Pesky, 1993b, p. 31)

As Steinbrecher intimated, soccer has become America's suburban, middle-class, *family* game, involving parents and children alike. Up until this point, this exposition of American soccer's demographic profile and location has concentrated on a very general level of analysis. Thus it is necessary to further this examination by focusing on the socio-spatial distribution of soccer within a specific metropolitan area. For this reason, we turn to a brief case study of Memphis, Tennessee.

Constituted by the City of Memphis and parts of Shelby County, the area herein referred to as metropolitan Memphis comprises some 779,169 people. Bounded to the west by the Mississippi River, in earlier times the city expanded both northward and southward. Postwar expansion has been dominated by the phenomenon of "white flight" (Marshall, 1979) to easterly suburban peripheries, as white (sub)urban Memphians sought refuge from the perils of the inner city and the economic/racial insecurities represented by aging inner suburbs. Bordered by a curtain of vibrant suburban employment and housing communities located on the eastern edge of the metropolitan area, contemporary Memphis represents an archetypal decentered and fragmented metropolitan space whose constituent sectors have evolved along definite class and racial lines. Within the boundaries of metropolitan Memphis, unofficial capital of the mid-south region, soccer is most definitely alive and kicking, thus refuting Sugden's (1994) assertions as to the underdeveloped nature of the game within the Southern United States. Yet as within the majority of America's metropolitan spaces, soccer is firmly anchored in some Memphis communities and most noticeably absent from others. This can be evidenced from the following brief demographic sketch, which draws data from the 1990 U. S. Census to constitute the five distinct residential zones that comprise the Memphis metropolitan area. Statistics from the Tennessee State Soccer Association also are provided related to the distribution of registered youth soccer players within each residential zone, for the period 1994–1995.[3]

Of the total estimated population for metropolitan Memphis, 54.04% (421,031) are white, and 44.66% (348,014) are black. Predictably this population is not equally distributed within the five residential zones and is spatially segregated along definite race and socioeconomic class lines. This can be illustrated by contrasting two residential zones, South Memphis (Zone 2) and East Suburban Memphis (Zone 5). The former comprises some 186,806 people and the latter 305,411. Whereas South Memphis is predominantly black (some 170,667 people, or 91.36% of the zone's population), East Suburban Memphis is predominantly white (some 259,319 people, or 84.90% of the zone's population). This racial bifurcation also is expressed in socioeconomic terms. Whereas the per capita income of the majority black population in South Memphis is $7,583 per annum ($14,751 p.a. for the zone's minority white population), that for the majority white population in East Suburban Memphis is $21,456 p.a. ($13,344 p.a. for the zone's minority black population). With regard to soccer, 3,067 (89.89%) of metropolitan youth soccer players reside in East Suburban Memphis, where 79,171 (37.01%) of the under-18 population of the entire metropolitan area reside. Conversely, although incorporating 58,002 (27.11%) of the under-18 population of metropolitan Memphis, the predominantly black and largely impoverished area of South Memphis contains only 18 (0.53%) metropolitan youth soccer players.

Despite not having figures available for the racial composition of registered youth soccer players, the vast overrepresentation of players from East Suburban Memphis, compounded by the statistical dominance of the white population within this residential zone, would inalienably suggest that, as in the rest of America, soccer in metropolitan Memphis has become the domain of the white, suburban middle class. However, as Stuart Hall (1986) would advance, there was no guarantee of either occurrence. The emergence of affluent and largely racially exclusive suburbs as the symbolic and material core of postindustrial America and the development of soccer's seemingly natural association with this *white* suburban space were both the result of corresponding intersections of social, economic, and political forces. For, as Bourdieu noted, there do exist logics "whereby agents incline towards this or that sporting practice" (1978, p. 833). Reconstructing the (sub)urban American context, and hence the logics, out of which soccer's suburban identity—and thereby raced demeanor—emerged provides the focus for the following section.

TERRITORIALIZING THE RACED METROPOLIS: PRODUCING (SUB)URBAN SPACE

There is a substantial body of research within urban sociology that has attempted to address the development of modern metropolitan spaces (for overviews, see Flanagan, 1993; Savage & Warde, 1993), however, perhaps the most suggestive framework pertaining to this study has been offered by Mark Gottdiener in his influential tome, *The Social Production of Urban Space* (1985). Within this work, Gottdiener promotes a synthetic understanding of the production of urban space based on

> an integrated understanding of the three-dimensional nature of sociospatial organization as deploying hierarchical linkages to places as well as contextual or interactive relations, such as those which foster agglomeration. Furthermore, this three-dimensional array, the spatio-temporal matrix of social activities which surrounds places, involves an interrelated meshing of cultural, political, and economic forces. (1985, p. 198)

Following Gottdiener, in order to fully understand the convergence of class and race around soccer within suburban America, it would appear necessary to—however briefly—highlight the social, economic, and political contingencies that fashioned the idealized postwar suburban space (Wright, 1983). This can only be achieved by recognizing the conjoined, contiguous, and hierarchical relations that emerged in the postwar era between increasingly decaying and demonized urban cores and evermore affluent and exalted suburban peripheries. Acknowledging the derivation and influence of contemporary socio-spatial relations—and indeed separations—within the deconcentrated metropolis provides a platform for understanding soccer's emergence as a marker of the culturally domineering, economically empowering, and racially differentiating *middle American* suburban agglomeration.

Although American suburbanization, the "decentralisation of population from the cities" (Savage & Warde, 1993, p. 76), predated the period beginning with the end of the Second World War, it was during this era that suburban expansion experienced its most startling rate of growth. Between 1950 and 1970, America's suburban population grew from 41 million to 76 million, or 27% of the nation's population in 1950 and 37% in 1970. By 1970, and for the first time in the evolution of the planet, the suburban population of a nation-state accounted for more than either its urban (31%) or rural populations (Holleb, 1975). By the advent of the 1990s, the number of American suburban dwellers neared an absolute majority of the national population (Kleinberg, 1995).

While earlier phases in the history of American suburbanization were engineered in order to accentuate very definite class and race divisions, the sheer scale of postwar suburbanization wrought the most profound influence on differentiating the collective experiences of class and race in (sub)urban America. Whereas the bulk of the American population living in the low-density, relatively affluent, suburban peripheries of the nation's 320 metropolitan areas are white, the nation's urban environments have become the site of highly concentrated black and hispanic poverty (Jacobs, 1992). In 1991, 42.4% of the black population (roughly half of which were located in inner city areas) lived in poverty, compared with 21.9% of the white population (U.S. Bureau of the Census, *Current Population Reports*, 1992, quoted in Fainstein, 1995, p. 127). As Rusk noted:

> In urban America, there are 10.8 million poor Whites compared with 6.9 million poor Blacks and 4.8 million poor Hispanics. In a typical metropolitan area, however, three out of four poor Whites live in middle-class neighborhoods scattered widely across the whole area; by contrast, three out of four poor Blacks and two out of three poor Hispanics live in poverty-impacted, inner-city neighborhoods. (1995, p. xv)

According to McCarthy, Rodriguez, Meacham, David, Wilson-Brown, Godina, Supryia, & Buendia (1996), the result of this racially articulated suburban-urban divide has been the creation of a widening gulf between the experiences of predominantly white suburban dwellers and predominantly black or Hispanic inner-city residents.

There are numerous interrelated reasons for the postwar deconcentration of American metropolitan space. First, the massive out-migration of mainly middle-income white inhabitants from the urban cores of Midwest and Northeastern cities, combined with large-scale in-migration of predominantly poor African Americans from the rural South into the evacuated urban centers, conclusively established residential racial segregation as the defining characteristic of the late-twentieth-century American city (McKay, 1977). Second, this pattern of racial segregation was reinforced through ill-conceived and implemented public housing policies, and the race-based discriminatory practices within the private housing industry (Wit, 1993). Third, further fracturing the postwar American city has been the criminal disinvestment and therefore collapse of the urban low-wage labor market, in favor of service-oriented suburban employment centers (Jacobs, 1992). Finally, over the last 15 years, and in the face of crippling postindustrial poverty, America's urban populace has had to contend with the massive retrenchment of a distinctly unambitious social welfare program (Neisser & Schram, 1994). The cumulative result of this concerted postwar neglect has been most visibly and catastrophically manifest in polarized patterns and experiences of postindustrial suburban socioeconomic growth and urban socioeconomic decline (Kleinberg, 1995; Wacquant, 1993, 1994; Wacquant & Wilson, 1989). Predominantly white and smugly affluent distending "technoburbs" (Lemann, 1989) have evolved in stark contrast to largely black (in some cities, Hispanic) "hyperghettos," crippled by the ravages of federal and corporate disinvestment (Wacquant, 1994).

Normalizing Suburban Space: All-Consuming Lifestyles and Soccer

Perhaps the most profound separation between urban and suburban spaces has formed around the uneven redistribution of capital between the two populations (Squires, 1994). In stark contrast to the fiscal disinvestment experienced by America's rapidly declining inner urban cores, the genesis and flowering of suburban culture was realized through a postwar ethos of unbridled economic expansion. Bolstered by significant growth in the disposable incomes of middle-class suburbanites, a concomitant enlargement of the commodity marketplace, and the advent of the era of mass commercial television, a new morality of commodity consumption was created that educated "(w)orkers who had become used to the rhetoric of thrift, hard work, and sobriety" to "appreciate a new discourse centred around the hedonistic lifestyle entailing new needs and desires" (Featherstone, 1982, p. 19). In this era, not far removed from the deprivations of the Great Depression, commodity consumption was advanced as *the* American way of life, and suburban existence became distinguished by the material commodities that conspicuously defined such lifestyles (see Ewen, 1976; Lasch, 1979).

With the maturation of America's consumer economy and culture in the decades following the 1945 watershed, previously class-exclusive goods, such as refrigerators, televisions, and video recorders, became available to a broader spectrum of the population. In light of this democratization of mass consumer durables, middle-class consumption practices became ever-more sophisticated in their search for class distinction, especially with regards to the advancement of differentiating lifestyle patterns (Bourdieu, 1984; Lee, 1993). According to Clarke:

> The new middle classes have constructed a system of equivalences be-
> tween their economic function and their cultural formation. Symbolic
> manipulation underpins these equivalences, along with the focus on
> creativity (as the production of difference), and the promotion of
> lifestyle as the purpose of consumption. (1991, p. 68)

As the twentieth century entered its final quarter, American middle-class consumption had become increasingly motivated by an ethos of cultural cosmopolitanism, through which the project of the self was fabricated via lifestyle markers
of worldly sophistication and refinement. Clarke (1991) argues that this commodified cosmopolitanism distinguishes and incorporates a new—reconfigured
along emerging race and gender lines—American middle class. However, in
terms of race, there appears little to suggest that the presence of a growing black
suburban middle class (Chideya, 1995) has had any effect upon dismantling the
racially charged, demonizing celebration of the "image of suburbia as a place of
refuge for the problems of race, crime, and poverty" (Jackson, 1985, p. 219). Indeed, it could be argued that the co-option of the black middle class, as atypical
embodiments and exponents of America's neocosmopolitan suburban *zeitgeist*,
has ever-more seductively reinforced the racial "borderline between the suburbs
and the traumatized inner city" (McCarthy et al., 1996, p. 138).

In Foucauldian fashion, Dumm (1993) identitied how the process of
racially territorializing suburban space was realized through the circulation and
consumption of an economy of commonly accepted lifestyle practices, values,
and identities. These observable markers of suburban existence coalesced the
fragmented subjectivities of America's suburban population into a necessarily
imagined *normalized* community that underpinned the normality of whiteness:

> No single person is ever average, and hence no one is ever normal.
> One's place in such a system is determined by the attributes one shares
> with others. . . . In the normalized community, the best that a minor-
> ity can be is "like a normal person." There is a range of deviations
> from the norm that only those who are "like" normal people will fall
> into. . . . And those who are *within* the range of the "normal" are likely
> to be discomfited by the very presence of those *outside* the "normal"
> for one other reason. By their presence (metaphorically more than
> physically), the nonnormal remind the normal of their own deviations
> from the law of the norm. (Dumm, 1993, p. 189, italics in original)

Bounded by a normalized *middle-class lifestyle* that mobilized operations of racial
inclusion and exclusion, this practice of territorialization effectively separated
"those who live in the suburbs from urban others" (Dumm, 1993, p. 189).

Undoubtedly the formation of normalized postwar suburban spaces of consumption has served as a compelling marker of the distance from the perceived "perdition" of inner urban material deprivation, structural decay, and moral decline travelled by the suburban dweller (McCarthy et al., 1996, p. 122). As Cole identitified, the meaning of racially coded spaces, as well as the raced bodies who inhabit them and the raced practices with which they are associated, is necessarily relational, for "the meaning of identity is not self-evident or self-contained, but is dependent on difference" (1996, p. 25). Thus postwar (white) suburban bodies, practices, and spaces have, in large part, been fabricated in response to their (black) inner urban equivalents. On the one hand, America's *new* cultural racism (see Denzin, 1991; Reeves & Campbell, 1994; Smith, 1994) fused the moral panics that enveloped issues of urban crime, violence, drug abuse, and welfare dependency around the "soft-bodied" irresponsibility, indolence, deviance, and promiscuity (Jeffords, 1993) of the stereotypical nonwhite urbanite. In response, middle-class norms have mobilized around the hard-bodied white suburbanite, who is necessarily "middle-class, straight, and law-abiding" (Dumm, 1993, p. 189).

Within this reconfiguring consumer culture, the healthy body has been rendered a conspicuous symbolic expression of lifestyle choice, morality and, thereby, status (see Howell, 1990; Ingham, 1985). For, as Bourdieu noted, the space of sport and physical activity is "not a universe closed in on itself. It is inserted into a universe of practices and consumptions themselves structured and constituted as a system" (1990, p. 159). Hence, the practice of *particular* sports and *particular* physical activities became synonymous with the emergence of this "consumerist body culture" (Ingham, 1985, p. 50), whose various physical manifestations represent compelling markers of normalized suburban existence. The most celebrated derivatives of the rigidly class-based *fitness movement* that enveloped suburban American life from the mid-1970s onward include jogging, aerobics (Markula, 1995; Whitson, 1994), and the expanding corporate health and wellness industry (Howell, 1990, 1991). Nevertheless, the rise of soccer within suburban America cannot be divorced from the metamorphosis of the body into a corporeal commodity through which self-worth is expressed.

The particular class articulation of soccer in the United States is reflective of a particular relation to the body, which itself is related to the suburban middle-class habitus—the system of dispositions, tastes, and preferences—that forms the basis of the suburban middle-class lifestyle (see Bourdieu, 1978, 1980, 1984, 1988). A central cog in Bourdieu's interpretation of the lived experience of class divisions is the differential relations through which class distinctions are advanced. Bourdieu pointed out that the different classes possess differing expectations with regard to the "perception and appreciation of the immediate or deferred profits accruing from the different sporting practices" (1978, p. 835). Put crudely, Bourdieu posited the working class as possessing an instrumental relation to the body and, hence, to sport. This manifests itself in an orientation toward practical sporting goals (i.e., the viewing of sport as an accepted path toward financial security). Conversely, the economic stability proffered by membership of the relatively privileged middle-class allows for the development of relationships with the body, based upon sports' ability to further the interrelated health and aesthetic dimensions of physical existence, both of which act as further sources of social distinction and differentiation.

Within the American suburban context, the bodies of the middle-classes and indeed those of their children are markers of upward social mobility, status, and achievement, self-actualized through involvement in the *right* healthy lifestyle practices (Howell, 1991). As Bourdieu noted, "Class habitus defines . . . the social value accruing from the pursuit of certain sports by virtue of the distinctive rarity they derive from their class distribution" (1978, p. 835). Soccer's particular class distribution within an American context has ensured that it contributes toward demarcating suburban bodies and spaces. Therefore, youth soccer participation has become an integral part of a normalized culture that marks suburban status and sameness as the antithesis of urban depravity and difference.

THE (NORMAL) PEOPLE'S GAME: VOICES FROM *MIDDLE* AMERICA

Soccer does not possess any innate, essential qualities that can explain its seeming affinity for the status-driven, suburban, middle-class habitus. Indeed, this articulation was only realized through the game's "objective polysemia, its partial indeterminacy" (Bourdieu, 1990, p. 163) within a post–civil rights American context. Although possessing a superficial ethnic gloss, soccer's indeterminate signification made it available for "different uses" (Bourdieu, 1990, p. 163) and allowed it to be appropriated by the suburban middle-class. In order to interrogate this strategic mobilization of soccer by the middle-class, this section borrows more explicitly from roughly 20 hours of nonstructured ethnographic interviews (see Denzin, 1989; Fontana & Frey, 1994; Thomas, 1993) with parents of children who play in the various leagues within the Germantown Area Soccer Association. Germantown was chosen as the site for the interviews as it represents the single most affluent community within East Suburban Memphis, and in Philip Langdon's (1995) words, minus the sardonic tone, it is viewed by many Memphians as "a better place to live."

Germantown's popular status as a suburban utopia is underscored by its self-conscious affluence and homogenous racial composition. With regard to the former, whereas the average per capita income in 1989 for East Suburban Memphis as a whole was $19,687 per annum, that for Germantown spiralled to $28,474 per annum. In terms of the latter, Germantown's 1989 population of 33,824 was 95.13% (32,177) white, 1.96% (662) black, and 2.91% (985) other. Germantown's status as an elite suburb demonstrates the diversity between suburban spaces, both in terms of racial and socioeconomic factors. As well as being the most affluent, Germantown also represents the most racially homogenous (in terms of the statistical dominance of the white population) sector within East Suburban Memphis.[4] Equally predictable, given these demographics, Germantown is a bastion of organized soccer, possessing some of the most established, organized, and successful youth soccer programs in the metropolitan area. Out of the six sectors within East Suburban Memphis, Germantown was one of only two areas whose percentage of the zone's youth soccer players exceeded the percentage of the zone's under-18 population.[5] Of the 3,067 registered youth soccer players from East Suburban Memphis, 21.1% (646) were located in Germantown, despite the fact that the area contained only 13.3% (10,520) of the residential zone's under-18 population. While there are no figures available that document the racial composition of the youth soccer-playing population in Germantown, it should be pointed out that of the hundreds of players observed during the interviewing process, only two were black. None of the parents interviewed were black.

The ethnographic interviews were carried out prior, during, and after games, at three of the venues at which Germantown Area Soccer Association games are played. The interviews were designed to elicit responses from parents pertaining to their perceptions of soccer, and their attitudes toward their children's participation in the game. In no way do these interviews offer a comprehensive ethnographic portrait of soccer in Germantown. They merely represent a preliminary, and we contend, suggestive, vehicle for delving into the common perceptions—and different symbolic uses—of soccer, both of which contributed to the territorialization of a specific suburban community. Thus during this discussion we intend to borrow judiciously from the ethnographic interviews and strategically position quotes from interviewees in such a way as to underscore, and thereby advance, wider social trends and logics as being responsible for fashioning soccer's suburban deportment.[6]

Part of soccer's ability to appeal to contemporary suburban values lies in its obtuse relationship with more established elements of American sporting culture. Given its residual indeterminacy, soccer was able to occupy a symbolic space created by vectors of popular opposition targeted at more traditionally American sporting pursuits. Specifically, both American football and basketball did not rest easily with the superficially progressive (often cloaked in a neo-reactionary traditionalism) mores of America's maturing (white) suburban hegemony. The exaggerated hypermasculinity and female marginalization celebrated by American football became increasingly incongruous with post–1960s' parents, many of whom strove for a semblance of gender equality in their children's lives, if not their own. Within this climate of increased gender awareness and activity in the realm of sport, and emerging as it was in the shadow of American football's physical and symbolic chauvinism, soccer assumed the mantle of the gender-inclusive American sport *par excellence:*

It's a sport that is not unfeminine, it's a good challenging sport that can be accepted. It's not a contact sport, or something like that, but it's a high quality game. I think people like it once it gets competitive, because it's something everyone can do.

Well, I was glad because this is a kid's sport. It's not violent. They get exercise, and she's on a team, so I think it's perfect for kids.

The tendency toward celebrating soccer as an agent of gender equality is countered by attitudes that divulge ingrained assumptions toward female physicality and correspondingly advance revealing attitudes toward soccer as a physical activity:

She does not have the interest or the skills. She likes it because it is fun. She is on a team, and she gets to play with the other kids. It is nothing that she takes seriously.

I don't know the reason why my daughter plays. It's just because the kids she goes to school with play, and it's something to do.

This is a kid's sport. It's not violent. They get exercise, and she's on a team, so I think it's perfect for kids.

The same rationale that made soccer a suitable physical activity for girls—its perceived encouragement of nonaggressive behavior, sociability, and the all-important *fun*—similarly made it attractive to parents seeking an alternative to American football for their sons. According to Wagg, " 'soccer' appeals to liberal and/or Democratic families concerned to promote equal opportunities but deterred by the aggressive masculinity" embodied within American football (1995, p. 182). As Hornung noted, soccer is "a sport preferred by middle- and upper-middle-class parents who want to protect their kids from the savagery of American football" (1994, p. 39). Certainly the thoughts of Germantown parents echoed similar sentiments:

I've seen too many children playing football [and] they hurt their knees. . . . It's physically a pretty punishing game, and I think a lot of them have this dream, "Oh I am going to be a Heisman Trophy[7] winner and I'm going on to the NFL," but statistically very few of them can do it, and a lot them end up with broken bodies along the way.

Not like football where you are using your upper body to knock people down. I mean, sometimes you knock people down, but not like that. But, he likes it. . . . He did not play football, and I am happy about that. As a mother I am pretty protective physically. The objective of soccer is not to knock someone down. That is really the major difference.

Soccer was thus popularized because it appeared to offer the *right* type of aerobic health benefits for boys *and* girls (Bondy, 1992; Pesky, 1993b), as dictated by the aesthetic and health directives of the suburban middle-class habitus:

> I think it provides overall higher aerobic exercise, conditioning, and coordination development than any of the other sports. I think it does more for them than any other sport.

> I think it's a conditioning sport and I think if you go out and do weights all day it's not going to help you as much as going out and running all the time, and being able to run and keep moving.

> I don't think it's a physical sport, but I think it's good for their bodies other than physical contact sports.

> Good team work, and the coordination, and the aerobic workout, it's a wonderful sport.

> It is a lot of running and endurance. I like to be outside . . . you do not see any fat kids here playing soccer.

According to a 1977 article in *U. S. News and World Report,* "Another possible reason for the growth of soccer in some suburbs—one that the game's proponents do not discuss publicly, but a few say privately—is that some white youths and their parents want a sport not as dominated by blacks as football and basketball" (Anonymous, 1977, p. 100). Over the last three decades of the twentieth century a racially charged "national fantasy" (Berlant, 1991) enveloped basketball. This centered upon the popular fears and fascinations associated with the perceived natural physicality of the urban African-American athlete, who, were it not for sport, would unerringly be involving his body in more deviant, promiscuous, and irresponsible pursuits (see Cole, 1996; Cole & Andrews, 1996; McCarthy et al., 1996; Reeves & Campbell, 1994). Unquestionably, the racial signifiers contained within popular basketball (and, to a lesser extent, American football) discourse have, in opposition, influenced soccer's symbolic location within the contemporary popular imaginary. In spatial (suburban/urban), racial (white/black), and corporal (cerebral/physical) senses, soccer became the antithesis of basketball:

> Yes, this is more of your suburban type of sport, it's not an urban sport.

It's mainly a white thing, there's not many blacks at all in Germantown, and there's no blacks in soccer here.

There's a lot of families, you know, you know it's mostly for white
players. You don't have a lot of black players in soccer right now, so the
city, you know isn't as strong.

As well as valorizing the suburban American family (which will be discussed
later), soccer was also cast as the appropriate activity for the *normal* suburban
athlete whose *innate* intelligence was counterpoised, even *in absentia*, by the
natural athletic ability of the black urbanite:

I think it takes a quicker mind, I mean to pick up where the play is
going and to set your things up. In basketball and football there is a
plan. With soccer, the sport is so fast, much like ice hockey, that it just
happens and you have to be prepared for what's going to happen, and
know how to interact with your teammates.

In soccer you have got to control two body parts, your head and your
feet.

Kids that do well are the ones that use their head. You can run all day,
but if you don't use your head, you're not going to necessarily do well.
So as far as the physical requirements, you need the mental requirements as well, if not more.

I don't believe that any of these kids have a burning desire to play soccer specifically, they just like playing a sport, and this is one that you
don't have to have a whole lot of expertise in. Anybody can play it, not
necessarily well, but anybody can play.

There also appears to be a widespread assumption that the standard of U. S.
soccer is hampered by the *type* of athlete (i.e. white/suburban/cerebral)
presently dominating the game, and that soccer in the United States would undoubtedly improve if the *right* populations (i.e., black/urban/physical) were encouraged to take up the sport. Accordingly, a *Chicago Sun-Times* columnist
noted, "soccer will never take off in America until the talent that still resides
within our cities is fully tapped and discovered. . . . Somewhere in the Robert
Taylor Homes[8] are a handful of Peles" (Hornung, 1994, p. 39).

Soccer also provided the suburban middle-class with an opportunity for
distancing itself from the instrumental relation to the body exemplified by the
pragmatic habitus of the black urban working class:

You don't get the big money. . . . You don't get $30 million or $40 million for playing soccer as you do being a quarterback on the NFL or any professional sports, something in basketball. . . . Usually black kids have something to look up to in football and basketball, because mainly, I would say probably 70% of all basketball teams are black.

In Memphis, a lot of the economic and racial considerations are that people look at traditional sports—football, baseball, and mostly basketball—as the way to go on to big money. Soccer is played in the local setting for sport.

Yeah, Germantown in all has better sports programs both in the schools and in the community, but I think you're dealing with a higher educated group of people that want their children to be involved in some type of sport. That's what it all boils down to. Basically, out of all of the parts of Memphis, the community supports all types of activities. Germantown has a swim team, they have a lot of diversified athletics, and other community things like theater and choirs and things like that. We pay higher taxes for this type of thing.

Evidently soccer is celebrated as a symbolic site for reaffirming the ascendant position of the suburban, middle-class lifestyle. On a more pernicious level, the use of soccer in sustaining the imagined and normalized suburban community necessarily—if discretely—advances notions of the moral and cultural superiority of (white) suburban practices, institutions, and individuals in relation to their (black) urban counterparts. Soccer is part of a middle-class lifestyle "that separates those who live in the suburbs from urban others. Those who are different . . . perceived as dangerous" (Dumm, 1993, p. 189). This is most vividly expressed in attitudes toward the family and child-rearing responsibilities. The hegemonic "pro-family" agenda, popularized by the intersecting forces of the Christian Right and the Reagan administration in the 1980s (Diamond, 1995), seemingly infused every aspect of suburban existence. Soccer is no exception:

It's good, like I said, it's a family affair here in Germantown.

It keeps the community close, keeps everybody . . . a big family.

The family support is big. If the kid is out here and he doesn't have parents watching, he may not really care as much.

I think the people here are more family oriented.

Such pro-family suburban sentiments are clearly fashioned in opposition to the zone of racial difference represented by the ghettoes of inner-urban America (Giroux, 1994). The New Right castigated the black urban populace for lacking the family oriented values, practices, and responsibilities, which were incredulously posited as the reasons for America's neglected, deteriorating and, hence, threatening inner cities. In response to this popular racial demonizing of anti-family urban spaces, many suburban dwellers display a hostility, resentment, and contempt for the urban populace (McCarthy et al., 1996). This frequently manifests itself in a conceited and self-righteous reinforcement of suburbanites' own status as responsible and caring members of the American family:

There's nothing more important than raising your kids.

Memphis is so diverse as far as the population, but also you don't have a lot of communities where you have a clump of middle-aged folks where they can all come together. . . . You have to have commitment from the parents, and you may not get that in the inner city.

In this area there's a lot more of a commitment to children in general . . . there's a lot more, there's a little more money.

The parents see that the kids have the opportunity if they want to take part, so people like me who are really too busy to do all of this, and to coach baseball and that sort of thing, we just say it's the most important thing that we're going to do besides making a living. This is a well-to-do community, and the parents are very motivated to see the kids happy.

As many of the quotes in this section suggest, soccer's articulation to suburban whiteness is rarely, if ever, expressed in overtly racial terms. Rather, racial and class references and hierarchies are more frequently inferred or implied through euphemistic (dis)association. In a Derridean sense, white suburban discourse is manufactured out of *différence* to the black urbanite, who is *always already there* (Smith, 1994).

In conclusion, this chapter has attempted to offer a preliminary examination of the ways soccer became complicit in the process of American suburban normalization, precisely because the game was able to resonate with the practices, values, and institutions that marked the boundaries of normalized suburban existence. In other words, the game became a sporting touchstone of raced, subdivision America (Jackson, 1985) and assumed the mantle of yet another taken-for-granted prerequisite of that mythologized existence:

Germantown is primarily a middle-age, family-type community and everybody has two or three kids. You play soccer in the fall and spring, and basketball leagues in the winter, and everybody plays baseball. You see the same people and the same parents throughout the different sporting seasons. I think it's good.

As an increasingly conspicuous presence in contemporary middle-class suburban American existence, soccer is heavily involved in the hierarchical territorialization of white suburban culture within the national popular imaginary. In rather trite, but nevertheless revealing, terms, Lawson commented, "soccer became a minor snob prop, like pet alligators and Tuscan extra virgin olive oil" (Lawson, 1993, quoted in Sugden, 1994, p. 247). Soccer's explicit articulation within the consumerist lifestyle (Clarke, 1991)—which demarcates the normalized racially coded inventory of suburban experience—resulted in the game being both articulated and experienced as the antithesis of America's unraveling urban dystopia. Participation in soccer expresses the type of normalized cultural values and ideals prized by suburban middle-class mores. Thus as with the other manifestations of the middle-class suburban habitus, soccer is nonchalantly, if unwittingly, experienced and advanced as a compelling, popular euphemism for both class and race superiority.

NOTES

1. This chapter represents a general introduction to a larger project that focuses on a critical ethnographic analysis of soccer within metropolitan Memphis. This broader study is itself part of a larger project that develops a social cartography of sport within Memphis.

2. As well as loosely drawing from ethnographic data derived from ongoing fieldwork carried out in the Memphis metropolitan area, this project also is informed by the authors' varied participatory experiences with youth soccer, in Connecticut, Illinois, and South Carolina.

3. The authors acknowledge the problems posed by the chronological distance that separates these two data sets. However, neither more recent reliable demographic information pertaining to metropolitan Memphis nor prior figures related to youth soccer registration are available. The authors have examined more up-to-date sample surveys and projected estimates, all of which point toward the accentuation of the spatialized demographic patterns outlined herein.

4. Interestingly, and as with some of America's elite suburban communities, the average per capita income of Germantown's miniscule black population actually exceeds that of the white population.

5. Collierville was the other area within the East Suburban area whose percentage of the zone's youth soccer players (38.8%) exceeded the percentage of the zone's under-18 population (6.8%). Despite the remarkable nature of the statistics for Collierville they are unreliable, because since the 1990 U. S. Census, the city has experienced

a staggering rate of population growth. Conversely, Germantown's population has remained relatively stable.

6. We have decided against identifying individual interviewees, as we prefer to use the responses to generate an understanding of the general patterns and common themes pertaining to the suburban consumption of soccer. It also should be pointed out that we carefully chose the interviewer—a German male in his late 20s—so respondents would feel that they were informing an *outsider* of their community, and the place of soccer therein.

7. The Heisman Trophy is awarded on an annual basis to the individual deemed best collegiate American football player.

8. The Robert Taylor Homes, a notorious public housing development, were built on the South Side of Chicago during the early to mid-1960s.

References

Anonymous. (1977, October 17). From kids to pros . . . : Soccer is making it big in U. S. *U.S. News & World Report,* 100.

Anonymous. (1993, December 4). Soccer's last frontier. *The Economist,* 100.

Anonymous. (1994, June 18). Stateside soccer: Will the World Cup diminish soccer in America? *The Economist,* 100.

Anonymous. (1995, August 21). Database. *U. S. News & World Report, 119,* 8.

Armijo, M. (1995, June 6). Youth soccer gaining popularity nationwide. *Arizona Republic,* p. E1.

Barclay, P. (1994). Foreword. In D. Cheeseman, M. Alway, A. Lyons, & P. Cornwall (Eds.), *This is soccer: Images of World Cup USA '94* (pp. 5–7). London: Gollancz/Witherby.

Berlant, L. (1991). *The anatomy of national fantasy: Hawthorne, utopia, and everyday life.* Chicago: University of Chicago Press.

Bondy, F. (1992, December 24). Soccer: Now kids, that's the way to use your heads! *New York Times,* p. B9.

Bourdieu, P. (1978). Sport and social class. *Social Science Information, 17(6),* 819–840.

Bourdieu, P. (1980). A diagram of social position and lifestyle. *Media, Culture, and Society, 2,* 255–259.

Bourdieu, P. (1984). *Distinction: A social critique of the judgement of taste.* Cambridge: Harvard University Press.

Bourdieu, P. (1988). Program for a sociology of sport. *Sociology of Sport Journal, 5(2),* 153–161.

Bourdieu, P. (1990). *Programme for a sociology of sport, In other words: Essays toward a reflexive sociology* (pp. 156–167). Stanford: Stanford University Press.

Cheeseman, D., Alway, M., Lyons, A., & Cornwall, P. (1994). *This is soccer: Images of World Cup USA '94*. London: Gollancz/Witherby.

Chideya, F. (1995). *Don't believe the hype: Fighting cultural misinformation about African Americans*. New York: Penguin.

Clarke, J. (1991). *New times and old enemies: Essays on cultural studies and America*. London: HarperCollins.

Cole, C. L. (1996). P. L. A. Y., Nike, and Michael Jordan: National fantasy and the racialization of crime and punishment. *Working Papers in Sport and Leisure Commerce (Bureau of Sport and Leisure Commerce: The University of Memphis), 1(1)*, www.honse.memphis.edu/WPSLC/number1.htm.

Cole, C. L., & Andrews, D. L. (1996). "Look—Its NBA *ShowTime!*": Visions of race in the popular imaginary. *Cultural Studies: A Research Volume, 1(1)*, 141–181.

Denzin, N. K. (1989). *The research act: A theoretical introduction to sociological methods*. Englewood Cliffs, NJ: Prentice Hall.

Denzin, N. K. (1991). *Images of postmodern society: Social theory and contemporary cinema*. London: Sage.

Diamond, S. (1995). *Roads to dominion: Right-wing movements and political power in the United States*. New York: Guilford Press.

Dumm, T. L. (1993). The new enclosures: Racism in the normalized community. In R. Gooding-Williams (Ed.), *Reading Rodney King: Reading urban uprising* (pp. 178–195). New York: Routledge.

Ewen, S. (1976). *Captains of consciousness: Advertising and the social roots of the consumer culture*. New York: McGraw-Hill.

Fainstein, N. (1995). Black ghettoization and social mobility. In M. P. Smith & J. R. Feagin (Eds.), *The bubbling cauldron: Race, ethnicity, and the urban crisis* (pp. 123–141). Minneapolis: University of Minnesota Press.

Featherstone, M. (1982). The body in consumer culture. *Theory, Culture, & Society, 1(2)*, 18–33.

Flanagan, W. G. (1993). *Contemporary urban sociology*. Cambridge: Cambridge University Press.

Fontana, A., & Frey, J. H. (1994). Interviewing: The art of science. In N. K. Denzin & Y. S. Lincoln (Eds.), *Handbook of qualitative research* (pp. 361–376). Thousand Oaks, CA: Sage.

Frankenberg, R. (1993). *The social construction of whiteness: White women, race matters*. Minneapolis: University of Minnesota Press.

Gardner, P. (1993). *The simplest game*. New York: Collier Books.

Giroux, H. A. (1994). *Disturbing pleasures: Learning popular culture*. New York: Routledge.

Gottdiener, M. (1985). *The social production of urban space*. Austin: University of Texas Press.

Grossberg, L. (1992). *We gotta get out of this place: Popular conservatism and postmodern culture.* London: Routledge.

Hall, S. (1986). The problem of ideology: Marxism without guarantees. *Journal of Communication Inquiry, 10(2),* 28–44.

Harpe, M. (1995, May 28). Soccer dollar limits blacks. *News & Record (Greensboro, NC),* p. C3.

Hayes-Bautista, D. E., & Rodriguez, G. (1994, July 4). L.A. story: Los Angeles, CA, soccer and society. *The New Republic,* 19.

Hersh, P. (1990, June 3). Soccer in U. S. at crossroads: World Cup seen as last resort to stir fan sport. *Chicago Tribune,* p. C1.

Holleb, D. B. (1975). The direction of urban change. In H. S. Perloff (Ed.), *Agenda for the new urban era* (pp. 11–43). Chicago: American Society of Planning Officials.

Hornung, M. N. (1994, June 17). 3 billion people can't be wrong. *Chicago Sun-Times,* p. 39.

Howell, J. (1991). "A revolution in motion": Advertising and the politics of nostalgia. *Sociology of Sport Journal, 8,* 258–271.

Howell, J. W. (1990). *Meanings go mobile: Fitness, health, and the quality of life debate in contemporary America.* Unpublished doctoral dissertation, University of Illinois, Urbana-Champaign.

Ingham, A. G. (1985). From public issue to personal trouble: Well-being and the fiscal crisis of the state. *Sociology of Sport Journal, 2(1),* 43–55.

Jackson, K. T. (1985). *Crabgrass frontier: The suburbanization of the United States.* New York: Oxford University Press.

Jacobs, B. D. (1992). *Fractured cities: Capitalism, community, and empowerment in Britain and America.* London: Routledge.

Jeffords, S. (1993). *Hard bodies: Hollywood masculinity in the Reagan era.* New Brunswick: Rutgers University Press.

Kleinberg, B. (1995). *Urban America in transformation: Perspectives on urban policy and development.* Thousand Oaks, CA: Sage.

Langdon, P. (1995). *A better place to live: Reshaping the American suburb.* New York: HarperPerennial.

Lasch, C. (1979). *The culture of narcissism: American life in an age of diminishing expectations.* New York: W.W. Norton.

Lee, M. J. (1993). *Consumer culture reborn: The politics of consumption.* London: Routledge.

Lemann, N. (1989, November). Stressed out in suburbia: A generation after the postwar boom, life in the suburbs has changed, even if our picture of it hasn't. *The Atlantic,* 34.

Malone, M. (1994, May–June). Soccer's greatest goal: Cultural harmony through sports. *Americas,* 64.

Markula, P. (1995). Firm but shapely, fit but sexy, strong but thin: The postmodern aerobicizing female bodies. *Sociology of Sport Journal, 12(4),* 424–453.

Marshall, H. (1979). White movement to the suburbs: A comparison of explanations. *American Sociological Review, 44*, 975–994.

McCarthy, C., Rodriguez, A., Meacham, S., David, S., Wilson-Brown, C., Godina, H., Supryia, K. E., & Buendia, E. (1996). Race, suburban resentment, and the representation of the inner city in contemporary film and television. In N. K. Denzin (Ed.), *Cultural Studies* (vol. 1, pp. 121–140). Greenwich, CT: JAI Press.

McKay, D. H. (1977). *Housing and race in industrial society: Civil rights and urban policy in Britain and the United States.* London: Croom Helm.

Messner, M. A., & Sabo, D. F. (1990). Introduction: Toward a critical feminist reappraisal of sport, men, and the gender order. In M. A. Messner & D. F. Sabo (Eds.), *Sport, men, and the gender order: Critical feminist perspectives* (pp. 1–15). Champaign: Human Kinetics.

Mormino, G. R. (1982). The playing fields of St. Louis: Italian immigrants and sport, 1925–1941. *Journal of Sport History, 9*, 5–16.

Neisser, P. T., & Schram, S. F. (1994). Redoubling denial: Industrial welfare policy meets postindustrial poverty. *Social Text (41)*, 41–60.

Omi, M., & Winant, H. (1994). *Racial formation in the United States: From the 1960s to the 1990s.* New York: Routledge.

Pesky, G. (1993a, March). The changing face of the game. *Sporting Goods Business, 32.*

Pesky, G. (1993b, April). On the attack: The growth of soccer in the United States. *Sporting Goods Business, 31.*

Post, T. (1994, Spring). Feet of the future. *Newsweek Special Issue, 60*–65.

Redhead, S. (1994). Media culture and the World Cup: The last World Cup? In J. Sugden & A. Tomlinson (Eds.), *Hosts and champions: Soccer cultures, national identities, and the USA World Cup* (pp. 291–309). Aldershot: Arena.

Reeves, J. L., & Campbell, R. (1994). *Cracked coverage: Television news, the anti-cocaine crusade, and the Reagan legacy.* Durham, NC: Duke University Press.

Rusk, D. (1995). *Cities without suburbs.* Baltimore: Woodrow Wilson Center Press.

Savage, M., & Warde, A. (1993). *Urban sociology, capitalism, and modernity.* London: Macmillan.

Schrof, J. M. (1995, June 19). American women: Getting their kicks. *Science & Society, 118*, 59.

Slack, J. D. (1996). The theory and method of articulation in cultural studies. In D. Morley & K. H. Chen (Eds.), *Stuart Hall: Critical dialogues in cultural studies* (pp. 112–127). London: Routledge.

Smith, A. M. (1994). *New right discourse on race and sexuality: Britain, 1968–1990.* Cambridge: Cambridge University Press.

Squires, G. D. (1994). *Capital and communities in black and white: The intersection of race, class, and uneven development.* Albany: State University of New York Press.

Steinbrecher, H. (1996, February). *Getting in on soccer: The hottest sport to reach interna-tional markets.* Unpublished paper presented at the Marketing with Sports Entities, Swissotel, Atlanta, GA.

Sugden, J. (1994). USA and the World Cup: American nativism and the rejection of the people's game. In J. Sugden & A. Tomlinson (Eds.), *Hosts and champions: Soccer cul-tures, national identities, and the USA World Cup* (pp. 219–252). Aldershot: Arena.

Thomas, J. (1993). *Doing critical ethnography.* Newbury Park, CA: Sage.

Toch, T. (1994, June 13). Football? In short pants? No helmets? *Science & Society, 116,* 76, 78.

Wacquant, L. J. D. (1993). The cost of racial and class exclusion in the inner city. In W. J. Wilson (Ed.), *The ghetto underclass: Social science perspectives* (pp. 25–42). New-bury Park, CA: Sage.

Wacquant, L. J. D. (1994). The new urban color line: The state and fate of the ghetto in post-Fordist America. In C. Calhoun (Ed.), *Social theory and the politics of identity* (pp. 231–276). Oxford: Blackwell.

Wacquant, L. J. D., & Wilson, W. J. (1989). Poverty, joblessness, and the social trans-formation of the inner city. In P. H. Cottingham & D. T. Ellwood (Eds.), *Welfare pol-icy for the 1990s* (pp. 70–102). Cambridge: Harvard University Press.

Wagg, S. (1995). The business of America: Reflections on World Cup '94. In S. Wagg (Ed.), *Giving the game away: Football, politics, and culture on five continents* (pp. 179–200). Leicester, England: Leicester University Press.

Waldrop, J. (1994, June). The world's favorite sport. *American Demographics,* 4.

Whitson, D. (1994). The embodiment of gender: Discipline, domination, and empow-erment. In S. Birrell & C. L. Cole (Eds.), *Women, sport, and culture* (pp. 353–371). Champaign, IL: Human Kinetics.

Wilson, W. J. (1980). *The declining significance of race: Blacks and changing American in-stitutions.* Chicago: University of Chicago Press.

Wilson, W. J. (1987). *The truly disadvantaged: The inner city, the underclass, and public pol-icy.* Chicago: University of Chicago Press.

Wilson, W. J. (1993). The underclass: Issues, perspectives, and public policy. In W. J. Wilson (Ed.), *The ghetto underclass: Social science perspectives* (pp. 1–24). Newbury Park, CA: Sage.

Wit, W. de (1993). The rise of public housing in Chicago, 1930–1960. In J. Zukowsky (Ed.), *Chicago architecture and design 1923–1993: Reconfiguration of an American metropolis* (pp. 232–245). Munich: Prestel.

Wright, G. (1983). *Building the dream: A social history of housing in America.* Cambridge: MIT Press.

12

The New Politics of Urban Consumption

Hoop Dreams, Clockers, and "America"

CL Cole and Samantha King

THE NEW ETHNOGRAPHIC

In this chapter, we discuss the popularly acclaimed, three-hour, low-budget, independent documentary *Hoop Dreams*. While documentaries are typically relegated to the margins of the film industry and popular media, *Hoop Dreams* was unexpectedly and immediately well received in the United States. Focusing on the lives of two African-American, inner-city youths who aspire to play professional basketball, it was declared "an American epic" that offered an atypically brutal and honest portrayal of the realities of urban life. Moreover, popular narrations aligned the film, the filmmakers, its audiences, and even its eventual corporate sponsors with some notion of "social cause." We suggest that the popular endorsement of *Hoop Dreams* as an official representation of urban America and the excitement surrounding the "realness" of the film are symptomatic of heightened desires to consume the ethnographic inner city. Moreover, we suggest that the film, its reception, and the general consumption of the ethnographic urban cannot be separated from America's representations and understanding of itself and all that that entails.

The question for us, then, is one of how to interpret "America's" investment in the film. While it is tempting to dismiss the mythic American Dream as it is celebrated in *Hoop Dreams*, succumbing to such temptation would provide limited understanding of the identificatory possibilities created through its narrative. Instead, we build on James Baldwin's assertion that "[t]he country's image of the [African American] which hasn't very much to do with the [African American], has never failed to reflect with a kind of frightening accuracy the state of mind of the country" (cited in Riggs, 1991). We advance Baldwin's thesis by taking seriously bell hooks' (1995) claim that *Hoop Dreams*

must take its place within the continuum of traditional anthropological and/or ethnographic documentary works that show us the "dark
other" from the standpoint of whiteness. Inner-city, poor, black communities, seen as "jungles" by many Americans, become in this film a
zone white filmmakers have crossed boundaries to enter, to document
. . . their subjects. (p. 24)

Building on accounts that link the historical (anthropological) ethnographic with desires to bring distant spaces closer in ways that encode and
enact evolution/progress through racial difference (Rony, 1996), we consider
Hoop Dreams an exemplary "formulaic hybrid." We use the term *formulaic hybrid* to draw attention to the dispersion of "the ethnographic" in popular and
diverse genres that rely on stereotypes drawn from the national archive of the
past and the present.[1] Rather than offering an atypically brutal and honest
portrayal of the realities of urban life, *Hoop Dreams*—as an element in the
ethnographic minutia of everyday life—is deeply embedded in that which is
"already known." The "already known" is configured through modern categories that enable and limit what/who are seeable and sayable.[2] In order to examine how the "already known" shapes *Hoop Dreams* and its reception, we
examine the familiar governing knowledges of racially codified inner-city
poverty. From the film's opening scene, familiar categories of racially coded
family breakdown, the struggle between sport and gangs, and prominent embodiments of violence are deployed to "make sense" of poverty, basketball, and
racially segregated urban America.[3] Moreover, origin stories of the film, trib-
utes to its honorable filmmakers, and filmic figures of displacement are crucial
extensions of that sense making.

We contrast the popular reception of *Hoop Dreams* to Spike Lee's *Clockers*
in our effort to demonstrate how *Hoop Dreams* functions as an expression of a
reactionary formation embedded in a particular configuration of American
identity. Like *Hoop Dreams*, *Clockers* ardently depicts and expresses the struggles
faced by coming-of-age, black urban youth (one of contemporary America's favorite new ethnographic themes [c.f., Massing, 1995]), as well as the social realities shaping their everyday lived experience.[4] Although each narrative
appears self-contained, each makes sense in relation to the dominant codes
governing America's understanding of "black urban youth" and itself as a "just"
nation. By investigating their points of divergence (including their different re-
ceptions) we demonstrate *Clockers'* force (however limited) as an anti-*Hoop
Dreams* narrative. Indeed, popular criticisms of *Clockers* provide insight into the
sort of anxieties contained by *Hoop Dreams*. While *Clockers* challenges easy
classifications of good and evil by drawing attention to material conditions,
Hoop Dreams actively discourages critical thinking about middle-class implications in the neglect of and poverty in the inner city as it facilitates the audience's sense of self as ethically and morally superior. Stated differently, the

categories organizing *Hoop Dreams* are crucial to America's imagination of itself as a democratic, caring, and compassionate nation in a period dominated
by heightened poverty, uncertainty, resentment, and acts of revenge directed at
the residents of America's poor inner cities.[5] In contrast, these categories are
configured in *Clockers* in ways that refuse "America" such comfort. This is not
to say that *Clockers* produces the ideal criticism of *Hoop Dreams'* logic and appeal. Indeed, and almost without exception, popular responses to *Clockers*—
both positive and negative—assess the film in terms of its truthfulness about
the reality of the pathologies presumably located in (and ostensibly the cause
of) the poor inner city. We contend that the persistence of this response is
symptomatic of the difficulty in seeing in ways that differ from the "already
known"—of seeing in ways that account for the real material differences organizing lived experience.

Given the historical weight of racist narratives that *Hoop Dreams* and
Clockers would need to overcome to even simply disturb "ways of seeing" urban
America and race, we ask: "What and who" are, and are not, the objects of criticism in both films? How are we to understand a configuration of national
identity that can embrace and celebrate a film like *Hoop Dreams* while it calls
for escalated punishments and policing directed at urban black youth? How
does *Clockers* complicate notions of truth, justice, and punishment as they operate in contemporary accounts of urban America, and how does this compli-
cation account for its reception? How is it that the makers of *Hoop Dreams*,
unlike Spike Lee, succeed, by the view of the critics and the *Hoop Dreams'* filmmakers themselves, in transcending boundaries of race and class? How might
we understand America's obsession with the reality-value of Spike Lee's films
in light of the historically conditioned ways of seeing the inner city and material conditions?

"America's" *Hoop Dreams*

Hoop Dreams is a three-hour documentary film made over a period of 5 years,
between 1986 and 1991. The film focuses on the lives of two African-American teenagers growing up in poor, racially segregated Chicago neighborhoods.
Not yet even in high school, the two teens, William Gates and Arthur Agee,
demonstrate basketball skills that suggest collegiate and professional poten-
tials.[6] The film begins as they prepare to enter high school; it highlights and or-
ganizes their high school years and concludes as they depart for college. Viewer
position and context are immediately established through a sequence of opening images in which viewers travel into Chicago. An elevated train running
parallel to the expressway and a group of young men playing basketball on a
graffiti-laden court below are almost simultaneously brought into view. The
camera follows a player (who viewers later recognize as William Gates) as he

moves toward the basket and shoots, and then moves around a concrete high-rise (perhaps *the* overdetermined sign of the ethnographic urban) to reveal Chicago Stadium, the site of the 38th annual NBA All-Star game.[7] A picture-perfect steal and dunk by the East's #23, Michael Jordan, is met by exuberant and overwhelmingly white spectators.

The elevated train takes us to Chicago's infamous Cabrini Green Projects, where we hear the televised All-Star game. Inside his family's home, we see Gates intensely watching the concluding moments of the game; the camera follows him outside and records his dunk on a rimless net that we see in slow motion. As Gates explains his dream to play in the NBA, the slow motion dunk is repeated, accompanied by the burst of applause we heard earlier in Chicago Stadium. His mother (Emma) and brother (Curtis) are introduced through close-ups, as each comments about Gates's dream to play in the NBA. The camera takes us to West Garfield Park, where Arthur Agee watches the game with his family. Again, Agee, his mother (Sheila), and his father (Bo) are captured in close-ups as each describes Agee's dream. In addition to Gates, Agee, and their families, much of the film focuses on "representatives" of the formal education-basketball network through which they will pursue their goals. Most specifically, the camera follows Gene Pingatore, head basketball coach at St. Joseph High School (a predominantly white, private Roman Catholic school in Westchester, a western suburb of Chicago), who preserves the school's ranking as one of Chicago's high school basketball powerhouses by recruiting players from across the city. We meet Pingatore after an unofficial scout for area high schools, Earl Smith, "discovers" Agee and arranges for him to attend St Joseph's summer basketball camp. Their trip from West Garfield Park to the Westchester suburbs makes clear that the distance Agee will negotiate daily exceeds the geographical.

Based on his basketball skills and performance at the camp, Agee is recruited to play for St. Joseph High School by Pingatore. In a conversation with Agee and his family, Pingatore not too cautiously promises that Agee's chances of securing a college scholarship will be enhanced by attending St. Joseph.

> Basketball has to be second to your academics, if you don't get your grades, you're not going to play. But if you work hard at your grades, and if you work hard at basketball, then I'll be able to help you as far as going to college. And I guarantee this ["Gene Pingatore, Head Basketball Coach" appears on the screen]—I can't promise you where you're going to go and if you're going to be a star, but I guaran*tee* that I will help you get into the school that will be best for you [cut to a photograph of alumnus Isiah Thomas, Agee's idol, the embodiment of his hopes and dreams, in his Indiana uniform]. I'm making this commitment to you, if you make a commitment to be part of this kind of program.

Both Agee and Gates are awarded partial scholarships to attend St. Joseph and, like Isiah Thomas, they will commute three hours each day by train to attend the school. Their first year, Gates is selected as a starter on the school's varsity team, while Agee wins the freshman team starting point guard position. Although both entered St. Joseph reading at a fourth-grade level, we routinely see Gates, whose academic skills drastically improve his first year, in the classroom. Agee's skills do not advance at the same rate. In response to a narrator's question that remains undefined, Pingatore verbalizes his hesitations about Agee's ability to adapt to the new environment:

> When Arthur first started at St. Joseph's, he was good kid from what we saw, but he was very immature. He might have been a little more disruptive, speaking out, getting into childish things. He wasn't used to the discipline and control. He reverted back to, maybe, his environment, where he came from.

In contrast to Pingatore's reservations, we see signs of Agee's desire to negotiate the distance between the inner city and suburban environment: a clip of him in preppy attire is followed by a clip of his mother, who says that she saw immediate changes in her son, particularly in terms of maturity. Meanwhile, through a series of upbeat, high-drama, last-minute game day scenes, we learn that Gates also is excelling on the basketball court and drawing attention from Division I schools and sportswriters who appear on a television talk show and identify him as the next Isiah Thomas.

A tuition increase during their sophomore year creates potential problems for Gates and Agee. Gates's concerns are alleviated when Patricia Wier, president of Encyclopedia Britannica, contributes to his tuition and gives him a summer job. Agee is expelled mid-semester because of his family's inability to make timely tuition payments. Sheila Agee and the coach at Marshall High, Agee's new school, conclude that the expulsion was not so much about tuition debt but Agee's failure to live up to Coach Pingatore's expectations. From this point on, Agee's story is narrated through the conventional categories of inner-city struggle: the dysfunctional family, individual will, and the seductions of local surroundings and friends. Almost immediately following Agee's expulsion, the narrator tells us that Bo has left the family; and Sheila, forced to quit her job due to chronic back pain, now depends on welfare and struggles to pay the bills and feed her four children.[8] Bo's next appearance, at a local playground where Agee plays basketball, is apparently less about Agee than about drugs. The camera lingers as Bo purchases drugs only yards away from where his son plays and then cuts back to show Agee's visible distress as he watches the transaction.

Gates's freshman and sophomore years, narrated in terms of his academic and athletic achievements at St. Joseph, clarify his central contribution to realizing Pingatore's dream of playing in the state finals. But, as media pundits identify Gates as the next Isiah Thomas, Gates suffers a potentially career-ending knee injury. Once injured, his story is most explicitly organized around his struggle with his knee. In a context dominated by uncertainty and Gates's knee surgery, his mother and older brother discuss their investment in Gates playing in the NBA. Here we learn that Curtis also was an exceptionally talented player who earned a scholarship to Florida State University. Apparently unable or unwilling to follow the rules, Curtis dropped out.

At Marshall, Agee improves dramatically and becomes a star in Chicago's public school league and the local media. His accomplishments on the basketball court are paralleled by the reuniting of his parents: Bo is released from jail and overcomes a drug addiction, and Sheila graduates as a nurses' assistant. His team eventually qualifies for and places third in the state championships in Champaign, Illinois, as Pingatore watches as a spectator. Because Agee cannot meet the SAT requirements, he accepts an athletic scholarship from Mineral Area Junior College in Missouri. In Missouri, Agee lives in the "Basketball House"—a dormitory located in the middle of a field, far removed from the rest of the campus—along with six of the seven black students at the college.

As Gates struggles with recurring knee injuries and to attain the minimum SAT score, he and his girlfriend, Catherine, have had a child, Alicia. After a strong performance at the Nike summer basketball camp, where Gates suffers another injury, he receives an "unconditional" athletic scholarship offer from Marquette University. The movie ends with Gates, uncertain of his desire to pursue a career in basketball, leaving for Marquette. In a written postscript, the filmmakers report that after graduating from Mineral Area with a C average, Agee continued to play at Arkansas State University, a Division I school, where he started point guard: "a national basketball magazine judged the team's success to be largely dependent on Agee's success. In his first start, Agee hit a 30-foot jump shot at the buzzer to win the game."[9] Gates, we are told, married Catherine, who moved to Marquette with their daughter. In his junior year, he became increasingly disillusioned with basketball and decided to drop out of school. His family persuaded him otherwise, and the university agreed to let him continue studying, without playing basketball.

"AMERICA" RESPONDS TO *HOOP DREAMS*

Since its premiere at the 1994 Sundance Film Festival in Park City, Utah (the premier showcase for independent films), *Hoop Dreams* received widespread and enthusiastic endorsement. It won Sundance's "Audience Award" and was the first documentary to claim the New York Film Festival's prestigious closing spot. The filmmakers signed a contract with Turner Broadcasting, who owns Fine Line Features (the distributor of the documentary). Turner immediately hired Spike Lee as executive producer and possibly director of its made-for-television counterpart. Additionally, Turner offered cross-promotion of the film during its airing of NBA games, bringing the cycle of takeovers and mergers that resulted from Reagan's deregulation policies into focus. Various teams in the NBA, including the Altanta Hawks and the Golden State Warriors, promoted the film by presenting trailers and conducting giveaway contests during games. Fine Line Features announced that it had "taken the film as a personal cause." Nike helped to establish an 800 number for local community group tickets and was credited with persuading *Sports Illustrated* to pay for the publication and mailing costs of a teacher/student guide that accompanied the release of the film. Nike, having never before endorsed a film, explained that they "really believed in the message of the film," a message they classified in terms of hope, spirit, sport, and family (Collins, 1994, p. B21).

Mainstream reviews (apparently diverging from Nike's depiction) endlessly applauded *Hoop Dreams* for eluding and exceeding the boundaries of seductive sport cliches. *Hoop Dreams*, we are repeatedly told, is about something of vastly greater significance than sport—that is, it is about real urban America. *Washington Post* film critic Hal Hinson (1994) suggests that "*Hoop Dreams* provides more emotion and human drama than 10 Hollywood movies" (p. F7). In the words of Michael Wilmington (1994a), "We get the true, raw emotion usually buried under the glitz and hoke of the average Hollywood-ized sports movie. . . . It isn't a slice of life—but a huge chunk of it" (p. 13:5). Popular critics pronounced the film "an American epic," as they declared Gates and Agee instant celebrities and the filmmakers heroes and filmic pioneers. *Hoop Dreams*, touted as a film that all Americans should see, was recognized as a timely, "warts and all" documentation of real urban life and, by extension, it was deemed a potent educational tool.

Indeed, reviews intimated that the youths' dreams to play professional basketball set the stage for a larger diagnosis of the poor inner city: a complex, realistic, and positive portrait of black inner-city life that was not, according to mainstream reviews, typically available to middle-class America. Mainstream media accounts repeatedly implied that America was prepared for—apparently even sought—an objective account of the conditions of the inner city that challenged the dominant versions offered. In a telling comment that punctuates the affective purchase of the documentary drama, Steve James told the *Chicago Tribune*, "White people have told us that the only contact they have with inner-city neighborhoods is what they see from their high-rise . . . but seeing a film like this, they really felt connection" (quoted in Wilmington, 1994a, p. 13:20).

Claims to the film's social consciousness are repeated in reviews and substantiated through declarations that distinguish *Hoop Dreams* from Hollywood films about urban America. While Patrick McGavin (1994) contends that "the film does not demonize inner-city life" (p. 26), academic critic Lee Jones (1996) extends that claim by suggesting that the film "decenters long-held stereotypes about residents who happen to live in the inner ghetto" (p. 8). Jones commended the film's intervention in routine representations of inner-city residents as less than human and improperly social:

> Within it [the film] lie simple stories about the strength of the often fragmented families, the importance of the extended family in the African-American community, the love shared at family celebrations and gatherings, the tremendous resilience in the face of too frequent setbacks, and the role that black women play in maintaining the family unit under the conditions of near Third World poverty. These themes take us on a journey to the other United States, capturing real human stories that remain ignored within popular debates about inner-city pathology. (p. 8)

Such pronouncements and conclusions were consistent with and reinforced that which director Peter Gilbert named as one of the filmmakers' primary concerns: "One of the things that was very important to us is that the people in the film are human beings. That they don't fit the stereotypes of inner city life" (quoted in McGavin, 1994, p. 26). The cornerstone of praise surrounding the film is linked, in many ways, to "felt connection" forged through a recognition of sameness—of the opportunity provided to viewers by the film (and, ultimately, by the filmmakers) to reassess the humanity of Gates, Agee, and their families. Although such declarations may sound promising, appeals to universal human forms, an invention of modernity, work to depoliticize the material circumstances that shape the everyday struggles of America's most vulnerable populations. That is, the celebrated "sameness" (which displaces material conditions and differences) contributes to both the viewers' intimate and pleasurable experience and the film's reality effect.

The *Chicago Tribune* depicted the film's excellence and realness in terms of its "big-picture" effect:

> *Hoop Dreams* has the movie-equivalent of all-court vision. It picks up everything happening in the gym, in the stands, and even outside. It gives us the thrill of the game, but it doesn't cheat on the vibrant social context of a deep human interest story. We understand the problems—racial, social, and economic—Arthur, Gates, and their families have to fight. And, because *Hoop Dreams* is real, happening right now in front of us, it involves our emotions on an exceptionally intense level. (Wilmington, 1994b, p. 7C)

Numerous media reviews depicted *Hoop Dreams* as an exemplar of realism, social advocacy, and media activism. As we have discussed, some reviewers identified its achievement in terms of its documentation of the real story of inner-city life. Others identified the film's contribution in terms of its making visible and comprehensible the humanity of poor, urban African Americans. Mainstream reviews lauded the film for its affective dimensions routinely attributed to both. Moreover, the filmmakers were commended for providing a much-needed critique of certain aspects of the sport entertainment system in the United States. Overall, *Hoop Dreams* was revered and imbued with the status of a vanguard film that furnished America with a unique educational opportunity. While such knowledge claims are most obviously made possible by the realist pretensions of documentary filmmaking, that aesthetic dimension was complemented with a narrative of integrity culled through a network of recurring themes that drew attention to the good intentions and personal virtues of its three white filmmakers: Steve James, Fred Marx, and Peter Gilbert. The congratulatory representations of these filmmakers celebrated for making truth available to mainstream audiences stand in stark contrast to the representations of *Clockers* and its director, Spike Lee.

SPIKE LEE'S *CLOCKERS*

Clockers opens with a series of images that disrupts now-familiar passageways and filmic invitations into urban America. While *Hoop Dreams* transports viewers by elevated train into poorer areas of inner-city Chicago (explicitly organizing the film as an ethnographic excursion of sorts), *Clockers* immediately confronts viewers with close-up images of African-American men, killed by gunshot.[10] Yellow and black police tape designates and contains the space of the crime and identifies the bodies as police territory. Their deaths are inscribed into local public memory by colorful murals produced by gang members. Before moving out of the film's documentary moment, Lee redirects the attention to a page from a handgun catalogue and an extract from a magazine story describing the accidental shooting death of a 12-year-old African-American boy by a police officer. The headline reads: "Toy Gun, Real Tragedy."

Viewing sensibility shifts as the film turns to familiar and overdetermined signs of urban America: a series of high-story, concrete buildings—the Nelson Mandella Homes in the Brooklyn projects—and a quintet of African-American male teens whose embodied display of caps, sports shirts, and sneakers resonate with rap's "gangsta" image. As the camera closes in on the group, we find them engaged in an animated and not so easily understood discussion about the "hardness" of rappers such as Chuck D, Tupac, and Dr. Dre.[11] At first glance, this appears to be a "slothful" scene, with the camera resting on a group of young men "hanging out" in the summer courtyard at the center of the homes. But as a white man, jittery and nervous, appears at the edge of the square, the men promptly disperse and spring into action. It quickly becomes apparent that this is the hub: the place, a social and an economic space, where drugs are bought and sold according to meticulous, prescribed, and intricate pattern of gestures and movements. The young men, viewers now realize, are "clockers"—low-ranking drug dealers who work around the clock.

Based on Richard Price's best-selling novel of the same name, *Clockers* tells the story of Ronald "Strike" Dunham, a 19-year-old Brooklyn clocker, who spends the majority of his time alongside his crew, selling drugs from the benches in front of the projects where he lives. Dunham works for Rodney, the local drug kingpin, his father figure and mentor, who watches from a safer distance as Dunham and friends deal with routine policing, harassment, and humiliation. A younger generation of youths, including 12-year-old Tyrone, who admires and emulates Dunham, also witnesses the selling and policing. As a demonstration of loyalty and means of career advancement, Rodney asks Dunham to murder Darryl Adams, a dealer who Rodney claims has been stealing from him. Dunham's ambivalence about the task is evident as he paces outside of Ahab's, the greasy spoon where Adams works as the night manager. As Dunham contemplates the task at hand, a huge anti-gun/anti-drug billboard looms in the background: "No More Packing." Unable to pull the trigger, Dunham stops in Cool Breeze, a local bar, in search of a chocolate Moo (a sweet dairy drink that provides temporary relief from his stomach ulcer, the source of chronic pain and bleeding). There he meets his old brother, Victor, and proceeds to tell him that Adams is a "wife beater" and a drug dealer who needs to "be got." Victor tells him that he knows someone who can do the job.

Dunham leaves the bar and once again stands outside of Ahab's. The image is compelling: Adams, a cartoonlike, buffoonish figure (who is unaware of the gun and decision facing him), stands in the doorway taunting and humiliating Dunham about his need for Mylanta and "pussy-bismo." The wall behind Dunham is covered with a massive black-and-white image of Michael Jordan. Across the bottom Nike's signature "Participate in the Lives of America's Youth P.L.A.Y." appears in large letters.

Red blinking lights of a police unit suggest Adams's murder. Inside the car are detectives Rocco Klein and Larry Mazilli, who are on their way to a gruesome crime scene. Adams is dead, with four bullets pummelled into his body, one caught in his teeth. Shortly after, Victor confesses to the murder. Victor is *not* a clocker: he is married and has two young children; in his effort to move his family out of the projects, he works two full-time jobs; in high school, he was a star athlete. Stated differently, Victor is *the* quintessential disciplined, hard-working, inner-city family man. Victor tells Klein that he killed Adams because he was "tired." He explains his mental and physical state the night of the murder in terms of exhaustion, of working two jobs that do not allow him to see his two children. Klein is convinced that Victor's confession is contrived, and that he is taking the fall for his younger brother. Pointing to the inconsistencies in his story, Klein demands the truth. Victor responds by telling him that "the truth is looking at you."

Determined to extract the truth from Dunham, Klein sets out on a course meant to facilitate justice. His plan is to create the illusion that Dunham has betrayed Rodney, but as his scheme unfolds, it initiates a chain of events that leads to the murder of Erole, another of Rodney's employees. Tyrone (the 12-year-old who admires Dunham) has shot and killed Erole in an effort to protect Dunham. By the film's end, Klein is forced to face the truth that Victor, the figure typically associated with individual achievement and community regeneration, killed Adams. Victor receives a "light sentence" (although the exact terms remain unclear), and Klein, perhaps as a means of alleviating his guilt, saves Tyrone from prison and helps Dunham leave the area, via Amtrak, in search of safety and a new life.

"AMERICA" RESPONDS TO *CLOCKERS*

Although *Clockers* is marked by a general absence of both basketball courts and references to dreams of playing in the NBA, the film can help us understand the curious place that "urban basketball" holds in the contemporary American imagination. Indeed, despite their apparent distance, *Clockers* and *Hoop Dreams* are implicated in similar themes: both are elements in a discursive formation whose widespread conventions (drugs, crime, rap, sneakers, and basketball) govern and organize America's prominent recognition of the inner city, its inhabitants, and violence. Specifically, *Clocker's* object of interrogation, the monstrosity/violence attributed to criminalized black masculinity, remains the invisible but necessary other of *Hoop Dreams*. It is the urban, criminal black youth, a central object of *Clockers*, that renders visible and intelligible the "urban basketball player," the NBA star, and, most specifically, Nike's Michael Jordan, who lurks in the background of both films.

Popular reviews of *Clockers* are mixed and differ in emphasis and tone; none offers the sort of praise, enthusiasm, and celebratory rhetoric that characterized the popular response to *Hoop Dreams*. While *Hoop Dreams* is applauded for its narrative integrity and good politics, Lee's film is criticized for its lack of realism, distracting camera work, insufficiently developed characters and scenes (particularly the murder scene), and unsatisfactorily resolved narrative.

That uninterrogated dyad of athlete and criminal, an element central to the weight and authority of liberal humanist categories underlying the apparent integrity of the *Hoop Dreams'* narrative, is part of *Hoop Dreams'* seduction. *Clockers* challenges, dislocates, and renegotiates that classificatory scheme by contesting the act/identity relation shaped by modern logic that undergirds the "athlete" and "criminal" categories. The dyad is most conspicuously exposed when Klein places individual photographs of Dunham and Victor side by side and rehearses the now-familiar classification constituting the primary pairing organizing America's racial imagination:

Klein [scrutinizing the photograph of Dunham while his left hand covers the picture of Victor]: What do I know? On the night of the shooting. Has the jumps. Never sat down. Left sober before the shooting. Yo's jacket shows possession with intent, possession of unlicensed firearm, and assault.

Mazilli [places hand over Dunham's picture and points to the photograph of Victor]: Listen to me now Rocco. He's all strung out on a few snortzovers, one night. He gets fried. Walks outta Cool Breeze with the heat in his gym bag. The Adams guy jumps out. Startles him. Pops the first guy who steps on his Nikes. Like a cappa on a bad day. Gets religion. Comes in. Gives it up. Pack it up. It's over.

Klein: Come on Larry. Can't you see? Larry [holding picture of Victor in his hand], Yo walks in, says he's the shooter. With no record, two adorable kids, two jobs, model citizen. Claims self-defense. Who's gonna argue? Now this other one [picks up picture of Dunham], if he tried to pull dat bullshit they'd throw the key away, he's an known scumbag. No wonder that his confession sounds like horseshit, he's lying. Victor never got off that barstool [cut to the picture of Victor]. Yo's taking the weight for his brother [cut to the picture of Dunham].

Mazilli: For what? Brotherly love? Fear? For Money? What?

Klein: They ran a game on me these two. 'Cos this cocksucker [picks up Victor's picture] is an innocent man.

Mazilli: Just because a nubian . . . got a wife, a job, two kids, a dog, a goldfish, and a bank account—he can't be a shooter? You did everything but stick your tongue down his throat. The kid didn't budge. Rocco, listen to me. Even if this Victor kid is selling us a line of shit on the tape, which is what they all do anyhow, even if they givin' it up. This is still a good, solid, close-by-arrest. And if I'm wrong. If Rodney conspired in on this, or Strike, or the fucking Medellen cartel, I don't give a fuck, 'cos we got da shoota.

Klein: . . . locked up the wrong brother . . .

This clarifies the act/identity relation that gives contemporary origin stories of crime, racial monstrosity, urban decay, and dystopic and utopic narratives their contemporary force. Although the strategies creating and sustaining these act/identity relations typically are erased, the bodies are presented as archival bodies—the bodies of recorded knowledges. While *Hoop Dreams* enacts and encodes the knowledges governing the national imagination, *Clockers* draws attention to and disturbs the primary dyad organizing and authorizing the American racial imagination.

While *Hoop Dreams'* success is inextricably linked to America's enthusiastic consumption of the African-American basketball player and corresponding narratives embodied by this figure, basketball players and their attendant meanings are strikingly absent in *Clockers'* landscape. Indeed, Dunham's obsession with miniature railways and trains punctuates the narrative in ways that disrupt ubiquitous inner-city basketball tales. The following exchange between Dunham and JoJo, a detective sent by Klein to convince Dunham to talk, illustrates this strategy by drawing attention to what is necessarily excluded and repressed to maintain the athlete/criminal dyad:

> JoJo: Dunham, my man! This is a new day, Strike. Dinkins out. Booty in. Law and order. Cut the budget. Party's over. Crack down on drugs, crime, niggers, spicks, the homeless, weepy men, African Americans. Have a seat [he pushes Strike down on the bench]. So, what's up?
>
> Dunham: Not a thing, detective.
>
> JoJo: Detective? Call me JoJo. You like basketball?
>
> Dunham: Nah, I don't like sports.
>
> JoJo: What do you like?
>
> Dunham: Trains [he opens his shirt to reveal a train T-shirt].
>
> JoJo: Choo-choo trains? You can't dunk a basketball?
>
> Dunham: Nahh.
>
> JoJo: Nah. Get the fuck outta here, man. You been slammin before you was crawlin!

The comparative invisibility of basketball does not in itself or by itself work to disturb the sport/gang dyad. Rather, it is Lee's attempts to make visible the socioeconomic conditions necessarily repressed by this dyad, which challenge its omnipotence. Thus rather than representing Dunham as the more familiar figure of racial monstrosity and source of inner-city violence, Lee continually underscores the conditions of everyday life as violent and as the source of violence. Victor's act of murder, Lee shows, cannot be separated from the insurmountable obstacles that he encounters in the simple, practical matter of making a living, and Dunham's decision to sell drugs appears as an adaptation to the conditions in which he lives. Clocking offers steady employment and a living wage for people who otherwise stand little chance of either.[12]

Klein's and Victor's exchange illustrates the ways in which *Clockers* draws attention to "already known truths," as Klein tries to consolidate Victor's identity as a hard-working, "good, decent, church-going, God-fearing" man, with the violent act that he claims to have committed. Particularly interesting is the explicit problematization of vision ("the truth is looking at you," and Lee's highly stylized shot of Klein's reflection in Victor's eyeball)—modernity's privileged strategy for assigning and locating deviance and threat.

Victor: Have you ever come home so tired you hated the sound of your own kids' crying? Your own flesh and blood? My wife Sharon says: "So quit a job, you've got two." What the hell she thinks I got these two jobs for in the first place, huh? I'm trying. I'm really trying to move us out of the projects. You know what I'm saying? I'm working. I'm saving. I'm trying to do the best I can. Provide those ends. I gotta work. I'm never late. I gotta work.

Klein: Victor, listen to me. You're a good, decent, church-going, God-fearing kid, and if you did pull the trigger, there has to be a reasonable answer other than what you've told me here. I gotta ask myself why would Darrell, the night manager at Ahab's, try to rob you in his own parking lot? So I think there had to be something personal.

Victor: No, I never saw him before in my life.

Klein: He flexed, you shot?

Victor: Look, I'm through with it. I told you what happened. I gave you the gun. What else do you want?

Klein: The truth, Victor.

Victor: The truth is looking at you man!

Klein: If the guy did something to you. If he threatened you, your family, this helps you. You were buggin'. Can't eat. Can't sleep. This helps you in court. What did that prick do to you?

Victor: It was self-defense.

Klein: Self-defense, huh? [Leaning toward Victor, Klein's reflection appears in Victor's eyeball] I wanna see what you see. I disagree. I don't think I look that fuckin' stupid.

Clocker's challenge to the sport/gang dyad is reinforced by the failure of the ascribed categories "drug dealer" and "productive family man" to render intelligible individual character. While drug dealers typically are represented through the breach of the work ethic, failed disciplined, incomprehensible violence, and pathological greed, Dunham is shown as disciplined, hard working, generous, and incapable of violence. When the public consumes *Hoop Dreams*, it also consumes a fantasy of racial sameness and politics through compassion: *Clockers* disavows both fantasies. While neither film fully interrogates the forces defining the post–Fordist city, *Hoop Dreams* relieves spectators of responsibility of critical reflection and their implication in exploitative spectator and consumption practices.

REALISM AND CONSUMPTION: CAN SPIKE LEE EVER GET IT RIGHT?

From the release of his first commercially successful film, *She's Gotta Have It* (1986), Spike Lee has been a controversial figure in the national imagination. Contention about Lee and his films has hinged on several recurring themes. While *She's Gotta Have It* stimulated debate among African-American feminists concerned (or not) with Lee's portrayal of women, the most prominent debate centers on the authenticity of his portrayal of African-American life: do his films capture some supposed "essence" of African-American culture, or are they, on the contrary, negative and stereotypical depictions of black, inner-city residents? *Do the Right Thing*, released in the summer of 1989, ignited a storm of popular and academic criticism (negative and positive) along these lines. The most widely circulated accusation came from critics who found the film so realistic that they denounced it as an incitement to violence. (This hysteria even prompted the *New York Times* to convene a panel of academics, law enforcement personnel, media pundits, and community activists to explore issues raised by the film.) While the ruckus surrounding *Do the Right Thing* was particularly intense, the controversy resurfaced with the release of *Clockers*. The response to *Clockers* proved to be uniform, as critics, almost without exception and regardless of their opinion, evaluated the film's correspondence to the reality of the inner city. Critics' support was linked to their understanding of the film as a critique of urban America, a cautionary tale and morality play about the evils and dangers of drugs: "The sanguine extravaganza is poetic pay-back for his [Dunham's] sin: dealing drugs" (Bradley, 1995, p. 32). "*Clockers* is about the curse of drugs on a sector of society that is especially vulnerable to them" (Kauffmann, 1995, p. 39). Lee has depicted "a compelling portrait of the self-destructive drug culture that rules our inner cities. America's most influential black filmmaker has clearly done the right thing, both as spokesman and as an artist (Schwager, "The Black Struggle in a White Society: Mr Show biz Archive reviews www.mrshowbiz.com"). While the dynamics and demands of the drug market are an important strain in the *Clockers* narrative, the film disrupts the liberal humanist premises (as it is expressed in terms of individualism, pathological self-destruction, the inherent evil of drugs, and logic of addiction) on which such comments are based.

The affective dimension of this disturbance appears in condemnations of *Clockers'* portrayal in the inner city. As a review in the *New York Times* demonstrates, these responses work as strategies to manage and redirect this disruption:

> Hell is missing from "Clockers." Though dialogue and cinematography present the drug trade's twisted economic concepts, the social effects only appear obliquely. . . . Even the urban ubiquity of drug litter is absent. (Bradley, 1995, 32)

Bradley extends the trope of vision as he argues that Lee's subjectivity cannot be translated into objectivity:

> Supposedly, an auteur's vision reveals the meaning of his subject. But what if his vision overwhelms that meaning? What if a director sees only what he wants to see? When does auteurism become egoism? (Bradley, 1995, 32)

Hoop Dreams' filmmaker Steve James's claim to objectivity stands in stark contrast to such criticisms as he implicitly criticizes not only Lee's style but challenges to what is already known:

> I admire some filmmakers who have carved out a distinctive aesthetic style, but their aesthetic style is about who they are. I'm always interested in capturing something about the world out there. And I plead guilty to being interested in films that are accessible. (quoted in Aufderheide, 1994, p. 34)

Harry Allen, critic for the *Village Voice*, interrogates the "reality" of *Clockers* as he cites "canyon-size gaps in character motivation and logic" that frequent the movie (1995, p. 84). Allen substantiates his view by invoking three experts' (an authentic drug dealer, a narcotics cop, and an emergency medical technician) assessment of filmic "reality." Ace, "a self-described on and off drug dealer" generally undermines the film's authenticity by claiming that he has never heard the term *clockers*. Ace's authority is established when Allen asks him about his experiences. Ace replies that he has had experiences "a lot." He continues, "I ain't ever been shot. I've been shot at. I've been in gunfights. Never been stabbed, never stabbed nobody, I don't know if I've shot anybody. Most likely, I probably did, but I don't know" (Allen, 1995, p. 84). Ace, unlike Dunham, does not take violence seriously: his attitude is clearly expressed when he identifies as this most realistic moment Dunham's crew beating him up for talking to Klein, as he lies on the ground writhing in agony with a burst ulcer. The portrayal of police is the most unrealistic in "narcotics cop" Luis Arroyo's view. Citing the dropped-pants search early in the film, and another scene in which Klein throws Dunham around an interrogation room, Arroyo says, "Here in New York City, that don't play well. Especially with all of the liberals we have living in the city, we have to play by a fine line, and with the new commissioner we have right now, something like that would have got all of those officers in the movie suspended or fired." For Arroyo the film's most realistic moment, something he has "all too often" seen, occurs when Dunham's mother refuses to take the "drug" money he offers for his brother's bail. Emergency medical technician (EMT) John Hancher criticizes the "overdone" crime-scene photos. "Murders that I've been to aren't usually this graphic looking, and I wondered if the graphics department at the film had actually doctored them up to make them look worse . . . I thought they were a little fake" (Allen, 1995, p. 84).

Hoop Dreams' realism is not questioned and is enhanced by media narratives which, to a great extent, distance the film production and motivation from capitalist imperatives and consumer-driven individualism. Media collaboration in the production of truth-effects, narrative integrity, and valorized identities is most easily observed in the disproportionate commentary devoted to the "actual making" of the film. Repeatedly, consumers are reminded that the filmmakers shot 250 hours of film over a period of 4½ years, that the film was made on an extremely low budget, and that all three filmmakers accumulated huge debts in the process. As Michael Wilmington (1994a) of the *Chicago Tribune* remarked, "The odds are so stacked against their [Agee's and Gates's] success. There's an obvious analogy with the long shot world of independent filmmaking itself" (p. 5). Along a related theme, Steve James told the *Washington Post* that the fact that he and his colleagues drove "rust bucket cars" was an important factor in gaining their subjects' trust (Howe, 1994, p. G4). Such unifying thematics rely on and generate easy slippages between the socioeconomic conditions of the filmmakers and the Agee and Gates families that trivialize the economic and social devastation defining the conditions of the concentrations of poverty in the post–Fordist inner city and the everyday lives of those who inhabitant such spaces. That reviewers felt able to draw parallels between the socioeconomic situation of two African-American youths from Chicago's poor inner city and the economic hardship that defines independent filmmaking is testament to the filmic and popular erasures of the historical forces shaping the lives of the urban poor. Such erasures allow for the recontextualization and production of the film's history, which contribute to filmic truth-effects.

More telling are the repetitions that portray filmmakers James, Marx, and Gilbert as being acutely loyal to Agee, Gates, and their families, which are inseparable from those lauding them for the financial and personal sacrifices made in order to complete the film. In what we think are symptomatic repetitions, the filmmakers appear repeatedly through the categories of loyalty and ethical superiority. We are told that unlike others before them, these filmmakers were persistently loyal, despite the difficulties that Agee and Gates confronted. That which the filmmakers take to be, by definition, the subject matter of the film—the predicaments encountered by Agee and Gates—is narrated as a "test" of the filmmakers' character. Numerous interviews recount Steve James's depiction of Agee's astonishment that the filmmakers continued filming him after he was expelled from St. Joseph. Similarly, several reviews draw attention to Emma Gates's initial ambivalence about the film and filmmakers, and her subsequent conversion experience: it was only after the filmmakers made clear that they would not abandon her son's story when a knee injury threatened his career that she came to trust them. For example, the *Washington Post* offered the following depiction as evidence of the filmmakers' loyalty:

> Initially, William's mother, Emma Gates—who felt she had been badly represented in a television program about the Cabrini Green housing project—didn't even want to appear on the film. But things changed after Gates faced a career set-back—a lingering knee injury—and the filmmakers did not desert him: Emma finally agreed to be interviewed.

"She realized," says Gilbert. "We weren't going to run away because things didn't fit the storybook ideal."

When a different kind of trouble threatened Agee's basketball future, "he was literally surprised when we showed up to film him," Gilbert says. "He told us, 'Why would you want to help me now?' We said, 'It's because we care about you'" (Howe, 1994, p. G4).

At first glance, such anecdotes may simply appear to be true, real-life, "behind the-scene" stories or background information; yet such anecdotes reveal America's "political unconscious" (to use Frederick Jameson's term), as they reshape America's historical consciousness and the public's reception of *Hoop Dreams*. Such repetitions suggest that the narrative is not simply about "trust"; instead, the narrative, which is most often and most explicitly organized around the unexpected material and financial success of the film and, by extension, the filmmakers, appears to be motivated by anxieties about guilt. The origin narrative repeatedly relieves anxieties about guilt by drawing attention to innocence, goodwill, personal virtues, and the highly principled, ethical behavior of the filmmakers.

While mainstream reviews underscore the philanthropy of *Hoop Dreams'* filmmakers, Lee is represented as "artistically misguided," "immature," and "excessively didactic" (Gorringe, 1995). Indeed, the concentrated attention to the philanthropy of the filmmakers reverses the critique that might have ensued through a different, more historical contextualization. For example, *Hoop Dreams'* origin story fails to account for the relationship between the rise of the NBA and its role in revitalizing America's post–Fordist cities. It neglects the correspondence between the making of the African-American NBA celebrity and America's war on inner-city youth. Not coincidentally, *Hoop Dreams* was initiated the same year that both Michael Jordan and crack became national preoccupations. Although elided by the origin story, the conditions of possibility of *Hoop Dreams* (by which we mean the *Hoop Dreams* portfolio, the comprehensive *Hoop Dreams* phenomenon) are embedded in a complex of transnational corporate interests, including the media, the NBA, and manufacturers of sports apparel that motivate the film and its popularity. The exclusions that govern the promotional *Hoop Dreams'* origin story effectively designate, establish, and stabilize the narrative integrity of the film.

Hoop Dreams' narrative integrity is inseparable from its representation as the offspring of hard work, loyalty, and selflessness. While it is seen as a purely accidental commercial success, Lee is regularly associated with celebrity, capitalism, and "sneaker-related violence." Jerome Christensen, in a piece entitled "Spike Lee, Corporate Populist," argues that the ultimate point of *Do the Right Thing* is the legitimation of Spike Lee's celebrity—a corporate populism that erases questions of power. Lee's independence, he argues, acquires its social silhouette and its political feel by his dramatized opposition to the major studios. Lee, unlike *Hoop Dreams'* filmmakers, can do business with the studios and maintain his independence, because they share the same social ontology and belong to the same corporate intertext. According to Christensen, Forty Acres aspires to the status of Touchstone Pictures; Spike's Joint is a nascent Walt Disney World.

CONCLUSION

As we have argued, popular narrations of *Hoop Dreams* suggest that its representation of urban America differs markedly from those previously available in the national popular. Its most important achievement is defined, by critics, in terms of its brutally real and honest portrayal of the realities of the poor inner city. Although its pedagogical value is routinely cast in terms of realness, we have argued that this realness is more accurately understood as a reality effect. This reality effect is symptomatic of a point of view whose limits and exclusions have been naturalized and are therefore not easily recognizable—an effect of the undisturbed, "already known." The exclusions that lend stability to categories such as sport/gangs, violence, humanity, and sameness work to produce contemporary deviant black masculinities. The introduction of Catherine (Gates's girlfriend) only after Alicia is born, for example, is an editing strategy that "reassures" viewers by making clear that Gates will take on the nationally sanctioned familial responsibility. The filmmakers may have been attempting to (wittingly or not) intervene in myths of the hypersexual black male, but rather than challenging cultural fears of black sexuality, such exclusions corroborate attributions of deviant sexuality to black men. That distancing strategy maintains the sharp differentiation between the inside/outside, the human/nonhuman, and the productive/unproductive governing and organizing the national imagination. In other words, while Gates figures the "human" (a stated authorial intention), the sport/gang dyad remains stable, marking what and who are deviant (both within the film and the national imagination). Again, as a means of translating subjectivity into objectivity, the images of African-American youths and African-American families in *Hoop Dreams* tell us more about the state of mind of the country than its does about real urban poverty and lived conditions. In contemporary America, the compassion and connection felt toward Agee, Gates, and their families suggest that revenge directed at criminalized African-American youth through excessive punitive measures is legitimate, since what calls for punishment (typically identified in terms of inexplicable acts of violence) is obvious and justified, and it requires no interrogation.

Steve James depicts the standing ovation received by *Hoop Dreams* at the New York Film Festival as an expression of the connection that the audience felt for the Gates and Agee families: the applause, at least on one level, is for the recognition of sameness, shared values, and desires. The audience's desire to recognize itself in the lives of a particular urban poor population and to celebrate that recognition is deeply problematic and symptomatic of the position from which identity is forged and judgements are made, America's quest for sameness and, relatedly, America's inability to think adequately about difference and inequality.[13] Easy slippages between the conditions of poor, primarily African-American, inner-city residents who face inhumane conditions of poverty, inadequate public assistance, and limited employment possibilities and "white, high-rise America," slippages routinely facilitated through the category of "family," are not necessarily something to be celebrated. Instead, in our view, they are indicative of the "knowledges" that govern the audience's understanding of the crisis of the inner city in ways that demonize single parents, welfare, welfare recipients, the underemployed and unemployed, and African-American youths in general. Moreover, these slippages, particularly as they are aligned with and call for a reconstitution of the family, work in concert with the neoconservative agenda of empowerment—will, self-sufficiency, and independence.

Although *Clockers* is perhaps most easily understood to be a film about drugs, even its most damning critics unwittingly acknowledge its complexity by pointing to the larger system of representation in which it accrues meaning. For example, when David Bradley (1995) contends that the ending of *Clockers* (which he defines in terms of Lee's vision) undercuts the story and Lee's best intentions (he asks, "For what is the point of showing dead bodies if you show a killer getting out of jail?" [p. 32]), he calls for justice in terms of punishment and revenge. Thus Bradley points to the relevance of topics such as responsibility, violence, justice, and punishment (as well as revenge) addressed by the film. Lee's film does not deny the violence associated with drugs, but, and more importantly, he does not deny the violence and destructive forces that are not easily imagined through modern logic. As a result, *Clockers* does not rely on categories in which the virtuous and vicious are easily distinguishable, and, therefore, troubles categories such as sameness, responsibility, freedom, and justice, which are foundational to America's identity. Dunham, the familiar figure of racial monstrosity in the national imagination, through which calls for revenge are justified, does not appear as the source of violence, and Victor's act is not abstracted from the monstrosities of the conditions in which he tries to survive. These conditions appear to be the insurmountable obstacles that he encounters in the simple, practical matter of making a living. Victor's state of physical and psychic exhaustion (the bodily habitus of poverty) exposes the deception of the promises shored up by America's foundational categories. In contrast, Dunham's decision to sell drugs appears as a rational adaptation to local conditions. In both cases, *Clockers* problematizes the sovereignty of acts, and in so doing, it problematizes the concepts of "choice" and "responsibility"—categories central to America's justice system.

Finally, figures like *Hoop Dreams'* Gene Pingatore work to displace guilt and implication onto easily identifiable agents.[14] We do not mean to suggest that these easily identifiable agents are not implicated in exploitative relations; instead, our intent is to direct attention to how such figures of displacement operate in the national popular to relieve guilt and to produce ethically superior subjects. In *Hoop Dreams*, "Gene Pingatore" helps mainstream audiences reconcile the conflict between inner-city poverty, their vengeful calls to punish, and the sense of themselves as compassionate, virtuous, and morally superior. In other words, guilt and the audience's implication in exploitative spectatorship and consumption practices are displaced onto Pingatore. The discomfort of *Clockers* is the moral ambiguity that is introduced into the foundational categories of America's truth. Indeed, while *Hoop Dreams'* Pingatore functions as a figure of displacement, allowing the American, middle-class audience to derive identification and pleasure, *Clockers* provides no easy escape.

NOTES

1. We label the diverse genres representing the racially coded urban spaces "ethnographic" because these images are generated through a racial relationship consistent with imperial ethnographies. During the late 1980s and the early 1990s, the ethnographic moments appeared in multiple forms of urban black, male, coming-of-age stories. This includes films like such as Spike Lee's (1989) *Do the Right Thing*, Matty Rich's (1991) *Straight Out of Brooklyn*, and John Singleton's (1991) *Boyz N the Hood* and the proliferation of popular books about the inner city, including Alex Kotlowitz's (1992) *There Are No Children Here*; Daniel Coyle's (1995) *Hardball: A Season in the Projects*; Greg Donaldson's (1994) *The Ville: Cops and Kids in Urban America*; and Darcy

Frey's (1994) *The Last Shot: City Streets, Basketball Dreams*. We also include newsclips, television dramas, NBA celebrity stories, and advertisements in this new ethnography. The popularity of these images has been interpreted as an indication of the commodification and mainstreaming of a multicultural agenda which, in the case of these films, is represented synecdochically through black masculinity and the black family.

2. "Archival bodies" (modern deviant corporeal subjectivities) and the ethnographic association of progress and racial hierarchies also are configured through modern categories. For an explanation of deviant corporeal subjectivities and modern power, particularly as they relate to sport and contemporary America, see Cole (1996a, 1996b).

3. In previous work, Cole has shown how what she refers to as the sport/gang dyad accrued prominence in the national imagination, particularly through the war on drugs. Although space does not permit an analysis of that dyad, this is based on that previous work. Readers unfamiliar with the ascendancy of that dyad should see Cole (1996a, 1996b) and Cole and King (1998). A key point in that work is the relationship between sport and gangs and the so-called "failed black family" (figured through the welfare mother and the absent, inseminating black male). That is, the "failed black family" (a historical mechanism for displacing the social, economic, and political forces shaping the lives of the urban poor) never simply lurked in the background, lending plausibility to the significance of sport and gangs in the lives of urban youth. Instead, the racially coded pathological family, urban sport, and gangs occupied the same symbolic space: violations of the nuclear family form were a subtext in coming-of-age narratives. The racially coded pathological family, the most powerful defining feature of the dyad, braced and intensified the psychic power of the racially coded sport/gang relation in the national imagination.

4. *Clockers* does not present itself as a documentary but as a more obviously scripted Hollywood film. As Rony (1996) explains, "scholars have overlooked the ways in which standard ethnographic film is linked to popular media entertainments and Hollywood spectacle" (p. 12).

5. The provisions established by recent U. S. crime bills have yielded substantial expansion in prison construction as well as prison populations. Since 1980, 600 new prisons have been built to house an incarcerated population that has increased from 500,000 to 1.5 million (Donzinger, 1996). As a result of the highly racialized patterns of arrest, conviction, and sentencing associated with the drug war, at least one third of African-American males between the ages of 18 and 34 who live in a major urban area are under some form of control by the criminal justice system (U. S. Department of Justice, 1995). The overall incarceration rate of young African Americans (ages 18 to 34) is an astounding six times that of whites. While what "calls for punishment" seems self-evident and apparently justifies the growth of America's prison-industrial complex, it is more likely that the murder rate and other serious crimes have actually and steadily declined. Moreover, the declaration of war by L. A. officials on African-American youth, the obvious criminalization of African-American urban males, and the increasing demand for harsher punishment directed at younger offenders suggest that what calls for punishment may be more complex than it appears. For a more detailed explanation of this dynamic, see Cole (1996b) and Connolly (1995).

6. Both Agee and Gates are familiar figures in the national imagination. Their achievement on the basketball court, their rejection of the gang and street options, and their motivation to leave their situation to have a better life are familiar terms. Although gang members and drug dealers are given limited visibility in the film, they are the Other over and against which Gates and Agee are defined in the national imagination. When gang members and drug dealers appear, they are visible in the dark, or they are shot from a distance: once Shannon is dismissed from Marshall's basketball team, he joins a gang and becomes peripheral to the narrative.

7. By overdetermined, we mean to draw attention to multiple meanings that are condensed in the signs. As such, these signs immediately evoke narratives of "what or who" (designating the modern translation of acts into identities) is responsible for the conditions of urban America.

8. Agee's best friend, Shannon, is experiencing problems at home and is also living with the Agees at this time. Later in the film, we are told that Shannon has been dropped from the Marshall basketball team and that he joined a gang.

9. In the cinema version of the movie, the postscript also told us that Agee had fathered two children. This announcement does not appear in the video release.

10. The images were recreated from real crime scene photos that Spike Lee obtained from police files.

11. The scene plays on the ethnographic desires of white America by taking the audience into the heart of the projects and allowing viewers a sense of knowledge about and intimacy with the racial other.

12. Compare this to the framing in *Hoop Dreams* of Bo, who suddenly is, and with little explanation of socioeconomic context, unemployed, estranged from his family, buying and selling drugs, and at one point in prison. The effect is to individualize and pathologize Bo's "downfall" and to ensure that structural forms of violence remain invisible.

13. Wilson (1996) argues that while Jim Crow arguments in support of racial segregation have largely disappeared, this movement has not been mirrored by increasing support for government programs that work to aggressively combat discrimination. Indeed, whites overwhelmingly oppose government interventions targeted to African Americans. For example, in 1991, only 1 in 5 whites believed that the federal government has a particular obligation to improve the living standards of African Americans. In 1975, this figure stood at over 1 in 4. Similarly, in 1990, 69.1% of whites opposed quotas for the admittance of black students into institutions of higher education, and 82.5% objected to the idea of preferential hiring and the promotion of blacks.

14. Gene Pingatore *is*, as argued by Caryn James (1994), the distillation of the exploitative relationships that we witness, but that distillation, which individuates and distances, is not simply revealed, nor is it easily achieved. Pingatore is positioned early in and throughout the film as the embodiment of social wrongs and exploitation through the considerable time devoted to visual narratives of long, intense practice sessions in which he appears ruthless, impatient, aggressive, and loud. Moreover, Pingatore's unemotional and frank interview style supports this characterization, and it is particularly jarring when, in a matter-of-fact manner, he (the label "Director of Development" identifies him in this scene) explains Agee's expulsion from St. Joseph's as an unfortunate but

unavoidable financial necessity. His opening conversation with the Agee family (here Pingatore was labeled "Head Basketball Coach"), coupled with Agee's dismissal, suggests that Pingatore has feigned care and concern, which makes him an especially despicable character. For an in-depth discussion of Pingatore's function in *Hoop Dreams*, see Cole & King (in press).

REFERENCES

Allen, H. (1995, October 3). Telling time: On Spike, Strike, and the reality of *Clockers*. *The Village Voice*, 84.

Andrews, D. (1996). The fact of Michael Jordan's blackness: Excavating a floating racial signifier. *Sociology of Sport Journal, 13(2)*, 125–128.

Aufderheide, P. (1994, October). The dream team. *The Independent*, 32–34.

Berkow, I. (1994, October 9). Dreaming hoop dreams. *New York Times*, pp. 2–1, 26, 27.

Berlant, L. (1993). National brands/national bodies: Imitation of life. In B. Robbins, (Ed.), *The phantom public sphere* (pp. 142–172). Minneapolis: University of Minnesota Press.

Berlant, L. (1996). The face of America and the state of emergency. In C. Nelson & D. P. Gaonkar (Eds.), *Disciplinarity and dissent in cultural studies* (pp. 367–440). New York: Routledge.

Bradley, D. (1995, September 10). Spike Lee's inferno: The drug underworld. *New York Times*, pp. 29, 32.

Carby, H. (1993). Encoding white resentment: *Grand Canyon*—A narrative of our time. In C. McCarthy & W. Crichlow (Eds.), *Race, identity, and representation in education* (pp. 236–250). New York: Routledge.

Carr, J. (1994, October 24). *Hoop Dreams:* A real-life slam-dunk. *Boston Globe*, pp. 47, 55.

Christensen, J. (1993). Spike Lee, corporate populist. *Critical Inquiry, 17*, 582–595.

Clark, M. (1994, October 13). "Hoop Dreams" reaches for the rafters and soars. *USA Today*, p. D1.

Cole, CL. (1996a.) P.L.A.Y., Nike, and Michael Jordan: National fantasy and the racialization of crime and punishment. *Working Papers in Sport and Leisure Commerce*, University of Memphis, 1.

Cole, CL. (1996b). American Jordan: P.L.A.Y., consensus, and punishment. *Sociology of Sport Journal, 13, 4*, 366–397.

Cole, CL. (forthcoming). *Heaven is a playground.* The Association for the Study of Play. (TASP) Newsletter.

Cole, CL, & Andrews, D. (1996). "Look—it's NBA ShowTime!": Visions of race in the popular imaginary. *Cultural Studies: A Research Annual, 1, 1*, 141–181.

Cole, CL, & King, S. (1998). Representing black masculinity and urban possibilities: Racism, realism, and hoop dreams. In G. Rail (Ed.), *Sport in postmodern times* (pp. 49–86). Albany: State University of New York Press.

Collins, G. (1994, November 7). Advertising. *New York Times*, p. B21.

Connolly, W. (1995). *The ethos of pluralization*. Minneapolis: University of Minnesota Press.

Coyle, D. (1995). *Hardball: A season in the projects*. New York: Harper Paperbacks.

Davis, M. (1990). *City of quartz: Excavating the future in Los Angeles*. London: Verso.

"Do the Right Thing": Issues and Images. (1989, July 9). *New York Times*, pp. 1, 23.

Donaldson, G. (1994). *The ville: Cops and kids in urban America*. New York: Anchor Books.

Donzinger, S. R. (Ed.). (1996). *The real war on crime: The report of the National Criminal Justice Commission*, New York: HarperCollins.

Dyson, M.E. (1996). *Race rules: Navigating the color line*. Reading, MA: Addison Wesley.

Feurer, J. (1995). *Seeing through the eighties*. Dunham, NC: Duke University Press.

Fraser, N., & Gordan, L. (1994). A genealogy of dependency: Tracing a keyword of the U. S. welfare state. *Signs: Journal of Women in Culture and Society, 19, 2*, 309–327.

Frey, D. (1994). *The last shot: City streets, basketball dreams*. Boston: Houghton Miflin.

Gray, H. (1995). *Watching race, television, and the struggle for blackness*. Minneapolis: University of Minnesota Press.

Gorringe, C. (1995). *Clockers* (review). www.nitrateonline.com/rclock.html.

Guerrero, E. (1993). *Framing blackness*. Philadelphia: Temple University Press.

Hinson, H. (1994, November 4). "Hoop Dreams": A slam-dunk shot of truth. *Washington Post*, pp. F1, F7.

hooks, b. (1995, April). Dreams of conquest. *Sight & Sound*, 22–23.

Howe, D. (1994, November 13). "Hoop Dreams": An overtime victory. *Washington Post*, p. G4.

James, C. (1994, October 7). Dreaming the dreams, realizing the realities. *New York Times*, pp. C1, C8.

Jones, L. (1996). Hoop realities. *Jump Cut, 40*, 8–14.

Kasarda, J. D. (1993). Inner-city concentrated poverty and neighborhood distress: 1970–1990. *Housing Policy Debate, 4, 3*, 253–302.

Kauffmann, S. (1995, October 2). Clockers. *New Republic, 213, 14*, 38–39.

Kotlowitz, A. (1992). *There are no children here*. New York: Anchor Books.

Kornheiser, T. (1994, November 3). Dreams; bring us back to reality. *Washington Post*, pp. B1, B6.

Massing, M. (1995, January 16). Ghetto blasting. *The New Yorker*, 32–37.

McGavin, P. Z. (1994, October 9). From the street and the gyms to the courtroom and beyond. *New York Times*, p. 26.

Miller, T. (1993). *The well-tempered self*. Baltimore: Johns Hopkins University Press.

Orlie, M. (1998). *Living ethically, acting politically*. Ithaca, NY: Cornell University Press.

Reeves, J., & Campbell, R. (1994). *Cracked coverage: Television news, the anticocaine crusade, and the Reagan legacy*. Dunham, NC: Duke University Press.

Reid, R. (1995). Death of the family or keeping human beings human. In J. Halberstam & I. Livingstone (Eds.), *Posthuman bodies* (pp. 177–199). Bloomington: University of Indiana Press.

Riggs, M. (1991). *Color adjustment*. San Francisco: California Newsreel.

Rony, F. (1996). *The third eye: Race, cinema and ethnographic spectacle*. Durham, NC: Duke University Press.

Sandell, J. (1995). Out of the ghetto and into the marketplace. *Socialist Review, 95, 2*, 57–82.

Schwager, J. (1995). The black struggle in a white society: Mr Show biz Archive reviews: www.mrshowbiz.com.

Seigel, J. (1994, January 31). Chicagoans' "Hoop Dreams" rises to the top at Sundance. *Chicago Tribune*, p. 16.

Sherman, B. (1994, October 16). The stuff of dreams. *Boston Sunday Globe*, pp. B11, B14.

Smith, C. (1997, March 3). Sneaker wars. *New York*, 40–47.

Smith, N. (1996). *The new urban frontier*. New York: Routledge.

Sperber, M. (1996). Hollywood dreams. *Jump Cut, 40*, 3–7.

Telander, R. (1976). *Heaven is a playground*. New York: St. Martin's Press.

U. S. Department of Justice. (1995, August). *Prisoners in 1994*. (NCJ-151654). Washington DC: U. S. Government Printing Office.

Wilmington, M. (1994a, October 2). When film dreams come true. *Chicago Tribune*, pp. 13:5, 20.

Wilmington, M. (1994b, October 21). Full court pressure: *Hoop Dreams* details the hope born of desperation. *Chicago Tribune*, pp. 7C, 7M.

Wilson, W. J. (1996). *When work disappears: The new world of the urban poor*. New York: Random House.

13

In Place of "Race," Space

"Basketball in Canada" and the Absence of Racism

Gamal Abdel-Shehid

And you? You go out there and you don't hustle. You don't move. You don't do any of the things you're supposed to do. You're acting just like a *nigger*![1]

Last year, I was a leading scorer on the team. This year, coach Shields tells me I just don't fit in. They [national team coaches] have a pre-conceived opinion of black players. They say you've got *attitude*. It's not my game that got me cut, it's because they think that if you have "Canada" written across your chest, you have to be white, because to them, Canada's white, and they'd rather lose than have too many black players on the team.[2]

This chapter is an analysis of racism and basketball. My particular focus will be the *Report of the Review Committee, Men's National Basketball Team,*[3] commissioned in the summer of 1994 by Basketball Canada, the governing body of the Canadian men's and women's national basketball teams. *The Report* examined allegations of racism in the men's national basketball program made by Cordell Llewellyn and Wayne Yearwood, two long-standing black team members who were cut just prior to the August 1994 "World Championship of Basketball" tournament, held in Toronto. Ken Shields, the white head coach of the national men's team at the time, was singled out in the allegations. Shields "vigorously denied" these allegations and delayed his planned resignation from the team until the allegations were investigated (R, p. 1). In November 1994, the Review Committee that authored *The Report* exonerated Shields and claimed that it

found no basis for allegations that overt, planned, or deliberate racism motivated decisions by Coach Shields in the selection or other aspects of operating the Men's National Basketball Team. (R, p. 11)

Instead, *The Report* offered alternative reasons for cutting Yearwood and Llewellyn, citing as more plausible causes "systemic barriers" and radical and incompatible differences in playing styles among the "Canadian University" and the "inner-city" or "high school" game (R, pp. 7–9).

In this chapter I stress how, despite the fact that its rationale was to investigate allegations of racism, *The Report* itself relied on racist knowledge categories, and in its findings it deployed a method of reasoning that erased even the possibility of racism. I show how instead of examining the practices of team members, coaches, and/or officials, the authors of *The Report* told a story about places and "styles." I argue that this is possible because of the culturally constructed nature of social space and its relation to identity. More to the point, I maintain that this construction is racist, in that it assumes to know people—who they are, what they like, and so on—on the basis of knowing where they come from. These assumptions are exemplified in the racist stereotypes of the Latin lover, the duplicitous Indian, and the lascivious black—all of which unite geography and personality.

This racist union of geography and personality also appears in the basketball discourse that *The Report* reproduces. This discourse, which I call "Hoop Dreams anthropology," accords a certain set of attributes to certain places in the basketball world. No word carries as much resonance in this discourse than "inner city." Inner city connotes blackness, crime, drug use, poverty, and basketball. It is this word, and its historical and political resonances, that comes to stand in for people in *The Report's* interpretive frame. I show how the historically racist practice of segregating nonwhite urban spaces and their attendant ideological associations supported a Manichean understanding in basketball, which in this case was used to absolve one of Basketball Canada's most senior officials in the face of allegations of racism.

I organize this chapter as follows. First, I begin by distinguishing two ways of perceiving "race" and racism: anti-racism and the assimilationist paradigm, of which *The Report* is an instance of the latter. Second, I outline the rhetorical structure of *The Report* to show how the investigation into allegations of racism is superseded by a discussion about space. Third, in light of the fact that *The Report* figures the inner city prominently, I provide background as to the incongruity of the inner city as a useful category in Canada. Fourth, I locate the discursive understanding of the inner city within two larger colonialist practices: (a) that of segregating and denigrating nonwhite urban locations, and (b) seeing space and "race" as one and the same. Fifth, I show how these colonialist practices work in "Hoop Dreams anthropology." Lastly, I argue that these processes have long-standing policy ramifications, since what results from this logic is the peculiar phenomenon of racism without racists—which makes allegations of racism, in sport and in other areas, impossible.

"Race," Racism, and Race Relations

The quotations cited at the beginning of this chapter exemplify a common way of understanding basketball in Canada and in the United States. They also point to one way that the category "race" works. As the first quote indicates, the work ethic so valorized in sports is opposed to what the racists call being "a nigger." This white coach's utterance accords with the racist typecasting of racialized "undesirables," in this case, blacks, as being lazy (Riggs, 1986).

In the second quote, a black player's utterance, "attitude" is akin to "nigger." What links both terms is the reduction of black people to generic and derogatory manifestations of a racialized essence. Llewellyn has attitude; Abdul-Jabaar is a nigger. Abdul R. JanMohamed (1986, p. 83) describes this as having the effect of

> commodif(ying) the native by negating his individuality, his subjectivity, so that he is now perceived as a generic being that can be exchanged for any other native (they all look alike, act alike, and so on).

These processes are not natural, they are racist, and in the eyes of Llewellyn, they are necessary to sustain unequal power relations within Canada's national program. In this sense, the excuse about having attitude is another way of excluding black players from representing Canadian basketball and keeping "Canada" white. Historically, there have been two dominant approaches to racist incidents such as the ones outlined above. They are the anti-racist approach and the race relations, or assimilationist, approach. Anti-racists believe, as I do, that racism is a sociohistorical act. Anti-racists (Davis, 1983; see also Gould, 1993; Lawrence, 1982) argue that "race" is not about biology or culture but more a social and historical category that accords power to certain people and denies it to others, based on what they look like. "Race," according to this view, does not exist per se in the body.[4] It is only possible as the actions of certain people, states, or institutions who stand to gain power, wealth, and so on by calling someone, for example, "nigger" and acting thereupon. The anti-racist response here is to see how these acts are located within socially constituted power relations such as colonialism, capitalism, sexism, and homophobia and for white and nonwhite citizens to resist racism.[5]

However, one of the most pernicious effects of racism is a constant denial, on the part of some, that there is even such a thing as racism. Those in the race relations school argue that racism is a natural by-product of "cultural exchange"—merely the result of ignorance or cultural unfamiliarity. In fact, the word "racism" often is not used; it is euphemistically described as "racial disharmony" or "racial conflict." This approach does not identify whiteness as an unequal social relation. Moreover, it holds a predetermined solution to the problem of disharmony, which is to accept "cultural difference" and to promote greater understanding and harmony "among the races." This approach, sometimes called "assimilationist."[6] does not understand racism as a personal and political act perpetrated by those interested in power.[7]

Moreover, the race relations approach, by naturalizing "race," allows one to think about places as having traits that make all of the people coming from such a place seem to be the same. How else would cultural or racial conflict emerge if people from a certain place were not presumed to be irreconcilably different from those of another place?

In what follows, I show how *The Report's* use of the category "inner city" is akin to both nigger and attitude in that it works to (re)produce the biological category "race" and thereby to occlude actual social relations of power and inequality. The rhetorical use of inner city, as we will see, has the effect of reducing a complex and varied social and historical terrain to a Manichean story without people. This act denies racism as a social relation and sees it as a matter of "culture" or space. In this manner, *The Report* works within a race relations paradigm. I will show that since place comes to equal "race," racism is therefore rendered impossible.

THE STATE OF "BASKETBALL IN CANADA," OR WHAT COLOUR IS YOUR GAME?

After establishing its objectivity and rationale, the Review Committee sets out its problematic. This is done by outlining the state of "Basketball in Canada." Three levels of basketball in Canada are laid out: they are the education system, the provincial basketball associations and city leagues, and Basketball Canada. What follows is a section entitled "growth of basketball." This growth, according to *The Report*, is limited to high school basketball:

> In recent years, basketball at the high school level has experienced significant *growth* in Canada. This is particularly true in Metropolitan Toronto, and to a lesser extent in other large urban areas. (R, p. 4, italics added)

After establishing the growth of urban high school basketball, the signifier "inner city" is used to further specify the place of growth:

> The Committee was told that in *inner city areas*, basketball has become the sport of choice among young athletes.... High school basketball stars often become community personalities and enjoy considerable popularity. (R, p. 4, italics added)

The effect of this inner-city growth is then characterized:

> While the growth and popularity at the high school level has in-
> creased the number of young people playing the game, it *may have also
> created some problems* in relation to both provincial development pro-
> grams and the national team programs. (R, pp. 4–5, italics added)

The Report then outlines the nature of the problem:

> The popularity of the NBA [National Basketball Association] and
> local basketball has tended to a considerable degree to obscure both
> the national team and developments in international basketball. Gen-
> erally speaking, international basketball is not well known in Canada
> and the *differences in style of play are not fully understood.* (R, p. 5, italics
> added)

Much later, the question of styles of play is explained in detail. After citing a Toronto newspaper journalist and a coach who discuss the differences between a "black game" and a "white game" (R, p. 14), *The Report* opposes the
"high school game," previously encoded as "inner city," to the Canadian game:

> The style of play in *Canadian universities* and internationally is quite
> *different* from the *high school* game. Coaches at higher levels in the sys-
> tem stress the need they see to integrate players into a *team structure* as
> opposed to a *highly individualistic style.* This style features a more
> technical, physical, and mental approach to the game. Most coaches at
> this level consider playing *discipline* a key part of the game. At this
> level coaches also try to instill in players the need to express them-
> selves through the team rather than individually . . . this can only be
> achieved by the experience of playing at higher levels, good coaching,
> and *willingness* on the part of players to accept coaching in these areas
> and *adapt to* playing in a different milieu. (R, p. 14, italics added)

Thus the interpretive frame is established: inner-city or high school basketball
and the popularity of the NBA have increased; this growth obscures the understanding of differences "in style of play," creating "problems" for the national team programs.[8] I want to stress that nowhere within this frame is the
word "racism" mentioned; moreover, there is no discussion about national team
racism or the actions of the coaches or players. *The Report* is not a story about
the power struggles and politics of men who play on and coach a basketball
team that represents Canada around the world. Rather, it is a story about places
and styles. *The Report's* dismissal of racism as a factor in national team selection
is *not* supported by detailed evidence in favor of Ken Shields and his practices.

Instead, *The Report* focuses on the landscape of basketball in Canada and the "problems" lying therein. The displacement of "race" or racism to space and style is where I now turn my attention.

MAKING HISTORY/ERASING HISTORY

Erasure, whether it relates to facts, people, or dates, is a classic method of writing and practicing both bourgeois nationalism and colonialism. Mary Louise Pratt (1986) has shown the extent to which European colonialist travellers' accounts of southern Africa relied on erasures of indigenous inhabitants in representation in order to present the land as empty, open, and inviting. This form of representation, or clearing the land, allows European colonialists to be represented as the sole actors and subjects in colonialism. In a similar fashion, Edward Sa'id (1980) describes how Zionist policy initiatives in Palestine understood the indigenous Palestinians as nonactive, invisible. Sa'id argues that this is necessary to achieve the presencing, both literal and figurative, of Europeans as colonialists. Speaking about Palestine, Sa'id (1980, p. 85, italics added) writes that Zionism and its proponents have rendered

> a whole territory essentially unused, unappreciated, misunderstood (if one can use such a term in this connection). Despite the people who lived on it, Palestine was therefore *to be made useful, appreciated, understandable*. The native inhabitants . . . *were not really there*.

While *The Report* is not about colonialism per se, I argue that it employs the colonial discursive practice outlined above of erasing certain members from the landscape of basketball in Canada in order to presence the landscape in another way, one amenable to achieve its ends: the absence of racism in Canada. Below I list the most glaring of *The Report's* erasures.

But before I do so, it is worth noting that the racial formation (Omi & Winant, 1986) in Canada is by no means accurately described in the manner that *The Report* attempts. While it is possible to claim that the term *inner city* is tenable in the United States owing to large sections of run-down urban areas largely populated by African and Chicana/o Americans, this is clearly not the case in Canada. There are only a few major urban centres in Canada, and none have what could clearly be called "inner cities" or "ghettos." The only comparable term to inner city within the Canadian context is "Jane-Finch" and "Regent Park," which are impoverished regions of Toronto typified by a high black presence. However, by and large, these terms only have local currency.

Moreover, the population and configuration of nonwhite populations in Canada are not homogeneous. Owing to Canada's position as an imperialist country within the British Empire, Canada has large portions of nonwhite citizens who have settled from India, Pakistan, and China. With reference to African Canadian populations, they are small in proportion to their American counterparts, and the forms of blackness vary in the sense that there is no history of plantation slavery, and that many African Canadians have come to Canada recently (since 1960). Also, blackness in Canada, unlike in the United States, is dominated by a distinct Caribbean element.[9]

This brief discussion helps highlight the incongruity of the category "inner city" as applied to the Canadian landscape and may help contextualize some of *The Report's* inconsistencies, some of which I will now list. First, no definition is provided for the geography of the inner city. Sometimes it is meant to refer to Toronto, or to Montreal; at other times it is difficult to tell. Second, *The Report* ignores the growth of high school basketball outside of the inner city, for example, in the *suburban* areas of Metro Toronto, such as Brampton and Mississauga. Third, no mention is made of inner-city basketball that is not played at high schools. Examples of this are (a) university basketball played in urban centres, (b) the community college system of men's basketball in Toronto, which contrary to *The Report's* claims, is arguably the top level of men's basketball in Canada, and (c) men's club basketball in Toronto, which is typified by high-level talent of differing ages, including former NCAA,[10] NBA, and European professional players.

This discussion of erasures provides an alternative description to what *The Report* offers as "basketball in Canada." These erasures are crucial to the reality structure of *The Report* in that they clear space for a set of inclusions restructuring the text. It is only after erasing and distorting the racial formation and the state of basketball in Canada that *The Report* can draw on the concept "inner city." What was and is a complex historical and political reality, local to Canada, is now rendered a neat and tidy binary: inner city versus Canadian university. Moreover, such a Manichean reduction belies the specific cultural context of Canada and the fact of its ethno-cultural diversity. This conceptual practice is akin to what Sa'id detailed about erasing indigenous subjectivities in order to render the terrain, whether discursive or material, "useful." It is as though the players, coaches, officials, fans, families, friends, and journalists who make up basketball in Canada are "not really there."

In order for the inner city to be legible and to hold such currency, these erasures are accompanied by a "Manichean allegory," which, according to Abdul R. JanMohamed (1986), is a feature of colonialist representation. He describes the Manichean allegory in representation as a way of understanding the colonized subject as completely opposite, or other, to the European colonialist. The allegory is

> a field of diverse yet interchangeable oppositions between white and black, good and evil, superiority and inferiority, civilization and

savagery, intelligence and emotion, rationality and sensuality, self
and other, subject and object. (1986, p. 82)

Moreover, *The Report's* binary, inner city versus Canadian university, is only
legible to an audience already in tune with such a way of thinking. In other
words, *The Report's* representation of basketball in Canada has to resonate with
those who understand, as Llewellyn did, that in racism, words do not always
mean what they say. Like attitude and nigger, inner city is not a literal reference.

The "Inner City" and Its Resonances

Two historical factors enable the inner city to resonate as it does. The first is
colonialism's history of administering and segregating nonwhite urban spaces;
the second is the Enlightenment/racist notion that place has an overdetermining and a homogenizing effect on peoples' habits, energies, and so on. While
the term *inner city* has a definitively American tone, we must note that this way
of representing and organizing nonwhite urban locations is not particular to
the United States. It is a common colonialist staple to perceive of these spaces
(and nonwhite spaces generally) as parochial and lacking in Reason, and to
administer them accordingly.[11]

In what follows I provide a background to the racist process of representing and administering the cities of racialized undesirables in Enlighten-
ment/colonialism. The reason for a sustained historical discussion of "race"
and the city here is that in basketball, as represented, both blackness and the
city are countervailing themes. It is thus impossible to understand representations of basketball in the city without an understanding of the racialized way
that city spaces have been, and continue to be, configured, either literally or
figuratively.

Max Weber's discussion of the city in *Economy and Society* is a paradig-
matic case.[12] Weber (1978) argues that "the Oriental city" lacked a series of
things found in the Occidental city, and these were, for him, the crucial differences in the Occidental ascent to superiority. One of the crucial negative criteria for Weber was the inability of men of Oriental cities to form what he calls
"autonomous associations." In a section entitled "Lack of Communal Features
in the Orient," Weber claims that the Oriental city was dominated by suspicion
and caste-like mentalities. In contrast to an "Occidental" separation of city and
country, which was necessary for rational advancement, the Oriental city was
lacking in this regard. According to Weber (1978, p. 1227):

Most importantly, the associational character of the city and the concept of a *burgher* (as contrasted to the man from the countryside)
never developed at all or existed only in rudiments.

He continues, in his description of Russian and Indian townsmen (1978, p. 1227), to note that

> (s)imilarly, the Russian member of a village community who earned his living in the city remained a "peasant" in the eyes of the law. The Indian townsman was, in addition, a member of his caste.

Weber is placing the urban center of racialized undesirables within the same frame of reference as the European countryside. Like the countryside, both have been historically understood as "dark" spheres residing outside of Enlightenment. In this sense, Weber (1978, p. 1229) sees Mecca, an example of an Oriental city, as marked by a "peculiar anarchy."[13]

It would be easy to dismiss this definition as the rambling of yet another dead white male philosopher/sociologist, but this serves as an important example, for two reasons. First, like *The Report*, Weber does not feel the need to talk about actual people in historical settings in detailed fashion. What is crucial here is Weber's use of a generic Russian or Indian and the subsequent linking of "race" to place. Weber's reader can now know[14] what kind of government is possible in each of these places. According to Pratt, this way of seeing/writing the Other was constant in European travel writing about the Africa of the eighteenth and nineteenth centuries. Both Weber and the travel writers share a similar rhetorical device, which Pratt (1986, p. 139) describes as follows:

> The people to be othered are homogenized into a collective "they" which is distilled even further into an iconic "he" (the standardized adult specimen).

Second, Weber's linking of "rudimentary" and "abortive" forms of government to "Oriental" urban space points to a long-standing colonialist staple of seeing only Occidental urban spaces as authentic. With respect to colonialist urban social organization, Fanon (1963, p. 39) writes

> The town belonging to the colonized people, or at least the native town, the Negro village, the medina, the reservation, is a place of ill fame, peopled by men of evil repute. They are born there, it matters little where or how; they die there, it matters not where, not how. It is a world without spaciousness; men live there on top of each other, and their huts are built on top of the other.

Moreover, what is crucial in this passage is that this is not simply a description of a kind of space. It describes both the inhabitants and the place. Fanon's analysis of the colonialist understandings of space shows the overdetermining (and overwhelming) similarity to space *and* people. The space comes to define the people. The biological characteristics descriptive of black bodies in colonialism are the same as those applied to the physical spaces in which these black bodies live.[15] This is evident in the following passage, where Fanon (1963, p. 42) notes that

> the settler . . . speaks of the stink of the native quarter, of breeding swarms, of foulness, of spawn, of gesticulations. When the settler seeks to describe the native fully in exact terms he constantly refers to the bestiary.

As Goldberg (1994) argues, this way of organizing and racializing *space* is central to "racist culture." With respect to urban location, he argues that one of the ways this control is exercised is through the production and maintenance of "urban peripheries." The city inhabited by colonized peoples is what Goldberg (1994, p. 188) calls a "*periphractic* space," which

> does not require the absolute displacement of persons to or outside city limits, to the literal margins of urban space. It merely entails their circumscription in terms of location and their limitation in terms of access—to power, to (the realization) of rights, and to goods and services.

Goldberg notes that in colonialist urban administration, the common racist fear of the colonized peoples spreading infectious disease in fact helped create slum-like living conditions initially, exacerbated by colonial officials acting upon these same fears. Goldberg's insight here points to the twin process of developing a paranoia and acting on it. In urban organization in racist culture, the creation of slums exists at the same time as the belief that nonwhites deserve such a place. This example highlights the way that identity, space, and "race" are interconnected in colonialism. The "native town," therefore, is both the embodiment *and* space of alterity and negativity; the inhabitants and the town come to mean the same thing. On the correlation between difference and distance, Goldberg (1994, p. 203) adds that:

> Distance is not, at least primarily, to be interpreted spatially or geographically but in terms of difference—and of the reinvented articulation of racist concepts.

By restricting, physically and/or discursively, the space of racialized undesirables, certain powers and privileges remain intact. This distancing process allows settlers to know that they are "healthy," "clean," "normal," and so on. Fanon and Goldberg detail the racist nature of this logic, built on the attempted Manichean separation of the races, to first "otherize" people and then to administer space, in this case, urban space, accordingly. In a periphractic space, who lives there is put and contained there by a series of colonial state and administrative practices. What follows is the racist belief and self-fulfilling prophecy that this town typified all of the values that are opposite, or negative, to those that characterize Enlightenment, or, in Weber's language, a peculiar anarchy.

The fact of "race"—that colonized peoples are seen as less civilized, dirtier, and less human—oriented and organized colonial administration and continues to do so in contemporary forms of segregated housing policy (Goldberg, 1994, pp. 187–192). Moreover, it allowed for a way of thinking that bound "race," space, and identity. And for those who argue that Canada does not know this reality, we need only recall Llewellyn's articulation of the racist relation between "race" and space when he says: "to them, Canada's white." This sentiment is echoed in the words of black Canadian folk singer Faith Nolan when she sings: "People always askin' me, where do you come from?"

BASKETBALL "STYLES" AND THE INNER CITY

The connection between "race," space, and identity also is evident in popular representations of sport. *The Report* is just one example of a genre of cultural production about basketball—which relies on racist assumptions about congenital black laziness and incorrigibility. I provisionally entitle this genre "Hoop Dreams anthropology." This enables the reader to know the kind of athlete (and, by extension, person) that one is—what style one will play, whether or not one will be "coachable," and so on—based on knowing one's geographical origin. It should come as no surprise that nonwhite spaces in this genre are negatively characterized, and that nonwhites are typified as more or less homogeneous. In this way, *The Report's* inner city is similar to Weber's Oriental city.

Here the bestiary manner of characterizing nonwhite urban spaces in colonialism is translated to a language of athletics and basketball, wherein the dominant and often interchangeable tropes are inner city and style. As I will show, *The Report's* use of these tropes works in two ways. First, it reinforces racist notions about blacks being lazy trouble makers and, relatedly, this understanding occludes a discussion of racist practices and is therefore indispensable in achieving the exoneration of Ken Shields.

Perhaps the most popular references to inner-city basketball are seen in the recent documentary film *Hoop Dreams*, and in fictional movies such as *White Men Can't Jump*.[16] These films represent the inner city as a black space where drug use, crime, poverty, and basketball flourish. Instead of the social conditions describing the basketball, basketball becomes the window to life on the inner city, and little is known about characters outside of "the game." In addition, this genre operates on the assumption that in black urban spaces, basketball is more "pure" and "physical"[17] than that played elsewhere. In fact, so heavy is the connection between basketball, the city, and black identity in this genre that I can recall no movie about basketball produced in the last 20 years that features either a white, inner-city player or a black player outside of the city.[18]

And, once again, space operates as the dominant trope in order to rewrite a story about politics, history, and human agency. While no sustained work has been done on the Orientalist foundations of sports literature, major parallels exist between sports writing and other anthropological work, such as travel writing. What characterizes much travel and sports writing is a monologic process of writing the Other into being, yet what also binds these genres is the prominence granted to physical space. Physical space is the subject that motivates biology, history, art, and so on. Pratt (1986, p. 142) notes that one form of nineteenth-century travel writing is typified by a "discursive configuration, which *centers landscape*, separates the people from place, and effaces the speaking self."

This is the ruling aesthetic of Rick Telander's *Heaven Is a Playground*, perhaps the foundational text of "Hoop Dreams anthropology." Telander treats the predominantly black urban center, Brooklyn's Bedford-Stuyvesant, as a state of nature in which urban living and blackness combine to produce great ballplayers, great games, and great stories. As Telander (1995, p. 2) writes in the introduction:

> Obviously, black superiority in basketball rises from a combination of many factors. But one would not be far wrong in saying that *in the cities, environment and black potential* have merged to form unusually fertile ground. Indeed, nowhere does the game of basketball thrive as it does in the ghetto.

For Telander, a mixture of "environment and black potential" makes basketball "thrive." Once again, it is space, the ghetto in Telander's words and the inner city in those of *The Report*, that overdetermines and homogenizes the individual athletes.

It is not far from this to the next stage, which is to argue about styles *as* racialized essences, which is exactly what *The Report* does. The effect of *The Report's* reference to a "black" game and a "white" game is to spatialize, naturalize, and split basketball in Canada. In similar fashion to attitude, style connotes "race" and erases the athletic achievement of individuals as a category to explain how players play. The notion of athletics as an individual and/or collective artistic performance, something central to C. L. R. James's (1992) insights, is inconceivable in this genre. More importantly, subjective experiences, which would seem to be necessary in an investigation of racism, give way to discussions of space and style. What *The Report* (p. 5) refers to as "differences in style of play" has nothing to do with individual differences, but in classically Manichean fashion, these rigid "differences" mean black or white, inner city or university. In the "common-sense racism" (Lawrence, 1982) of "Hoop Dreams anthropology," one's place is one's style.

A profound dehumanization occurs through the reduction of a social and historical reality to a landscape of basketball in Canada ruled by "race." The complex racial formation that is Canada[19] is reduced to black and white. This process resonates with Marx's (1986, p. 77) discussion of commodity fetishism, where he writes that "a definite social relation between men . . . assumes . . . the fantastic form of a relation between things." What Marx signals is a shift from a way of understanding a process organized by people to one organized by things, in this case, the commodities themselves. In "Hoop Dreams anthropology," space, not commodities, stands in as the defining social relation.

In sum, *The Report* relies on these ways of representing reality to produce a series of what Bryan Green (1983) calls "knowledge effects," which, in keeping with the Manichean consciousness of colonialism, equate space with "race." *The Report* draws on a genre of basketball writing to tell a story not about players and coaches—which would be necessary for an investigation of basketball and racism—but about style and place. Unfortunately, for victims of racism in basketball, this has devastating effects.

CONCLUSION: RACISM WITHOUT RACISTS

It is only because the inner city has such powerful resonances that *The Report's* reliance on it works to exonerate Shields. These resonances are (a) the history of colonialist practices of subjugating nonwhite urban spaces and (b) a colonialist epistemological framework that equates space, "race," and identity. Thus instead of investigating allegations of racism, the textual option is to resort to a racist and Manichean form of splitting off reality into neat and tidy racialized essences. The category "inner city" acts as a semiotic briefcase that is brought into the body of the text and then opened up so that its attendant meanings can refigure the text itself.

Having done so, *The Report* does not need to investigate Ken Shields's practices, whether as a coach or elsewhere, or determine whether or not they were racist. In *The Report*, racism is, in a sense, *nothing personal*. Yet racism, as I stated in the beginning, is personal if nothing else. It is a social relation, a human act effected by subjects onto other subjects. How is it that this phenomenon of erasure works? The answer has already been given. If *The Report* understands "race" to be more about place and style than anything else, then who can be racist? The answer, regrettably, is nobody! Therefore, it is not only wrong to call Ken Shields a racist, but it is wrong to call anybody a racist. This thematic accords with the assimilationist paradigm of race relations that I described earlier, which accepts a biological (and a *geographical!*) entity called "race" and sees the eradication of racism as possible through greater understanding and tolerance among people of different races. It is thus not surprising that one of *The Report's* recommendations (p. 18) is not to develop vigilance against racism but to aid "coaches in understanding cultural and other differences in a multi-cultural society." This approach to thinking about "race" as being natural and reducible to place, culture, or style exonerates everyone from the charge of racism.

This has significant ramifications, the most important being that *The Report*, by textually establishing the impossibility of racism, poses dangerous political consequences for victims of racism in sports in general but also specifically for members of national team programs in the future. *The Report* is an official policy document at Basketball Canada and thereby provides historical "proof" to racism's impossibility. Thus *The Report* is more than an exoneration of Ken Shields. It stands as evidence that cultural difference and inner-city styles are the cause of racial disharmony.

In fact, in a bizarre and violent reversal that accords with racism's understanding of black bodies as "trouble,"[20] it is not Shields or anyone else who is at fault, but rather it is the fault of those black men who, according to *The Report*, play a certain "game." In order to "just say no" to racism, *The Report* says that it is the responsibility of black players, from national team members such as Cordell Llewellyn to former NBA legend Kareem Abdul-Jabaar to any kid on any playground or gym, victimized by racism, to listen to Donohue's advice and to stop "acting like niggers." I do not think so!

NOTES

1. Former Canadian national basketball men's head coach Jack Donohue. Donohue, who preceded Ken Shields in that position, uttered these words to former NBA basketball star Kareem Abdul-Jabaar, then named Lew Alcindor, while he was Alcindor's high school coach at Power Memorial High school in New York City in the mid-1960s. This quote is from Abdul-Jabaar, (1983, p. 66, italics added).

2. Former Canadian national men's basketball team member Cordell Llewellyn, as quoted in the *Globe and Mail*, August 23, 1994, p. C2. This article is Appendix 1 in *The Report of the Review Committee, Men's National Basketball Team* (1994, italics added).

3. This report was issued November 1994. Hereinafter, I will refer to it as "*The Report.*" In what follows, when I cite *The Report* and, where necessary, provide in-text citations, I will refer to it as "R," followed by the page number.

4. Because of the dubious nature of this category, I will refer to race in double quotation marks throughout this chapter when the word stands on its own.

5. This, unfortunately, is a brief explanation. For a more detailed explanation, see Lawrence (1982); Appiah (1992); Davis (1983); Gould (1993).

6. For a summary of this approach, see Li & Singh-Bolaria (1985, pp. 18–22).

7. When it does see racism as personal, it is understood that racism perhaps exists among "evil" people, such as neo-Nazis, and the assumption is that if these people are "weeded out," racism will vanish with them.

8. These changes in basketball in Canada can be referred to as the "objective crisis" that necessitates *The Report*. According to Green (1983, pp. 84–90), the existence and narration of a crisis are crucial in policy research. It helps achieve what he calls "constitutive innocence," thereby establishing itself as impartial. In this case, what is crucial is that the crisis here is not the allegations of racism.

9. It is worth mentioning that blackness, at least in Toronto, has recently undergone shifts owing to the large-scale immigration of Somalis, Eritreans, and Ethiopians. For more on the racial formation of Canada, see Li & Singh-Bolaria (1988).

10. NCAA is the acronym for the National Collegiate Athletic Association. It is the organization that oversees intercollegiate athletics in the United States. The men's basketball programs of some NCAA schools feature some of the best basketball in the world.

11. While a discussion of the connection between "race" and Reason is outside the purview of this chapter, those interested can refer to Goldberg (1994, chap. 2, 3); also see Gould (1993).

12. For a detailed discussion of the category "Islamic city" in Orientalist knowledge production, please see Al-Azmeh (1976).

13. In short, the problem is that the men of these towns have not advanced beyond their families. The sexist-racist foundations of this explanation are worth examining further, especially given the presence of white men being rational in cultural productions about basketball, such as *Hoop Dreams* and *White Men Can't Jump*. Unfortunately, this is beyond my purview here.

14. I use the notion of knowing here similar to the way that Edward Sa'id (1979) uses it.

15. For a description of the hypersexualization of black female bodies, please see Gilman (1986).

16. It may be argued that since these films are American, they may not translate well into a very different Canadian context. These films translate owing to the similarity of commonsense racist ideas about blacks in both the United States and in Canada. In terms of the applicability of these films to any cultural context, including the United States, I wonder to what extent these anthropological pieces tell us more about whiteness than they do about blackness?

17. I will leave the notion of a basketball game, which is less "physical," to the racist imagination.

18. There was the recent *Air Up There*, which featured black ballplayers in Africa and a white American coach. But in this case, the themes of blackness and biology were featured prominently. The only "rural" basketball film I can cite is *Hoosiers*, which features no black players.

19. Or anywhere else, for that matter.

20. In this regard, please see Butler (1993).

REFERENCES

Abdul-Jabaar, K., & Knobler, K. (1983). *Giant steps: The autobiography of Kareem Abdul-Jabaar.* Toronto: Bantam.

Al-Azmeh, A. (1976). What is the Islamic City? *Review of Middle Eastern Studies, 2(5),* 1–13.

Appiah, K. A. (1992). *In my father's house.* New York: Oxford University Press.

Butler, J. (1993). Endangered/Endangering: Schematic representations and white paranoia. In R. Gooding-Williams (Ed.), *Reading Rodney King, Reading Urban Uprising* (pp. 15–22). London: Routledge.

Davis, A. (1983). *Women, race, and class.* New York: Vintage.

Fanon, F. (1963). *The wretched of the earth.* New York: Grove Weidenfeld.

Fanon, F. (1967). *Black skin, white masks.* New York: Grove Press.

Gilman, S. L. (1986). Black bodies, white bodies: Toward an iconography of female sexuality in late-nineteenth century art, medicine, and literature. In H. L. Gates (Ed.), *"Race," writing, and difference* (pp. 171–197). Chicago: University of Chicago Press.

Goldberg, D. T. (1994). *Racist culture.* Oxford: Blackwell.

Gould, S. J. (1993). American polygeny and craniometry before Darwin: Blacks and Indians as separate, inferior species. In S. Harding (Ed.), *The racial economy of science* (pp. 23–57). Bloomington: Indiana University Press.

Green, B. (1983). *Knowing the poor.* London: Routledge and Kegan Paul.

James, C. L. R. (1992). What is art? In A. Grimshwaw (Ed.), *The C. L. R. James Reader* (pp. 15–32). Oxford: Blackwell.

JanMohamed, A. R. (1986). The economy of Manichean allegory: The function of racial difference in colonialist literature. In H. L. Gates (Ed.), *"Race," writing, and difference* (pp. 96–129). Chicago: University of Chicago Press.

Lawrence, E. (1982). Just plain common sense: the "roots" of racism. In Center For Contemporary Cultural Studies (Ed.), *The empire strikes back* (pp. 79–97). London: Hutchinson.

Li, P., & Singh Bolaria, B. (1985). *Racial oppression in Canada.* Toronto: Garamond.

Marx, K. (1986). *Capital.* Moscow: Progress.

Omi, M., & Winant, M. (1986). *Racial formation in the United States.* New York: Routledge.

Pratt, M. L. (1986). Scratches on the face of the country; or, what Mr. Barrow saw in the land of the Bushmen. In H. L. Gates (Ed.), *"Race," writing, and difference* (pp. 130–156). Chicago: University of Chicago Press.

Review Committee, Men's National Basketball Team. (1994). *The Report of the Review Committee, Men's National Basketball Team.*

Riggs, M. *Ethnic notions.* (1986). (Video, color, 60 min.). San Francisco: California Newsreel.

Sa'id, E.W. (1979). *Orientalism.* New York: Vintage.

Sa'id, E.W. (1980). *The question of Palestine.* New York: Vintage.

Sekyi-Otu, A. (1996). *Fanon's dialectic of experience.* Cambridge: Harvard University Press.

Telander, R. (1995). *Heaven is a playground.* Lincoln: University of Nebraska Press.

Weber, M. (1978). *Economy and society.* Berkeley: University of California Press.

14

Driving the Lane against the Raptor

The Production and Racialization of (Transgressive) Subjects on the Streets of Toronto

Andrew D. Thornton

INTRODUCTION

In this chapter I present a "reading against the grain" (Simon, 1992) of the "Raptorfest KFC 3-on-3 Basketball Challenge," which was held for the second year on a major "downtown" street in Toronto. I discuss the ways in which this event's symbolic terrain produces racialized logics and the possibilities of how and who should or can be the "on the streets." The "Raptorfest" was sponsored by several large corporations: Kentucky Fried Chicken, Nike, Ford, Gatorade, the Toronto Raptors Basketball Team, and the National Basketball Association. Many, if not the majority of, participants, were male, black African-Canadians and Afro-Americans. This geographical space also was the site of a sustained, high-profile, public protest against a racist exhibit "Into the Heart of Africa" at the Royal Ontario Museum (ROM). Organized and maintained by a local coalition of black activists and supporters, it was heavily policed and was a regular feature in Toronto's mainstream media for several months. The Raptorfest, on the other hand, was policed in the manner of a street festival: low visibility and numbers of uniformed police redirecting local traffic.

By placing the ROM protest in the same frame as the Raptorfest, I highlight the complexities of how definitions of (urban) space transform and reproduce forms of social regulation. I also gesture to the limits of the social regulation of space. "Where" you "are" contains and constrains how "you" are identified and identifiable. Urban space as such is part of the "politics of representation" (Mercer, 1994) and the "new cultural politics of difference" (West, 1990).

The Setting: A Mini-Ethnography
of Toronto's Streets

The Raptorfest is a 3-on-3 street basketball tournament sponsored by several large (American) corporations. It has become, in two short years, a highly visible public consumer spectacle and athletic competition in Toronto. The event took place on University Avenue, which is a major route for cars in the city going from the downtown core to northern parts of Toronto and provides access north and south to expressways and highways that border the city. It is six lanes wide and bordered by the entrance to the ROM, a few other smaller museums, the University of Toronto campus, the provincial parliament buildings, and, recently, a warehouse sized "Club Monaco" store. Thousands of cars use this street every day, and it often is lined with school buses on visits to the museum located at the corner of Bloor Street and University Avenue. It is a sterile, concrete place with few trees and no grass. The street splits into two as it heads south to form a circle around the parliament buildings. The entire area is called "Queen's Park Crescent." There are trees and grass in the crescent, and usually street people mingle with office workers amongst the trees. During the Raptorfest, the streets that constitute the "crescent" were filled with portable basketball hoops, and the connecting streets were blocked from access by barricades and local, uniformed police.

This chapter is grounded in my experience and description of events using participant observation.[1] My research method was critical ethnography,[2] informed most heavily by symbolic interactionist (Becker, 1970, 1990; Rock, 1979) theory of social relations and neo-Marxist, feminist, and poststructuralist theory, which has problematized how power relations are produced, contested, rehearsed, and strengthened in sport (Lenskyj, 1986, 1994; Hall, 1987; Gruneau & Whitson, 1993; Pronger, 1990; Messner, 1991; Andrews, 1996). A key feature of my analysis is the acknowledgment and mapping of the "instability of categories, signs, and their meanings" (Lather, 1992).

During the two days of the tournament, I was a spectator to many games, walked about the site for several hours each day, and collected some information pamphlets from the various promotional kiosks. Subsequently I made some "field notes" on what I observed, heard, and felt. The idea for this chapter came to me when I saw advertisements for the tournament on local television. I had seen and participated briefly in the protest against the "Into the Heart of Africa" exhibit. I had never actually been into the ROM up until that point. My "normal" vision of the ROM was disrupted by the reconfiguration created by the Raptorfest. I was particularly struck by the low visibility of the police. Surprisingly, the ROM continued to operate during the tournament, and the museum goers were gawking at the basketball players, taking many pictures.

The "entrance" to the Raptorfest was marked by a huge, 40-foot-high, inflated (balloon) replica of the Toronto Raptor's mascot and team namesake. It was located at the corner of University Avenue and Bloor Street and was visible from at least a half mile away. Each backboard had the Raptor's logo on it, and there were other corporate logos on just about every flat surface. Most prominent among these were Ford, Nike, and Kentucky Fried Chicken. The Nike "swoosh" was on the team jerseys that each player received as part of his registration ($100 per team, with a maximum of four players to a team[3]). There were approximately 300 teams participating, and the competitive structure was organized by age, gender, and skill levels (e.g., Elite or "First" division players who were current or ex-university players. I did not hear any mention of "ex-pros" playing). There were noticeably fewer female teams, but they had as many levels of competition. There were no "coed" competitions.

The highly public, controversial protest against the "Into the Heart of Africa" was conducted on the steps of the main entrance to the ROM in 1989. The protesters were a coalition of social activists led by local black activist groups. The protest lasted several months and finally resulted in the premature closing of the exhibit, the resignation of the exhibit's curator from her teaching job, and the cancellation of the rest of the exhibit's tour (Mackey, 1995).

There was an inordinately heavy and violent response from local police authorities. On two separate occasions, there were violent confrontations between police and protesters, and 11 protesters were arrested (Mackey, 1995, p. 405).

Police violence against African-Canadian men, in particular, was already in the public consciousness due to several incidents of police shootings in the months prior to and during the exhibit. It is a common feature of blacks' day-to-day experience in Toronto to be stopped, monitored, and harassed by police (Mackey, 1995, p. 419). Around this time, a young black man, Marlon Neal, was shot in the back of the head by police for not stopping at a radar speed trap (Mackey, 1995). These events had irrevocably placed race and racism on the agenda of the public and popular consciousness of Toronto's people. In this context, players stepping onto the basketball court and onto the streets of downtown Toronto are, by definition, engaged in the politics of race and racism. Paul Gilroy (1987) and Sallie Westwood (1990) have made similar points about black men's experiences of public spaces in the cities of England. Sense of place and space is a key feature of understanding marginalized men's subjectivity and community (Westwood, 1987). In particular, how men identify with and relate to sport is a significant component of their knowledge of themselves and relations of power and oppression (Messner, 1991).

In this chapter I do not look too closely at the protest itself. Instead, I point to the meanings and discourses that were brought to bear on it as an in-road to understanding how the Raptorfest is in many ways a form of protest and struggle over public space, identity, and representation. It is not simply another sports tournament or consumer spectacle. "The Raptorfest" intertwines the pedagogy of desire and the politics of consumption (Giroux, 1994; Grossberg, 1992). It is an example of the Great Urban (White) myth perpetrated on black bodies: Sport makes good "citizens" and is a ticket "out of the ghetto."

I think the fact that these two events took place in the same physical space raises serious and important questions about understanding sport, race, racism, and cultural politics in Canada and beyond.

MAPPING TORONTO THE GOOD'S IMAGINED WHITELINESS: OTHER(S) SPACES?

Where do we normally see "blacks" and athletes in our own lives, in the media, and in the "popular imaginary" (Simon, 1992)? What are they normally represented as doing? In Toronto, as in other large cities in North America and Europe we generally see in the media black men, especially when they are "misbehaving" (Clarke, 1991). But these mostly young black men were "behaving": playing basketball. In racist discourse, this was another "normal" thing for black men to do. The historical construction of racist discourse, or what Dei (1996) calls "race knowledge," has been built up over time and constructed as whiteness being distinct and superior to blackness, or, more correctly, all that is not "white" is other.

> Distinctions between "them" and "us" were thus enforced through the popular representation of the savage, bestial, and uncivilized black African, in difference to the restrained, cerebral, and civilized white European Americans. (Andrews, 1996, p. 127)

Race is conceived here, then, not as a natural or a biological fact nor as an attribute of any body or identity, and along with a host of other binary oppositions, it forms the logics of racist discourse (Dei, 1996). Of particular salience here is the ongoing fear/fascination of the white imaginary with black (male) bodies:

> Mass media stereotypes of black men—as criminals, athletes, and entertainers—bear witness to the contemporary repetition of such colonial fantasy . . . the rigid and limited grid of representations through which black male subjects become publicly visible continues to reproduce certain idées fixes, ideological fictions, and psychic fixations. (Mercer, 1994, p. 176)

How, then, might we understand black (and white) athletic men and women who were seen to be "behaving" in the white space of downtown Toronto? The space in front of the ROM and other institutions of "intellectual" production signifies restraint and "civility" as people come and go in suits and ties, and children stream into the museum to consume knowledge of themselves and others. Museums thus tend to signify what can be considered "mindful," "rational," and, thereby, "civil" (read "white"). The Raptorfest signifies the opposite of restraint, as its players are extremely physically active and "unrestrained" in their play. They are the bodily half of the racist mind, and while play transgresses the normative aspects of the ROM's restrained demeanor, it only does so as a point of difference. The Raptorfest's central logic of play, festival, and physicality marks its participants outside of propriety (i.e., bourgeois masculine whiteness), and not simply because they are doing something that normally occurs "elsewhere."

One of the claims of the "Into the Heart of Africa" producers was that it allowed white, Euro-Anglo viewers an opportunity to engage with the violence of (their own) white colonialism in a critical and an ironic manner (Mackey, 1995). The possibility that such an exhibit could reinforce racist stereotypes of African peoples was apparently not seen as a likely reading. The basketball tournament constructs a similar set of potential readings, one of which is that basketball is helping to bring together players from all social backgrounds. On the court, players are all the same, and all that counts is that one cares about playing the game:

> Within Canada's official multiculturalism, cultural difference has generally been defined as a benign variation rather than as historically specific and related to issues of power. Until very recently the dominant rhetoric of multiculturalism spoke of ethnicity, and not of race and racism. (Mackey, 1995, p. 417)

The Raptorfest plays around the edges of multiculturalism and opens up recognition of the racial politics embedded in the tournament, never quite admitting to either, but trying to discursively represent both as a possibility. The erasure of the racial politics of the Raptorfest is necessary to imagine an egalitarian, a nonracial, and a nonracist basketball universe, and thereby a multicultural city. As Anderson (1991b) suggests, "Communities are to be distinguished not by their falsity/genuineness, but by the style in which they are imagined" (p. 6).

Paul Gilroy points out how "black people are represented in racist discourse as either problem or victim" (1987). This plays out in interesting ways in the representation of the Raptorfest and of basketball in Toronto. The participants were, in much of the imaging on television and in print, constructed as occupying the "urban jungle." The discursive space of "sport," in this case, 3-on-3 basketball, serves as a site for the construction of particular athletic masculine subject positions that use racialized signifiers to produce their logics. The notion of the "urban jungle" is openly used in the first-ever television commercial for the Raptors. In computer-generated simulation, a basketball court is pictured as being surrounded by palm trees and other "tropical" (read black and/or "exotic") signifiers, such as birds chirping and monkeys screeching. Then we hear a growl, and as the camera moves into and parts the undergrowth, a red arm and claw flings a basketball the length of the court and sinks the shot. This is followed by a voice-over, "The Toronto Raptors. The hungriest team in the NBA."

The imagined community of this image is potentially broad, but for my purposes here, it seems to me to blend with the 3-on-3 in an attempt to bring the urban jungle "downtown." This constructs an exotic space for whites to tour in what is signified as black spaces. It works to reinscribe dominant discourses of the "black beast" and his imagined physical superiority (Clarke, 1991). The players explode this stereotype and play with it in many ways in the Raptorfest. By exaggerating and mimicking extreme physical play, they do not signify a unity with racist conceptions of the superhuman black. I would argue that the performance is instead a sign of their refusal to conform to white standards of public display and propriety. They emphasized and celebrated those aspects of the game that have come to be understood as signifiers of "blackness." Dunks, blocked shots, and physical intimidation were collectively acknowledged by all watchers and participants. Players literally played to the crowd. They ran to the sidelines and gave "high fives" to friends and "got in the face" of people cheering for the other team. The crowd was not spectator, but an essential part of many of the games.

Basketball, I would argue, has been bought and sold to largely the same white, urban, middle-class audiences that consume rap and hip-hop music (Walcott, 1995). This trend fits in with the overall transformations in the consumer base of professional sport. The majority of spectators are no longer committed to the local team, nor are they generally familiar with the technical and historical aspects of the various sports events that they attend (Gruneau & Whitson, 1993). Seeing the top stars from the best teams is of more interest than supporting the local team. The fact that every city that Michael Jordan plays in sells out attests to this feature of the postmodernity of sport (Andrews, 1996). Professional sport is now fully a commodity that one consumes. Games and arenas are designed as "pure entertainment," with the actual games' structure and length a mere platform for a larger spectacle.

The game of 3-on-3 is an "inner-city" object that has undergone a similar transformation. In this case, it has been appropriated by corporations and commodified and shipped "downtown" to the (public) white space of Toronto and other major cities. Part of the postmodern city, it became redefined as a "playground" for (black) basketball players, if only momentarily for the players from "the inner city" and "Jane and Finch" (a locally racialized term for the working-class and/or blacks). At the center of this event is the Raptor's Foundation. It is the Raptor's good corporate citizen arm that has "community partnerships" with local schools and governments. Recently one of its events was a co-sponsored event called "Team Up," which was more or less a news conference with the pro basketball players talking about the value of participating in "thoughtfully organized community service" and ways of dealing with the "dangers of violence":

> Violence makes victims of us all," states the TV ad. How true! Someone else may be the actual victim but, in the end, we all feel a little more threatened.
>
> There are ways to make things better—to make our businesses, our homes, our streets and schools and subway safer and more secure. And be alerted! The Big Guys and the Good Guys are on the same team.
>
> We can end violence. We just need the skills.
>
> (Toronto Transit Commission, 1996)

NBA Rookie of the Year Damon Stoudamire supported the program when he said, "You gotta work hard and stay out of trouble if you want to be successful" (*Toronto Star*, November 30, 1996, p. 14) Meritocracy and individualism are still the dominant ethos of (professional) sports, and they are clearly racialized discourses, as the "Team Up" event illustrated. The general message of the program was that crime can be prevented through "social skills," such as learning negotiation to deal with "violence." The fact that "violence" was (and is) regularly directed at black and working-class youth by "The Good Guys" (i.e., Toronto police) is conveniently left out of the discussion.

The middle-class whiteness implied in this "social skills"[4] rhetoric has not been widely analyzed for its racial and cultural bias. Those who need to "develop better social skills" are not imagined to be part of the community that already has the "proper social skills." There is a clear class and race bias in this discourse, but for my purposes, I will just mention how I see it as being implicated in the "Team Up" news event.

The assumptions of such programs effectively erase the history of exclusion and discrimination of black people and other marginalized groups. Such a discourse of blame constructs an image of the "enemy from within" (Mercer, 1994), destroying the fabric of "civilized" culture. Reinerman and Levine (1989) unveil the logic of such discourses:

> Unemployment, poverty, urban decay, school crises, and all their attendant forms of human trouble are spoken of and acted upon as if they were the result of individual deviance, immorality or weakness. (p. 127, quoted in Andrews, 1996)

The "Team Up" program neatly appropriates this paradigm to make it seem as though they are doing good for the downtrodden: The "Big

Guys and the Good Guys" program implicitly individualizes the complex relations of oppression through suggesting that youth get active in "productive community partnerships," implying that they are currently not doing anything and are simply victims of their craftier evil black brother and sisters and their own inherent inability to be "good citizens." This is problematic on many levels, especially given the large and diverse number of black identified community organizations and public figures in Metropolitan Toronto. I don't know if there is any support from black political organizations in Toronto for the Raptors Foundation. There is, though, a strong link with high school basketball, as indicated by the "Raptors Real Skills Sessions"[5] which targets young basketball players to partake in "Camp Raptors" basketball skills summer camps.

The pathologizing disavowal of historically grounded race based discrimination and differentiation actively disparages the relevances of racially oriented welfare policies and justified (and will justify) the slashing of billions of dollars from the welfare budget. (Wacquant, 1994, pp. 258–260, quoted in Andrews, 1996)

The question must be rethought not as a "lack" of social skills (whatever those might be) but rather as whose "social skills" are we talking about? What behaviors and identities does "social skills" training target for "correction," and whose are assumed to be the norm?

RACIALIZATION OF SPACE:
POLICING AND COMMODIFICATION

The television advertisements leading up to the Raptorfest emphasized the "Dunking" competition. Dunking has come to be associated with so-called "black" playing styles. The ads contained only images of black men dunking the ball. The racialized logic of athletic bodies is pervasive in regard to dunking. For example, there was some considerable discussion last year when Brett Barry (a white player) won the NBA's Dunking Championship. The old racist myth that "white men can't jump," and its necessary corollary, that black men are natural jumpers, was momentarily disrupted. However, the association of dunking (physical prowess) with blackness is a persistent racial metaphor, and this was realized in the "Dunk-Off" at the Raptorfest, where there were no white contestants. The space "above the rim"[6] and on the courts is a clearly racialized one, and everyone at the tournament abided by the ideology. Above the rim is a common description of, in particular, black aesthetics and practice in basketball circles, although arguably just about everyone in professional and college basketball plays "above the rim." It also is a competitive masculine metaphor suggesting superior ability and quality of play rather than lowly mortals, who are, like the mythical non-jumping white man, earthbound. Assumptions and ideologies of naturalized biological difference are ever present in sport culture, and we can see some of their racist connotations in these examples. There also is a gendered practice at work here, since there was no dunking competition for women.

The Raptorfest never publicly acknowledges (cannot acknowledge) that the majority of the participants are black African Canadians and Americans. Even though they use black players to sell the game to the general public, in particular to black fans, the Raptorfest is the presentation and performance of blackness to not only the white public's gaze but to the black communities of Toronto. This constitutes it as an important cultural politics.

The meanings and definitions of the court are worth looking at as well. Both legal and sport courts are sustained by similar rules and organizational assumptions. Sport and the law assume a level playing field in their space. Blacks in Toronto know that the court system is not fair, and they have little control over the definition or outcome of an engagement with the law (Mackey, 1995). In these 3-on-3 games, they have more control and can demonstrate personal control of their emotions and bodies (both of which are assumed, in a racist ideology to be "out of control"). Inside the lines of the court, they show that they can work out whatever problems arise. Inside the line, they are free to perform a collective, communal politics. Players can show that they are athletes and performers, transforming space and time into a small stage of intense play and fun: "I'm only here to play basketball, but the fact that I am here has nothing to do with basketball." If nothing else, the Raptorfest reminds a forgetful city that there is a large population of black people, and that they are part of this community, despite every effort to demonize and criminalize them.

TRANSGRESSION AND PERFORMANCE

There is an intense monitoring of black male bodies in Toronto by police, the media, and schools (Mackey, 1995). Overt policing was diminished at the Raptorfest, because sporting events are structured to depoliticize their spaces. The ideology of sport as being uplifting and as not involved in or interested in politics is contradicted by the high-profile presence and emphasis of the community involvement ideology of the "Raptor Foundation.". The assumption is that sport can construct "pro-social" behavior (i.e., nonblack identified behavior).

Significantly, the "Team Up' event took place in a subway platform where a 13-year-old black male was knifed to death by another young black man. The bringing together of these events blends a series of racial metaphors and histories that otherwise could not make sense. Many black and other marginalized groups regularly travel through this subway station. The Raptor Foundation promotes its project of urban renewal through the participation in an "organized community" organization such as basketball. It feeds off of the moral panic of the construction of the urban "bad (black) boys."

It seemed to me that a lot of people knew each other. There were many greetings exchanged and laughter, hugs, and handshakes: a broad sense of community was apparent, as well as a coming together of people who do not often get the chance to do so. I think that there is an easy reading of the players being co-opted by the corporate machines, and that consumer culture is a form of social control in its own right. However, as Fiske (1993) suggests, people can and do appropriate the material and discursive resources of their dominance and bend them to their own purposes:

> The social order constrains and oppresses the people, but at the same time offers them the resources to fight against those constraints. Oppression is always economic. Yet the everyday culture of the oppressed can take the signs of that which oppresses them and use them for their own purposes. Commodities can be abstracted from the economic system of the dominant and made into the things of the people. (p. 219)

The identification of oneself with the basketball community was of primary importance, not drinking Gatorade and wearing the "right" shoes. The identification was not constrained by association with different parts of Toronto, by different ethnicities or racial categories. This identification was not a construction of the "sponsors" of the event. I am suggesting that this tournament is the site of resistance to racist representations of blackness. Those who participated, regardless of racial identification, transgress normative notions and practices of urban(e) whiteness. Certainly there are problems within this masculine sporting culture, such as cut-throat competition. However, the complexities of 3-on-3 are precisely configured through the intersections of race, class, masculinity, and sport culture. Westwood (1990) put it succinctly:

> To consider black masculinities as part of the cultures of resistance to racism is not to suggest that they are in themselves contradictory. These areas, the streets and football, are important to consider, because it is precisely in these areas that current stereotypes about black men have been generated and have become part of commonsense racism today. (p. 59)

The forgetting and remembering of the history of urban spaces are crucial in understanding the politics of resistance and marginalization in different "locales" (Fiske, 1993), such as University Avenue in Toronto. The way things are remembered defines how particular spaces are used and known. Toronto is a highly racially, class-segregated city. University Avenue is rarely the sight of anything but traffic and other corporate-endorsed sporting spectacles, such as "Shopper's Drug Mart Annual 10K Run." It is a major route for the middle class of Toronto to vacate the downtown core to return to their homes in Forest Hill and North Toronto. It is rarely used on the "top end" (i.e., the area where Bloor Street meets Avenue Road) for anything but traffic. Further south toward the parliament buildings is a regular site of protest against whichever government happens to be in power.

The ROM protest is implicated here as it too struggled over the racist representations of the white imaginary. It also was the transgression of a space controlled by dominant white groups that wished to close down the possibilities of particular types of black visibility: Toronto wants to forget or negate the possibilities of black identities and bodies that do not fit into the noble black/savage beast dichotomy. Humane, caring, "normal" black and working-class identities are never affirmed in the popular imaginary. However, I think that at moments, the players in the Raptorfest actively refused their demonization, and that the insidious logic of sport as a "civilizing" process obscures such an analysis. To my surprise, the Raptorfest received little mainstream print or television coverage, a further negation of black and sport culture.

The space of "downtown" is ambiguous in Toronto. University Avenue is "downtown" but only in relation to "North Toronto" (i.e., historically white, middle-class Anglos) or Scarborough (a suburban, white, working-class area that includes recent immigrant populations from East Asia and South Asia) and the "Jane-Finch Corridor" (populated by white, poor, and working-class groups and recent immigrants from Northern and Western Africa). Nothing about "Jane-Finch" strikes me as particularly odd or fantastic in terms of the urban landscape. Geographically, in a universe where the "center" is Yonge and Bloor, Jane-Finch is arguably the "burbs," not the inner city. It has been categorized as "inner city," because the social and economic structures of Toronto have created conditions where crime, poverty, drug trade, and schooling crises are business as usual. Arguably, Toronto's major media focus an inordinate amount of energy on this area's "problems," furthering stereotypes about blacks and other marginalized groups.

> . . . because there is no real difference between the self and other, an imaginary line must be drawn . . . this line is as dynamic in its ability to alter itself as is the self. (Gilman, 1985, pp. 17–18, quoted in Andrews, 1996, p. 127)

"Toronto the white" likes to imagine that social problems arise out of the "inner city." However, I would argue that the inner city is nowhere in particular. It is a discursively manufactured social object. The precision of the ideological effect (and affect) of evoking the "inner city" as the source and site of "social ills" depends on its indeterminacy as an actual geographical locale. The result is the displacement of social and historical oppressions as events that only happen in "that part of the city." Crime and violence do not happen in relation to one's own privilege or around the corner or next door. Thus again we see the ideological bases of the "Team Up" program which, although laudable, serves to reinforce a series of racially oppressive ideologies. It works because of the desire of racist ideology to fix the signifiers of blackness and to ignore or obscure the actualities of daily life.

In this way the dominant, white, middle-class groups construct a "safe space," and they distance themselves from acknowledging and confronting racism and other forms of injustice and violence, thus the astonishment of many people who are interviewed on television after their neighbor kills his wife: "He was such a quiet man." Perceived attacks on this safe space, of course, allow for the logic of increased surveillance and the policing of "deviants." This is why one can look at the Raptorfest as being racially configured, as it suggests to me that black males are welcome in downtown Toronto, but only if they can be perceived to be there temporarily and for very "obvious" reasons. Otherwise, it seems to me that surveillance of Toronto streets would categorize what they are doing as "just hanging out." A related example was the mainstream media response to the "Just Desserts" restaurant murder that brought forth a massive cry of outrage from the wealthy, white, upper-middle-class residents of that neigborhood. The images of two young black men from the in-store surveillance cameras were played again and again on television and reproduced in Toronto's daily newspapers for weeks on end. Today, some five years later, they are often held out as an example of how "dangerous the streets of the city" have become. Dressed as they were in sneakers and hooded jackets, the identification with all other black (and white and Asian) males who wore similar attire became a sign of "trouble." Such an outfit is common among most urban youth who identify with sport, hip-hop, and other related popular cultural forms. Although sport as a form of social and moral regulation has been a common practice of British colonialism in Canada and North America (Hall, Slack, Smith, & Whitson, 1991; Gruneau & Whitson, 1993), it has rarely been interrogated for how "youth" in particular take up and appropriate its symbols and meanings in resistant or counterhegemonic or subaltern ways. The dominant representations though of such embodiment present youth, in particular, black, male youth, as menacing and as threats to social order.

Conclusion: Towards an Understanding of Racism, Sport, and Popular Culture

The Raptorfest (and basketball in general) has arguably become a terrain of racial identification and struggle in the same way as, for example, cricket was and continues to be in the West Indies. In *Beyond a Boundary*, C. L. R. James discussed the politics of playing cricket as a site of resistance to British colonialism. He illustrated how Afro-Caribbean players transformed the actual play of the game and beat the colonizers at their own game using their own "style." Do the players in the Raptorfest turn back and appropriate the colonizers' "games" to form some space of cultural expression inside of a larger system of control and oppression? What possibilities does it suggest for political transformation in the context of sport in "the late, late twentieth century capitalist show" (Grossberg, 1995)?

Mackey (1995) points out that, "Multiculturalism and Post-Modernism (can be) deployed offensively and defensively by powerful groups when their authority is being challenged by less socially or politically powerful groups" (p. 430). Mackey was talking about the ability of a museum to use notions of the multiplicity of truths and the instability of meaning to avoid responsibility for the actual harms of racist representations. The postmodern as such is not necessarily the site of emancipation and the democratization of existing inequalities. A postmodern stance acknowledges the opening up of space literally and metaphorically for the reinterpretation and reconstruction of meaning, knowledge/power, and history. Who, how, and what will fill in such a space is not predetermined, and the existing dominant groups already have control over the existing modes of representing and creating our culture. In such a context, it seems pertinent to ask whether or not the Raptorfest is another example of the "Saris Samosas and Steelbands" model of multiculturalism, which diffuses the three Rs of an anti-racism politics: "Resistance, rebellion, and rejection" (Dei, 1996). I do not think that it is easily contained inside such a narrow either/or categorization. It is perhaps better understood as constituting both possibility and negation. It must be understood as something else.

NOTES

1. For a more in-depth discussion of Participant Observation and Ethnographic research see Spradley (1980); Kirby & McKenna (1989); Strauss & Corbin (1990); Denzin (1989); Becker (1990).

2. For critiques of and possibilities in doing "critical" ethnography, see Thomas (1993); Lather (1992); Clifford & Marcus (1986); Van Maanen (1988).

3. I found this information by calling the Raptors head office in Toronto. It was relayed via a voice mail message, and although I made a request that a registration form be mailed to my home, I have yet to receive one.

4. Recent Canadian immigrants who speak English as a second language are targeted for "social skills training" by schools. They largely come from Northern and Western African and South Asian backgrounds.

5. Camp Raptors!: Raptors Real Skills Sessions. (Application form). Toronto Raptors Basketball Team, 20 Bay Street, Suite 1702, Toronto, Ontario.

6. See George (1992).

References

Anderson, B. (1991). *Imagined communities: Reflections on the origin and spread of nationalism.* London: Verso.

Andrews, D. L. (1996) The fact(s) of Michael Jordan's blackness: Excavating a floating racial signifier. *Sociology of Sport Journal, 13(2),* 125–158.

Becker, H. (1970). *Sociological work.* Englewood Cliffs, NJ: Prentice Hall.

Becker, H. (1990). *Doing things together.* Englewood Cliffs, NJ: Prentice Hall.

Clarke, S. A. (1991). Fear of a black planet. *Socialist Review, 21(2),* 37–59.

Clifford, J., & Marcus, G. (1986). *The poetics and politics of ethnography.* Berkeley: University of California Press.

Dei, G. S. (1996). *Anti-Racism: Theory and practice.* Halifax, NS: Fernwood.

Denzin, N. (1989). *The research act.* Englewood Cliffs, NJ: Prentice Hall.

Fiske, J. (1993). *Power plays, power works.* London: Verso.

George, N. (1992). *Elevating the game: Black men and basketball.* New York: HarperCollins.

Gilman, S. (1985). *Difference and pathology: Stereotypes of sexuality, race, and madness.* Ithaca, NY: Cornell University Press.

Gilroy, P. (1987). *"There ain't no black in the union jack.": The cultural politics of race and nation.* Chicago: University of Chicago Press.

Gilroy, P. (1991). Sounds authentic: Black music, ethnicity, and the challenge of a changing same. *Black Music Research Journal, 11,* 2.

Giroux, H. (1994). *Disturbing pleasures: Learning popular culture.* New York: Routledge.

Grossberg, L. (1992). *We gotta get out of this place: Popular conservatism and postmodern culture.* London: Routledge.

Gruneau, R., & Whitson, D. (1993). *Hockey night in Canada.* Toronto: Garamond.

Hall, M. A. (1987). Knowledge and gender: Epistemological questions in the social analysis of sport. In Greta Hofmann Nemiroff (Ed.), *Women and men: Interdisciplinary readings on gender* (pp. 80–102). Montreal: Fitzhenry & Whiteside.

Hall, M. A., Slack, T., Smith, G., & Whitson, D. (1991). *Sport in Canadian society.* Toronto: Mclelland and Stewart.

James, C. L. R. (1983). *Beyond a boundary.* New York: Pantheon Books.

Kirby, S., & McKenna, K. (1989). *Experience, research, social change.* Toronto: Garamond.

Lather, P. (1992). *Getting smart: Feminist pedagogy and research with/in the post-modern.* New York: Routledge.

Lenskyj, H. (1986). *Out of bounds: Women, sport, and sexuality.* Toronto: Women's Press.

Lenskyi, H. (1994). Sexuality and feminity in sport contexts: Issues and alternatives. *Journal of Sport and Social Issues, 18(4),* 356–376.

Mackey, E. (1995). Postmodernism and cultural politics in a multicultural nation: Contests over truth in the "Into the Heart of Africa" controversy. *Public Culture, 7,* 403–431.

Mercer, K. (1994). Welcome to the jungle: New positions in black cultural studies. London: Routledge.

Messner, M. (1991). *Power at play: Sports and the problem of masculinity.* Boston: Beacon Press.

Pronger, B. (1990). *The arena of masculinity: Sports, homosexuality, and the meaning of sex.* Toronto: Summerhill.

Reinerman, C., & Levine, H. G. (1989). The crack attack: Politics and media in America's latest drug scare. In J. Best (Ed.), *Images of issues: Typifying contemporary social problems.* (pp. 115–137). New York: Aldine de Gruyter.

Rock, P. (1979). *The making of symbolic interactionism,* London: Macmillan.

Simon, R. (1992). *Teaching against the grain.* Toronto: OISE Press.

Spradley, J. (1980). *Participant observation.* New York: Holt, Reinhart, and Winston.

Strauss, A., & Corbin, J. (1990). *Basics of qualitative research: Grounded theory and techniques.* Newbury Park, CA: Sage.

Thomas, J. (1993). *Doing critical ethnography.* Newbury Park, CA: Sage.

Toronto Transit Commission. (1996, September). *Customer News, 42(8),* 1.

Van Maanen, J. (1988). *Tales of the field: On writing ethnography.* Chicago: University of Chicago Press.

Wacquant, L. J. D. (1994). The new urban color line: The state and fate of the ghetto in post–Fordist America. In C. Calhoun (Ed.), *Social theory and the politics of identity* (pp. 231–276). Oxford: Blackwell.

Walcott, R. (1995). *Performing the post-modern: Rap, hip-hop, and the black Atlantic.* Unpublished doctural dissertation, University of Toronto, Canada.

West, C. (1990). The new cultural politics of difference. In Fergusson et al. (Eds.), *Out there: Marginalization and contemporary cultures* (pp. 19–36). Boston: MIT/New Museum.

Westwood, S. (1990). Racism, black masculinity, and the politics of space. In J. Hearn & D. Morgan (Eds.), *Men, masculinities, and social theory* (pp. 55–71). London: Unwin Hyman.

Contributors

Gamal Abdel-Shehid
Gamal Abdel-Shehid is Assistant Professor in the Faculty of Physical Education and Recreation at the University of Alberta. He teaches in the areas of sport and popular culture.

Darren Ambrose
Darren Ambrose is the Head Women's soccer Coach at The University of Pennsylvania. Born in Sheffield, England, Ambrose earned his Management Accounting Degree at USC-Spartanburg while playing in goal for the top ranked Rifle soccer team. He moved on to Rhodes College as a men's and women's assistant soccer coach while taking his M.S. in Sport and Leisure Commerce at the University of Memphis. While in Memphis, Ambrose spent five years involved in youth soccer as a club and an Olympic Development Program coach. He currently resides in Philadelphia along with his wife Sherry and daughter Madison Naomi.

David L. Andrews
David L. Andrews is an Associate Professor of Sport and Cultural Studies in the Department of Human Movement Sciences and Education at the University of Maryland at College Park, and a Senior Visiting Research Fellow at De Montfort University, UK. He is an associate editor of the *Journal of Sport and Social Issues,* and an editorial board member of the *Society of Sport Journal, Leisure Studies,* and *International Sport Studies.* He has published on a variety of topics related to the critical, theoretically informed, analysis of sport as an aspect of contemporary commercial culture.

Michael F. Atkinson

Michael Atkinson is an Assistant Professor in the Department of Sociology at the Memorial University of Newfoundland. He received his PhD in Sociology at the University of Calgary in 2001. His teaching, research, and writing interests revolve around cultural issues related to sports violence, organized crime, youth subcultures, and body modification. In addition, through a series of interrelated participant-observation based studies on deviance in Canada, he is currently developing a general process-sociological model of crime and deviance.

Gene Burd

Gene Burd Ph.D. is an Associate Professor of Journalism, at the University of Texas-Austin. He does research on urban communication, including sports, media and cities; and use of sports reporting techniques to explain urban issues. His career at the *Kansas City Star, Houston Chronicle, Albuquerque Journal* and in suburban Los Angeles and Chicago included sports reporting. He also taught at Marquette and Minnesota and was educated at UCLA, Iowa and Northwestern. His research has appeared in the *Journal of Urban Affairs, Urban Affairs Annual Reviews, Nation's Cities, National Civic Review, Journalism Quarterly, Journal of Communication Inquiry, Journalism History,* and *American National Biography.*

Michael Clark

Michael Clark is an adjunct Assistant Professor with the Youth Sports Institute at Michigan State University. He holds the B.A, M.A., and Ph.D. degrees from MSU. His research interests include coach education and the effects of rule changes on skill development and safety in youth sports.

CL Cole

CL Cole is an Associate Professor in the Departments of Kinesiology and Sociology, and The Program for Studies of Women, Gender, and Sexualities at the University of Illinois at Urbana-Champaign.

Alan G. Ingham

Alan G. Ingham was born in Manchester, England. He attended Carnegie College of Physical Education and obtained a B.Ed from the University of Leeds. His Master's degree in physical education was obtained from Washington State University and his Ph.D in sociology from the University of Massachusetts. He has taught at the University of Washington, and is currently a senior professor of Sport Studies at Miami University, Ohio. He has published articles in journals such as the *Journal of Experimental and Social Psychology, Journal of Social History, Theory, Culture & Society, Sociology of Sport Journal, The International Review for the Sociology of Sport,* and *Quest* to name but a few. In conjunction with John W. Loy, he edited a book, *Sport in Social Development*. From 1984 to 1987, he was the President of the International Sociology of Sport Association.

Samantha King

Samantha King is an Assistant Professor in the Physical Education Program at the University of Arizona where she researches and teaches the cultural politics of sport, health, and leisure. Her essays have appeared in *Social Text*, the *International Journal of Sport Marketing and Sponsorship*, the *Journal of Sport and Social Issues*, and the *Sociology of Sport Journal*.

Mary McDonald

Mary G. McDonald is Associate Professor in the Department of Physical Education, Health and Sport Studies and an affiliate with the Women's Studies program at Miami University in Oxford, Ohio, USA. Her scholarship focuses on feminist and cultural studies of sport, the media, and popular culture and explores power relations as constituted along the axes of race, class, gender and sexuality. Her research has appeared in several journals including the *Sociology of Sport Journal*, *American Studies* and the *International Review for the Sociology of Sport*. She is coeditor with Susan Birrell of *Reading Sport: Critical Essays on Power and Representation* (Northeastern University Press, 2000), an anthology that ties particular highly publicized sporting events and personalities to larger cultural, economic and political realms.

Robin Mathy

Robin M. Mathy earned her Honors B.S. *summa cum laude* in Sociology from the Honors College at Arizona State University. She has postgraduate credentials from Indiana University—Bloomington, the University of Minnesota–Twin Cities, and the University of Oxford. She is completing a Master's in International Relations at the University of Cambridge. She was Executive Director of The Phoenix Clinic in Arizona, while taking postgraduate courses in Anthropology at Arizona State University. She is currently a Clinical Research Fellow in Child & Adolescent Psychiatry at the University of Minnesota–Twin Cities, with an NIMH Supplemental Grant to study Prevention Science.

Robert Pitter

Robert Pitter is an Assistant Professor in the School of Recreation Management and Kinesiology at Acadia University in Wolfville, Nova Scotia, Canada. He teaches courses addressing social and political issues relevant to sport and physical activity. His research interests include political, economic, and social aspects of sport and recreation; urban social development; organizational politics; social and organizational change; and microcomputer-assisted qualitative analysis.

Steven A. Riess

Steven A. Riess is Professor of History at Northeastern Illinois University. He is the author of several books on sport including *City Games: The Evolution of American Society and the Rise of Sports*, and *Touching Base: Professional Baseball and American Culture in the Progressive Era*, former editor of the *Journal of Sport History*, and edits the series "Sport and Entertainment" for Syracuse University Press. He is currently writing a book examining the relationship between horse racing, politics, and crime in New York and Chicago from 1870 to 1940.

Danny Rosenberg

Danny Rosenberg, PhD, is an Associate Professor in the Department of Physical Education and Kinesiology at Brock University in St. Catharines, Ontario, Canada. His teaching areas and research interests include sport philosophy and the ethics of sport, sport history, and the administration of physical education and sport. He is co-author with Joy DeSensi (1996) of *Ethics in Sport Management* and has published works in several anthologies and proceedings, the *Journal of the Philosophy of Sport*, *Journal of Sport History*, *International Journal of Physical Education*, *Canadian Journal of Sport History* and others. He is currently researching and writing a book on Jews and sport in Toronto during the interwar years, and with DeSensi, is completing a second edition of their sport management ethics book.

Synthia Sydnor Slowikowski

Synthia Sydnor is an Associate Professor at the University of Illinois at Urbana-Champaign where she holds appointments in Kinesiology, Criticism & Interpretive Theory; the Interdisciplinary Concentration in Cultural Studies & Interpretive Research; and the John Henry Newman Institute of Catholic Thought. Her research has appeared in a range of journals and books including *Quest*, *Journal of Sport History*, *Sport and Postmodern Times*, and *Games, Sports and Cultures*.

Andrew Thornton

Andrew Thornton is Lecturer in the School of Sport, Exercise and Leisure at the University of Surrey Roehampton (London, UK). His PhD thesis (Toronto) was *Ultimate Masculinities: An Ethnography of Power and Social Difference in Sport*. His main interests are cultural studies of sport and leisure, in particular how social difference operates within the experience and organisation of sport. He is studying 'new' sports and is interested in the relation between whiteness, race, racism and masculinities in sport and culture. He has recently begun research on the cultural significance of video games under the title *Will the Real Lara Croft Please Stand Up?*

Phil White

Phil White is a Professor of Kinesiology at McMaster University, Canada. He has contributed many articles and book chapters in various areas of scholarly inquiry in the sociology of sport. He is also co-editor (with Kevin Young) of *Sport and Gender* in Canada (Oxford University Press, 1999). In recent years, Phil has coached the Canadian Men's Rugby team that went to the Maccabiah Games in Israel and the Ontario Women's Rugby Programme.

Ralph C. Wilcox

Ralph C. Wilcox is Interim Vice President and CEO at the University of South Florida St. Petersburg and was formerly Professor and Chair of the Department of Human Movement Sciences and Education at The University of Memphis. He holds degrees from The University of Alberta, Canada (PhD, 1982), Washington State University (MSc, 1978), and Exeter University, England (BEd Hons, 1977). He has served as an Izaak Walton Killam Scholar and Fellow of the American Council on Education. His current research interests focus on cross-cultural dimensions of the sport industry with particular reference to ethics in the expanding global marketplace. He has published his work in a variety of academic arenas including the *European Journal for Sport Management, The Journal of the British Society of Sports History*, the *Journal of Sport History, The International Journal of the History of Sport*, together with *Comparative Physical Education and Sport. Cross-Cultural and International Studies.*

Brian Wilson

Brian Wilson is an Assistant Professor in the School of Human Kinetics at the University of British Columbia. His research interests include media representations of race and gender, audience studies, youth culture, social movements, and the sociology of sport. His most recent research focuses on the production and consumption of alternative media by youth subcultural groups, with a concentration on the "anti-jock" (cyber)movement. He has published his work in journals such as the *Sociology of Sport Journal*, the *International Review for the Sociology of Sport*, the *Journal of Sport and Social Issues*, and the *Canadian Journal of Communication.*

Detlev Zwick

Detlev Zwick is Assistant Professor of Marketing and Consumer Behavior at York University, Toronto, Canada. His current research interest focuses on the political, cultural, and social effects of new information and communication technologies on exchange relationships. His work has been published in the *European Journal of Marketing, Electronic Markets*, and the *Journal of Research for Consumers*. His dissertation entitled *The Speed of Money: Investing as Consumption in the Age of Computer-Mediated Communication*, won a national award from the Marketing Science Institute. Recently, he was visiting researcher at the Computer Science department at the University of Aalborg, Denmark, and Visiting Assistant Professor in the Kogod School of Business at American University, Washington, DC.

Index

Books in SUNY series on
Sport, Culture, and Social Relations

Alan M. Klein, *Little Big Men: Bodybuilding Subculture and Gender Construction.*

Todd W. Crosset, *Outsiders in the Clubhouse: The World of Women's Professional Golf.* Winner North American Society for the Sociology of Sport (NASSS) Book Award.

Wanda Ellen Wakefield, *Playing to Win: Sports and the American Military, 1898–1945.*

Laurel R. Davis, *The Swimsuit Issue and Sport: Hegemonic Masculinity in Sports Illustrated.*

Jim McKay, *Managing Gender: Affirmative Action and Organizational Power in Australian, Canadian, and New Zealand Sport.*

Juan-Miguel Fernandez-Balboa, (ed.), *Critical Postmodernism in Human Movement, Physical Education, and Sport.*

Genevieve Rail, (ed.), *Sport and Postmodern Times.*

Shona M. Tompson, *Mother's Taxi: Sport and Women's Labor.*

Nancy Theberge, *Higher Goals: Women's Ice Hockey and the Politics of Gender.* Winner, North American Society for the Sociology of Sport (NASSS) Book Award.

Helen Jefferson Lenskyj, *Inside the Olympic Industry: Power, Politics, and Activism.*

C. Richard King and Charles Fruehling Springwood, *Beyond the Cheers: Race as Spectacle in College Sport.*

David Andrews (ed.), *Michael Jordan, Inc: Corporate Sport, Media Culture, and Late Modern America.*

Margaret Gatz, Michael A. Messner, and Sandra J. Ball-Rokeach (eds.), *Paradoxes of Youth and Sport.*

Helen Jefferson Lenskyj, *The Best Olympics Ever? Social Impacts of Sydney 2000.*

Anne Bolin and Jane Granskog (eds.), *Athletic Intruders; Ethnographic Research on Women, Culture, and Exercise.*

Ralph C. Wilcox, David L. Andrews, Robert Pitter, and Richard L. Irwin (eds.), *Sporting Dystopias: The Making and Meaning of Urban Sport Cultures.*

Robert E. Rinehart and Synthia Sydnor (eds.), *To the Extreme: Alternative Sports, Inside and Out.*